# Morals and Values

7.45"
SM 7525

PYM JN
(Sin)

B45981

# Morals and Values

*Readings in Theoretical
and Practical Ethics*

*Edited by Marcus G. Singer*

CHARLES SCRIBNER'S SONS    NEW YORK

Copyright © 1977 Charles Scribner's Sons

**Library of Congress Cataloging in Publication Data**
Main entry under title:

Morals and values.

Bibliography: p. 446
Includes index.
1. Ethics—Addresses, essays, lectures.
I. Singer, Marcus George, 1926–
BJ1012.M636      170      76-28974
ISBN 0-684-14813-7

*This book is for*
*Esther Kobre Singer*
*my mother*
*and for Mimi*

# PREFACE

*It is the fate of those who toil at the lower employments of life, to be rather driven by the fear of evil, than attracted by the prospect of good: to be exposed to censure, without hope of praise; to be disgraced by miscarriage, or punished for neglect, where success would have been without applause, and diligence without reward.*

*Among those unhappy mortals is the writer of dictionaries. . . .*

With these wry words Samuel Johnson prefaced his great *Dictionary*. It might be supposed, without stretching the truth too far, that they apply as well to the anthologist or, in the academic community, to the writer of either a textbook or a popular work.

Dr. Johnson went on to say, "I have, notwithstanding this discouragement, attempted a dictionary of the English language." And I have, notwithstanding Dr. Johnson's discouragement—which did not really trouble me much—attempted this work, more text than treatise and mainly anthology.

This book has been prepared in the conviction that moral philosophy—ethical theory, reflection on morality—can influence and inform conduct, action, morality itself, that it properly can, and that, all things considered, it ought to—unless it is very bad philosophy or confused reflection. (But only further reflection can determine whether reflection is confused.) And it has been designed so as to test and prove this conviction.

I have long considered that a philosophically valuable collection of readings in ethics must itself be based on a theory, a theory of ethics as well as a theory of how it should be taught and can best be learned. The present collection is based on such a theory, which is sketched in the General Introduction and the Introductions to the various parts. This theory provides the main basis of selection and also the method of classification of the materials selected. Hence, one of the distinguishing features of this book is the emphasis on the application of theory to practice.

Another distinguishing feature of the book is the inclusion of a large number of Statements on Morality, as I have called them, arranged in ten series. These are quotations of varying length, too short to merit the title of a selection, which provide useful and stimulating materials for reflection and discussion. With many I managed to extract the essence of what is ethically relevant or useful from a work that in its original form would have strayed too far from the topic. This feature constitutes what can be called a mini-anthology (I owe the name to Professor Hector-Neri Castañeda) and there is interplay within the mini-anthology itself as well as between the mini-anthology and the main anthology.

The arrangement of selections within each part is in many cases necessary and logical, in some of no special significance. I have indicated connections that are not brought out by the arrangement by means of cross references in editorial footnotes. The numbered footnotes are those of the authors of the selections in which they appear. All others are editorial and are indicated by other signs. The sources of selections are fully indicated. I have sometimes changed or supplied the title of a selection; this is always indicated. Similarly, all editorial omissions are marked by ellipses; editorial additions, by brackets. Most selections are complete, though a number are extracts. Where I judged it important or useful (and was allowed to do so), I have edited selections and omitted parts that would not contribute to the purpose for which the selection was originally included.

A few issues that some practitioners have come to regard as standard in the presentation of the subject have been deliberately omitted from this collection. These are, preeminently, the problem of moral motivation, often expressed in the question "Why should I be moral?"; egoism and other theories of motivation; and what John Stuart Mill called "the celebrated controversy concerning the freedom of the will." It is my conviction that none of these issues or theories has a significant relation to deliberation and the informing of practice. With regard to "the theoretical question as to the freedom of the will," I agree with Sidgwick in thinking that "the ethical importance of deciding it one way or another is liable to be exaggerated":

> In all ordinary cases . . . it does not seem to me relevant to ethical deliberation to determine the metaphysical validity of my consciousness of freedom to choose whatever I may conclude to be reasonable, unless the affirmation or negation of the Freedom of the Will somehow modifies my view of what it would be reasonable to choose to do if I could so choose. . . . When we are

> endeavoring to ascertain . . . what choice it is reasonable to make between two alternatives of present conduct, Determinist conceptions are . . . irrelevant. . . . And from neither point of view does it seem practically important, for the general regulation of conduct, to decide the metaphysical question at issue in the Free-Will Controversy. . . .[1]

These points, like everything else connected with this celebrated controversy, are themselves likely to generate controversy, and this would be a good thing, for these arguments of Sidgwick's, on the moral relevance of the free will issue, have rarely if ever been considered on their own merits. Similarly, when in a particular situation one is attempting to determine what ought to be done, it is irrelevant to consider whether egoism or some other theory of human motivation is true, and thus it cannot logically enter as a factor into deliberation. If a particular theory can be shown to have practical bearings, then let it be shown and let it be considered, but it is unwise to suppose that just because some issue has reference to conduct it therefore has relevance to it.

Although this book is designed for introductory and intermediate level courses on ethics, it is for anyone who cares to learn what ethical thought, at its best and most significant, is about. Consequently it can be used with some profit at higher levels of study, even though it has not been designed for following arguments to the ultimate reaches of philosophical subtlety. (Still, there is plenty of subtlety in such selections as 4, 16, 41, 45, and 53.) My aim has been to demonstrate, consistent with providing material for a good course in ethics, "the genuine interplay of practical issues and theoretic philosophy."[2] The book has developed out of my own teaching of introductory ethics and has been projected for some years. It has benefited immeasurably from the stimulation I received from my students and also from the comments, criticisms, and advice of the marvelous graduate students, most now happily embarked on their own careers, I have been fortunate enough to have as my assistants: Hans Oberdiek, Michael Reiter, Ellen Kappy, Norman Gillespie, Maria Lugones, Stephen Luebke, and Abel Pablo Iannone. It also benefited from the years I spent as chairman of my department, which enabled me to see at firsthand the limits of principle and the vital importance of judgment and discretion in the administration of policy and the resolution of disputes.

---

[1] Henry Sidgwick, *The Methods of Ethics* (1st ed., 1874; 7th ed., London: Macmillan and Co., Limited, 1907), pp. 66, 68, 70. The quotation from Mill is from his *System of Logic* (1st ed., 1843), Bk. VI, ch. ii.

[2] Morris R. Cohen, *Reason and Nature* (New York: Harcourt, Brace and Company, 1931), p. xv.

I have also learned a great deal, in ways which affected the structure and the substance of this book, from my friends Kurt Baier, James Griffin, A. Phillips Griffiths, A. I. Melden, John Rawls, Richard Rudner, John Silber, and Theodore Waldman. I am further grateful, for similar stimulation, to my colleagues at Wisconsin; I must mention, in particular, Carl Bögholt, Claudia Card, Donald Crawford, Haskell Fain, William Hay, Jon Moline, and the late Julius Weinberg. Claudia Card and Hector-Neri Castañeda read selected portions of the manuscript and enabled me to benefit from their acute and judicious comments. The substance of Part II of the General Introduction, "Moral Problems and the Study of Ethics," earlier appeared, in another form and under another title, in *The Monist,* vol. 58 (1974), and I am grateful to the editor, Eugene Freeman, for permission to use it here.

Finally, I must express my gratitude and appreciation to Blanche, Karen, Debra, and Josephine Samovna, who all contributed in their own special ways to the preparation of the manuscript and to the thinking that led to it.

M. G. S.

*Madison, Wisconsin*
*February 11, 1976*

# A NOTE TO THE STUDENT

Although this book is primarily for use in courses, it is also for the reader who wishes to study the subject independently, without benefit of tuition. This can be done, though some guidance may be needed. This note is for just such readers.

In addition to the General Introduction, there is an Introduction to each part of the book. I would suggest a preliminary reading of these introductions. This should enable you to get your bearings and to familiarize yourself with the subject matter as well as the organization of the book. The individual parts of the book can be read independently of one another, but they are intended to be integrated, and the ordering of parts (though not necessarily of individual selections in each part) has significance. Therefore, you would do well to start formal study with one or two of the selections from Part I, say 1 and 5. Where you go from there, if you choose to depart from the formal organization (a course that is certainly feasible) is up to your own inclination, taste, and interests.

But before reading any selections, you might find it interesting to begin by reading some of the Statements on Morality, the relatively brief quotations, something like epigraphs, that either begin or end each section of the book. Though for the most part arranged so as to have special relevance to the section in which they are contained, they often have connections with selections or topics in other parts of the book. Although these quotations have all been labeled Statements on Morality, it is not strictly true to say that they are all statements on *morality,* that is, not all of them deal with morality or questions of right and wrong. Some have to do with other things, more or less closely related, such as questions of good and bad. These are not, strictly speaking, matters of morality. Others, such as those in the ninth and tenth series, deal with such matters as the nature of institutions or the nature of war and are not, by themselves, statements on morality. These differentiations, if not clear already, will become clear with further sophistication in the subject.

In the source notes to the selections there are cross references to other selections (and sometimes statements) with which the given selection may usefully be compared, either because of a sharp contrast between them or because one supplements and completes the other. Contiguous selections are often closely related, in an obvious way, but not always. You will discover for yourself as you go along other connections and points of agreement and disagreement.

In reading any of the passages contained in this book, either the shorter statements in the mini-anthology or the longer selections in the anthology proper, it is essential to have certain questions in mind. The important thing to consider in connection with any piece is what is being said in it, whether it is sound, and what its further implications are. So ask yourself: What exactly is being said here? Why is it being said? What problem is it relevant to? Is it convincing? If it is not convincing, why isn't it? If it is, what other ideas am I familiar with that go against it? And what reasons does the author have for what is being maintained? Are there better ones?

Ethics is a subject that deals with matters that are of great importance and interest to nearly everyone but on which there exist great differences of opinion. The whole subject is enormously controversial. There is even controversy on what the controversy is about and how it can be resolved. This fact is discouraging to some but to others it is a challenge and a stimulus. Intellectual power does not develop automatically; it must be exercised to be developed, and it can be exercised only through the overcoming of obstacles. Similarly, one's power to make moral judgments can be developed only by making moral judgments and testing them against the facts, relevant principles, and the opinions of others.

But what moral judgments can be tested against is itself one of the matters about which there is such controversy. As you will see.

# CONTENTS

# PART III   VALUES AND IDEALS

# PART IV   THE VARIETIES
# OF MORAL SKEPTICISM

# PART V CASUISTRY AND CONFLICT

# PART VI CONFLICT, WAR, AND MORALITY

# PART VII INSTITUTIONAL ETHICS

# Morals and Values

# General Introduction

## I. THEORETICAL AND PRACTICAL ETHICS

*I suppose if there is no question, there is no answer.*

GERTRUDE STEIN

This remark, reportedly the last words ever uttered by Gertrude Stein, encapsulates a profound insight. There can be questions without answers—there are many questions without answers—but there can be no answers without questions. Thus what one must ask first is, "What is the question?" not "What is the answer?" And if only an answer is provided, one must determine just what question it is an answer to.

### I

A moral philosophy is essentially a set of concepts, relations, and propositions designed to clarify and to answer both certain theoretical questions—those that arise out of the process of theorizing itself—and certain practical questions: those that arise out of the practice, and the difficulties in practice, that give rise to the theoretical activity in the first place.

There are some who maintain that it does not matter what ethical theory one holds—what one's moral philosophy is—so far as the determination of one's duties goes. Paley, for example, remarked that

> moralists, *from whatever different principles they set out,* commonly meet in their conclusions: that is, they enjoin the same conduct, prescribe the same rules of duty, and with a few exceptions, deliver upon dubious cases the same determinations.[1]

[1] William Paley, *The Principles of Moral and Political Philosophy* (1785), bk. II, ch. 1 (italics added).

There is an opposite view, however, according to which two persons can hold exactly the same principles and still arrive at conflicting conclusions about conduct. It is interesting to note that both these views, apparently so opposed, actually agree in their implication that moral theory is irrelevant to moral practice, since both maintain that one's abstract or general moral principles do not determine one's conclusions about moral right and wrong in particular cases.

There is, certainly, some truth in each of these views. Persons whose principles are fundamentally different can agree on some concrete questions of conduct, and those with the same or similar principles can arrive at widely divergent conclusions. But this is not evidence that moral philosophy is irrelevant to moral problems; it only underlines what should already have been obvious, that factors other than one's abstract theory play a role in determining the conclusions one arrives at about what is right or wrong in concrete cases. And that theory is not the only thing relevant is no evidence that it is irrelevant.

This book is designed to show how theory is relevant to practice by tracing out the implications of different forms and types of ethical theory for certain basic questions of moral practice.

## II

One's idea of what an ethical theory is and what it can and should be expected to do essentially determines the kind of theory one is likely to find congenial. But the very question whether moral philosophy—ethical theory—has moral relevance is one that itself has moral relevance, since any answer to it has implications for practice. Thus at the very outset we find controversy about what moral philosophy is about and what it can reasonably or properly be expected to do, and this controversy is both theoretically and practically important.

On one main tradition the task of moral philosophy is purely critical, descriptive, or analytical, and it is not to issue in moral judgments or to have any moral relevance. On this view, in other words, moral theory—ethics in the theoretical sense—is to be morally neutral. Such a view is set out in the following way by A. J. Ayer:

> There is a distinction, which is not always sufficiently marked, between the activity of a moralist, who sets out to elaborate a moral code, or to encourage its observance, and that of a moral philosopher, whose concern is not primarily to make moral judgments but to analyze their nature.[2]

[2] A. J. Ayer, Editorial Foreword to P. H. Nowell-Smith, *Ethics* (Baltimore: Penguin Books, 1954), p. 7.

Similarly, in his influential work *Ethics and Language,* C. L. Stevenson tells us that "there is a marked distinction between the conclusions that are drawn *about* normative ethics and those that are drawn *within it,*" and explains that his book

> is related to normative (or "evaluative") ethics in much the same way that conceptual analysis and scientific method are related to the sciences. One would not expect a book on scientific method to do the work of science itself; and one must not expect to find here any conclusions about what conduct is right or wrong.[3]

Strangely enough, a very similar example of this point of view, now—or recently—so much in fashion, was presented some time ago, when it was not in fashion, by F. H. Bradley (a metaphysical idealist and an unapologetic metaphysician), who maintained that

> there cannot be a moral philosophy which will tell us what in particular we are to do, and . . . it is not the business of philosophy to do so. All philosophy has to do is "to understand what is", and moral philosophy has to understand morals which exist, not to make them or give directions for making them . . . ethics has not to make the world moral, but to reduce to theory the morality current in the world.[4]

Certainly there are great differences in the ways in which Bradley (19 and 34), on the one hand, and Ayer (24) and Stevenson on the other, view philosophy, and in what they would regard as constituting "understanding what is," but the similarity in import is obvious.[5]

The enterprise or discipline that draws conclusions *about* normative ethics, and not *within* it, to use Stevenson's point of distinction, has come to be called "metaethics," presumably on the theory that a difference in name will mark off an important difference in function.

Metaethics, then, is a discipline containing problems and assertions about ethics. Any statement about ethics belongs, by definition, to meta-

---

[3] C. L. Stevenson, *Ethics and Language* (New Haven: Yale University Press, 1944), pp. vii, 1. On p. 159 great emphasis is placed on the importance of scientific detachment in studying "controversy about ethical methods," in order that the study itself will not have any effect in altering these methods. But why should it not?

[4] F. H. Bradley, *Ethical Studies* (Oxford: The Clarendon Press, 1876; 2nd ed., 1927), p. 193. See selection 19 (p. 167), where the passage appears.

[5] In addition to the selections mentioned, the point of view just delineated is represented in this volume by E. F. Carritt (2). An opposing point of view is represented by John Dewey (1) and Arthur Murphy (3). An interesting variant of the position of Ayer and Stevenson is presented by Stephen Toulmin, who holds that "an ethical theory of the traditional kind is no substitute for a descriptive account of the function of ethical concepts," which, he tells us, is "what we need" and what his book supplies (*The Place of Reason in Ethics* [Cambridge: The University Press, 1950], pp. 193–194).

ethics. Thus the question how moral judgments and moral principles can be justified is a question in (or of) metaethics. But what is ethics? That is a problem of metaethics. Is it also a problem of ethics? If the answer to the question has implications in and for ethics, then it is. And if the argument I have presented in selection 5 ("The Nature of Ethics") is sound, then it is. And if it is, then the question "What is ethics?" is not simply a question of metaethics but also a question of ethics. If this is so, then the problems of metaethics are not irrelevant to the problems of ethics, and metaethical analyses are not morally neutral—or not necessarily so—but have ethical and therefore practical moral bearings.

But perhaps this conclusion is only a trivial consequence of an essentially arbitrary definition of metaethics. Well, the literature of metaethics is not especially conspicuous for consistency of definition. Thus the question arises "What is metaethics?" Perhaps we should say, by analogy, that this is a question of metametaethics, except that, in addition to the stimulus it provides to stuttering, the analogy indicates that this is just a way of generating an interminable series of questions of no consequence. The important question is whether metaethics is ethically or morally neutral. (And not, in turn, whether this question is a question of metametaethics.) If "metaethics" is understood as just a name for philosophical inquiries into the nature and basis and methods of ethics and morality, it may be a useful piece of terminology. What should be evident is that such philosophical inquiry is not morally neutral. Consequently moral philosophy, which is what such inquiry is, is relevant to moral problems.

This is the main point distinguishing the other main tradition in moral philosophy, and it is well brought out by John Dewey when he says:

> If inquiries are to have any substantial basis, if they are not to be wholly up in the air, the theorist must take his departure from the problems which men actually meet in their own conduct. . . . If he gets away from them he is talking about something which his own brain has invented, not about moral realities.[6]

But what are these moral problems to which moral philosophy is supposed to be relevant? In one sense we all know, for we all face them and have constantly to deal with them in one way or another. In another sense, we do not, for the precise analysis of the nature of moral problems is itself a problem of moral philosophy, and one that is decidedly difficult.[7]

---

[6] John Dewey and James H. Tufts, *Ethics* (New York: Henry Holt and Company, 1908), p. 212.

[7] Something about this is said in selection 5, "The Nature of Ethics," and there are other selections and statements that are relevant. For example, selection 1 (Dewey) and statement 13.

A moral problem, like any problem, arises out of conflicting considerations, in this case conflicting moral considerations. Of course, if one does not feel the conflict, feel the force of the opposing considerations—which can be rules, duties, obligations, claims, rights, needs, interests, impulses, wants, or desires—one does not feel the problem, though perhaps it can be claimed that one ought to. But apart from this, moral problems can be of various kinds. At one extreme, a moral problem may be both personal and private: a person feels the pull of conflicting considerations and asks himself, "What should I do?" The answer he arrives at will almost invariably determine what he actually does. At the other extreme, a moral problem may be relatively abstract and impersonal: a person considers a question about social policy, or about something someone has done in the past, and asks, "Which policy should be adopted?" or "Should Caesar have crossed the Rubicon?" Unless one happens to be in a position of power or influence, which is extremely unlikely (and in fact impossible when dealing with the past), the answer that one arrives at will have no effect on conduct. So, although all moral problems seem to involve some reference to conduct, not all are such that the answers to them will, or even can, have a bearing on conduct. Moreover, not all decisions or problems about conduct—not even those expressed by the question "What should I do?"—are moral in character. (Consider, for example, the manager who asks himself, "What should I do? Should I let him hit away or give him the signal to bunt?" and arrives at a decision before the question can even be formulated in words. The problem in this case, though it may be important, is clearly not moral.) Again, though it is clear that not all questions involving or affecting the interests of others are moral problems, it remains a matter of controversy whether a moral problem necessarily involves a reference to the interests of others, and apparently it is one's moral philosophy that determines whether one regards this characteristic as essential.

In between the extremes mentioned—the private problems where the answers definitely affect conduct, and questions of public policy where the answers one arrives at are unlikely to affect conduct—there is subtle gradation and variation. A very common type of problem arises when two (or more) persons have made up their minds about what ought to be done and each tries to persuade or convince the other to adopt his point of view, either in order to resolve some question of the sort "What should be done?" or simply as a matter of abstract discussion. Where there exist strong differences of opinion on opposing sides of some moral question we have what might be called a moral issue, rather than a moral problem. The discussions that are resorted to as means of settling them often turn into disputes, controversies, or conflicts, some of which, owing to the failure of other mutually agreed-on means of resolving them, may be resolved only by threats, intimidation, or warfare.

Now what I am maintaining, and what I trust this book will help to bring out, is that moral philosophy must be applicable to all kinds of moral problems, issues, and conflicts—even to the point of determining when moral considerations, in any traditional sense, are irrelevant to the genuine interests involved.

## III

The initial focus of the book is provided by such questions as the following: (1) What makes right acts right? What makes wrong acts wrong? Is there something common to and characteristic of all right actions in virtue of which they are right? Or is what makes a right action right something peculiar to that particular action and not a general characteristic necessarily shared by all other right actions? (2) How can it be determined which actions are right and which wrong? What is the difference between right and wrong anyway? What is the basis of this distinction? Are there any tests that can be applied, in particular cases or in general, for determining whether an act ought or ought not to be done? (3) Is the distinction between right and wrong a genuine and objective distinction, or is it merely a matter of convention, feeling, taste, or opinion?

Questions of the first set are about what constitutes rightness, what *makes* an act right. But one can know what *makes* an act right without knowing *whether* the act is right, because one may not know whether the conditions for rightness are satisfied. Thus questions of the second set are, for purposes of practical ethics, more fundamental, for they raise the questions how we can know whether an act is right or wrong and what would be good and accessible reasons for a moral belief. If one thinks of an ethical theory as designed to provide a test of right and wrong, from this point of view questions of the first set are mainly metaphysical in character, and no matter how fundamental they may be philosophically, they are not fundamental morally. It is these questions about morality, the epistemological and logical, and of course the various answers that have been given to them, that I have chosen to emphasize. Questions of the third set are typical, though not exhaustive, of moral skepticism, and it is evident that no satisfactory answers can be given to the epistemological or logical questions of ethics without some satisfactory way of settling the doubts generated by moral skepticism.

Because of what has been said about the basic importance of one's view of what ethics is and can do, Part I of the book contains a number of selections presenting different views of the nature and function of moral philosophy, and the second part of this Introduction presents some moral problems both for consideration in their own right and for the purpose of stimulating the reader to think of other problems in the light of which the theories presented can be considered. The ideal reader of this book is one who is prepared to think of moral theory in relation to a number of moral questions, problems, and issues derived from his own reading, experience, knowledge, or imagination. These problems should serve as tests of the theories to be considered, and the theories, in turn, should serve as tests for the solutions to the problems.

This leads directly to Part II of the book in which several different theories, or tests, are presented and a number are discussed, defended, elaborated, criticized, or further explained.

A moral judgment is a judgment, or assessment, of the morality of an action, person, or institution. It should be distinguished (though not every writer does so) from a judgment of value, or an evaluation. An evaluation is an estimate, opinion, or assessment of the value, quality, worth, or desirability of something. It ought to be clear that one can make a value judgment without committing oneself to or presupposing any moral judgment or moral theory. When eggs are graded A or B, this is a process of evaluation, but it commits no one to any judgment of the morality of eating eggs or raising chickens to lay them. The evaluation of one automobile as a better buy than another—as is constantly made by an organization such as Consumers Union—implies no judgment about the morality of buying or driving automobiles. When one grades examinations as A, B, C, D, or—does it still happen?—F, one is not necessarily committing oneself to any judgment of the morality of the grading system or even to any judgment about the adequacy of the five-fold division of grades. Such distinctions are central to the main topic of Part III, "Values and Ideals," but they also play a role in part II. Bentham's Hedonic Calculus (10) is intended to provide a procedure for determining the value of a quantity of pleasure or pain. Its moral relevance, its relevance to the question of what ought to be done, is determined by the principle of utility, presented by Bentham in selection 9 (and also by Urmson in selection 11 and Sidgwick in 13).

To speak of theories as tests, or even to speak of the distinction between right and wrong at all, raises the inevitable, and important, question of moral skepticism. A number of varieties of this complex attitude, as well as rebuttals or criticisms of some of them, are presented in Part IV. But even some forms of skepticism turn out to have practical relevance. For ethical relativism, as one of the varieties of moral skepticism, raises doubts about the possibility of valid transcultural moral judgments, judgments made by a person in one culture about the practices, traditions, or institutions of another. However, if it is possible to make critical judgments of the institutions of one's own society, then it should be possible to make such judgments about the institutions of another, and this point is suggested, albeit dimly and unwittingly, in the selection by Ruth Benedict (27), and further suggested in the critique of relativism presented by Murphy (29). So this part of the section on skepticism has further relevance to the later parts of the book, on practical ethics.

But what, after all, is practical ethics? This is explained in the second part of this Introduction, "Moral Problems and the Study of Ethics," where a distinction is also drawn between ethics in the sense of a theory about conduct, and ethics in the sense of a code of conduct (p. 11). But something needs to be said about it now.

The traditional view of practical ethics is that it is that species of learning or instruction that teaches one (or *learns* one) one's duties. Thus a work entitled *Practical Ethics,* dating from 1892, says that

> Such a book must be direct and practical. It must contain clear-cut presentation of duties to be done, virtues to be culti-vated, temptations to be overcome, and vices to be shunned: yet this must be done, not by preaching and exhortation, but by showing the place these things occupy in a coherent system of reasoned knowledge.[8]

This, however, is not my conception of practical ethics. Virtue can be learned, but it is not to be taught, and certainly it is not to be inculcated. One cannot be taught one's duties, though one can learn them, because one cannot be taught how one ought to act, though one can develop one's capacity for moral judgment. However, only one who wants to learn them—who has moral beliefs and genuine moral problems—is capable of learning them and of developing moral understanding. Practical ethics, then, is that branch of ethics that deals directly with questions of moral practice rather than questions of ethical theory. It is not an exercise in moral catechism, for neither the answers nor the questions are determined in advance. Its aim is the development of the moral understanding, sense, or judgment and the resolution of moral problems and issues, not the indoctrination of moral dogma.

Hence, the emphasis in this collection is on casuistry, both its possibility and desirability; on the resolution of conflicts; and on the nature and evaluation of social institutions, including war.

[8] William DeWitt Hyde, *Practical Ethics* (New York: Henry Holt and Company, 1892), p. iv.

## IV

I mentioned earlier some things ethical theory can be expected to do. There are at least two things, however, that an ethical theory definitely cannot be expected to do, though on occasion theories have been devised for doing one or the other. No theory can be expected to provide a justification for every existing social institution or arrangement. Nor can any theory be expected to overturn and reject every existing institution or social arrangement.

No theory can possibly justify every existing institution because not all are justifiable. There are conflicts and clashes between them, which need adjudicating, so no wholesale justification is possible. And no theory can possibly provide grounds for rejecting every existing institution or practice, all at once and *in toto*, because if it attempted to do so, it could not get a purchase on our judgment, and hence could not possibly provide anyone with any reasons for accepting the theory itself.[9]

A good example of an ethical theory that attempts to justify every existing institution is Paley's. This attempt is epitomized by his argument in support of the human practice of eating the flesh of animals. Where this practice cannot be justified on his utilitarian criterion (as tending to increase the happiness of the whole sentient creation), and he finds that it cannot, he resorts to the interpretation of some cryptic scriptural declarations to determine that such an arrangement is in accordance with the will of God—as good an example as can be imagined of the use of a *deus ex machina* in philosophy. (See selection 6, section 9, pp. 52–54.)

Though it may not always be as artificial and unconvincing as the instance just mentioned, such a procedure simply will not work. For it is the feeling or conviction that things are somehow not right that gives rise to ethical theory in the first place, and this feeling or conviction, though it may in particular instances be wrong, is not to be eliminated or satisfied by any attempt at wholesale justification.

These two opposing attitudes towards the task of ethical theory are matched by analogous opposing attitudes towards morality itself. What may be called the Puritan (or Victorian, or Authoritarian) attitude towards morality maintains that all of our natural impulses are evil and should be suppressed. What may be called the Bohemian attitude towards morality maintains just the opposite: that all our natural impulses should be given free reign and that their suppression or restraint is evil. This often takes the form of antagonism towards morality as such.

---

[9]Some further explanation on these points is provided in selections 5, 15, and 16.

As I have described them, these attitudes are at the opposite and extreme ends of a continuous scale, and my description is, of course, only a caricature. No one could exist who adopted whole-heartedly and consistently what I have called the Puritan attitude towards morality. Some natural impulses, at least, must be followed if we are not to perish. And it is obvious that not all natural impulses can be given free reign, since they are so often in conflict with one another. So each of these attitudes, as here delineated, is equally unreasonable, though on different grounds. Yet I suspect that some of both is present in each of us.

Thus we have the limits of ethical theory, limits that ethical theory can itself determine. But given these extreme aberrations and variations of attitudes, which make for a basic unreasonableness in human nature, is there anything that can reasonably be regarded as the fundamental or overriding moral problem of our time?

I believe that there is, but that the overriding moral problem of our time is not something specific, or particular, or peculiar to our time. It is actually identical with the fundamental moral problem of all times: the problem of establishing a moral order in which moral issues and conflicts, and conflicts on other issues as well, can be resolved in a way that is fair and reasonable, and in a way that will be accepted as fair and reasonable by all who think about and are concerned about the matter.

I have not presented this idea as a prescription for a utopia. For one thing, it is not a prescription at all; for another, I doubt that the situation envisaged would actually be a utopia. It would certainly be much better than the situation that exists now, or any situation that has ever existed on this earth. Yet this would not make it a utopia. The moral order envisaged is something to be brought about, and to be brought about it must be worked for. It is, in other words, an ideal, and to the extent that it is attained the world would be a much better place than it is. Is this situation attainable, in any substantial degree whatever? Can such a moral order be established? I do not know—no one knows or can know—but it would be nice to think so. And not only would it be nice to think so, but we ought to think so, because this much at least we do know, that if we do not think so then we cannot do so.

# II. MORAL PROBLEMS AND THE STUDY OF ETHICS*

There are a number of different ways of teaching ethics. I am sure that there is no one way that is right, but I am also sure that there are many ways that are wrong. For example, it is wrong, in my judgment, to teach ethics—at least introductory ethics—by simply presenting and discussing a number of ethical theories in isolation from the actual or imagined problems of morality that these theories were developed in response to. It is wrong, in other words, to present ethics as a set of disembodied abstractions.

But I do not want to dwell here on ways that I regard as wrong. Rather I want to suggest a way that is right and that can be very effective if executed with at least some virtuosity.

Let us distinguish between moral education and the study of ethics. Moral education is the attempt by instructional means to expand the student's capacity to grasp moral principles, to develop the student's moral sense, and to increase the student's moral motivation. This may or may not be a worthy or possible enterprise. But to engage in moral education is not the same as teaching ethics, which is clearly something that is both possible and desirable. Good moral character is not a prerequisite for the study of ethics, nor is it a guaranteed, or even an expected, end product.

A distinction must also be made between at least two different senses of the term "ethics." At a lower level of abstraction, the term is used to refer to a code of conduct; in this sense we can speak of a given person's ethics, or the ethics of a certain profession. At a higher level of abstraction, the term is used to mean a theory of, or philosophical reflection about, morality or ethics in the sense just delineated. Let us call the first sense "the code of conduct sense" and the second sense "theoretical ethics." It is ethics in the second, or theoretical, sense with which I am here concerned. When one asks "Can ethics be practical?" what one is asking is whether ethics in the theoretical sense can apply to, alter, or be used to resolve problems about ethics in the sense of a code of conduct. The application of theoretical ethics to these tasks is what is meant by practical ethics.

I am convinced that in an introductory course it is a mistake to try to study theoretical and practical ethics in isolation from one another; there should be some reasonable mix. Therefore the teaching of ethics, if it is

*This material, "Moral Problems and the Study of Ethics," is based upon "The Teaching of Introductory Ethics" by Marcus Singer, an article that previously appeared in *The Monist*, Vol. 58, No. 4 (October 1974), pp. 616–629.

done right and done well, involves an appropriate combination of the theoretical and the practical, and such teaching can affect character (though perhaps it ought not to) by affecting the understanding.

How can this be done right and done well? One way is by the use of what can be called a modified case method. To use simply a case method—that is, simply to present a series of actual cases for discussion, with the idea that appropriate principles and standards will somehow be generated inductively through the process of reflection and discussion—though it could prove an interesting enterprise for a time, will not do. There must be some knowledge of "ethical laws," or moral principles, *ab initio,* in order to know what the problem is supposed to be. For unless one has moral beliefs, one cannot have or even recognize any moral problems. So to fail to assume a knowledge of these laws, a knowledge of relevant moral standards and principles, at the outset, is to go wrong at the outset. And the fact that a case in ethics is a made-up one, and is not drawn veraciously from some real life happening, is not a drawback. It can actually be an advantage. In a modified case method, real cases have no better claim to authenticity and utility than imaginary ones, and one does not suppose that the mind, in approaching the study of morality, is a moral *tabula rasa.* And this is perfectly all right. For it does not matter so much what people have actually done or judged as it does what they ought to have done or judged; and as long as one does not alter reality *too much,* one is on safe ground. But one cannot suppose, for example, that human beings become immortal, or immune to physical harm, or incapable of being deceived or otherwise injured; this would simply change the subject. One may imagine, and even create, cases and circumstances, but one may not invent a world where the laws of nature are different, or so different as to generate a morally relevant difference; and the determination of when this has been done is itself a problem of morality.

In an ethics text using a modified case method, the following "case," as it is called, is presented:

> As I make out the grades for a logic class, I am tolerably sure of the following facts. Student No. 1 will not get into law school next fall unless he receives a B. He has earned a C. To miss entering in the fall means having to wait another entire year. Student No. 2 will be dropped from college by the dean if he fails to get a C in each of his courses. He has earned a D. The logic course was not in any sense necessary to him in his future work; he registered for it because he had heard that it was interesting and not too difficult. Student No. 3 will be able to graduate if he receives merely a D. If he receives an F, he will not. He has earned an F. His low mark

was probably due to a combination of laziness and indifference. What ought I to do in each case?[1]

Let us add to the list of examples by making up some more. Student No. 4, let us imagine, needs a B to get into medical school. His great ambition in life is to become a physician, and he grew up in a family immersed in medical life. Both his mother and his father are doctors, as are both his grandfathers. He has earned a D. Student No. 5, let us suppose, needs an A in order to retain a fellowship he has been awarded by a graduate school. He has earned a B. What ought I to do in each of *these* cases? To add further examples is to sharpen and define the moral judgment that needs to be made. Should all these cases be handled in the same way; that is to say, should the grade be changed in each case in accordance with the specified need of the student? Or, rather, should the grade be determined in each case by the instructor's judgment of what grade the student has earned? If one is to distinguish one case from another and say that the grade should be raised in some cases but not in others, on what standard can this distinction be made? Does treating these cases differently need justification? If so, what would justify it? Suppose my grading is determined, not by any evaluation of what grade a student has "earned" or by any consideration of what grade a student needs to attain some predetermined end, but rather by whether I like the student or not. Would this be fair? Would this be right? Ought it to be done? Ought it to be tolerated?

What is especially interesting about this case is the way it tends almost inexorably to generate questions about the relevant or related institution of grading. In a system where this institution does not exist, no such problems can arise. Where the institution operates under radically different rules— where, for example, there is only a Pass/Fail option—the only question that can arise concerns student No. 3. Is this a reason for changing or abolishing the institution of grading? Someone who, in considering the problems that are raised by this case, asks such questions as "What are grades for, anyhow? What does a grade mean? How are grades used?" is raising questions about the institution of grading, not about the particular case. This may be perfectly sensible and appropriate. Then again it may not. For if one is operating within the confines of the institution of grading as it is determined in a particular college or university, it may not be open to one, in those circumstances, to raise the question about the appropriateness, fairness, or reasonableness of the institution. Of course, one might decide to subvert the institution—or "the system," as it is so quaintly called—by giving everyone A's. Such a person would not, and could not, have any of

---

[1] Alburey Castell, *An Elementary Ethics* (Englewood Cliffs: Prentice-Hall, Inc., 1954), p. 5.

the particular problems detailed above. He would, presumably, give each of the students the grade he needed or wanted, or something even higher. But another question arises, though our subversive grader might not recognize it, and that is whether anyone has the right to subvert the institution of grading in this way. Does the responsibility of grading convey the right to grade as one pleases?

These are just some of the questions, which in turn lead to further problems, generated by the case cited. And to introduce ethical theory as a device for clarifying these questions and their circumstances and for providing guidance towards reasonable answers is what I would suggest as a proper and sensible mode for the teaching of introductory ethics. Though the actual case may be made up, it is certainly real enough to generate a moral problem and to raise the various questions that one would expect an ethical theory to be able to deal with and provide some means for answering.

Let us consider another example, which I adapt from a newspaper article of some years ago, in which a number of persons, selected at random, were asked to give their answers to a question. The question was: "According to scientists, about fifty years from now people will be able to determine the sex of their child and decide whether they want one or more at a time. Do you think that would be a good thing?" (The question as it actually appeared was: "Would you like that?" Is that the same question?)

Here are some sample answers:

1. Woman, office worker: "I really don't think it will ever come to that. Anyway it should not—it should be up to nature to determine. Nature has done a good job up till now and I don't think it should be meddled with. A lot of people might wish it could be done but I don't want to see it."

2. Woman, student: "I don't know too much about it. Personally I think it should be the province of God. It should not be in our realm. Part of the joy and hope of having children is wondering and expecting. I don't think it should be up to the individual. For one thing it might cause an unbalance of one sex or the other."

3. Man, businessman: "Identifying the sex after conception, if it would positively work, would make it easier for parents to shop and decorate the nursery. It would make showers for babies easy and cut out the disappointment if the parents' hearts were set on one or the other. However, to decide sex before the child is conceived would be destroying nature and would be morally wrong."

4. Woman, teacher: "It would be very welcome—as long as this is

optional and up to the individual and he is legally and mentally capable of choice. I suppose there would be some religious objection and there is always the chance of unbalance of the sexes. However, I think a family should have the right to determine which sex they prefer."

5. Woman, lab assistant: "I'd rather leave it up to nature and have the surprise as it comes. It is not the sort of thing that should be meddled with. It might lead to all sorts of complications and abnormalities, too. It is outside the sphere of man's influence, and in the hands of God. It might be applied to animals but not humans."

This is another case worthy of discussion, though obviously it is a case of an entirely different sort from the one presented before. The student can contemplate the question independently of these responses and try to decide how he would answer it and why. Then he can, and perhaps should, go on to consider the answers given and try to determine if any of the differences manifested can be reconciled. If they can, how? On what basis? What different theories, not just about morality but about the universe, are presupposed in the answers? What effects do they have? Which points made in the answers are genuinely responsive to the question asked and which are irrelevant? Which are merely personal reactions and which provide genuine moral judgments? Which judgments are backed by reasons and what reasons are given? Are these reasons sound or unsound? How can this be determined?

Here the main task, then, is to consider the role of theory in resolving controversy, and not simply in helping one make up one's own mind where there is no question of disagreement with another. And the fact that the questions and answers are drawn from an article that actually appeared in print makes absolutely no difference. For all the reader knows, the whole thing could have been made up. What difference would that make?

Let us consider one more case, of a somewhat similar nature, but in which the fact that a question is being raised about a practice or institution is more readily apparent.

Question: "Should men and women receive equal pay for equal services?"

Answers:

1. Man, salesman: "I don't think so. There are a lot of positions that a woman is not qualified to fill—through no fault of her own, of course. Further, the average man is a family man, and the rest of his family is dependent on him for support. It's still a man's world from a business standpoint."

2. Man, physician: "I am a doctor and my wife is a doctor, and if she does the same work I do I don't see any reason why she shouldn't receive the same renumeration. Men and women are equal in mental capabilities. My answer to your question would not, of course, apply to some forms of manual labor."

3. Woman, housewife: "I don't think so. Men should receive more money than women; they generally exhibit better judgment in most lines of work than women do. In my opinion women should, as a general rule, stay out of business. There are exceptions, naturally. I think women were intended to take care of children."

4. Man, executive: "If their responsibilities are comparable, men and women should be paid alike. That's if they're doing precisely the same kind of work. However, in the normal business organization consideration should be given to men if they have family status and home responsibilities. And you can ask a man to do some things on a job—attend night meetings, travel alone, etc.—that might make him worth more money than a woman."

5. Woman, farm housewife: "I haven't thought much about that, but I guess if men and women do the same kind and quality of work they should be paid alike. I really do think men should have the work that is available in the business world, because most men have homes and family responsibilities and should be enabled to earn the necessary money."

What is of special interest in this case is not so much the right answer to the question as the reasoning that supports these various answers. Some of the responses are totally irrelevant to the question at issue; others are more to the point; but there is none that does not commit a fallacy of irrelevance at some point. What this brings out is that we can distinguish between relevant and irrelevant considerations and that consequently there is such a thing as reasoning in support of a moral judgment, which suggests that a distinction can be made between good moral reasoning and bad moral reasoning. The making of such a distinction, or the formulation of standards for making it, is, indeed, one of the tasks of an ethical theory. And it makes no difference that none of the above responses has been made up and that all have been reproduced exactly as they appeared in print. (The astute reader might already have inferred that these answers were given at a time somewhat prior to the relatively recent revival of the Women's Liberation Movement.) Let us go on to make up some additional responses to the question in order to provide a somewhat wider range of moral opinions for analysis and criticism.

6. Woman, magazine editor: "Of course they should. Only a pig would ask such a question. Actually, women should receive higher pay to make up for the years of repression they have had to suffer and to redress the balance. This would also bring more women into various jobs that have been pre-empted by men but that women can do just as well or better."

7. Man, union organizer: "No, they should not. Equal services have nothing to do with it. Each person should be paid according to his or her years of service and seniority in the organization. If a woman has greater seniority than a man, then she should get higher pay; if a man has greater seniority in the same organization than a woman, then he should get paid more. It is very simple, and sex has nothing to do with it." .

8. Person of indeterminate sex, occupation not given: "No, I don't think so. Because they can never perform equal services. What should determine a person's pay is the number of people in his or her family dependent on him or her for support. It is solely a matter of need. The person who has more people to support should get more money, whether that person is a man or a woman."

9. Woman, unemployed: "Yes, I think so. If two people perform the same services they should receive the same pay. That just stands to reason. It's only because it's been taken for granted for so many years that a man would have greater family responsibilities that men have almost always received more pay for the same amount of work. But that's no longer true. Lots of women today have just as many family responsibilities as men."

10. Woman, go-go dancer: "No, women should receive more pay. They work harder and do all sorts of things that a man couldn't do. If women received more pay than men, the world would be a better place. They would quickly take on positions of greater responsibility and put an end to war, poverty, racism, and sexism."

Anyone who doesn't like these imaginary answers is invited to make up his (or her) own. In either case, the end in view, the more effective teaching of ethics, would be closer to achievement. For although one here is not confronted by a "case" in the usual sense of that term, complete with a recital of the facts together with the reasoning (opinion) that presumably led to the decision (judgment), one has something that is at least as valuable. One has a range of moral opinions, each answering the same moral question and each backed up by more or less relevant moral reasons, and this provides an impetus to the development of one's own powers of moral judgment by stimulating one to exercise them. To the extent that one is self-conscious about the reasoning and about the reasons (as distinct from the causes) for the differences of opinion represented, one has the stimulus to consider, and possibly try to formulate, an ethical theory whose object would be to try to bring some semblance of order out of this chaos.

This is what ethical theory is all about, and to study it in isolation from its source and subject matter is not only to take the life out of it but is morally and philosophically naive.

The following passage may be pondered: "The ultimate good may be what you will,—pleasure, self-realization, the greatest good of the greatest number, or the will of God—but in any case its practical manifestation must be in relations with men in some society; and I think that students—professional students—of ethics have largely lost sight of this fact. They leave the application of their theories to clergymen and social reformers, thinking their duty to be merely to discover the correct principles upon which all should act. Doubtless this would be a sufficient task if it were performed. But it is not performed; and one of the reasons, at least, why it is not performed is that the students have not borne in mind what the ultimate object of the study was." [2]

Precisely. And if we bear this in mind, I am confident that we shall be in a better position to discover and to formulate and establish the correct and ultimate principles of morality, and also know better how to apply them in the resolution of concrete problems and controversies.

[2] George Clarke Cox, *The Public Conscience: Social Judgments in Statute and Common Law* (New York: Henry Holt and Company, 1922), pp. 15–16.

# Part I

## Moral Problems
## and Moral Philosophy

For best understanding the selections in this part (and also the next), the reader would do well to keep in mind some clearly formulated moral problem. The grading problem presented in the General Introduction (pp. 12–14) can serve both as an example in its own right and as a model on which the reader can go on to formulate similar problems of his own. And the precise formulation is important. (Look back at the General Introduction, pp. 5–6, where an account of the nature of a moral problem is given.) Without a range of practical problems of conduct to serve as stimuli and to determine the relevance of the subject, the reader will get no adequate idea of the nature of ethical theory or the purpose of moral philosophy.

This last claim, of course, is the expression of a philosophical opinion, and it is as well to note that, while it is argued for further in selection 5, it is disputed in selections 2 (Carritt) and 19 (Bradley).

# STATEMENTS ON MORALITY

## *First Series*

1. *Foundations of morality are like all other foundations; if you dig too much about them the superstructure will come tumbling down.*
Samuel Butler

2. *What we call "morals" is simply blind obedience to words of command.*
Havelock Ellis (1923)

3. *So far, about morals, I know only that what is moral is what you feel good after and what is immoral is what you feel bad after and judged by these moral standards, which I do not defend, the bullfight is very moral to me because I feel very fine while it is going on and have a feeling of life and death and mortality and immortality, and after it is over I feel very sad but very fine.*
Ernest Hemingway (1932)

4. *Now what's the* use *of prying into the philosophical basis of morality? We all know what morality is: it is behaving as you were brought up to behave, that is, to think you ought to be punished for not behaving. But to believe in thinking as you have been brought up to think defines* conservatism. *It needs no reasoning to perceive that morality is conservatism. But conservatism again means, as you will surely agree, not trusting to one's reasoning powers. To be a moral man is to obey the traditional maxims of your community without hesitation or discussion.*
Charles Sanders Peirce (1898)

5. *So far are business men from being without moral standards that the majority of them, like the majority of other people, have three. There is first the standard which John Smith applies to his treatment of other people—his competitors, his customers, his*

*employees, and those from whom he purchases his supplies. There is, second, the
standard which he expects them to apply to him. Finally there is the standard which he
applies to other people's treatment of each other.*
F. C. Sharp and P. G. Fox (1937)

6. *The more I see, the more sure I am that it does not matter why people do the
right thing so long only as they do it, nor why they may have done the wrong if they have
done it. The result depends upon the thing done and the motive goes for nothing.*
Samuel Butler (1903)

7. *It is entirely on the motives and dispositions of the mind that the* moral
*character of any one's conduct depends. An action, indeed, which is done from a bad or
from an inferior motive, may be in itself right, as being what a good man would be
disposed to do; as when a man pays his debts for fear of being imprisoned, or having his
goods seized; but this does not make him an honest man.*
Richard Whately (1859)

8. *The fact that people generally desire something does not prove that they should
do so, for by following their desires they may bring on themselves an evil even greater
than that of struggling in vain to get what they want—the evil of getting it and
experiencing regret and disappointment, if not worse calamities. What people* ought to
*desire is what they* would *desire if they were enlightened and knew both what they
really wanted and what natural means would bring it about. Morality is thus wisdom
applied to the conduct of life, and yields rules which we would follow if we thought out
all the implication of our choices and knew in advance their consequences.*
Morris Cohen and Ernest Nagel (1934)

9. *It is one of the drawbacks of philosophy that it is always difficult to make its
problems—necessarily abstract and technical—appear to have much bearing on the
practical concerns that engage the ordinary man; and this is rather notably the case with
theories of value. What matters to people generally is the claim of values in particular;
and when they are asked to divest themselves temporarily of concrete interests and to
consider, not how best to plead some favorite cause, but what they mean when they call
anything at all a valuable end, the inquiry will seem not only barren and disappointing
but very likely mischievous as well, since it has the appearance of putting in doubt the
things to which it is most of all important that we should wholeheartedly yield assent.
It may be, however, that circumstances will at times arise to bring home the recognition
to a wider circle that such a preliminary task of criticism is after all not as unimportant
as it looks at first to be; and something like this situation is now actually confronting us.
So far as morals go, there probably has never been an age quite so perplexed and torn by
discord as the present one, or so little disposed to be submissive to the admonitions of*

*the good and great; and the reason is that for large numbers of people the things valued in the past have lost their motive power, and no one seems to know just how to go to work to replace them.*

A. K. Rogers (1934)

*10. All morality consists in a system of rules, and the essence of all morality is to be sought for in the respect which the individual acquires for these rules.*

Jean Piaget (1932)

# 1

## The Moral Situation*

### JOHN DEWEY
### (1859-1952)

. . . The moral situation is one which . . . involves a voluntary factor. . . . A voluntary act may . . . be defined as one *which manifests
character,* the test of its presence being the presence of desire and deliberation; these sometimes being present directly and immediately, sometimes
indirectly and remotely through their effects upon the agent's standing
habits. But we do not judge all voluntary activity from the moral standpoint. Some acts we judge from the standpoint of skill or awkwardness;
others as amusing or boring; others as stupid or highly intelligent, and so
on. We do not bring to bear the conceptions of right and wrong. And on the
other hand, there are many things called good and bad which are not
voluntary. . . .

. . . *Wherever one end is taken for granted by itself without any consideration of
its relationship to other ends.* . . . [it is] a technical rather than a moral affair. It
is a question of taste and of skill—of personal preference and of practical
wisdom, or of economy, expediency. There are many different roads to
most results, and the selection of this path rather than that, on the assumption that either path actually leads to the end, is an intellectual,
aesthetic, or executive, rather than an ethical matter. I may happen to
prefer a marine view to that of the uplands—that is an aesthetic interest. I
may wish to utilize the time of the walk for thinking, and may find the
moor path less distracting; here is a matter of intellectual economy. Or I
may conclude that I shall best get the exercise I want by going to the water
fall. Here it is a question of "prudence," of expediency, or practical wisdom.
Let any one of the ends, aesthetic, intellectual, hygienic, stand alone and it

*From *Ethics* by John Dewey and James H. Tufts (New York: Henry Holt and Company,
1908), Pt. II, pp. 201-202, 203, 206-10. Compare with statement 13.

is a fit and proper consideration. The moral issue does not arise. . . . But let the value of one proposed end be felt to be really incompatible with that of another, let it be felt to be so opposed as to appeal to a different kind of interest and choice, in other words, to different kinds of disposition and agency, and we have a moral situation. This is what occurs when one way of traveling means self-indulgence; another, kindliness or keeping an engagement. There is no longer one end, nor two ends so homogeneous that they may be reconciled by both being used as means to some more general end of undisputed worth. We have alternative ends so heterogeneous that choice has to be made; an end has to be developed out of conflict. The problem now becomes what *is* really valuable. It is the *nature* of the valuable, of the desirable, that the individual has to pass upon.

Suppose a person has unhesitatingly accepted an end, has acquiesced in some suggested purpose. Then, starting to realize it, he finds the affair not so simple. He is led to review the matter and to consider what really constitutes worth for him. The process of attainment calls for toil which is disagreeable, and imposes restraints and abandonments of accustomed enjoyments. An Indian boy, for example, thinks it desirable to be a good rider, a skilful shot, a sagacious scout. Then he "naturally," as we say, disposes of his time and energy so as to realize his purpose. But in trying to become a "brave," he finds that he has to submit to deprivation and hardship, to forego other enjoyments and undergo arduous toil. He finds that the end does not mean in actual realization what it meant in original contemplation—something that often happens, for, as Goldsmith said: "In the first place, we cook the dish to our own appetite; in the latter, nature cooks it for us."

This change in apparent worth raises a new question: Is the aim first set up of the value it seemed to be? Is it, after all, so important, so desirable? Are not other results, playing with other boys, convivial companionship, which are reached more easily and pleasantly, really more valuable? The labors and pains connected with the means employed to reach an end, have thrown another and incompatible end into consciousness. The individual no longer "naturally," but "morally," follows the selected end, whichever of the two it be, because it has been chosen after conscious valuation of competing aims.

Such competitions of values for the position of control of action are inevitable accompaniments of individual conduct, whether in civilized or in tribal life. A child, for example, finds that the fulfillment of an appetite of hunger is not only possible, but that it is desirable—that fulfillment brings, or is, satisfaction, not mere satiety. Later on, moved by the idea of this sort of value, he snatches at food. Then he is made aware of other sorts of values involved in the act performed—values incompatible with just the value at which he aimed. He brings down upon himself social disapproval and reproach. He is termed rude, unmannerly, greedy, selfish. He acted in accordance with an unhesitatingly accepted idea of value. But while reaching one result he accomplished also certain other results which he did not intend, results in the way of being thought ill of, results which are disagreeable: *negative values.* He is taught to raise the question of what, after all, in such cases is the *really* desirable or valuable. Before he is free to deliberate upon means, he has to form an estimate of the relative worth of various possible ends, and to be willing to forego one and select the other. . . .

. . . Moral experience is . . . that kind of conduct in which there are ends so discrepant, so incompatible, as to require selection of one and rejection of the other. This perception of, and selection from, incompatible alternatives, discriminates moral experience from those cases of conduct which are called out and directed by ideas of value, but which do not necessitate passing upon the *real worth,* as we say, of the value selected. It is incompatibility of ends which necessitates consideration of the *true* worth of a given end; and such consideration it is which brings the experience into the moral sphere. Conduct as moral may thus be defined as *activity called forth and directed by ideas of value or worth, where the values concerned are so mutually incompatible as to require consideration and selection before an overt action is entered upon.*

Many questions about ends are in reality questions about means: the artist considers whether he will paint a landscape or a figure; this or that landscape, and so on. The general character of the end is unchanged: it is to paint. But let this end persist and be felt as desirable, as valuable; let at the same time an alternative end present itself as also desirable (say keeping an engagement), so that the individual does not find any way of adjusting and arranging them into a common scheme (like doing first one and then the other), and the person has a moral problem on his hands. Which shall he decide for, and why? . . .

# 2

## The Purpose of Moral Philosophy*

### E. F. CARRITT
(1876–1964)

If, then, moral philosophy cannot prove either that we have duties or what in detail they are, it may well be asked why we study it. I think we all in some degree want, and also believe we have some obligation, to make ourselves and others capable of thinking and speaking clearly, especially about important matters such as conduct. All who have listened to discussions about morals in chance company, unused and untrained to such arguments, will know the profound dissatisfaction in which they conclude. Everybody contradicts everybody, including himself; nobody could conceal his obvious fallacies except by red herrings; misunderstandings are universal; the disputant who comes off best is the one who talks most and loudest because least aware of his own ignorance and of the intricacies in the subject. A discussion between trained thinkers will be as different from all this as a first-class match from one where the players know neither the rules nor the ropes. There will still be plenty of disagreement, but the disputants will know what they disagree about; they will understand each other's language and even the reasons for conclusions from which they differ; all parties will generally feel enlightened by the argument, and see that they have much in common. In such talks it is far more usual to hear "I believe after all you are right," or at least "There is something in what you say."

The cause of this improvement is that in moral philosophy we learn to use language with much greater care and discrimination. In ordinary talk, where no great consistency or accuracy is expected, we use terms like

*From E. F. Carritt, *Ethical and Political Thinking* (Oxford: The Clarendon Press, 1947), pp. 5–7. By permission of The Clarendon Press, Oxford. The title of this selection has been modified by the editor.

"right," "moral," "virtuous," "good," "meritorious," "obligatory," as if they all meant much the same; but when we have to speak accurately we find that actions and characters can be ethically commended on different grounds, and that we must either invent new words to indicate these differences or select which among the names we have hitherto used loosely is most appropriate to each. Even popular language begins to recognize this when it is said that an opponent is acting wrongly though honestly; that "an honest man is the noblest work of God" though honesty is merely the best policy. Moral philosophy distinguishes the ethical from the nonethical meaning of terms and also one ethical meaning from another.

Is the benefit of moral philosophy, then, purely intellectual and in no degree practical? I think that it does not and should not affect our conduct directly, for like other sciences it has no other basis than our apprehension of the facts and we must not juggle with facts to support our theory. If a moral philosopher's arguments led to practical precepts directly contradictory to men's reflective conclusions on simple moral questions, we should have the best possible reason for thinking that he was in error, that he had either argued fallaciously or assumed false premisses. In our most ordinary casuistry we have already embarked for an ethics; our more considered judgements are the philosopher's only data; and if he pretends to contradict them except by still more careful analysis of their meaning, he is like an astronomer who should declare a crescent moon gibbous because it must be so by his cosmology.

Philosophy, then, can only clarify our ethical thinking and help us to avoid taking for granted that uncriticized taboos or prejudices or fashions are moral judgements. The case is similar with logic, which can neither contradict nor confirm our immediate certainty that if all A is B and all B is C, all A is C, but may remind us of our uncertainty about the premisses, and by analyzing more complicated arguments help us to see that they are only specious fallacies, though in the end we must see it for ourselves.

So there comes about an indirect influence of moral philosophy upon conduct. Every sane person has done some moral philosophizing, but since most of us are intellectually lazy, if he has not been specially stimulated, this probably consisted in accepting high-sounding generalities of other people, who may either have been as superficial as himself or had some axe to grind. And for bad philosophy the only cure is better.

# 3

## The Use of Moral Theory*

### ARTHUR E. MURPHY
(1901–1962)

. . . The question with which the "practical" reader is likely to confront the sort of theory developed in the preceding chapter is simply and bluntly, "What of it?" Even if it were granted that the argument seemed cogent on the somewhat lofty level on which it appeared to proceed, what difference would the acceptance or rejection of it make in the more concrete areas of experience in which our thinking habitually, and more comfortably, moves? I think the question is a fair one, and in this chapter I propose to answer it.

The first step toward such an answer, however, is to ask another question. How should we expect a moral theory to make a difference in practical thinking and thus in practical affairs? The answer to this question was given in the previous section. The business of theories and abstractions, as we there discovered, is not to reproduce our direct experiences or to provide a ghostly duplicate of the experienced world in some allegedly super-sensible realm beyond. Their function is to extend and deepen the range of significant experience by showing us what to look for and what is significant in situations where mere gaping and pointing would quite certainly have missed the point, and where action without a grasp of relevant and salient factors is bound to be shortsighted and confused. The alternative to an adequately articulated theory in such cases is not the hard-headed rejection of "mere theory," which simple-minded "realists" like to think they have achieved. It is the uncritical use of theories whose preconceptions are so familiar and habitually accepted that they can be

---

*From A. E. Murphy, *The Uses of Reason* (New York: Macmillan, 1943), pp. 136–40. Reprinted with the kind consent of Dr. Frederick H. Ginascol, executor of the Murphy estate. Compare with selection 29. The title of this selection was supplied by the editor.

assumed without the painful mental effort which, for many, is required for a first-hand examination of principles. Where such acceptance works well and suffices for the purpose at hand, no further practical question need arise. But preconceptions which make adequate sense for one purpose, under limited conditions, or in a restricted area of experience, may prove altogether inept and confusing where a different or more extended application is called for. Those who persist in employing them under such circumstances are simply not able to make essential identifications and discriminations within the field in which they are trying to work. They cannot even report fairly what they find, for their unacknowledged preconceptions commit them in advance to its systematic misdescription. They literally do not know what they are talking about, for they lack that intellectual mastery of their subject-matter which only a just, discriminating and pertinent articulation of its structure—that is, a good theory—could provide.

Popular and practical discussions of the issues of conduct have suffered much in recent years for lack of a commonly understood theory capable of performing this enlightening function. There is a great tradition of moral teaching to which appeal is made from time to time for edifying and ceremonial purposes. And there are vested interests in "spiritual" values eager to claim for this tradition, and for themselves as its spokesmen, an absolute and unassailable authority in thought and conduct. In times of stress and uncertainty, and in moments of nostalgic reminiscence, we are inspired by the affirmation that the eternal values stand unshaken and heartened to see that there is still a group of men who can speak with such righteous assurance as to their nature. For the rest such transcendent values enter but little into our effective thinking on more mundane issues. Indeed, the nature of their incidence upon such issues is a subject for endless and not very profitable dispute. But we still like to think that they are there, and we are made uncomfortable and resentful by any overt denial of their unconditional validity. Hence the "plain man" is, as a rule, an absolutist on moral issues or, at least, is likely to become one as soon as he hears that familiarly accredited maxims of conduct are being openly questioned. A full-blown moral theory emerges when this incipient absolutism is made the basis for an ethical doctrine, its primary assurances—in a purged and rarefied form, to be sure—accorded the status of self-evident truths, and its conclusions bulwarked by reference to a "reality" which is held "in the end" to guarantee the deliverances of rightly instructed moral judgment.

Such ethical absolutism has its merits, and it has done good service in preserving for our generation—though sometimes in a mummified form—the great insights of the past on which any adequate moral theory must build. But it does not operate in an atmosphere, or on a level, which has proved conducive to the intellectual mastery of our current problems. What it provides is not so much a means of thinking accurately and adequately about these problems as an assurance that, when our thinking fails, we can still confidently claim that what we antecedently wished to affirm is "somehow" true. And if the ground for this assurance is questioned, the absolutist is all too likely to interpret a criticism of his ethical theory as an attack on the foundations of public morals. The ensuing controversies have their uses, but the rational organization of experience is not among them.

In recent years the chief alternative to this sort of absolutism has been the brand of popular enlightenment which goes by the general name of "relativism." It is an odd but, for many, a persuasive amalgam of methodological positivism masquerading as intellectual honesty, of a sharp and still surprised awareness of the diversity of moral codes and customs, and of a brand of "liberalism" or "tolerance" which sums up its somewhat attenuated moral insight in the judgment that no moral judgments are morally legitimate or scientifically respectable. The excellent motives and often plausible theoretical considerations which lead good men and competent thinkers to adopt this theory will become apparent as we proceed. It will be equally apparent, however, that the attempt to apply it in the analysis and evaluation of moral behavior can only end in failure. It can be eloquently defended as a program for the generalization of scientific enlightenment and social benevolence, but it cannot be put to use without incoherence and confusion, for the categories which constitute its intellectual equipment are radically inappropriate to the subject-matter to which they are applied. We are harvesting today, in quite "practical" affairs, the fruits of that confusion.

I propose in this chapter to discuss the nature and consequences of these two ways of dealing with moral problems, as examples of the way in which an "ethical abstraction" does make a difference in the way we think and act. It is not a matter of indifference to such thought and action that those who chiefly function in our society as the spokesmen for the "higher" values have been able to express their moral enthusiasms—and ours— chiefly in the form of vaguely edifying generalities and/or angry attacks on those who differ from them with respect to the dogmatic foundations, theological or metaphysical, on which these generalizations have traditionally been based. Nor is it an inconsiderable factor in our present confusions that those earnest souls who turn to science for intellectual nourishment have so often received the stony negations of moral positivism as the best that critical thinking in this field has to offer. That we have failed so often to estimate rightly the nature of our moral responsibilities and resources in the contemporary world is a consequence, at least in part, of our failure to know where to look for pertinent enlightenment, or how to interpret what we found. This is an intellectual failure with moral implications and practical effects. It is an illustration of how "ethical abstractions" operate when they are inadequate to their task.

The only cure for an inadequate theory is a better and more adequate one. It is, indeed, only in terms of such a theory that the inadequacies of current views and the possibilities for improvement can fruitfully be exhibited. I believe that, in the theory outlined in the preceding chapter, we have the means for making this sort of correction, not through a polemical destruction of rival doctrines, but by a use of discriminations there developed to set the relevant factors involved in the issues of conduct in such order and relationship that their factual basis and ideal or moral significance can be justly and reliably determined. The true—to repeat our quotation from Spinoza—is the norm or standard for itself, and for the false as well. If we can see, in the terms this theory provides, how and where the mistakes were made which have in the past contributed to our confusion, and what corrections are required to clarify and organize our moral purposes, then its use as an ethical abstraction will have been exhibited. This is what we should expect an adequate moral theory to do for us. . . .

# 4

## Ethics As a Science*

### W. D. LAMONT
### (1901–    )

So far, in our account of the nature and subject-matter of ethics, we have been able to proceed along traditional lines. Ethics is the study of human conduct in respect of its rightness or wrongness in the light of some supreme standard and it is a purely theoretical inquiry, although it may be undertaken with a view to the practical application of the conclusions which it establishes. But we come now to an important problem for which traditional modes of thought offer no clear solution. The problem is this: when we say that the central problem of ethics is to explain the nature of the standards or principles upon which our moral judgements are based, do we mean standards which we "ought" to use, or standards which we "do in fact" use? It appears that most writers on the subject have not devoted much attention to this distinction; and their arguments suggest that they approach the problem of moral standards now from the one point of view and again from the other. They sometimes speak of the task of ethics as that of "explaining and defending" the principles upon which the "plain man" bases his moral ideas. In other words, they conceive of their task as that of showing both that these are the principles which we actually use, and also that they are the ones which we ought to use. But I cannot see how any "ought" can enter into the question at all. The only question in moral theory which we can legitimately ask about moral standards is, "What are the standards actually employed?" We involve ourselves in self-contradiction if we try to argue that they, or some other set of standards, ought to be employed.

I do not base this contention upon any general view of the place of

*From W. D. Lamont, *The Principles of Moral Judgement* (Oxford: The Clarendon Press, 1946), pp. 9–12. By permission of The Clarendon Press, Oxford.

value judgements in a process of theoretical reasoning. It is sometimes said that value judgements cannot form either premisses or conclusions in strictly logical thinking. This view seems to me to be very doubtful. It is perfectly logical to argue: All good children go to heaven; Mary is a good child; Therefore Mary goes to Heaven. Or: All German optical instruments are good; This is a German optical instrument; Therefore this instrument is good. My difficulty about the view that ethics is concerned to establish moral standards which we ought to follow is not founded upon any theory about value judgements in general and their place in theoretical reasoning, but arises from the particular case of moral standards.

The difficulty is this: any statement of an "ought" implies some standard of judgement from which the "ought" follows. Therefore if we assert that there is some supreme standard in accordance with which we ought to pass judgements on actions, we are asserting, on the one hand, that the standard is supreme (and that there can, therefore, be no higher standard), and, on the other hand, implying by the "ought" a further higher standard of judgement in accordance with which we judge our "supreme" standard (and which cannot then be supreme). Now the standard or standards of moral judgement is or are supreme (we are at present leaving it an open question whether we have a number of separate standards or only one); that is presupposed in the conception of "moral" rightness. Hence we cannot intelligibly ask whether the moral standard ought to be followed as a standard of judgement. We can only ask what is the nature of the standard or standards which we do in fact use in making moral judgements.

It may be said that, if a person is anxious to attain to a consistent moral perspective, it is not sufficient to explain to him the principles which he does, in fact, use. He will want to know more than this. Are these principles good, the best ones which it is possible to use, the ones, in short, which he "ought" to use? How can we satisfy him on such points if it is "unintelligible" to ask whether the standard which he uses as supreme is really the one which he ought to use?

In replying to this point, it is necessary to consider two possible alternatives. (*a*) Our analysis of moral ideas may show that there are several different standards in use by men, and that there is nothing to suggest that these are all merely subordinate forms of a single more general principle. That is to say, we may have a number of different ultimate criteria. (*b*) Our investigation may show that all the standards which men consciously use are but different expressions of one ultimate principle.

(*a*) If there are different standards, and if we can find no single supreme principle in accordance with which we can show that one rather than the others ought to be used, that is to say, if there are several independent "supremes," it is still possible to institute the further inquiry as to whether the use of the different standards is correlated with differences in level of civilization, mental development in the individual, &c., and whether there is any order in which they tend to displace each other. If no such correlations are seen to exist, this will suggest an irrational factor in the very heart of the moral consciousness, and that the individual's question as to whether his standard is a "good" one is equally irrational. All sorts of possibilities are opened up if we suppose that there may be various supreme principles of judgement; and it is profitless to speculate as to what we shall do if we find this to be the case, until we have gone into the matter and tried to discover whether it really is so.

(*b*) If, on the other hand, our investigation shows that all the standards actually in use imply some single ultimate principle, the further question will naturally arise as to why this one and not another lies at the basis of moral judgement. It may be found that the principle follows from certain fundamental characteristics in human nature itself. Should this turn out to be so, the question as to whether a person ought to use this standard will still be meaningless; for, following as it does from something in his own essential nature, he cannot avoid using it in making moral judgements. It will be analogous to the "principles of understanding" in Kant's theory of knowledge. There are certain "categories of thought," he holds, such as "substance and quality" and "cause and effect," the operation of which is assumed in every judgement we make about what "is." These categories are grounded in the nature of the human mind. In like manner, it may be that the principles we actually use in our moral judgements are so fundamental to our nature that their operation is assumed in every judgement we make about what "ought to be." Here again I am not attempting to pre-judge the issue of our investigation into moral ideas. I am simply suggesting a possibility which has to be kept in mind as an ultimate result of this investigation.

The central question of ethics, then, with which we shall be concerned in the following chapters, is: What are the principles on which we base our moral judgements of right and wrong? We shall be concerned here with the analysis of moral ideas, and particularly with the analysis of moral judgements on conduct, in order to discover the standards implied in those judgements; and I have described this as the central problem in the "science" of ethics. . . .

# 5

## The Nature of Ethics*

### MARCUS SINGER

(1926–      )

Ethics, as a branch of inquiry, is the study of the principles, standards, and methods for distinguishing right from wrong, good from bad, and better from worse. It thus involves reflection upon the phenomena of morality, and it differs from ordinary reflection on these phenomena in being more searching, systematic, and self-conscious. It is characteristic of philosophical inquiry generally not to be satisfied with immediate practical solutions, but to aim at a clarified and comprehensive understanding.

The phenomena of morality are, basically, moral beliefs, which in turn issue in standards, codes, and laws, and sometimes even influence conduct. We all have moral beliefs, beliefs about what is right and what is wrong, on which we base our moral judgments. For example, many people believe that it is wrong to punish a person for a crime he did not commit. Some people believe that capital punishment is wrong and ought to be abolished. There are some who believe that it is all right to cheat as long as you can get away with it, or that what has come to be known as payola is all right because it is a widespread business practice. That something is all right because "everyone is doing it" is itself a moral belief, though an absurd one.

It is on such moral beliefs, some sensible and some not, that we base our specific moral judgments, on a person's conduct, on his character, and on social practices and institutions. Frequently people restrict their moral judgments to the conduct and character of others, but there are a few over-conscientious people who do not always operate with this restriction.

Not only do we all have moral beliefs, but we also have moral

*Prepared especially for this volume. A somewhat modified version, entitled "Metaethics and the Nature of Ethics," appeared (in Polish translation only) in *Etyka,* Vol. 11 (Warsaw, 1973), pp. 121–25.

problems, problems about what ought to be done, whether a certain course of action would be right or wrong or morally permissible. These can arise at many different levels, for example, at the personal level: "Should I stay away from work on the pretense that I'm ill in order to play golf?" or "Is it all right for me to sleep with my best friend's wife, or should I break up my friendship first?"; or at a somewhat more exalted level: "Should the practice of euthanasia be legalized?" or "Should the practice of birth control be enforced by the State?" This last is, of course, a problem of politics, law, economics, and ecology, but it is also a problem of morality. For it involves the question whether the arrangement referred to is fair and justifiable. To have a moral problem, or to recognize a problem as a moral one, is not to have a sick conscience. It is a perfectly natural phenomenon. For moral problems arise out of our moral beliefs—from the fact that they are not always adequate, often vague, and frequently in conflict. These beliefs, and the problems to which they give rise, provide both the data and the starting point for ethical theory, which attempts to coordinate these beliefs, to systematize them and to make them coherent, and to find ways of answering moral questions and settling moral issues. An ethical theory, in essence, is a theory about the nature and basis of morality and the appropriate standards for moral judgment, and it most naturally arises out of reflection on the actual moral perplexities of everyday life.

There are many such theories that have been put forward in the history of human thought, and there is much to be learned from them. The problems have not all been solved, or even formulated, and new ideas are constantly being put forth. This often leaves a confused impression, and it is obviously an aid in considering the rival arguments to have some criteria for evaluating these theories themselves. There are at least three.

The first criterion is derived from the first task of an ethical theory, which is to make clear the reasons why certain kinds of acts are right and others wrong—what makes right actions right and wrong actions wrong. This naturally presupposes that some actions are right and others wrong, and this is a supposition that must be defended in the development of the theory. But the first test of an ethical theory is how well it performs this task of *explanation.*

Secondly, an ethical theory should be *coherent,* both (1) with itself and (2) with what on other grounds is known to be true, and (3) should help to make our moral ideas and beliefs coherent.

Thirdly, such a theory should *enlighten,* in the sense of being relevant to the solution of moral problems. This does not mean that it must provide automatic solutions to them. This is out of the question, for in morality the factor of judgment can never be totally eliminated, and the problems of morality often depend upon determinations of fact for which no theory can provide a guarantee. What it means is that an ethical theory should throw some light on the factors that are relevant to and the conditions to be met by a satisfactory solution. It should, in other words, help to bring order out of confusion.

One such confusion is the idea that the standards and practices of one's own particular community are inherently right, while others, where they differ, are wrong. But ethics, in searching for the basis of morality, while it may support some present or local standards, will certainly reject others. It must, because they are not all consistent with one another. The opposite of this sort of *parochialism* is *relativism,* the idea that there are no valid standards, because there are so many. This often leads to the supposedly enlightened view that no one ought ever to make any moral judgments, because it is unfair for anyone to impose his own values on others. The contradiction in this last statement ought to be obvious, but it apparently is not, perhaps because the contradiction is compounded, which is, as we all know, a mark of profundity.

It ought to be obvious that the claim that one ought never to make any moral judgments is itself a moral judgment, and not just a universal judgment, and it is here presented, in a rather whimsical way, as supported by another moral judgment, that it is unfair for anyone to impose his own values on others. No doubt it is unfair to impose one's own values on others, but it by no means follows that in simply making a moral judgment one is thereby imposing one's own values on others. Both these views, parochialism and relativism, confuse mores or customs with morality—what happens to be or what is thought to be with what ought to be—which shows that they are not so old-fashioned after all.

Another such confusion is the idea that morality is essentially dependent on the firmness of religious belief, so that a person who lacks religious faith must be immoral, since he has no reason not to be. It has even been propounded from on high, and occasionally made a rallying cry of some new committee for moral disarmament, that the moral virtues of democracy are founded solely on the firmness of God-given religious faith. One who lacks the tenacity of this faith, or confesses to occasional doubts, is branded as immoral or un-American or worse—supposing there could be anything worse. Thus immorality is defended on high and mighty moral grounds, and the faith in question is buttressed in the quicksands of passion, so the basically egoistic theory underlying this view remains unnoticed. "He that spits against the wind," as Ben Franklin warned Tom Paine, "spits in his own face," and where the wind is the shifting wind of doctrine no one is safe who spits. Better then to swallow one's own phlegm?

The problem here is obvious, as is its source. It is only its solution that is not, since there is no ready way of easing human fears.

Still another confusion is the idea that morality is limited to the rules and sentiments governing sexual behavior, an idea common enough to be reflected in our language and in our folklore, as in such expressions as "a woman of easy virtue" and in the idea that "immorality" is an euphemism for unorthodox sexual behavior. Sex, however, is only a part of life. It may play a particularly prominent role in the lives of people between, say, 15 and 55, but it is still not their sole concern—or seldom is—and it is not reported to play any role in heaven. Morality, on the other hand, extends to the whole of life, and does not relate solely or even primarily to phenomena connected with sex. To keep a proper balance betwen whole and part, between means and ends, and between what is good and what is better, is the part of wisdom, which the study of ethics helps to inculcate. For ethics aims at attaining a sensible scale of values, and at delineating the elements involved in a good life.

So there is no part of life, and consequently no public practice or social institution, that is not subject to moral criticism. These include the practices of law, politics, business, advertising, education, religion, medicine, the press, and many more. But, of course, there is no shortage of moral judgments and criticisms. There is hardly anything in more abundant supply. What is needed is more reasoned moral judgment, and it is the task of ethics to supply a basis for this. So what is needed is more thought and less declamation, as well as some measure of human feeling and understanding. It would be well to keep this in mind in considering discussions of the practical side of ethics, and before hurling judgments about with abandon. In dealing with individuals, at any rate, if to understand is not necessarily to forgive—and it is not—at least it helps, and it is worthwhile for its own sake. Compassion is not yet out-dated, nor is it the cure-all some seem to think it to be.

# STATEMENTS ON MORALITY
## *Second Series*

*11. The aim of Ethics is to systematise and free from error the apparent cognitions that most men have of the rightness or reasonableness of conduct, whether the conduct be considered as right in itself, or as the means to some end commonly conceived as ultimately reasonable.*

H. Sidgwick (1901)

*12. Of one thing we may be sure. If inquiries are to have any substantial basis, if they are not to be wholly up in the air, the theorist must take his departure from the problems which men actually meet in their own conduct. He may define and refine these; he may divide and systematize; he may abstract the problems from their concrete contexts in individual lives; he may classify them when he has thus detached them; but if he gets away from them he is talking about something his own brain has invented, not about moral realities.*

John Dewey and James Tufts (1908)

*13. Specifically moral problems arise in just those cases in which a man is concerned with the interests and the happiness of others beside himself, either because he values their satisfaction directly as an end worth working for, or because he acknowledges an obligation to respect it.*

Arthur E. Murphy (1943)

*14. Logically the problem of ethics is just as legitimate as the problem of physics. In both cases we may be said to begin with a set of primitive judgments—in the first case that certain things exist and in the second case that they are good or ought to be. We deal with these judgments scientifically if we examine them critically and elaborate them in the form of a rational system determined by principles. The greater difficulties of a theory of ethics are due to the greater variability of man's moral judgments and their dependence on all sorts of conventions which differ according to time and place. Diverse people who agree in condemning murder, incest, theft, etc., as immoral do not necessarily mean the same thing by these terms. Christians who accept the command "thou shalt not kill," do not think it wrong to kill at the command of a military officer. Few see anything wrong in long-distance killing, e.g., in our starving other peoples . . . by monopolizing the fertile lands that keep us in luxury. The Old Testament horror of incest does not touch Abraham's marrying his half sister.*

*Moral feelings are very strong, but this does not prevent them from appearing as irrational taboos to those who do not share our conventions. This should warn us against the tendency to make ethical philosophy an apology or justification of the conventional customs that happen to be established. Suppose that someone were to offer our country a wonderfully convenient mechanism, but demand in return the privilege of killing thousands of our people every year. How many of those who would indignantly refuse such a request will condemn the use of the automobile now that it is already with us?*

Morris R. Cohen (1949)

*15. The most crucial and difficult of all political questions is that which turns on the difference between public and private morality. The problem which it presents in the relations between States is a commonplace. But, since its essence is the difficulty of applying the same moral standard to decisions which affect large masses of men as to those in which only individuals are involved, it emerges in a hardly less acute form in the sphere of economic life, as soon as its connections ramify widely, and the unit is no longer the solitary producer, but a group. To argue, in the manner of Machiavelli, that there is one rule for business and another for private life, is to open a door to an orgy of unscrupulousness before which the mind recoils. To argue that there is no difference at all is to lay down a principle which few men who have faced the difficulty in practice will be prepared to endorse as of invariable application, and incidentally to expose the idea of morality itself to discredit by subjecting it to an almost intolerable strain. The practical result of sentimentality is too often a violent reaction towards the baser kinds of* Realpolitik.

R. H. Tawney (1926)

*16. The contribution which science has to make to ethics, quite apart from questioning its fundamental presuppositions, but merely by revealing facts which were previously unknown or commonly overlooked, is very much greater than is usually admitted. The adoption of methods of thought which are commonplaces in science would bring before the bar of ethical judgment whole groups of phenomena which do not appear there now. For instance, our ethical notions are fundamentally based on a system of individual responsibility for individual acts. The principle of statistical correlation between two sets of events, although accepted in scientific practice, is not usually felt to be ethically completely valid. If a man hits a baby on the head with a hammer, we prosecute him for cruelty or murder; but if he sells dirty milk and the infant sickness or death rate goes up, we merely fine him for contravening the health laws. And the ethical point is taken even less seriously when the responsibility, as well as the results of the crime, falls on a statistical assemblage. The whole community of England and Wales kills 8,000 babies a year by failing to bring its infant mortality rate down to the level reached by Oslo as early as 1931, which would be perfectly feasible; but few people seem to think this a crime.*

C. H. Waddington (1948)

*17. The last century of philosophic and psychological discussion has again demonstrated that morality is a relative concept; that it differs widely according to places and circumstances; that people in a given locality rarely reach a unanimous decision as to what is truly "good" or "bad"; and most people, when even they theoretically "know" or accept certain standards of "good" conduct, easily and unconsciously rationalize their own behavior and find "good" reasons for doing the "wrong" things. To excoriate humans for their difficulties in defining and accepting "good" behavior is therefore unrealistic and unjust.*

Albert Ellis and Robert A. Harper (1969)

*18. To be moral is simply to be intelligent, to be right-minded and open-minded in the unavoidable business of living. Morality is a collection of formulas and models based solidly on experience of acts and their consequences; it offers the most competent advice as to how to proceed with an enterprise, whether large or small. It is the theory and technique which underlies the art of conduct.*

Ralph Barton Perry (1909)

*19. As man's conscience is not infallible, you must not at once conclude that you are right when you are acting according to the dictates of conscience. And yet you may be sure that you are wrong if you are acting against it. For if you do what you believe to be wrong, even though you may be mistaken in thinking so, and it may be in reality right, still you yourself will be wrong.*

Richard Whately (1855)

# Part II

## Theories and Tests

In this part a number of different and sharply contrasting ethical theories are presented. There are some selections that argue for them, others that elaborate their implications, others that defend them against objections, and still others that sharply criticize them. The specific interconnections are often brought out by the titles and are also indicated in the editorial footnotes.

The underlying idea is that these theories should be regarded as differing tests for determining the morality of acts and practices and as means for solving moral problems and resolving moral issues. An ethical theory, as that term is used here, consists in the formulation, elaboration, and defense of one or more moral principles, which are intended to clarify the moral situation and to test the morality of conduct. It is possible, however, to have a test without a theory, and then the question is whether the test, apart from any theory, is as usable or as intelligible as it would be in the light of some theory that would explain it and the procedures for applying it. The Golden Rule is probably the outstanding example of a widely accepted moral principle—test of conduct—that seems to be independent of any theory; hence selections 14 and 15.

An idea of perennial appeal is the notion that what makes acts right or wrong is the will of God or, depending on one's theology, the commands of some other superior and supremely powerful being. Beyond a doubt the clearest, most provocative, and most influential presentation of this point of view is Paley's. A good label for Paley's theory is theological utilitarianism, for it attempts to combine the theological principle with a utilitarian criterion for knowing when it applies, at least when scripture is insufficiently explicit on the matter. (See selection 6, sections 4–6, pp. 48–50.) Just

*43*

what a utilitarian criterion is is explained by Bentham (9) and Sidgwick (13), and also, in a somewhat different fashion, by Urmson (11). But the reason for including the selection from Paley's work is not that it can be regarded as a form of utilitarianism or that it can somehow be combined with utilitarianism but that it is a presentation of the theological principle. Paley said in his Preface that the chief faults that he had noticed in the treatises on morals that he had met with were "either that the principle was erroneous, or that it was indistinctly explained, or that the rules deduced from it were not sufficiently adapted to real life and to actual situations . . . to answer precisely the design of a system of ethics—the direction of private consciences in the general conduct of human life." This is what Paley was concerned with, and within the limits determined by the circumstance that his own principle was erroneous, he dealt with it very well. So it is no accident that other selections from Paley's work appear in other parts of this book (46 and 48), since they serve to show how his theory is to be applied and what it implies, and these applications and implications of the theory in turn can serve as tests of it.

Paley is now out of fashion, and one seldom sees discussions of or selections from his work, which is all the more reason for including the treatment of it by Whately (7). But Paley had another great merit, that of avoiding what he had the perspicacity to point out as a fault of other moralists, as he called them, "namely, the dwelling upon verbal and elementary distinctions, with a labour and prolixity proportioned much more to the subtlety of the question, than to its value and importance in the prosecution of the subject." Unfortunately, this fault is not itself out of fashion and probably never will be. But I am satisfied that it is avoided by most of the writings included herein.

One does not usually find nowadays any actual selection from the writings of Thomas Reid, but since there is no better example to be found of traditional intuitionism in ethics, a selection (8) is included here. A collection of traditional ethical theories, moreover, must not altogether omit utilitarianism and the Kantian theory. I have chosen Bentham (9 and 10) to represent utilitarianism, rather than Mill, for at least two reasons. One of them is that, although Mill's *Utilitarianism* is of nearly transcendent importance, both in its own right and in the development of the subject, it is available in inexpensive paperback editions, and I decided to use the space it would have occupied for other selections not so available. The other is that, in the course of his presentation of the principle of utility, Bentham also presents hints of a type of argument that can be used in proving an ultimate principle, which is what the principle of utility is supposed to be, though he never actually follows through and sets forth the proof. (See selection 9, secs. xi–xiv, pp. 73–74. Compare with statement 48.) This section of Bentham has never received the attention it deserves. Bentham claims that the principle of utility cannot be proved, at least in the way other, subordinate, principles can be proved. But he also claims that a proof of it is not necessary. Does it follow that the ultimate principle of morality is self-evident (as an intuitionist presumably would claim) or that it is arbitrary (as a skeptic would claim)? Actually, neither follows. Whether the ultimate principle of morality, if there is one, is self-evident or arbitrary, or eminently reasonable, depends on what the principle is and what it implies, and whether it is the right one. But how can it be determined whether it is the right one? That, of course, is one of the most difficult questions there is, and the source of much philosophizing, perplexity, and debate. It is pretty clear that no one-line answer to it can be given.

The question of the justification of principles, which in turn are to serve as tests of the morality of conduct, is the topic of the essay by Rawls (16) and also comes up again and again in the course of this book. A procedure for testing principles in the light of other moral beliefs, and moral beliefs in the light of moral principles, is sketched in selection 15. (See also statements 14, 32, and 58.)

# 6

## Morality and
## the Will of God*

### WILLIAM PALEY
(1743–1805)

1. Virtue is *"the doing good to mankind, in obedience to the will of God, and for the sake of everlasting happiness."*

According to which definition, "the good of mankind" is the subject; the "will of God," the rule; and "everlasting happiness," the motive, of human virtue. . . .

2. A man is said to be *obliged, "when he is urged by a violent motive resulting from the command of another."*

I. "The motive must be violent." If a person, who has done me some little service, or has a small place in his disposal, ask me upon some occasion for my vote, I may possibly give it to him, from a motive of gratitude or expectation: but I should hardly say that I was *obliged* to give it him; because the inducement does not rise high enough. Whereas if a father or a master, any great benefactor, or one on whom my fortune depends, require my vote, I give it him of course: and my answer to all who ask me why I voted so and so is, that my father or my master *obliged* me; that I had received so many favours from, or had so great a dependence upon, such a one, that I was *obliged* to vote as he directed me.

Secondly, "It must result from the command of another." Offer a man a gratuity for doing anything, for seizing, for example, an offender, he is not *obliged* by your offer to do it; nor would he say he is; though he may be *induced, persuaded, prevailed upon, tempted.* If a magistrate or the man's immediate superior command it, he considers himself as *obliged* to comply,

---

*From William Paley, *The Principles of Moral and Political Philosophy* (London, 1785), Bk. I, ch. 7; Bk. II, chs. 2, 3, 4; Bk. I, ch. 4; Bk. II, chs. 4, 5, 9, 11. The title of this selection has been supplied by the editor. Compare with selections 7, 9, and 12.

though possibly he would lose less by a refusal in this case than in the former.

I will not undertake to say that the words *obligation* and *obliged* are used uniformly in this sense, or always with this distinction: nor is it possible to tie down popular phrases to any constant signification: but wherever the motive is violent enough, and coupled with the idea of command, authority, law, or the will of a superior, there, I take it, we always reckon ourselves to be *obliged*.

And from this account of obligation it follows, that we can be obliged to nothing, but what we ourselves are to gain or lose something by; for nothing else can be a "violent motive" to us. As we should not be obliged to obey the laws, or the magistrate, unless rewards or punishments, pleasure or pain, somehow or other, depended upon our obedience; so neither should we, without the same reason, be obliged to do what is right, to practice virtue, or to obey the commands of God.

3. Let it be remembered, that to be *obliged*, is "to be urged by a violent motive, resulting from the command of another."

And then let it be asked, Why am I *obliged* to keep my word? and the answer will be, "because I am urged to do so by a violent motive" (namely the expectation of being after this life rewarded, if I do, or punished for it if I do not), "resulting from the command of another" (namely of God).

This solution goes to the bottom of the subject, as no further question can reasonably be asked.

Therefore, private happiness is our motive, and the will of God our rule.

When I first turned my thoughts to moral speculations, an air of mystery seemed to hang over the whole subject; which arose, I believe, from hence,—that I supposed, with many authors whom I read, that to be *obliged* to do a thing, was very different from being induced only to do it; and that the obligation to practice virtue, to do what is right, just, &c., was quite another thing, and of another kind, than the obligation which a soldier is under to obey his officer, a servant his master; or any of the civil and ordinary obligations of human life. Whereas, from what has been said it appears, that moral obligation is like all other obligations; and that *obligation* is nothing more than an *inducement* of sufficient strength, and resulting, in some way, from the command of another.

There is always understood to be a difference between an act of *prudence* and an act of *duty*. Thus, if I distrust a man who owed me a sum of money, I should reckon it an act of prudence to get another person bound with him; but I should hardly call it an act of duty. On the other hand, it would be thought a very unusual and loose kind of language to say, that, as I had made such a promise, it was *prudent* to perform it; or that, as my friend, when he went abroad, placed a box of jewels in my hands, it would be *prudent* in me to preserve it for him till he returned.

Now in what, you will ask, does the difference consist? inasmuch as, according to our account of the matter, both in the one case and the other,—in acts of duty as well as acts of prudence,—we consider solely what we ourselves shall gain or lose by the act.

The difference, and the only difference, is this; that in the one case, we consider what we shall gain or lose in the present world: in the other case, we consider also what we shall gain or lose in the world to come.

Those who would establish a system of morality, independent of a future state, must look out for some different idea of moral obligation, unless they can show that virtue conducts the possessor to certain happiness in this life, or to a much greater share of it than he could attain by a different behaviour.

To us there are two great questions:

I. Will there be after this life any distribution of rewards and punishments at all?

II. If there be, what actions will be rewarded, and what will be punished?

The first question comprises the credibility of the Christian religion, together with the presumptive proofs of a future retribution from the light of nature. The second question comprises the province of morality. Both questions are too much for one work. The affirmative therefore of the first, although we confess that it is the foundation upon which the whole fabric rests, must in this treatise be taken for granted. . . .


4. As the will of God is our rule; to inquire what is our duty, or what we are obliged to do, in any instance, is, in effect, to inquire what is the will of God in that instance? which consequently becomes the whole business of morality.

Now there are two methods of coming at the will of God on any point:

I. By his express declarations, when they are to be had, and which must be sought for in Scripture.

II. By what we can discover of his designs and disposition from his works; or, as we usually call it, the light of nature. . . .


5. Whoever expects to find in the Scriptures a specific direction for every moral doubt that arises, looks for more than he will meet with. And

to what a magnitude such a detail of particular precepts would have enlarged the sacred volume, may be partly understood from the following consideration:—The laws of this country, including the acts of the legislature, and the decisions of our supreme courts of justice, are not contained in fewer than fifty folio volumes; and yet it is not once in ten attempts that you can find the case you look for, in any law-book whatever: to say nothing of those numerous points of conduct, concerning which the law professes not to prescribe or determine anything. Had then the same particularity which obtains in human laws so far as they go, been attempted in the Scriptures, throughout the whole extent of morality, it is manifest they would have been by much too bulky to be either read or circulated; or rather, as St. John says, "even the world itself could not contain the books that should be written."

Morality is taught in Scripture in this wise.—General rules are laid down, of piety, justice, benevolence, and purity: such as, worshipping God in spirit and in truth; doing as we would be done by; loving our neighbour as ourself; forgiving others, as we expect forgiveness from God; that mercy is better than sacrifice; that not that which entereth into a man, (nor, by parity of reason, any ceremonial pollutions,) but that which proceedeth from the heart, defileth him. These rules are occasionally illustrated, either by *fictitious examples,* as in the parable of the good Samaritan; and of the cruel servant, who refused to his fellow-servant that indulgence and compassion which his master had shown to him: *or in instances which actually presented themselves,* as in Christ's reproof of his disciples at the Samaritan village; his praise of the poor widow, who cast in her last mite; his censure of the Pharisees who chose out the chief rooms,—and of the tradition, whereby they evaded the command to sustain their indigent parents: *or, lastly, in the resolution of questions, which those who were about our Saviour proposed to him;* as his answer to the young man who asked him, "What lack I yet?" and to the honest scribe, who had found out, even in that age and country, that "to love God and his neighbour, was more than all whole burnt-offerings and sacrifice."

And this is in truth the way in which all practical sciences are taught, as Arithmetic, Grammar, Navigation, and the like.—Rules are laid down, and examples are subjoined: not that these examples are the cases, much less all the cases, which will actually occur; but by way only of explaining the principle of the rule, and as so many specimens of the method of applying it. The chief difference is, that the examples in Scripture are not annexed to the rules with the didactic regularity to which we are now-a-days accustomed, but delivered dispersedly, as particular occasions suggested them; which gave them, however, (especially to those who heard them, and were present on the occasions which produced them,) an energy and persuasion, much beyond what the same or any instances would have appeared with, in their places in a system.

Besides this, the Scriptures commonly presuppose in the persons to whom they speak, a knowledge of the principles of natural justice; and are employed not so much to teach *new* rules of morality, as to enforce the practice of it by *new* sanctions, and by a *greater certainty;* which last seems to be the proper business of a revelation from God, and what was most wanted.

Thus the "unjust, covenant-breakers, and extortioners," are condemned in Scripture, supposing it known, or leaving it, where it admits of doubt, to moralists to determine, what injustice, extortion, or breach of covenant, are.

The above considerations are intended to prove that the Scriptures do not supersede the use of the science of which we profess to treat, and at the same time to acquit them of any charge of imperfection or insufficiency on that account. . . .

6. The method of coming at the will of God concerning any action, by the light of nature, is to inquire into "the tendency of the action to promote or diminish the general happiness." This rule proceeds upon the presumption, that God Almighty wills and wishes the happiness of his creatures; and, consequently, that those actions, which promote that will and wish, must be agreeable to him; and the contrary.

As this presumption is the foundation of our whole system, it becomes necessary to explain the reasons upon which it rests.

7. When God created the human species, either He wished their happiness, or He wished their misery, or He was indifferent and unconcerned about both.

If He had wished our misery, He might have made sure of his purpose, by forming our senses to be so many sores and pains to us, as they are now instruments of gratification and enjoyment; or by placing us amidst objects so ill-suited to our perceptions, as to have continually offended us, instead of ministering to our refreshment and delight. He might have made, for example, everything we tasted, bitter; everything we saw, loathsome; everything we touched, a sting; every smell, a stench; and every sound, a discord.

If He had been indifferent about our happiness or misery, we must impute to our good fortune (as all design by this supposition is excluded) both the capacity of our senses to receive pleasure, and the supply of external objects fitted to produce it. But either of these (and still more both of them) being too much to be attributed to accident, nothing remains but the first supposition, that God, when He created the human species, wished their happiness; and made for them the provision which He has made, with that view, and for that purpose. . . .

We conclude, therefore, that God wills and wishes the happiness of his creatures. And this conclusion being once established, we are at liberty to go on with the rule built upon it, namely, "that the method of coming at the will of God, concerning any action by the light of nature, is to inquire into the tendency of that action to promote or diminish the general happiness." . . .

8. Right and obligation are reciprocal; that is, wherever there is a right in one person, there is a corresponding obligation upon others. If one man has a "right" to an estate; others are "obliged" to abstain from it:—If parents have a "right" to reverence from their children; children are "obliged" to reverence their parents:—and so in all other instances.

Now, because moral *obligation* depends, as we have seen, upon the will of God; *right,* which is correlative to it, must depend upon the same. Right therefore signifies, *consistency with the will of God.* . . .

But if the divine will determine the distinction of right and wrong, what else is it but an identical proposition to say of God, that He acts *right?* or how is it possible to conceive even that He should act *wrong?* Yet these assertions are intelligible and significant. The case is this: By virtue of the two principles, that God wills the happiness of his creatures, and that the will of God is the measure of right and wrong, we arrive at certain conclusions; which conclusions become rules; and we soon learn to pronounce actions right or wrong, according as they agree or disagree with our rules, without looking any further: and when the habit is once established of stopping at the rules, we can go back and compare with these rules even the divine conduct itself: and yet it may be true (only not observed by us at the time) that the rules themselves are deduced from the divine will.

Right is a quality of persons or of actions.

Of persons; as when we say, such a one has a "right" to this estate; parents have a "right" to reverence from their children; the king to allegiance from his subjects; masters have a "right" to their servants' labour; a man has not a "right" over his own life.

Of actions; as in such expressions as the following: it is "right" to punish murder with death; his behaviour on that occasion was "right"; it is not "right" to send an unfortunate debtor to gaol; he did or acted "right," who gave up his place rather than vote against his judgment.

In this latter set of expressions, you may substitute the definition of right above given, for the term itself: *e.g.* it is "consistent with the will of God" to punish murder with death;—his behaviour on that occasion was "consistent with the will of God"—it is not "consistent with the will of God" to send an unfortunate debtor to gaol;—he did, or acted, "consistently with the will of God," who gave up his place rather than vote against his judgment.

In the former set, you must vary the construction a little, when you introduce the definition instead of the term. Such a one has a "right" to this estate, that is, it is "consistent with the will of God" that such a one should have it;—parents have a "right" to reverence from their children, that is, it is "consistent with the will of God" that children should reverence their parents;—and the same of the rest.


9. By the General Rights of Mankind, I mean the rights which belong to the Species collectively; the original stock, as I may say, which they have since distributed among themselves.

These are,

I. A right to the fruits or vegetable produce of the earth.

The insensible parts of the creation are incapable of injury; and it is nugatory to inquire into the right, where the use can be attended with no injury. But it may be worth observing, for the sake of an inference which will appear below, that, as God had created us with a want and desire of food, and provided things suited by their nature to sustain and satisfy us, we may fairly presume, that He intended we should apply these things to that purpose.

II. A right to the flesh of animals.

This is a very different claim from the former. Some excuse seems necessary for the pain and loss which we occasion to brutes, by restraining them of their liberty, mutilating their bodies, and, at last, putting an end to their lives (which we suppose to be the whole of their existence), for our pleasure or conveniency.

The reasons alleged in vindication of this practice are the following: that the several species of brutes being created to prey upon one another, affords a kind of analogy to prove that the human species were intended to feed upon them; that, if let alone, they would overrun the earth, and exclude mankind from the occupation of it; that they are requited for what they suffer at our hands, by our care and protection.

Upon which reasons I would observe, that the *analogy* contended for is extremely lame; since brutes have no power to support life by any other means, and since we have; for the whole human species might subsist entirely upon fruit, pulse, herbs, and roots, as many tribes of Hindoos actually do. The two other reasons may be valid reasons, as far as they go; for, no doubt, if Man had been supported entirely by vegetable food, a great part of those animals which die to furnish his table would never have lived: but they by no means justify our right over the lives of brutes to the extent in which we exercise it. What danger is there, for instance, of fish interfering with us, in the occupation of their element? or what do *we* contribute to their support or preservation?

It seems to me, that it would be difficult to defend this right by any arguments which the light and order of nature afford; and that we are beholden for it to the permission recorded in Scripture, Gen. ix. 1, 2, 3: "And God blessed Noah and his sons, and said unto them, Be fruitful, and multiply, and replenish the earth; and the fear of you, and the dread of you, shall be upon every beast of the earth, and upon every fowl of the air, and upon all that moveth upon the earth, and upon all the fishes of the sea; into your hand are they delivered: every moving thing shall be meat for you; even as the green herb, have I given you all things." To Adam and his posterity had been granted, at the creation, "every green herb for meat," and nothing more. In the last clause of the passage now produced, the old grant is recited, and extended to the flesh of animals; "even as the green herb, have I given you all things." But this was not till after the flood; the inhabitants of the antediluvian world had therefore no such permission, that we know of. Whether they actually refrained from the flesh of animals, is another question. Abel, we read, was a keeper of sheep; and for what purpose he kept them, except for food, is difficult to say (unless it were sacrifices): might not, however, some of the stricter sects among the antediluvians be scrupulous as to this point? and might not Noah and his family be of this description? for, it is not probable that God would publish a permission, to authorize a practice which had never been disputed.

Wanton, and, what is worse, studied cruelty to brutes, is certainly wrong, as coming within none of these reasons.

[Editor's note: Paley's work was for over sixty years a standard text at Cambridge, and was an almost canonical work at a great many American colleges and universities for most of the 19th century. Its influence has now waned, to the point where it is almost forgotten. This is a pity, since the point of view it represents is of almost perennial interest. In comprehensiveness of coverage (see, for example, selections 46 and 48) it is well in advance of most of the ethical texts of our own day, and its style is exemplary. For a sample of a view very closely allied with Paley's, in *some* respects, consider the following passage from Thomas Hobbes's *Leviathan* (1651), ch. 31:

> The right of nature, whereby God reigneth over men, and punisheth those that break his laws, is to be derived not from his creating them, as if he required obedience, out of gratitude for his benefits; but from his *Irresistible Power*. I have formerly shown, how the sovereign right ariseth from pact: to show how the same right may arise from nature, requires no more, but to show in what case it is never taken away. Seeing all men by nature had right to all things, they had right every one to reigne over all the rest. But because this right could not be obtained by force, it concerned the safety of every one, laying by that right, to set up men (with sovereign authority) by common consent, to rule and defend them: whereas if there had been any man of Power Irresistible; there had been no reason, why he should not by that power have ruled, and defended both himselfe, and them, according to his own discretion. To those therefore whose power is irresistible, the dominion of all men adhaereth naturally by their excellence of power; and consequently it is from that power, that the Kingdome over men, and the right of afflicting men at his pleasure, belongeth naturally to God Almighty; not as Creator, and Gracious; but as Omnipotent.]

# 7

## Annotations on
## Paley's Moral Philosophy*

### RICHARD WHATELY
(1787–1863)

Although some of the Works of the justly celebrated Archdeacon Paley, especially his *Natural Theology* and *Evidences,* are more read than his *Moral Philosophy,* and have met with more unmixed approbation, this last has been exercising great influence, not only directly, but indirectly. Having long been an established Text-book at a great and flourishing University, it has laid the foundation of the Moral Principles of many hundreds—probably thousands—of Youths while under a course of training designed to qualify them for being afterwards the Moral instructors of Millions. Such a Work therefore cannot fail to exercise a very considerable and extensive influence on the Minds of successive generations. And accordingly, to supply any needful explanations, illustrations, or modifications of its principles, and above all, to correct any considerable errors in them, cannot be deemed a superfluous or an unimportant task. . . .

1. *"Virtue is the doing good to Mankind, in obedience to the Will of God."* [*Paley, p. 46*]

This simple system of Morals (as doubtless it appeared to him) Paley adopted, denying the existence of a Moral-faculty! on account of the great *discrepancy* in men's Moral judgments. But he forgot to inquire whether

---

*Whately, Fellow of Oriel College and Archbishop of Dublin, published his edition of *Paley's Moral Philosophy: With Annotations* in 1859 (London: John W. Parker and Son). What follows are a number of these Annotations, correlated with the appropriate passage from Paley's text, as it appears in this volume. (There is no exact correspondence, however, between the enumeration of the sections; hence the bracketed references to Paley are to the pages of this volume.) The passages herein included are taken from pp. iii; 51–52; 58; 60–63; 16–17; and 88–91.

nearly as great discrepancies do not exist in their notions of what *is* the Will of God, and what *is* doing good to Mankind. We have it on the highest authority that those who killed the disciples of Jesus "thought they were doing God service"; and doubtless they thought also that they were "doing good to mankind" in putting down a pestilent heresy. Such also was the belief of Paul (while a persecutor) who "verily thought that he ought to do many things contrary to the name of Jesus." And among professing Christians, no one can doubt that some at least of the Romish Inquisitors were convinced that they were conforming to the Will of God, and doing good to Mankind, in burning heretics. Such also was no doubt, the belief of Cranmer when he brought Anabaptists to the stake, and of Calvin in burning Servetus.

And let no one suppose that such notions are confined to Ages or Countries far remote from ours, and are quite obsolete among us at the present day. The following is a passage from a History of England—an Educational Book—which, it may fairly be said, is circulated throughout England at the *public expense;* being used in Roman Catholic Schools receiving Government grants under what is called the "separate system," the system which some are desirous to introduce into Ireland also: "At last the Queen and her council had Cranmer and a great many Protestant bishops put in prison, and they were burnt for heresy. It is very difficult to say now what should or should not have been done. The whole country was unsettled and diseased with heresy, and it was clearly impossible to stop it by gentle means. In this case, you know, when men are determined to destroy not only their own souls, but the souls of many others, they have to be treated as malefactors, and are given over by the church to the law, to be punished. It was very shocking that people should be burned; but it was much more shocking that they should be leading so many more people to be burned in the flames of hell for ever; and this was what Bishop Gardiner thought." [1]

Many other passages might be cited from various authors, showing what notions men entertain of doing good to Mankind in obedience to the Will of God.

Among others, a *Protestant* writer, in a work published a few years ago, maintains that "the magistrate who restrains, coerces and *punishes* those who seek to propagate an erroneous religion," (which he will of course think any to be that differs from his *own,*) "obeys the will of God, and is not a persecutor!"

---

[1] *The History of England for Catholic Children.* London: Burns and Lambert, 17, Portman Street. Birmingham: Lauder, Powell and Co. 1850.

2. *"I will not undertake to say that the words 'obligation' and 'obliged' are used uniformly in this sense." [Cf. Paley, p. 47]*

Certainly no one can be fairly called on to give a definition that shall embrace every sense of these words. But Paley's definition would be thought by most persons to be not applicable at all to the case of what is called *moral* obligation. A planter's slave, for instance, is urged by a violent motive—a *very* violent one,—to work in the fields at his master's command, and sometimes to assist in flogging his fellow-labourers. But though he is *obliged* to do this, few, except slave-owners, would call this a *moral* obligation, or would deny his being justified in escaping when he had an opportunity, into a free country.

If it should be said that the master has no *just* right *over* him, and is not therefore a *rightful* "superior," this would be to recognise a Moral-faculty. But if every one is a "superior" who has *power* to enforce submission, the slave-owner is such; and so is the robber who holds a pistol to your head.

3. *"Why am I obliged to keep my word?" [Cf. Paley, p. 47]*

"The irrelevancy," says Professor Whewell, "of Paley's mode of treating the question of the Moral sense is so generally allowed at present that we need not dwell on it here. But we may observe, that other mistakes, flowing from a like misapprehension, affect his analysis of virtue. He endeavours to make an advance in this inquiry by the question, 'Why am I obliged to keep my word, or to do any other moral act?' And by his answer to this question, he reduces Moral obligations to two elements—external restraint, and the command of a superior. This attempt at an analysis of Morality is singularly futile: for, of the two supposed elements, external constraint annihilates the morality of the act, and the reference to a superior presupposes Moral obligation, since a *superior is one whom it is our duty to obey.* If Paley had stated his question in the simpler form, 'Why *ought* I to keep my word?' he would have had before him a problem more to the purpose of Moral philosophy, and one to which his answer would have been palpably inapplicable."

It has been suggested that Paley might, conceivably, have maintained, that perhaps there had been an ancient revelation (though there is no record of it in the Book of Genesis) teaching that God would reward or punish in another world certain kinds of actions; and that men thereupon, adopting Paley's ground of distinction, applied the word *"Duty"* in cases where they calculated on what they were to "gain or lose in the next world"; and *"Prudence,"* in cases where the present world alone is concerned;

that this revelation was afterwards forgotten, along with the knowledge of the true God; but that the *custom* remained, and prevailed throughout all languages, of thus distinguishing the two classes of actions. It might be replied that there is nothing but unsupported conjecture for such a theory, and there are many improbabilities in it. But I think the main consideration is, that men never do, and, apparently, never did, account any conduct virtuous which they believe to have proceeded *entirely* from *calculations of self-interest;* even though the external act itself be such as they conceive *would* have been done by a virtuous man.

*"There is always understood to be a difference between an act of prudence and an act of duty." [Cf. Paley, p. 47]*

Not only is this true, but the distinction is fully recognised by those who had no notion of a "World to come," and who made no reference to any divine command: by Aristotle, for instance, in his *Ethics,* who speaks therein of death as the "boundary, beyond which there is neither good nor evil"; and by Cicero in his *De Officiis,* who gives distinct treatises on the [Honestum] *virtuous,* and the [Utile] expedient; and who derides the idea of fearing the wrath of Jupiter, and evidently believed in no personal existence after death.

And all the ancient heathen writers use words which evidently signify what we call "Virtue"—"Duty"—"Moral-goodness"; which words could not possibly have found their way into the languages of men destitute (as most of them were) of any belief in a future state of retribution, if Paley's theory were correct. It is disproved not by any supposed truth and *soundness* in the views of the ancient Writers, but by the very *words* they employ.

Some few individuals, it is well known, are to be found who labour under that curious defect of vision, the non-perception of *colours.* Though their sight is good in other respects, they perceive only darker and lighter shades, as we do in a *print,* or a pencil-drawing. Now if we could conceive a whole *Nation* labouring under this defect, we might be sure they would not have in their language any such words as red, green, yellow, and blue. And we may be no less certain that a nation having no more belief in a "world to come" than the ancient Greeks and Romans, would have had no words in their language answering to "Virtue," or "Duty," supposing men's notions on the subject were wholly and solely derived from considerations relating to the next world.

Some persons are apt to fall into indistinctness of language, and confusion of thought, on this subject, from not taking care to distinguish between our moral judgment on some *particular cases,* and our notion of

Duty *generally*. On any particular point, a pious man will be ready, if he is convinced that a divine command has been given, to obey it at once without further inquiry; taking for granted that it is right, though he may not see the reason of it. But this is not from his having no notion at all, generally, of *anything* being in itself right or wrong, and knowing no meaning of the word "good," except "what is commanded by a superior power." On the contrary, he acts as he does from his general trust in God's goodness, and just claim to obedience. For, in this or that *particular point,* a divine command may *make* that a duty which was not so before. But this can only be when the command is given to a Being endowed with a moral sense, which enables him to perceive that there is *such a thing* as Duty, and that God has a rightful claim to be obeyed, even when the reason of his commands is not perceived.

In like manner, a telescope will enable a man possessing the sense of sight, to see objects invisible to the naked eye. But the revelation of a divine command could no more *originate* the notion of Duty, generally, in a Being destitute of Moral Faculty, and to whom, therefore, the word "duty" would have no meaning at all (though he might be *afraid* to disobey), than a telescope could confer sight on a blind man.

*"He who would establish a system of Morality independent of a future state, must look out for a different idea of Moral obligation."* [Cf. Paley, p. 48]

But on Paley's theory, they manifestly could not possibly form *any* such idea at all. For if, as he maintains, the only foundation of that idea is the expectation of reward and punishment in the next world, those who have no knowledge or no belief of this, could never have a notion of such a thing as Duty. It would be thought ridiculous to say "Men see with their eyes, and cannot see any otherwise; and those who have no eyes, must see as well as they can without them."

Yet it is an indisputable fact that the ancient Heathen did, without the knowledge of a future state, entertain a notion of Duty. Whether their views of it were or were not reasonable and well-founded, is nothing to the present purpose. The *fact,* that they did entertain *some,* is a disproof of the theory in question.

4. It is highly important that the Student should attentively notice, and steadily keep in mind, Paley's remark . . . that *"the Scriptures presuppose in the persons addressed a knowledge of the principles of natural justice, and are employed not so much to teach new rules of Morality, as to enforce the practice of it,"* &c. [Cf. Paley, p. 50]

This is most true and highly important; but I do not see how it is to be reconciled with the subsequent parts of the Treatise. For supposing Man a Being destitute of all Moral-faculty, and deriving all notions of right and wrong that he can ever possess, entirely from a consideration of the Will of God, and the expectation of reward and punishment in the next World from Him, one does not see how those to whom our Scriptures were addressed—the *Gentile*-Converts at least—could have had any notion at all of "Natural Justice." Not only must they have needed "New Rules of Morality," but the very idea of any such thing as Morality must have been entirely a Novelty to them. Of the Eternal Supreme Creator they seem to have scarcely had a thought. The gods they worshipped were little better than evil Demons. And as for a future state of retribution, they had little, if any, belief in any such thing. Paul accordingly speaks of "the rest,"—*i.e.* all the unconverted Gentiles as sorrowing for their departed friends, from "having *no hope.*" Now, on Paley's theory, these persons could have had no more idea of moral right and wrong than a blind-born man has of light and colours. And yet he speaks of their being addressed as understanding what (on his theory) must have been a totally unknown language.

5. *"Yet these assertions are intelligible and significant."* [*Cf. Paley, p. 51*]

Arguing in a *circle* is very common; with crafty sophists, from design, and with bad reasoners, from confusion of thought. But the former are careful to conceal the fallacy; and the latter do not perceive it.

It is very strange that Paley should perceive and acknowledge that he is involved in a circle, and should yet adhere to it. The procedure is (as I have above remarked) something like that of the Mahometans, who give as a proof of the divine origin of the Koran, that its *style* is so eminently beautiful; all other works being reckoned the better or worse Arabic according as they approach more or less to the style of the Koran. But then it comes out that they have *made* the Koran the standard of good Arabic, and have deduced *from* that all their rules of style. So that the argument when thus exposed, merely amounts to this, that "the style of the Koran is—the style of the Koran!"

On this point I have remarked in the *Lessons on Morals* that "the sacred Writers always speak of God as *just* and *good,* and his commands as *right* and reasonable. 'Are not my ways,' said He by a prophet, 'equal? Are not your ways unequal?' And again, 'Why, even of yourselves judge ye not what is right?'" Now all this would have been quite unmeaning, if Man had no idea of what is good or bad in itself, and meant by those words merely what is *commanded* or *forbidden* by God. For then, to say that God's commands are just and good, would be only saying that his commands are his commands. If Man had not been originally endowed by his Maker with any power of distinguishing between moral good and evil, or with any preference of the one to the other, then, it would be mere trifling to speak of the divine *goodness;* since it would be merely saying that "God is what He is"; which is no more than might be said of any Being in the universe.

Whenever, therefore, you hear any one speaking of our having derived all our notions of morality from the will of God, the sense in which you must understand him is, that it was God's will to create Man a Being endowed with conscience, and capable of perceiving the difference of right and wrong, and of understanding that there is such a thing as Duty. And if any one should use expressions which seem not to mean this, but to imply that there is no such thing as natural-Conscience—no idea in the human mind of such a thing as Duty—still you may easily prove that his real meaning must be what we have said. If any persons tell you that our first notion of right and wrong is entirely derived from the divine Law, and that those words have no meaning except obedience and disobedience to the declared will of God, you may ask them whether it is a matter of *duty* to obey God's will, or merely a matter of *prudence,* inasmuch as He is able to punish those who rebel against Him? Whether they think that God is *justly entitled* to obedience, or merely that it would be very *rash* to disobey one who has power to enforce his commands?

They will doubtless answer, that we *ought* to obey the divine commands as a point of duty, and not merely on the ground of expediency—that God is not only powerful, but good—and that conformity to his will is a thing right in itself, and should be practised, not through mere fear of punishment, or hope of reward, but *because* it is *right.*

Now this proves that they must be sensible that there is in the human mind some notion of such a thing as Duty, and of things being right or wrong in their own nature. For, when any persons submit to the will of another merely because it is their interest, or because they dare not resist, we never speak of this submission as a matter of *duty,* but merely of prudence. If robbers were to seize you and carry you off as a slave, threatening you with death if you offered to resist or to escape, you might think it *advisable* to submit, if you saw that resistance would be hopeless: but you would not think yourself bound in *duty* to do so. Or again, if you were offered good wages for doing some laborious work, you might think it *expedient* to accept the offer, but you would not account it a moral duty. And when a farmer supplies his cattle, or a slave-owner his slaves, with abundance of the best food, in order that they may be in good condition, and do the more work for himself, or fetch a better price, and not from benevolence to them, every one would regard this as mere *prudence,* and not virtue. And we judge the same in every case where a man is acting solely with a view to his own advantage.

You can easily prove, therefore, that when people speak of a knowledge of the divine will being the origin of all our moral notions, they cannot mean exactly what the words would seem to signify; if, at least, they admit at the same time that it is a matter of *duty,* and not merely of prudence, to obey God's will, and that He has a just claim to our obedience.

It is urged by some that Man's judgment on Moral questions is an utterly incompetent tribunal, because his notions of right and wrong have been grievously perverted by the fall. Now it is very true that the Moral-faculty is imperfect and fallible: but the same may be said of the *Reasoning*-faculty also. And there is no need of putting in the qualification of "since the fall"; because our first parents manifestly showed an imperfection, both moral and intellectual, in listening to the arguments of the Tempter. Had they been perfect both in point of conscience and of reason, they would never have transgressed the divine command. If then, on the ground of the imperfection of the Moral-faculty, we are to forego all employment of it, we must do the same by the Reasoning-faculty also; and then Revelation itself would be of no use to us. How do you know, it may be asked, that so and so is declared in the Bible? You will say, "I so understand the words": but it may be answered, "Lean not to thine own understanding." How do you know that the Bible itself contains the revelation of God's will? or that there is a God at all? You think you have good reason for the belief; your Reason leads you to that conclusion: but your Reason is imperfect, fallible, and impaired; and is therefore "an utterly incompetent tribunal." Your argument therefore is completely suicidal; it leaves you no ground to stand on; no just assurance for believing anything at all.

But in truth the Reasoning-faculty, and the Moral-faculty,—and in short every faculty of the human mind, though imperfect and fallible, are to be employed, but with due allowance for that imperfection and fallibility, and with caution to guard against their occasional errors. . . .

# 8

# *Of the First Principles of Morals\**

## THOMAS REID

(1710–1796)

Morals, like all other sciences, must have first principles, on which all moral reasoning is grounded.

In every branch of knowledge where disputes have been raised, it is useful to distinguish the first principles from the superstructure. They are the foundation on which the whole fabric of the science leans; and whatever is not supported by this foundation can have no stability.

In all rational belief, the thing believed is either itself a first principle, or it is by just reasoning deduced from first principles. When men differ about deductions of reasoning, the appeal must be made to the rules of reasoning, which have been very unanimously fixed from the days of Aristotle. But when they differ about a first principle, the appeal is made to another tribunal; to that of common sense.

How the genuine decisions of common sense may be distinguished from the counterfeit, has been considered in Essay sixth, on the Intellectual Powers of Man, Chapter fourth, to which the reader is referred. What I would here observe, is, That as first principles differ from deductions of reasoning in the nature of their evidence, and must be tried by a different standard when they are called in question, it is of importance to know to which of these two classes a truth which we would examine belongs. When they are not distinguished, men are apt to demand proof for every thing they think fit to deny: And when we attempt to prove by direct argument, what is really self-evident, the reasoning will always be inconclusive; for it will either take for granted the thing to be proved, or something not more

*From Thomas Reid, *Essays on the Active Powers of Man* (1788), Essay V, ch. 1. Compare with selections 9, 15, 16, and 24.

evident; and so, instead of giving strength to the conclusion, will rather tempt those to doubt of it, who never did so before.

I propose, therefore, in this chapter, to point out some of the first principles of morals, without pretending to a complete enumeration.

The principles I am to mention, relate either to virtue in general, or to the different particular branches of virtue, or to the comparison of virtues where they seem to interfere.

1. There are some things in human conduct, that merit approbation and praise, others that merit blame and punishment; and different degrees either of approbation or of blame, are due to different actions.

2. What is in no degree voluntary, can neither deserve moral approbation nor blame.

3. What is done from unavoidable necessity may be agreeable or disagreeable, useful or hurtful, but cannot be the object either of blame or of moral approbation.

4. Men may be highly culpable in omitting what they ought to have done, as well as in doing what they ought not.

5. We ought to use the best means we can to be well informed of our duty, by serious attention to moral instruction; by observing what we approve, and what we disapprove, in other men, whether our acquaintance, or those whose actions are recorded in history; by reflecting often, in a calm and dispassionate hour, on our own past conduct, that we may discern what was wrong, what was right, and what might have been better; by deliberating coolly and impartially upon our future conduct, as far as we can foresee the opportunities we may have of doing good, or the temptations to do wrong; and by having this principle deeply fixed in our minds, that as moral excellence is the true worth and glory of a man, so the knowledge of our duty is to every man, in every station of life, the most important of all knowledge.

6. It ought to be our most serious concern to do our duty as far as we know it, and to fortify our minds against every temptation to deviate from it; by maintaining a lively sense of the beauty of right conduct, and of its present and future reward, of the turpitude of vice, and of its bad consequences here and hereafter; by having always in our eye the noblest examples; by the habit of subjecting our passions to the government of reason; by firm purposes and resolutions with regard to our conduct; by avoiding occasions of temptation when we can; and by imploring the aid of him who made us in every hour of temptation.

These principles concerning virtue and vice in general, must appear self-evident to every man who hath a conscience, and who hath taken pains to exercise this natural power of his mind. I proceed to others that are more particular.

1. We ought to prefer a greater good, though more distant, to a less; and a less evil to a greater.

A regard to our own good, though we had no conscience, dictates this principle; and we cannot help disapproving the man that acts contrary to it, as deserving to lose the good which he wantonly threw away, and to suffer the evil which he knowingly brought upon his own head.

We observed before, that the ancient moralists, and many among the modern, have deduced the whole of morals from this principle, and that when we make a right estimate of goods and evils according to their degree, their dignity, their duration, and according as they are more or less in our power, it leads to the practice of every virtue: More directly, indeed, to the virtues of self-government, to prudence, to temperance, and to fortitude; and, though more indirectly, even to justice, humanity, and all the social virtues, when their influence upon our happiness is well understood.

Though it be not the noblest principle of conduct, it has this peculiar advantage, that its force is felt by the most ignorant, and even by the most abandoned.

Let a man's moral judgment be ever so little improved by exercise, or ever so much corrupted by bad habits, he cannot be indifferent to his own happiness or misery. When he is become insensible to every nobler motive to right conduct, he cannot be insensible to this. And though to act from this motive solely may be called *prudence* rather than *virtue,* yet this prudence deserves some regard upon its own account, and much more as it is the friend and ally of virtue, and the enemy of all vice; and as it gives a favourable testimony of virtue to those who are deaf to every other recommendation.

If a man can be induced to do his duty even from a regard to his own happiness, he will soon find reason to love virtue for her own sake, and to act from motives less mercenary.

I cannot therefore approve of those moralists, who would banish all persuasives to virtue taken from the consideration of private good. In the present state of human nature these are not useless to the best, and they are the only means left of reclaiming the abandoned.

2. As far as the intention of nature appears in the constitution of man, we ought to comply with that intention, and to act agreeably to it.

The Author of our being hath given us not only the power of acting within a limited sphere, but various principles or springs of action, of different nature and dignity, to direct us in the exercise of our active power.

From the constitution of every species of the inferior animals, and especially from the active principles which nature has given them, we easily perceive the manner of life for which nature intended them; and they uniformly act the part to which they are led by their constitution, without any reflection upon it, or intention of obeying its dictates. Man only, of the inhabitants of this world, is made capable of observing his own constitution, what kind of life it is made for, and of acting according to that intention, or contrary to it. He only is capable of yielding an intentional obedience to the dictates of his nature, or of rebelling against them.

In treating of the principles of action in man, it has been shewn, that as his natural instincts and bodily appetites are well adapted to the preservation of his natural life, and to the continuance of the species; so his natural desires, affections, and passions, when uncorrupted by vicious habits, and under the government of the leading principles of reason and conscience, are excellently fitted for the rational and social life. Every vicious action shews an excess, or defect, or wrong direction of some natural spring of action, and therefore may, very justly, be said to be unnatural. Every virtuous action agrees with the uncorrupted principles of human nature.

The Stoics defined virtue to be a life according to nature. Some of them more accurately, a life according to the nature of man, in so far as it is superior to that of brutes. The life of a brute is according to the nature of the brute; but it is neither virtuous nor vicious. The life of a moral agent cannot be according to his nature, unless it be virtuous. That conscience, which is in every man's breast, is the law of God written in his heart, which he cannot disobey without acting unnaturally, and being self-condemned.

The intention of nature, in the various active principles of man, in the desires of power, of knowledge, and of esteem, in the affection to children, to near relations, and to the communities to which we belong, in gratitude, in compassion, and even in resentment and emulation, is very obvious, and has been pointed out in treating of those principles. Nor is it less evident, that reason and conscience are given us to regulate the inferior principles, so that they may conspire, in a regular and consistent plan of life, in pursuit of some worthy end.

3. No man is born for himself only. Every man, therefore, ought to consider himself as a member of the common society of mankind, and of those subordinate societies to which he belongs, such as family, friends, neighbourhood, country, and to do as much good as he can, and as little hurt to the societies of which he is a part.

This axiom leads directly to the practice of every social virtue, and indirectly to the virtues of self-government, by which only we can be qualified for discharging the duty we owe to society.

4. In every case, we ought to act that part towards another, which we would judge to be right in him to act towards us, if we were in his circumstances and he in ours; or, more generally, what we approve in

others, that we ought to practise in like circumstances, and what we condemn in others we ought not to do.

If there be any such thing as right and wrong in the conduct of moral agents, it must be the same to all in the same circumstances.

We stand all in the same relation to him who made us, and will call us to account for our conduct; for with him there is no respect of persons. We stand in the same relation to one another as members of the great community of mankind. The duties consequent upon the different ranks and offices and relations of men are the same to all in the same circumstances.

It is not want of judgment, but want of candour and impartiality, that hinders men from discerning what they owe to others. They are quick-sighted enough in discerning what is due to themselves. When they are injured, or ill treated, they see it, and feel resentment. It is the want of candour that makes men use one measure for the duty they owe to others, and another measure for the duty that others owe to them in like circumstances. That men ought to judge with candour, as in all other cases, so especially in what concerns their moral conduct, is surely self-evident to every intelligent being. The man who takes offence when he is injured in his person, in his property, in his good name, pronounces judgment against himself if he act so toward his neighbour.

As the equity and obligation of this rule of conduct is self-evident to every man who hath a conscience; so it is, of all the rules of morality, the most comprehensive, and truly deserves the encomium given it by the highest authority, that *it is the law and the prophets.*

It comprehends every rule of justice without exception. It comprehends all the relative duties, arising either from the more permanent relations of parent and child, of master and servant, of magistrate and subject, of husband and wife, or from the more transient relations of rich and poor, of buyer and seller, of debtor and creditor, of benefactor and beneficiary, of friend and enemy. It comprehends every duty of charity and humanity, and even of courtesy and good manners.

Nay, I think, that, without any force or straining, it extends even to the duties of self-government. For, as every man approves in others the virtues of prudence, temperance, self-command and fortitude, he must perceive, that what is right in others must be right in himself in like circumstances.

To sum up all, he who acts invariably by this rule will never deviate from the path of his duty, but from an error of judgment. And, as he feels the obligation that he and all men are under to use the best means in his power to have his judgment well informed in matters of duty, his errors will only be such as are invincible.

It may be observed, that this axiom supposes a faculty in man by which he can distinguish right conduct from wrong. It supposes also, that, by this faculty, we easily perceive the right and the wrong in other men that are indifferent to us, but are very apt to be blinded by the partiality of selfish passions when the case concerns ourselves. Every claim we have against others is apt to be magnified by self-love, when viewed directly. A change of persons removes this prejudice, and brings the claim to appear in its just magnitude.

5. To every man who believes the existence, the perfections, and the providence of God, the veneration and submission we owe to him is self-evident. Right sentiments of the Deity and of his works, not only make the duty we owe to him obvious to every intelligent being, but likewise add the authority of a divine law to every rule of right conduct.

There is another class of axioms in morals, by which, when there seems to be an opposition between the actions that different virtues lead to, we determine to which the preference is due.

Between the several virtues, as they are dispositions of mind, or determinations of will to act according to a certain general rule, there can be no opposition. They dwell together most amicably, and give mutual aid and ornament, without the possibility of hostility or opposition, and, taken altogether, make one uniform and consistent rule of conduct. But, between particular external actions, which different virtues would lead to, there may be an opposition. Thus, the same man may be in his heart, generous, grateful and just. These dispositions strengthen, but never can weaken one another. Yet it may happen, that an external action which generosity or gratitude solicits, justice may forbid.

That in all such cases, unmerited generosity should yield to gratitude, and both to justice, is self-evident. Nor is it less so, that unmerited beneficence to those who are at ease should yield to compassion to the miserable, and external acts of piety to works of mercy, because God loves mercy more than sacrifice.

At the same time, we perceive, that those acts of virtue which ought to yield in the case of a competition, have most intrinsic worth when there is no competition. Thus, it is evident that there is more worth in pure and unmerited benevolence than in compassion, more in compassion than in gratitude, and more in gratitude than in justice.

I call these *first principles*, because they appear to me to have in themselves an intuitive evidence which I cannot resist. I find I can express them in other words. I can illustrate them by examples and authorities, and perhaps can deduce one of them from another; but I am not able to deduce them from other principles that are more evident. And I find the best moral reasonings of authors I am acquainted with, ancient and modern, Heathen and Christian, to be grounded upon one or more of them.

The evidence of mathematical axioms is not discerned till men come to a certain degree of maturity of understanding. A boy must have formed the general conception of *quantity,* and of *more* and *less* and *equal,* of *sum* and *difference;* and he must have been accustomed to judge of these relations in matters of common life, before he can perceive the evidence of the mathematical axiom, that equal quantities, added to equal quantities, make equal sums.

In like manner, our moral judgment, or conscience, grows to maturity from an imperceptible seed, planted by our Creator. When we are capable of contemplating the actions of other men, or of reflecting upon our own calmly and dispassionately, we begin to perceive in them the qualities of honest and dishonest, of honourable and base, of right and wrong, and to feel the sentiments of moral approbation and disapprobation.

These sentiments are at first feeble, easily warped by passions and prejudices, and apt to yield to authority. By use and time, the judgment, in morals as in other matters, gathers strength, and feels more vigour. We begin to distinguish the dictates of passion from those of cool reason, and to perceive, that it is not always safe to rely upon the judgment of others. By an impulse of nature, we venture to judge for ourselves, as we venture to walk by ourselves.

There is a strong analogy between the progress of the body from infancy to maturity, and the progress of all the powers of the mind. This progression in both is the work of nature, and in both may be greatly aided or hurt by proper education. It is natural to a man to be able to walk or run or leap; but if his limbs had been kept in fetters from his birth, he would have none of those powers. It is no less natural to a man trained in society, and accustomed to judge of his own actions and those of other men, to perceive a right and a wrong, an honourable and a base, in human conduct; and to such a man, I think, the principles of morals I have above mentioned will appear self-evident. Yet there may be individuals of the human species so little accustomed to think or judge of any thing, but of gratifying their animal appetites, as to have hardly any conception of right or wrong in conduct, or any moral judgment; as there certainly are some who have not the conceptions and the judgment necessary to understand the axioms of geometry.

From the principles above mentioned, the whole system of moral conduct follows so easily, and with so little aid of reasoning, that every man of common understanding, who wishes to know his duty, may know it. The path of duty is a plain path which the upright in heart can rarely mistake. Such it must be, since every man is bound to walk in it. There are some intricate cases in morals which admit of disputation; but these seldom occur in practice; and, when they do, the learned disputant has no great advantage: For the unlearned man, who uses the best means in his power to know his duty, and acts according to his knowledge, is inculpable in the sight of God and man. He may err, but he is not guilty of immorality.

# 9

# The Principle of Utility*
## JEREMY BENTHAM
### (1748–1832)

I. Nature has placed mankind under the governance of two sovereign masters, *pain* and *pleasure*. It is for them alone to point out what we ought to do, as well as to determine what we shall do. On the one hand the standard of right and wrong, on the other the chain of causes and effects, are fastened to their throne. They govern us in all we do, in all we say, in all we think: every effort we can make to throw off our subjection, will serve but to demonstrate and confirm it. In words a man may pretend to abjure their empire: but in reality he will remain subject to it all the while. The *principle of utility*[1] recognises this subjection, and assumes it for the foundation of that system, the object of which is to rear the fabric of felicity by the hands of reason and of law. Systems which attempt to question it, deal in sounds instead of sense, in caprice instead of reason, in darkness instead of light.

But enough of metaphor and declamation: it is not by such means that moral science is to be improved.

*From Jeremy Bentham, *An Introduction to the Principles of Morals and Legislation* (1780, 1789), ch. 1. Should be read in conjunction with selection 10.

[1]Note by the Author, July 1822.

To this denomination has of late been added, or substituted, the *greatest happiness* or *greatest felicity* principle: this for shortness, instead of saying at length *that principle* which states the greatest happiness of all those whose interest is in question, as being the right and proper, and only right and proper and universally desirable, end of human action: of human action in every situation, and in particular in that of a functionary or set of functionaries exercising the powers of Government. The word *utility* does not so clearly point to the ideas of *pleasure* and *pain* as the words *happiness* and *felicity* do: nor does it lead us to the consideration of the *number*, of the interests affected; to the *number*, as being the circumstance, which contributes, in the largest proportion, to the formation of the standard here in question; the *standard of right and wrong*, by which alone the propriety of human conduct, in every situation, can with propriety be tried. This want of a sufficiently manifest connexion between the ideas of *happiness* and *pleasure* on the one hand, and the idea of *utility* on the other, I have every now and then found operating, and with but too much efficiency, as a bar to the acceptance, that might otherwise have been given, to this principle.

II. The principle of utility is the foundation of the present work: it will be proper therefore at the outset to give an explicit and determinate account of what is meant by it. By the principle[2] of utility is meant that principle which approves or disapproves of every action whatsoever, according to the tendency which it appears to have to augment or diminish the happiness of the party whose interest is in question: or, what is the same thing in other words, to promote or to oppose that happiness. I say of every action whatsoever; and therefore not only of every action of a private individual, but of every measure of government.

III. By utility is meant that property in any object, whereby it tends to produce benefit, advantage, pleasure, good, or happiness, (all this in the present case comes to the same thing) or (what comes again to the same thing) to prevent the happening of mischief, pain, evil, or unhappiness to the party whose interest is considered: if that party be the community in general, then the happiness of the community: if a particular individual, then the happiness of that individual.

IV. The interest of the community is one of the most general expressions that can occur in the phraseology of morals: no wonder that the meaning of it is often lost. When it has a meaning, it is this. The community is a fictitious *body,* composed of the individual persons who are considered as constituting as it were its *members.* The interest of the community then is, what?—the sum of the interests of the several members who compose it.

V. It is in vain to talk of the interest of the community, without understanding what is the interest of the individual.[3] A thing is said to promote the interest, or to be *for* the interest, of an individual, when it tends to add to the sum total of his pleasures: or, what comes to the same thing, to diminish the sum total of his pains.

VI. An action then may be said to be conformable to the principle of utility, or, for shortness sake, to utility, (meaning with respect to the community at large) when the tendency it has to augment the happiness of the community is greater than any it has to diminish it.

---

[2] The word principle is derived from the Latin principium: which seems to be compounded of the two words *primus,* first, or chief, and *cipium,* a termination which seems to be derived from *capio,* to take, as in *mancipium, municipium;* to which are analogous, *auceps, forceps,* and others. It is a term of very vague and very extensive signification: it is applied to any thing which is conceived to serve as a foundation or beginning to any series of operations: in some cases, of physical operations; but of mental operations in the present case.

The principle here in question may be taken for an act of the mind; a sentiment; a sentiment of approbation; a sentiment which, when applied to an action, approves of its utility, as that quality of it by which the measure of approbation or disapprobation bestowed upon it ought to be governed.

[3] Interest is one of those words, which not having any superior *genus,* cannot in the ordinary way be defined.

VII. A measure of government (which is but a particular kind of action, performed by a particular person or persons) may be said to be conformable to or dictated by the principle of utility, when in like manner the tendency which it has to augment the happiness of the community is greater than any which it has to diminish it.

VIII. When an action, or in particular a measure of government, is supposed by a man to be conformable to the principle of utility, it may be convenient, for the purposes of discourse, to imagine a kind of law or dictate, called a law or dictate of utility: and to speak of the action in question, as being conformable to such law or dictate.

IX. A man may be said to be a partizan of the principle of utility, when the approbation or disapprobation he annexes to any action, or to any measure, is determined by and proportioned to the tendency which he conceives it to have to augment or to diminish the happiness of the community: or in other words, to its conformity or unconformity to the laws or dictates of utility.

X. Of an action that is conformable to the principle of utility one may always say either that it is one that ought to be done, or at least that it is not one that ought not to be done. One may say also, that it is right it should be done; at least that it is not wrong it should be done: that it is a right action; at least that it is not a wrong action. When thus interpreted, the words *ought*, and *right* and *wrong*, and others of that stamp, have a meaning: when otherwise, they have none.

XI. Has the rectitude of this principle been ever formally contested? It should seem that it had, by those who have not known what they have been meaning. Is it susceptible of any direct proof? it should seem not: for that which is used to prove every thing else, cannot itself be proved: a chain of proofs must have their commencement somewhere. To give such proof is as impossible as it is needless.

XII. Not that there is or ever has been that human creature breathing, however stupid or perverse, who has not on many, perhaps on most occasions of his life, deferred to it. By the natural constitution of the human frame, on most occasions of their lives men in general embrace this principle, without thinking of it: if not for the ordering of their own actions, yet for the trying of their own actions, as well as of those of other men. There have been, at the same time, not many, perhaps, even of the most intelligent, who have been disposed to embrace it purely and without reserve. There are even few who have not taken some occasion or other to quarrel with it, either on account of their not understanding always how to apply it, or on account of some prejudice or other which they were afraid to examine into, or could not bear to part with. For such is the stuff that man is made of: in principle and in practice, in a right track and in a wrong one, the rarest of all human qualities is consistency.

XIII. When a man attempts to combat the principle of utility, it is with reasons drawn, without his being aware of it, from that very principle itself.[4] His arguments, if they prove any thing, prove not that the principle is *wrong*, but that, according to the applications he supposes to be made of it, it is *misapplied*. Is it possible for a man to move the earth? Yes; but he must first find out another earth to stand upon.

XIV. To disprove the propriety of it by arguments is impossible; but, from the causes that have been mentioned, or from some confused or partial view of it, a man may happen to be disposed not to relish it. Where this is the case, if he thinks the settling of his opinions on such a subject worth the trouble, let him take the following steps, and at length, perhaps, he may come to reconcile himself to it.

1. Let him settle with himself, whether he would wish to discard this principle altogether; if so, let him consider what it is that all his reasonings (in matters of politics especially) can amount to?

2. If he would, let him settle with himself, whether he would judge and act without any principle, or whether there is any other he would judge and act by?

3. If there be, let him examine and satisfy himself whether the principle he thinks he has found is really any separate intelligible principle; or whether it be not a mere principle in words, a kind of phrase, which at bottom expresses neither more nor less than the mere averment of his own unfounded sentiments; that is, what in another person he might be apt to call caprice?

4. If he is inclined to think that his own approbation or disapprobation, annexed to the idea of an act, without any regard to its consequences, is a sufficient foundation for him to judge and act upon, let him ask himself whether his sentiment is to be a standard of right and wrong, with respect to every other man, or whether every man's sentiment has the same privilege of being a standard to itself?

5. In the first case, let him ask himself whether his principle is not despotical, and hostile to all the rest of human race?

6. In the second case, whether it is not anarchial, and whether at this rate there are not as many different standards of right and wrong as there are men? and whether even to the same man, the same thing, which is right to-day, may not (without the least change in its nature) be wrong to-

4"The principle of utility, (I have heard it said) is a dangerous principle: it is dangerous on certain occasions to consult it." This is as much as to say, what? that it is not consonant to utility, to consult utility: in short, that it is *not* consulting it, to consult it.

morrow? and whether the same thing is not right and wrong in the same place at the same time? and in either case, whether all argument is not at an end? and whether, when two men have said, "I like this," and "I don't like it," they can (upon such a principle) have any thing more to say?

7. If he should have said to himself, No: for that the sentiment which he proposes as a standard must be grounded on reflection, let him say on what particulars the reflection is to turn? if on particulars having relation to the utility of the act, then let him say whether this is not deserting his own principle, and borrowing assistance from that very one in opposition to which he sets it up: or if not on those particulars, on what other particulars?

8. If he should be for compounding the matter, and adopting his own principle in part, and the principle of utility in part, let him say how far he will adopt it?

9. When he has settled with himself where he will stop, then let him ask himself how he justifies to himself the adopting it so far? and why he will not adopt it any farther?

10. Admitting any other principle than the principle of utility to be a right principle, a principle that it is right for a man to pursue; admitting (what is not true) that the word *right* can have a meaning without reference to utility, let him say whether there is any such thing as a *motive* that a man can have to pursue the dictates of it: if there is, let him say what that motive is, and how it is to be distinguished from those which enforce the dictates of utility: if not, then lastly let him say what it is this other principle can be good for?*

*The first paragraph of chapter 2 runs this way: "If the principle of utility be a right principle to be governed by, and that in all cases, it follows from what has been just observed, that whatever principle differs from it in any case must necessarily be a wrong one. To prove any other principle, therefore, to be a wrong one, there needs no more than just to show it to be what it is, a principle of which the dictates are in some point or other different from those of the principle of utility: to state it is to confute it." Bentham's inference here is a fascinating one. Does "it follow," or is this just a *non sequitur?* Compare statements 21 and 22.

# 10

## The Hedonic Calculus*

### JEREMY BENTHAM
### (1748–1832)

I. Pleasures then, and the avoidance of pains, are the *ends* which the legislator has in view: it behoves him therefore to understand their *value*. Pleasures and pains are the *instruments* he has to work with: it behoves him therefore to understand their force, which is again, in other words, their value.

II. To a person considered *by himself*, the value of a pleasure or pain considered *by itself*, will be greater or less, according to the four following circumstances[1]:

1. Its *intensity*.
2. Its *duration*.
3. Its *certainty* or *uncertainty*.
4. Its *propinquity* or *remoteness*.

III. These are the circumstances which are to be considered in estimating a pleasure or a pain considered each of them by itself. But when the value of any pleasure or pain is considered for the purpose of estimating the

---

*From Jeremy Bentham, *An Introduction to the Principles of Morals and Legislation* (1789), ch. 4, with the omission of the last paragraph. The title of this selection has been supplied by the editor. Should be read in conjunction with selection 9.

[1]These circumstances have since been denominated *elements* or *dimensions* of *value* in a pleasure or a pain.

Not long after the publication of the first edition, the following memoriter verses were framed, in the view of lodging more effectually, in the memory, these points, on which the whole fabric of morals and legislation may be seen to rest.

*Intense, long, certain, speedy, fruitful, pure—*
Such marks in *pleasures* and in *pains* endure.
Such pleasures seek, if *private* be thy end:
If it be *public*, wide let them *extend*.
Such *pains* avoid, whichever be thy view:
If pains *must* come, let them *extend* to few.

tendency of any *act* by which it is produced, there are two other circumstances to be taken into the account; these are,

5. Its *fecundity,* or the chance it has of being followed by sensations of the *same* kind: that is, pleasures, if it be a pleasure: pains, if it be a pain.

6. Its *purity,* or the chance it has of *not* being followed by sensations of the *opposite* kind: that is, pains, if it be a pleasure: pleasures, if it be a pain.

These two last, however, are in strictness scarcely to be deemed properties of the pleasure or the pain itself; they are not, therefore, in strictness to be taken into the account of the value of that pleasure or that pain. They are in strictness to be deemed properties only of the act, or other event, by which such pleasure or pain has been produced; and accordingly are only to be taken into the account of the tendency of such act or such event.

IV. To a *number* of persons, with reference to each of whom the value of a pleasure or a pain is considered, it will be greater or less, according to seven circumstances: to wit, the six preceding ones; *viz.*

1. Its *intensity.*

2. Its *duration.*

3. Its *certainty* or *uncertainty.*

4. Its *propinquity* or *remoteness.*

5. Its *fecundity.*

6. Its *purity.*

And one other; to wit:

7. Its *extent;* that is, the number of persons to whom it *extends;* or (in other words) who are affected by it.

V. To take an exact account then of the general tendency of any act, by which the interests of a community are affected, proceed as follows. Begin with any one person of those whose interests seem most immediately to be affected by it: and take an account,

1. Of the value of each distinguishable *pleasure* which appears to be produced by it in the *first* instance.

2. Of the value of each *pain* which appears to be produced by it in the *first* instance.

3. Of the value of each pleasure which appears to be produced by it *after* the first. This constitutes the *fecundity* of the first *pleasure* and the *impurity* of the first *pain.*

4. Of the value of each *pain* which appears to be produced by it after the first. This constitutes the *fecundity* of the first *pain,* and the *impurity* of the first pleasure.

5. Sum up all the values of all the *pleasures* on the one side, and those of all the pains on the other. The balance, if it be on the side of pleasure, will give the *good* tendency of the act upon the whole, with respect to the interests of that *individual* person; if on the side of pain, the *bad* tendency of it upon the whole.

6. Take an account of the *number* of persons whose interests appear to be concerned; and repeat the above process with respect to each. *Sum up* the numbers expressive of the degrees of *good* tendency, which the act has, with respect to each individual, in regard to whom the tendency of it is *good* upon the whole: do this again with respect to each individual, in regard to whom the tendency of it is *good* upon the whole: do this again with respect to each individual, in regard to whom the tendency of it is *bad* upon the whole. Take the *balance;* which, if on the side of *pleasure,* will give the general *good tendency* of the act, with respect to the total number or community of individuals concerned; if on the side of pain, the general *evil tendency,* with respect to the same community.

VI. It is not to be expected that this process should be strictly pursued previously to every moral judgment, or to every legislative or judicial operation. It may, however, be always kept in view: and as near as the process actually pursued on these occasions approaches to it, so near will such process approach to the character of an exact one.

VII. The same process is alike applicable to pleasure and pain, in whatever shape they appear: and by whatever denomination they are distinguished: to pleasure, whether it be called *good* (which is properly the cause or instrument of pleasure) or *profit* (which is distant pleasure, or the cause or instrument of distant pleasure,) or *convenience,* or *advantage, benefit, emolument, happiness,* and so forth: to pain, whether it be called *evil,* (which corresponds to *good*) or *mischief,* or *inconvenience,* or *disadvantage, or loss,* or *unhappiness,* and so forth.

VIII. Nor is this a novel and unwarranted, any more than it is a useless theory. In all this there is nothing but what the practice of mankind, wheresoever they have a clear view of their own interest, is perfectly conformable to. An article of property, an estate in land, for instance, is valuable, on what account? On account of the pleasures of all kinds which it enables a man to produce, and what comes to the same thing the pains of all kinds which it enables him to avert. But the value of such an article of property is universally understood to rise or fall according to the length or shortness of the time which a man has in it: the certainty or uncertainty of its coming into possession: and the nearness or remoteness of the time at which, if at all, it is to come into possession. As to the *intensity* of the pleasures which a man may derive from it, this is never thought of, because it depends upon the use which each particular person may come to make of it; which cannot be estimated till the particular pleasures he may come to derive from it, or the particular pains he may come to exclude by means of it, are brought to view. For the same reason, neither does he think of the *fecundity* or *purity* of those pleasures. . . .*

*The second sentence of chapter 5 is: "Pains and pleasures may be called by one general word, interesting perceptions."

# 11

# The Moral Philosophy
# of J. S. Mill*

## J. O. URMSON
(1915–     )

... Mill, in his *Utilitarianism* attempts to do two things; first, he attempts to state the place of the conception of a *summum bonum* in ethics, secondly, he attempts to give an account of the nature of this ultimate end. We shall be concerned only with the first of these two parts of Mill's ethical theory; we shall not ask what Mill thought the ultimate end was, and how he thought that his view on this point could be substantiated, but only what part Mill considered that the notion of an ultimate end, whatever it be, must play in a sound ethical theory. This part of Mill's doctrine is logically independent of his account of happiness.

## Two Mistaken Interpretations of Mill

Some of Mill's expositors and critics have thought that Mill was attempting to analyse or define the notion of right in terms of the *summum bonum*. Thus Mill is commonly adduced as an example of an ethical naturalist by those who interpret his account of happiness naturalistically, as being one who defined rightness in terms of the natural consequences of actions. Moore, for example, while criticising Mill's account of the ultimate end says: "In thus insisting that what is right must mean what produces the best possible results Utilitarianism is fully justified." [1] Others have been less

*From J. O. Urmson, "The Interpretation of the Moral Philosophy of J. S. Mill," *The Philosophical Quarterly*, Vol. 3 (1953), pp. 33–39, with the omission of the first paragraph and the first sentence of the second paragraph. Permission to reprint was granted by the author and the editors of *The Philosophical Quarterly*. Compare with selections 9 and 13.
[1] *Principia Ethica*, reprinted 1948, p. 106.

favourable in their estimation of this alleged view of Mill's. But right or wrong, it seems clear to me that Mill did not hold it. Mill's only reference to this analytic problem is on page 27 (of the Everyman edition, to which all references will be made), where he refers to a person "who sees in moral obligation a transcendent fact, an objective reality belonging to the province of 'Things in themselves,'" and goes on to speak of this view as an irrelevant opinion "on this point of Ontology," as though the analysis of ethical terms was not part of ethical philosophy at all as he conceived it, but part of ontology. It seems clear that when Mill speaks of his quest being for the "criterion of right and wrong" (p. 1), "concerning the foundation of morality" (p. 1) for a "test of right and wrong" (p. 2), he is looking for a "means of ascertaining what is right or wrong" (p. 2), not for a definition of these terms. We shall not, therefore, deal further with this interpretation of Mill; if a further refutation of it is required it should be sought in the agreement of the text with the alternative exposition shortly to be given.

The other mistaken view avoids the error of this first view, and indeed is incompatible with it. It is, probably, the received view. On this interpretation Mill is looking for a test of right or wrong as the ultimate test by which one can justify the ascription of rightness or wrongness to courses of action, rightness and wrongness being taken to be words which we understand. This test is taken to be whether the course of action does or does not tend to promote the ultimate end (which Mill no doubt says is the general happiness). So far there is no cause to quarrel with the received view, for it is surely correct. But in detail the view is wrong. For it is further suggested that for Mill this ultimate test is also the immediate test; the rightness or wrongness of any particular action is to be decided by considering whether it promotes the ultimate end. We may, it might be admitted, on Mill's view sometimes act, by rule of thumb or in a hurry, without actually raising this question; but the actual justification, if there is one, must be directly in terms of consequences, including the consequences of the example that we have set. On this view, then, Mill holds that an action, a particular action, is right if it promotes the ultimate end better than any alternative, and otherwise it is wrong. However we in fact make up our minds in moral situations, so far as justification goes no other factor enters into the matter. It is clear that on this interpretation Mill is immediately open to two shattering objections; first, it is obviously and correctly urged, if one has, for example, promised to do something it is one's duty to do it at least partly because one has promised to do it and not merely because of consequences, even if these consequences are taken to include one's example in promise-breaking. Secondly, it is correctly pointed out that on this view a man who, *ceteris paribus,* chooses the inferior of two musical comedies for an evening's entertainment has done a moral wrong, and this is preposterous.[2] If this were in fact the view of Mill, he would indeed be fit for little more than the halting eristic of philosophical infants.

## A Revised Interpretation of Mill

I shall now set out in a set of propositions what I take to be in fact Mill's view and substantiate them afterwards from the text. This will obscure the subtleties but will make clearer the main lines of interpretation.

   A. A particular action is justified as being right by showing that it is in accord with some moral rule. It is shown to be wrong by showing that it trangresses some moral rule.

   B. A moral rule is shown to be correct by showing that the recognition of that rule promotes the ultimate end.

   C. Moral rules can be justified only in regard to matters in which the general welfare is more than negligibly affected.

   D. Where no moral rule is applicable the question of the rightness or wrongness of particular acts does not arise, though the worth of the actions can be estimated in other ways.

As a terminological point it should be mentioned that where the phrase "moral rule" occurs above Mill uses the phrase "secondary principle" more generally, though he sometimes says "moral law." By these terms, whichever is preferred, Mill is referring to such precepts as "Keep promises," "Do no murder," or "Tell no lies." A list of which Mill approves is to be found in *On Liberty* (p. 135).

There is, no doubt, need of further explanation of these propositions; but that, and some caveats, can best be given in the process of establishing that these are in fact Mill's views. First, then, to establish from the text that in Mill's view particular actions are shown to be right or wrong by showing that they are or are not in accord with some moral rule. (i) He says with evident approbation on p. 2: "The intuitive, no less than what may be termed the inductive, school of ethics, insists on the necessity of general laws. They both agree that the morality of an individual action is not a question of direct perception, but of the application of a law to an individual case. They recognize also, to a great extent, the same moral laws." Mill reproaches these schools only with being unable to give a unifying rationale of these laws (as he will do in proposition B). (ii) He says on page 22: "But to consider the rules of morality as improvable is one thing; to

---

[2] For one example of this interpretation of Mill and the first and more important objection, see Carritt, *The Theory of Morals,* Ch. IV.

pass over the intermediate generalisations entirely, and endeavour to test each individual action directly by the first principle, is another. It is a strange notion that the acknowledgment of a first principle is inconsistent with the admission of secondary ones." He adds, with feeling: "Men really ought to leave off talking a kind of nonsense on this subject which they would neither talk nor listen to on other matters of practical concernment." (iii) Having admitted on p. 23 that "rules of conduct cannot be so framed as to require no exceptions," he adds (p. 24) "We must remember that only in these cases of conflict between secondary principles is it requisite that first principles should be appealed to. There is no case of moral obligation in which some secondary principle is not involved; and if only one, there can seldom be any real doubt which one it is, in the mind of any person by whom the principle itself is recognized." This quotation supports both propositions A and D. It shows that for Mill moral rules are not merely rules of thumb which aid the unreflective man in making up his mind, but an essential part of moral reasoning. The relevance of a moral rule is the criterion of whether we are dealing with a case of right or wrong or some other moral or prudential situation. (iv) The last passage which we shall select to establish this interpretation of Mill (it would be easy to find more) is also a joint confirmation of propositions A and D, showing that our last was not an *obiter dictum* on which we have placed too much weight. In the chapter entitled "On the connection between justice and utility," Mill has maintained that it is a distinguishing mark of a just act that it is one required by a specific rule or law, positive or moral, carrying also liability to penal sanctions. He then writes this important paragraph (p. 45), which in view of its importance and the neglect that it has suffered must be quoted at length: "The above is, I think, a true account, as far as it goes, of the origin and progressive growth of the idea of justice. But we must observe, that it contains, as yet, nothing to distinguish that obligation from moral obligation in general. For the truth is, that the idea of penal sanction, which is the essence of law, enters not only into the conception of injustice, but into that of any kind of wrong. We do not call anything wrong, unless we mean to imply that a person ought to be punished in some way or other for doing it; if not by law, by the opinion of his fellow-creatures; if not by opinion, by the reproaches of his own conscience. This seems to be the real turning point of the distinction between morality and simple expediency. It is a part of the notion of Duty in every one of its forms, that a person may rightfully be compelled to fulfil it. Duty is a thing which may be exacted from a person, as one exacts a debt. Unless we think that it may be exacted from him, we do not call it his duty. . . . There are other things, on the contrary, which we wish that people should do, which we like or admire them for doing, perhaps dislike or despise them for not doing, but yet admit that they are not bound to do; it is not a case of moral obligation; we do not blame them, that is, we do not think that they are proper objects of punishment. . . . I think there is no doubt that this distinction lies at the bottom of the notions of right and wrong; that we call any conduct wrong, or employ, instead, some other term of dislike or disparagement, according as we think that the person ought, or ought not, to be punished for it; and we say, it would be right to do so and so, or merely that it would be desirable or laudable, according as we would wish to see the person whom it concerns, compelled, or only persuaded and exhorted, to act in that manner." How supporters of the received view have squared it with this passage I do not know; they do not mention it. If they have noticed it at all it is, presumably, regarded as an example of Mill's inconsistent eclecticism. Mill here makes it quite clear that in his view right and wrong are derived from moral rules; in other cases where the ultimate end is no doubt affected appraisal of conduct must be made in other ways. For example, if one's own participation in the ultimate end is impaired without breach of moral law, it is (*Liberty,* p. 135) imprudence or lack of self respect, it is not wrong-doing. So much for the establishment of this interpretation of Mill, in a positive way, as regards points A and D. We must now ask whether there is anything in Mill which is inconsistent with it and in favour of the received view.

It is impossible to show positively that there is nothing in Mill which favours the received view against the interpretation here given, for it would require a complete review of everything that Mill says. We shall have to be content with examining two points which might be thought to tell in favour of the received view.

(*a*) On p. 6 Mill says: "The creed which accepts as the foundation of morals, Utility, or the Greatest Happiness Principle, holds that actions are right in proportion as they tend to promote happiness, wrong as they tend to promote the reverse of happiness." This seems to be the well-known sentence which is at the bottom of the received interpretation. Of course, it could be taken as a loose and inaccurate statement of the received view, if the general argument required it. But note that strictly one can say that a certain action tends to produce a certain result only if one is speaking of type- rather than token-actions. Drinking alcohol may tend to promote exhilaration, but my drinking this particular glass either does or does not produce it. It seems, then, that Mill can well be interpreted here as regarding moral rules as forbidding or enjoining types of action, in fact as making the point that the right moral rules are the ones which promote the ultimate end (my proposition B), not as saying something contrary to proposition A. And this, or something like it, is the interpretation which consistency requires. Mill's reference to "tendencies of actions" at the top of p. 22 supports the stress here laid on the word "tend," and that context should be examined by those who require further conviction.

(*b*) Mill sometimes refers to moral rules as "intermediate generalisations" (e.g., p. 22) from the supreme principle, or as "corollaries" of it (also p. 22). These are probably the sort of phrases which lead people to think that they play a purely heuristic role in ethical thinking for Mill. As for the expression "intermediate generalisation," Mill undoubtedly thinks that we should, and to some extent do, arrive at and improve our moral rules by such methods as observing that a certain type of action has had bad results of a social kind in such an overwhelming majority of cases that it ought to be banned. (But this is an over-simplification; see the note on p. 58 on how we ought to arrive at moral rules, and the pessimistic account of how we in fact arrive at them in *Liberty*, pp. 69–70). But this account of the genesis of moral rules does not require us to interpret them as being anything but rules when once made. It really seems unnecessary to say much of the expression "corollary"; Mill obviously cannot wish it to be taken literally; in fact it is hard to state the relation of moral rules to a justifying principle with exactitude and Mill, in a popular article in *Fraser,* did not try very hard to do so.

## Moral Rules and the Ultimate End

We have already been led in our examination of possible objections to proposition A to say something in defence of the view that Mill thought that a moral rule is shown to be correct by showing that the recognition of that rule promotes the ultimate end (proposition B). A little more may be added on this point, though it seems fairly obvious that if we are right in saying that the supreme principle is not to be evoked, in Mill's view, in the direct justification of particular right acts, it must thus come in in an indirect way in view of the importance that Mill attached to it. And it is hard to think what the indirect way is if not this. (i) On p. 3 Mill reproaches other moral philosophers with not giving a satisfactory account of moral rules in terms of a fundamental principle, though they have correctly placed moral rules as governing particular actions. It would be indeed the mark of an inconsistent philosopher if he did not try to repair the one serious omission which he ascribes to others. (ii) Mill ascribes to Kant (p. 4) the use of utilitarian arguments because, Mill alleges, he in fact supports the rules of morality by showing the evil consequences of not adopting them or adopting alternatives. Thus Mill is here regarding as distinctively utilitarian the justification or rejection of moral rules on the ground of consequences. He could hardly have wished to suggest that Kant would directly justify, even inadvertently, particular actions on such grounds. But it is perhaps not to the point to argue this matter more elaborately. If anyone has been convinced by what has gone before, he will not need much argument on this point; with others it is superfluous to make the attempt.

## In What Fields are Moral Rules of Right and Wrong Applicable?

The applicability of moral rules is, says Mill, "the characteristic difference which marks off, not justice, but morality in general, from the remaining provinces of Expediency and Worthiness" (p. 46). Mill says little or nothing in *Utilitarianism* about the boundary between morality and worthiness (surely it would be better to have said the boundary between right and wrong on the one hand and other forms of both moral and non-moral appraisal on the other?). It seems reasonable to suppose that he would have recognised that the use of moral rules must be confined to matters in which the kind of consequence is sufficiently invariable for there not to be too many exceptions. But this is a pragmatic limitation; Mill does have something to say about a limitation in principle in *Liberty* which I have crudely summarised in my proposition C—moral rules can be justifiably maintained in regard only to matters in which the general welfare is more than negligibly affected.

It is important to note that Mill in *Liberty* is concerned with freedom from moral sanctions as well as the sanctions of positive law. The distinction between self-regarding and other actions is regarded by him as relevant to moral as well as to political philosophy. The most noteworthy passage which bears on the scope of moral rules is on page 135. Here he mentions such things as encroachment on the rights of others as being "fit objects of moral reprobation, and, in grave cases, of moral retribution and punishment." But self-regarding faults (low tastes and the like) are "not properly immoralities and to whatever pitch they are carried, do not constitute wickedness. . . . The term duty to oneself, when it means anything more than prudence, means self-respect or self-development." Self-regarding faults render the culprit "necessarily and properly a subject of distaste, or, in extreme cases, even of contempt," but this is in the sphere of worthiness not of right and wrong.

So much then for Mill's account of the logic of moral reasoning. It must be emphasised that no more has been attempted than a skeleton plan of Mill's answer, and that Mill puts the matter more richly and more subtly in his book. Even on the question of general interpretation more store must be laid on the effect of a continuous reading in the light of the skeleton plan than on the effect of the few leading quotations introduced in this paper. It is emphatically not the contention of this paper that Mill has given a finally correct account of these matters which is immune to all criticism; an attempt has been made only to give a sympathetic account without any criticism favourable or unfavourable. But I certainly do maintain that the current interpretations of Mill's *Utilitarianism* are so unsympathetic and so incorrect that the majority of criticisms which have in fact been based on them are irrelevant and worthless.

# 12

# The Good Will
## and the Categorical Imperative*
### IMMANUEL KANT
(1724–1804)

## I. The Good Will

Nothing can possibly be conceived in the world, or even out of it, which can be called good without qualification, except a *good will.* Intelligence, wit, judgment, and the other *talents* of the mind, however they may be named, or courage, resolution, perseverance, as qualities of temperament, are undoubtedly good and desirable in many respects; but these gifts of nature may also become extremely bad and mischievous if the will which is to make use of them, and which, therefore, constitutes what is called *character,* is not good. It is the same with the *gifts of fortune.* Power, riches, honor, even health, and the general well-being and contentment with one's condition which is called *happiness,* inspire pride, and often presumption, if there is not a good will to correct the influence of these on the mind, and with this also to rectify the whole principle of acting, and adapt it to its end. The sight of a being who is not adorned with a single feature of a pure and good will, enjoying unbroken prosperity, can never give pleasure to an impartial rational spectator. Thus a good will appears to constitute the indispensable condition even of being worthy of happiness.

There are even some qualities which are of service to this good will itself, and may facilitate its action, yet which have no intrinsic unconditional value, but always presuppose a good will, and this qualifies the esteem that we justly have for them, and does not permit us to regard them

*From Immanuel Kant, *Fundamental Principles* (or *Groundwork,* or *Foundations*) *of the Metaphysic of Morals* (1785), translated by T. K. Abbott (1873), the bulk of the First Section (chapter) and relevant portions of the Second Section. The title of this selection has been supplied by the editor, as has the sectioning. Compare with selection 41 and statements 25, 37, and 40.

as absolutely good. Moderation in the affections and passions, self-control, and calm deliberation are not only good in many respects, but even seem to constitute part of the intrinsic worth of the person; but they are far from deserving to be called good without qualification, although they have been so unconditionally praised by the ancients. For without the principles of a good will, they may become extremely bad; and the coolness of a villain not only makes him far more dangerous, but also directly makes him more abominable in our eyes than he would have been without it.

A good will is good not because of what it performs or effects, not by its aptness for the attainment of some proposed end, but simply by virtue of the volition—that is, it is good in itself, and considered by itself is to be  esteemed much higher than all that can be brought about by it in favor of any inclination, nay, even of the sum-total of all inclinations. Even if it should happen that, owing to special disfavor of fortune, or the niggardly provision of a step-motherly nature, this will should wholly lack power to accomplish its purpose, if with its greatest efforts it should yet achieve nothing, and there should remain only the good will (not, to be sure, a mere wish, but the summoning of all means in our power), then, like a jewel, it would still shine by its own light, as a thing which has its whole value in itself. Its usefulness or fruitfulness can neither add to nor take away anything from this value. It would be, as it were, only the setting to enable us to handle it the more conveniently in common commerce, or to attract to it the attention of those who are not yet connoisseurs, but not to recommend it to true connoisseurs, or to determine its value. . . .

We have then to develop the notion of a will which deserves to be highly esteemed for itself, and is good without a view to anything further, a notion which exists already in the sound natural understanding, requiring rather to be cleared up than to be taught, and which in estimating the value of our actions always takes the first place and constitutes the condition of all the rest. In order to do this, we will take the notion of duty, which includes that of a good will, although implying certain subjective restrictions and hindrances. These, however, far from concealing it or rendering it unrecognizable, rather bring it out by contrast and make it shine forth so much the brighter.

I omit here all actions which are already recognized as inconsistent with duty, although they may be useful for this or that purpose, for with these the question whether they are done *from duty* cannot arise at all, since they even conflict with it. I also set aside those actions which really conform to duty, but to which men have *no* direct *inclination*, performing them because they are impelled thereto by some other inclination. For in this case we can readily distinguish whether the action which agrees with duty is done *from duty* or from a selfish view. It is much harder to make this distinction when the action accords with duty, and the subject has besides a *direct* inclination to it. For example, it is always a matter of duty that a dealer should not overcharge an inexperienced purchaser; and wherever there is much commerce the prudent tradesman does not overcharge, but keeps a fixed price for everyone, so that a child buys of him as well as any other. Men are thus *honestly* served; but this is not enough to make us believe that the tradesman has so acted from duty and from principles of honesty; his own advantage required it; it is out of the question in this case to suppose that he might besides have a direct inclination in favor of the buyers, so that, as it were, from love he should give no advantage to one over another. Accordingly the action was done neither from duty nor from direct inclination, but merely with a selfish view.

On the other hand, it is a duty to maintain one's life; and, in addition, everyone has also a direct inclination to do so. But on this account the often anxious care which most men take for it has no intrinsic worth, and their maxim has no moral import. They preserve their life *as duty requires,* no doubt, but not *because duty requires.* On the other hand, if adversity and hopeless sorrow have completely taken away the relish for life, if the unfortunate one, strong in mind, indignant at his fate rather than de-sponding or dejected, wishes for death, and yet preserves his life without loving it—not from inclination or fear, but from duty—then his maxim has a moral worth.

To be beneficent when we can is a duty; and besides this, there are many minds so sympathetically constituted that, without any other motive of vanity or self-interest, they find a pleasure in spreading joy around them, and can take delight in the satisfaction of others so far as it is their own work. But I maintain that in such a case an action of this kind, however proper, however amiable it may be, has nevertheless no true moral worth, but is on a level with other inclinations, for example, the inclination to honor, which, if it is happily directed to that which is in fact of public utility and accordant with duty, and consequently honorable, deserves praise and encouragement, but not esteem. For the maxim lacks the moral import, namely, that such actions be done *from duty,* not from inclination. Put the case that the mind of that philanthropist was clouded by sorrow of his own, extinguishing all sympathy with the lot of others, and that while he still has the power to benefit others in distress, he is not touched by their trouble because he is absorbed with his own; and now suppose that he tears himself out of this dead insensibility and performs the action without any inclination to it, but simply from duty, then first has his action its genuine moral worth. Further still, if nature has put little sympathy in the heart of this or that man, if he, supposed to be an upright man, is by temperament cold and indifferent to the sufferings of others, perhaps because in respect of his own he is provided with the special gift of patience and fortitude, and supposes, or even requires, that others should have the same—and such a man would certainly not be the meanest product of nature—but if nature had not specially framed him for a philanthropist, would he not still find in himself a source from whence to give himself a far higher worth than that of a good-natured temperament could be? Unquestionably. It is just in this that the moral worth of the character is brought out which is incomparably the highest of all, namely, that he is beneficent, not from inclination, but from duty.

To secure one's own happiness is a duty, at least indirectly; for discontent with one's condition, under a pressure of many anxieties and amidst unsatisfied wants, might easily become a great *temptation to transgression of duty.* But here again, without looking to duty, all men have already the strongest and most intimate inclination to happiness, because it is just in this idea that all inclinations are combined in one total. But the precept of happiness is often of such a sort that it greatly interferes with some inclinations, and yet a man cannot form any definite and certain conception of the sum of satisfaction of all of them which is called happiness. It is not then to be wondered at that a single inclination, definite both as to what it promises and as to the time within which it can be gratified, is often able to overcome such a fluctuating idea, and that a gouty patient, for instance, can choose to enjoy what he likes, and to suffer what he may, since, according to his calculation, on this occasion at least, he has [only] not sacrificed the enjoyment of the present moment to a possibly mistaken expectation of a happiness which is supposed to be found in health. But even in this case, if the general desire for happiness did not influence his will, and supposing that in his particular case health was not a necessary element in this calculation, there yet remains in this, as in all other cases, this law—namely, that he should promote his happiness not from inclination but from duty, and by this would his conduct first acquire true moral worth.

It is in this manner, undoubtedly, that we are to understand those passages of Scripture also in which we are commanded to love our neighbor, even our enemy. For love, as an affection, cannot be commanded, but beneficence for duty's sake may, even though we are not impelled to it by any inclination—nay, are even repelled by a natural and unconquerable aversion. This is *practical* love, and not *pathological*—a love which is seated in the will, and not in the propensions of sense—in principles of action and not of tender sympathy; and it is this love alone which can be commanded.

The second* proposition is: That an action done from duty derives its moral worth, *not from the purpose* which is to be attained by it, but from the maxim by which it is determined, and therefore does not depend on the realization of the object of the action, but merely on the *principle of volition* by which the action has taken place, without regard to any object of desire. It is clear from what precedes that the purposes which we may have in view in our actions, or their effects regarded as ends and springs of the will, cannot give to actions any unconditional or moral worth. In what, then, can their worth lie if it is not to consist in the will and in reference to its expected effect? It cannot lie anywhere but in the *principle of the will* without regard to the ends which can be attained by the action. For the will stands between its *a priori* principle, which is formal, and its *a posteriori* spring, which is material, as between two roads, and as it must be determined by something, it follows that it must be determined by the formal principle of volition when an action is done from duty, in which case every material principle has been withdrawn from it.

The third proposition, which is a consequence of the two preceding, I would express thus: *Duty is the necessity of acting from respect for the law.*† I may have *inclination* for an object as the effect of my proposed action, but I cannot have *respect* for it just for this reason that it is an effect and not an energy of will. Similarly, I cannot have respect for inclination, whether my own or another's; I can at most, if my own, approve it; if another's, sometimes even love it, that is, look on it as favorable to my own interest. It is only what is connected with my will as a principle, by no means as an effect—what does not subserve my inclination, but overpowers it, or at least in case of choice excludes it from its calculation—in other words, simply the law of itself, which can be an object of respect, and hence a command. Now an action done from duty must wholly exclude the influence of inclination, and with it every object of the will, so that nothing remains which can determine the will except objectively the *law,* and subjectively *pure respect*

---

*What was the first proposition? Kant apparently neglected to tell us explicitly, and most translators have felt the need to help the reader, even the reader who knows German, by supplying what Kant apparently failed to supply. Thus Abbott's footnote at this point reads: "The first proposition was that to have moral worth an action must be done from duty," and there is nearly universal agreement on this. This seems very likely, but how do we know that this is so? Actually, we cannot be certain that "the first proposition" is not something else, such as the first proposition of the chapter: "Nothing can possibly be conceived in the world, or even out of it, which can be called good without qualification, except a *good will.*"

†This presents another problem of interpretation. What exactly are "the two preceding," is the third really a consequence of them, and what exactly does this "third proposition" mean? Perhaps a better way of rendering it would be: "An action done from duty is an action done out of respect for the law."

for this practical law, and consequently the maxim[1] that I should follow this law even to the thwarting of all my inclinations.

Thus the moral worth of an action does not lie in the effect expected from it, nor in any principle of action which requires to borrow its motive from this expected effect. For all these effects—agreeableness of one's condition, and even the promotion of the happiness of others—could have been also brought about by other causes, so that for this there would have been no need of the will of a rational being; whereas it is in this alone that the supreme and unconditional good can be found.* The preeminent good which we call moral can therefore consist in nothing else than *the conception of law* in itself, *which certainly is only possible in a rational being,* in so far as this conception, and not the expected effect, determines the will. This is a good which is already present in the person who acts accordingly, and we have not to wait for it to appear first in the result.

But what sort of law can that be the conception of which must determine the will, even without paying any regard to the effect expected from it, in order that this will may be called good absolutely and without qualification? As I have deprived the will of every impulse which could arise to it from obedience to any law, there remains nothing but the universal conformity of its actions to law in general, which alone is to serve the will as a principle, that is, I am never to act otherwise than so *that I could also will that my maxim should become a universal law.* Here, now, it is the simple conformity to law in general, without assuming any particular law applicable to certain actions, that serves the will as its principle, and must so serve it if duty is not to be a vain delusion and a chimerical notion. The common reason of men in its practical judgments perfectly coincides with this, and always has in view the principle here suggested. Let the question be, for example: May I when in distress make a promise with the intention not to keep it? I readily distinguish here between the two significations which the question may have: whether it is prudent or whether it is right to make a false promise? The former may undoubtedly often be the case. I see clearly indeed that it is not enough to extricate myself from a present difficulty by means of this subterfuge, but it must be well considered

---

[1]A *maxim* is the subjective principle of volition. The objective principle (i.e., that which would also serve subjectively as a practical principle to all rational beings if reason had full power over the faculty of desire) is the practical *law.*

*In the Preface, Kant makes the following statement, which is useful in understanding the point he is making here: "For in order that an action should be morally good, it is not enough that it *conform* to the moral law, but it must also be done *for the sake of the law,* otherwise that conformity is only very contingent and uncertain; since a principle which is not moral, although it may now and then produce actions conformable to the law, will also often produce actions which contradict it."

whether there may not hereafter spring from this lie much greater inconvenience than that from which I now free myself, and as, with all my supposed *cunning,* the consequences cannot be so easily foreseen but that credit once lost may be much more injurious to me than any mischief which I seek to avoid at present, it should be considered whether it would not be more *prudent* to act herein according to a universal maxim, and to make it a habit to promise nothing except with the intention of keeping it. But it is soon clear to me that such a maxim will still only be based on the fear of consequences. Now it is a wholly different thing to be truthful from duty, and to be so from apprehension of injurious consequences. In the first case, the very notion of the action already implies a law for me; in the second case, I must first look about elsewhere to see what results may be combined with it which would affect myself. For to deviate from the principle of duty is beyond all doubt wicked; but to be unfaithful to my maxim of prudence may often be very advantageous to me, although to abide by it is certainly safer. The shortest way, however, and an unerring one, to discover the answer to this question whether a lying promise is consistent with duty, is to ask myself, Should I be content that my maxim (to extricate myself from difficulty by a false promise) should hold good as a universal law, for myself as well as for others; and should I be able to say to myself, "Every one may make a deceitful promise when he finds himself in a difficulty from which he cannot otherwise extricate himself"? Then I presently became aware that, while I can will the lie, I can by no means will that lying should be a universal law. For with such a law there would be no promises at all, since it would be in vain to allege my intention in regard to my future actions to those who would not believe this allegation, or if they over-hastily did so, would pay me back in my own coin. Hence my maxim, as soon as it should be made a universal law, would necessarily destroy itself.

I do not, therefore, need any far-reaching penetration to discern what I have to do in order that my will may be morally good. Inexperienced in the course of the world, incapable of being prepared for all its contingencies, I only ask myself: Canst thou also will that thy maxim should be a universal law? If not, then it must be rejected, and that not because of a disadvantage accruing from it to myself or even to others, but because it cannot enter as a principle into a possible universal legislation, and reason extorts from me immediate respect for such legislation. I do not indeed as yet *discern* on what this respect is based (this the philosopher may inquire), but at least I understand this—that it is an estimation of the worth which far outweighs all worth of what is recommended by inclination, and that the necessity of acting from *pure* respect for the practical law is what constitutes duty, to which every other motive must give place because it is the condition of a will being good *in itself,* and the worth of such a will is above everything.

Thus, then, without quitting the moral knowledge of common human reason, we have arrived at its principle. And although, no doubt, common men do not conceive it in such an abstract and universal form, yet they always have it really before their eyes and use it as the standard of their decision. Here it would be easy to show how, with this compass in hand, men are well able to distinguish, in every case that occurs, what is good, what bad, conformable to duty or inconsistent with it, if, without in the least teaching them anything new, we only, like Socrates, direct their attention to the principle they themselves employ; and that, therefore, we do not need science and philosophy to know what we should do to be honest and good, yea, even wise and virtuous. Indeed we might well have conjectured beforehand that the knowledge of what every man is bound to do, and therefore also to know, would be within the reach of every man, even the commonest. Here we cannot forbear admiration when we see how great an advantage the practical judgment has over the theoretical in the common understanding of men. In the latter, if common reason ventures to depart from the laws of experience and from the perceptions of the senses, it falls into mere inconceivabilities and self-contradictions, at least into a chaos of uncertainty, obscurity, and instability. But in the practical sphere it is just when the common understanding excludes all sensible springs from practical laws that its power of judgment begins to show itself to advantage. It then becomes even subtle, whether it be that it chicanes with its own conscience or with other claims respecting what is to be called right, or whether it desires for its own instruction to determine honestly the worth of actions; and, in the latter case, it may even have as good a hope of hitting the mark as any philosopher whatever can promise himself. Nay, it is almost more sure of doing so, because the philosopher cannot have any other principle, while he may easily perplex his judgment by a multitude of considerations foreign to the matter, and so turn aside from the right way. Would it not therefore be wiser in moral concerns to acquiesce in the judgment of common reason, or at most only to call in philosophy for the purpose of rendering the system of morals more complete and intelligible, and its rules more convenient for use (especially for disputation), but not so as to draw off the common understanding from its happy simplicity, or to bring it by means of philosophy into a new path of inquiry and instruction?

Innocence is indeed a glorious thing; only, on the other hand, it is very sad that it cannot well maintain itself, and is easily seduced. On this account even wisdom—which otherwise consists more in conduct than in knowledge—yet has need of science, not in order to learn from it, but to secure for its precepts admission and permanence. Against all the commands of duty which reason represents to man as so deserving of respect, he feels in himself a powerful counterpoise in his wants and inclinations, the entire satisfaction of which he sums up under the name of happiness. Now reason issues its commands unyieldingly, without promising anything to the inclinations, and, as it were, with disregard and contempt for these claims which are so impetuous and at the same time so plausible, and which will not allow themselves to be suppressed by any command. Hence there arises a natural *dialectic,* that is, a disposition to argue against these strict laws of duty and to question their validity, or at least their purity and strictness; and, if possible, to make them more accordant with our wishes and inclinations, that is to say, to corrupt them at their very source and entirely to destroy their worth—a thing which even common practical reason cannot ultimately call good. . . .

## II. The Categorical Imperative

### Imperatives in General

. . . From what has been said, it is clear that all moral conceptions have their seat and origin completely *a priori* in the reason, and that, moreover, in the commonest reason just as truly as in that which is in the highest degree speculative; that they cannot be obtained by abstraction from any empirical, and therefore merely contingent, knowledge; that it is just this purity of their origin that makes them worthy to serve as our supreme practical principle, and that just in proportion as we add anything empirical, we detract from their genuine influence and from the absolute value of actions; that it is not only of the greatest necessity, in a purely speculative point of view, but is also of the greatest practical importance, to derive these notions and laws from pure reason, to present them pure and unmixed, and even to determine the compass of this practical or pure rational knowledge, that is, to determine the whole faculty of pure practical reason; and, in doing so, we must not make its principles dependent on the particular nature of human reason, though in speculative philosophy this may be permitted, or may even at times be necessary; but since moral laws ought to hold good for every rational creature, we must derive them from the general concept of a rational being. In this way, although for its *application* to man morality has need of anthropology, yet, in the first instance, we must treat it independently as pure philosophy, that is, as metaphysic, complete in itself (a thing which in such distinct branches of science is easily done); knowing well that, unless we are in possession of this, it would not only be vain to determine the moral element of duty in right actions for purposes of speculative criticism, but it would be impossible to base morals on their genuine principles, even for common practical purposes, especially of moral instruction, so as to produce pure moral dispositions, and to engraft them on men's minds to the promotion of the greatest possible good in the world.

But in order that in this study we may not merely advance by the natural steps from the common moral judgment (in this case very worthy of respect) to the philosophical, as has been already done, but also from a popular philosophy, which goes no further than it can reach by groping with the help of examples, to metaphysic (which does not allow itself to be checked by anything empirical and, as it must measure the whole extent of this kind of rational knowledge, goes as far as ideal conceptions, where even examples fail us), we must follow and clearly describe the practical faculty of reason, from the general rules of its determination to the point where the notion of duty springs from it.

Everything in nature works according to laws. Rational beings alone. have the faculty of acting according *to the conception* of laws—that is, according to principles, that is, have a *will*. Since the deduction of actions from principles requires *reason*, the will is nothing but practical reason. If reason infallibly determines the will, then the actions of such a being which are recognized as objectively necessary are subjectively necessary also, that is, the will is a faculty to choose *that only* which reason independent on inclination recognizes as practically necessary, that is, as good. But if reason of itself does not sufficiently determine the will, if the latter is subject also to subjective conditions (particular impulses) which do not always coincide with the objective conditions, in a word, if the will does not *in itself* completely accord with reason (which is actually the case with men), then the actions which objectively are recognized as necessary are subjectively contingent, and the determination of such a will according to objective laws is *obligation*, that is to say, the relation of the objective laws to a will that is not thoroughly good is conceived as the determination of the will of a rational being by principles of reason, but which the will from its nature does not of necessity follow.

The conception of an objective principle, in so far as it is obligatory for a will, is called a command (of reason), and the formula of the command is called an Imperative.

All imperatives are expressed by the word *ought* [or *shall*], and thereby indicate the relation of an objective law of reason to a will which from its subjective constitution is not necessarily determined by it (an obligation).

They say that something would be good to do or to forbear, but they say it to a will which does not always do a thing because it is conceived to be good to do it. That is practically *good,* however, which determines the will by means of the conceptions of reason, and consequently not from subjective causes, but objectively, that is, on principles which are valid for every rational being as such. It is distinguished from the *pleasant* as that which influences the will only by means of sensation from merely subjective causes, valid only for the sense of this or that one, and not as a principle of reason which holds for every one.[2]

A perfectly good will would therefore be equally subject to objective laws (viz., laws of good), but could not be conceived as *obliged* thereby to act lawfully, because of itself from its subjective constitution it can only be determined by the conception of good. Therefore no imperatives hold for the Divine will, or in general for a *holy* will; *ought* is here out of place because the volition is already of itself necessarily in unison with the law. Therefore imperatives are only formulae to express the relation of objective laws of all volition to the subjective imperfection of the will of this or that rational being, for example, the human will.

Now all *imperatives* command either *hypothetically* or *categorically.* The former represent the practical necessity of a possible action as means to something else that is willed (or at least which one might possibly will). The categorical imperative would be that which represented an action as necessary of itself without reference to another end, that is, as objectively necessary.

Since every practical law represents a possible action as good, and on this account, for a subject who is practically determinable by reason as necessary, all imperatives are formulae determining an action which is necessary according to the principle of a will good in some respects. If now the action is good only as a means *to something else,* then the imperative is *hypothetical;* if it is conceived as good *in itself* and consequently as being

---

[2]The dependence of the desires on sensations is called inclination, and this accordingly always indicates a *want.* The dependence of a contingently determinable will on principles of reason is called an *interest.* This, therefore, is found only in the case of a dependent will which does not always of itself conform to reason; in the Divine will we cannot conceive any interest. But the human will can also *take an interest* in a thing without therefore acting *from interest.* The former signifies the *practical* interest in the action, the latter the *pathological* in the object of the action. The former indicates only dependence of the will on principles of reason in themselves; the second, dependence on principles of reason for the sake of inclination, reason supplying only the practical rules how the requirement of the inclination may be satisfied. In the first case the action interests me; in the second the object of the action (because it is pleasant to me). We have seen in the first section that in an action done from duty we must look not to the interest in the object, but only to that in the action itself, and in its rational principle (viz., the law).

necessarily the principle of a will which of itself conforms to reason, then it is *categorical.*

Thus the imperative declares what action possible by me would be good, and presents the practical rule in relation to a will which does not forthwith perform an action simply because it is good, whether because the subject does not always know that it is good, or because, even if it know this, yet its maxims might be opposed to the objective principles of practical reason.

Accordingly the hypothetical imperative only says that the action is good for some purpose, *possible* or *actual.* In the first case it is a *problematical,* in the second an *assertorial* practical principle. The categorical imperative which declares an action to be objectively necessary in itself without reference to any purpose, that is, without any other end, is valid as an *apodictic* (practical) principle.

Whatever is possible only by the power of some rational being may also be conceived as a possible purpose of some will; and therefore the principles of action as regards the means necessary to attain some possible purpose are in fact infinitely numerous. All sciences have a practical part consisting of problems expressing that some end is possible for us, and of imperatives directing how it may be attained. These may, therefore, be called in general imperatives of *skill.* Here there is no question whether the end is rational and good, but only what one must do in order to attain it. The precepts for the physician to make his patient thoroughly healthy, and for a poisoner to ensure certain death, are of equal value in this respect, that each serves to effect its purpose perfectly. Since in early youth it cannot be known what ends are likely to occur to us in the course of life, parents seek to have their children taught a *great many things,* and provide for their *skill* in the use of means for all sorts of arbitrary ends, of none of which can they determine whether it may not perhaps hereafter be an object to their pupil, but which it is at all events *possible* that he might aim at; and this anxiety is so great that they commonly neglect to form and correct their judgment on the value of the things which may be chosen as ends.

There is *one* end, however, which may be assumed to be actually such to all rational beings (so far as imperatives apply to them, viz., as dependent beings), and, therefore, one purpose which they not merely *may* have, but which we may with certainty assume that they all actually *have* by a natural necessity, and this is *happiness.* The hypothetical imperative which expresses the practical necessity of an action as means to the advancement of happiness is *assertorial.* We are not to present it as necessary for an uncertain and merely possible purpose, but for a purpose which we may presuppose with certainty and *a priori* in every man, because it belongs to his being. Now skill in the choice of means to his own greatest well-being may be called *prudence,*[3] in the narrowest sense. And thus the imperative which refers to the choice of means to one's own happiness, that is, the precept of prudence, is still always *hypothetical;* the action is not commanded absolutely, but only as means to another purpose.

Finally, there is an imperative which commands a certain conduct immediately, without having as its condition any other purpose to be attained by it. This imperative is *categorical.* It concerns not the matter of the action, or its intended result, but its form and the principle of which it is itself a result; and what is essentially good in it consists in the mental disposition, let the consequence be what it may. This imperative may be called that of *morality.*

There is a marked distinction also between the volitions on these three sorts of principles in the *dissimilarity* of the obligation of the will. In order to mark this difference more clearly, I think they would be most suitably named in their order if we said they are either *rules* of skill, or *counsels* of prudence, or *commands* (*laws*) of morality. For it is *law* only that involves the conception of an *unconditional* and objective necessity, which is consequently universally valid; and commands are laws which must be obeyed, that is, must be followed, even in opposition to inclination. *Counsels,* indeed, involve necessity, but one which can only hold under a contingent subjective condition, viz., they depend on whether this or that man reckons this or that as part of his happiness; the categorical imperative, on the contrary, is not limited by any condition, and as being absolutely, although practically, necessary may be quite properly called a command. We might also call the first kind of imperatives *technical* (belonging to art), the second *pragmatic* (belonging to welfare), the third *moral* (belonging to free conduct generally, that is, to morals).

Now arises the question, how are all these imperatives possible? This question does not seek to know how we can conceive the accomplishment of the action which the imperative ordains, but merely how we can conceive the obligation of the will which the imperative expresses. No special explanation is needed to show how an imperative of skill is possible. Whoever wills the end wills also (so far as reason decides his conduct) the means in his power which are indispensably necessary thereto. This proposition is, as regards the volition, analytical; for in willing an object as my

---

[3]The word *prudence* is taken in two senses: in the one it may bear the name of knowledge of the world, in the other that of private prudence. The former is a man's ability to influence others so as to use them for his own purposes. The latter is the sagacity to combine all these purposes for his own lasting benefit. This latter is properly that to which the value even of the former is reduced, and when a man is prudent in the former sense, but not in the latter, we might better say of him that he is clever and cunning, but, on the whole, imprudent.

effect there is already thought the causality of myself as an acting cause, that is to say, the use of the means; and the imperative educes from the conception of volition of an end the conception of actions necessary to this end. Synthetical propositions must no doubt be employed in defining the means to a proposed end; but they do not concern the principle, the act of the will, but the object and its realization. For example, that in order to bisect a line on an unerring principle I must draw from its extremities two intersecting arcs; this no doubt is taught by mathematics only in synthetical propositions; but if I know that it is only by this process that the intended operation can be performed, then to say that if I fully will the operation, I also will the action required for it, is an analytical proposition; for it is one and the same thing to conceive something as an effect which I can produce in a certain way, and to conceive myself as acting in this way.

If it were only equally easy to give a definite conception of happiness, the imperatives of prudence would correspond exactly with those of skill, and would likewise be analytical. For in this case as in that, it could be said whoever wills the end wills also (according to the dictate of reason necessarily) the indispensable means thereto which are in his power. But, unfortunately, the notion of happiness is so indefinite that although every man wishes to attain it, yet he never can say definitely and consistently what it is that he really wishes and wills. The reason of this is that all the elements which belong to the notion of happiness are altogether empirical, that is, they must be borrowed from experience, and nevertheless the idea of happiness requires an absolute whole, a maximum of welfare in my present and all future circumstances. Now it is impossible that the most clear-sighted and at the same time most powerful being (supposed finite) should frame to himself a definite conception of what he really wills in this. Does he will riches, how much anxiety, envy, and snares might he not thereby draw upon his shoulders? Does he will knowledge and discernment, perhaps it might prove to be only an eye so much the sharper to show him so much the more fearfully the evils that are now concealed from him and that cannot be avoided, or to impose more wants on his desires, which already give him concern enough. Would he have long life? Who guarantees to him that it would not be a long misery? Would he at least have health? How often has uneasiness of the body restrained from excesses into which perfect health would have allowed one to fall, and so on? In short, he is unable, on any principle, to determine with certainty what would make him truly happy; because to do so he would need to be omniscient. We cannot therefore act on any definite principles to secure happiness, but only on empirical counsels, for example, of regimen, frugality, courtesy, reserve, etc., which experience teaches do, on the average, most promote well-being.

Hence it follows that the imperatives of prudence do not, strictly speaking, command at all, that is, they cannot present actions objectively as practically *necessary;* that they are rather to be regarded as counsels (*consilia*) than precepts (*praecepta*) of reason, that the problem to determine certainly and universally what action would promote the happiness of a rational being is completely insoluble, and consequently no imperative respecting it is possible which should, in the strict sense, command to do what makes happy; because happiness is not an ideal of reason but of imagination, resting solely on empirical grounds, and it is vain to expect that these should define an action by which one could attain the totality of a series of consequences which is really endless. This imperative of prudence would, however, be an analytical proposition if we assume that the means to happiness could be certainly assigned; for it is distinguished from the imperative of skill only by this that in the latter the end is merely *possible,* in the former it is *given;* as, however, both only ordain the means to that which we suppose to be willed as an end, it follows that the imperative which ordains the willing of the means to him who wills the end is in both cases analytical. Thus there is no difficulty in regard to the possibility of an imperative of this kind either. . . .

## The Principle of Universal Law

When I conceive a hypothetical imperative, in general I do not know beforehand what it will contain until I am given the condition. But when I conceive a categorical imperative, I know at once what it contains. For as the imperative contains besides the law only the necessity that the maxims[4] shall conform to this law, while the law contains no conditions restricting it, there remains nothing but the general statement that the maxim of the action should conform to a universal law, and it is this conformity alone that the imperative properly represents as necessary.

There is therefore but one categorical imperative, namely this: *Act only on that maxim whereby thou canst at the same time will that it should become a universal law.*

Now if all imperatives of duty can be deduced from this one imperative as from their principle, then, although it should remain undecided whether what is called duty is not merely a vain notion, yet at least we shall be able to show what we understand by it and what this notion *means.*

---

[4]A "maxim" is a subjective principle of action, and must be distinguished from the *objective principle,* namely, practical law. The former contains the practical rule set by reason according to the conditions of the subject (often its ignorance or its inclinations), so that it is the principle on which the subject *acts;* but the law is the objective principle valid for every rational being, and is the principle on which it *ought to act*—that is an imperative.

Since the universality of the law according to which effects are produced constitutes what is properly called *nature* in the most general sense (as to form)—that is, the existence of things so far as it is determined by general laws—the imperative of duty may be expressed thus: *Act as if the maxim of thy action were to become by thy will a universal law of nature.*

We will now enumerate a few duties, adopting the usual division of them into duties to ourselves and to others, and into perfect and imperfect duties.[5]

1. A man reduced to despair by a series of misfortunes feels wearied of life, but is still so far in possession of his reason that he can ask himself whether it would not be contrary to his duty to himself to take his own life. Now he inquires whether the maxim of his action could become a universal law of nature. His maxim is: From self-love I adopt it as a principle to shorten my life when its longer duration is likely to bring more evil than satisfaction. It is asked then simply whether this principle founded on self-love can become a universal law of nature. Now we see at once that a system of nature of which it should be a law to destroy life by means of the very feeling whose special nature it is to impel to the improvement of life would contradict itself, and therefore could not exist as a system of nature; hence that maxim cannot possibly exist as a universal law of nature, and consequently would be wholly inconsistent with the supreme principle of all duty.

2. Another finds himself forced by necessity to borrow money. He knows that he will not be able to repay it, but sees also that nothing will be lent to him unless he promises stoutly to repay it in a definite time. He desires to make this promise, but he has still so much conscience as to ask himself: Is it not unlawful and inconsistent with duty to get out of a difficulty in this way? Suppose, however, that he resolves to do so, then the maxim of his action would be expressed thus: When I think myself in want of money, I will borrow money and promise to repay it, although I know that I never can do so. Now this principle of self-love or of one's own advantage may perhaps be consistent with my whole future welfare; but the question now is, Is it right? I change then the suggestion of self-love into a universal law, and state the question thus: How would it be if my maxim were a universal law? Then I see at once that it could never hold as a universal law of nature, but would necessarily contradict itself. For sup-

[5] It must be noted here that I reserve the division of duties for a future *metaphysic of morals;* so that I give it here only as an arbitrary one (in order to arrange my examples). For the rest, I understand by a perfect duty one that admits no exception in favor of inclination, and then I have not merely external but also internal perfect duties. This is contrary to the use of the word adopted in the schools; but I do not intend to justify it here, as it is all one for my purpose whether it is admitted or not.

posing it to be a universal law that everyone when he thinks himself in a difficulty should be able to promise whatever he pleases, with the purpose of not keeping his promise, the promise itself would become impossible, as well as the end that one might have in view in it, since no one would consider that anything was promised to him, but would ridicule all such statements as vain pretenses.

3. A third finds in himself a talent which with the help of some culture might make him a useful man in many respects. But he finds himself in comfortable circumstances and prefers to indulge in pleasure rather than to take pains in enlarging and improving his happy natural capacities. He asks, however, whether his maxim of neglect of his natural gifts, besides agreeing with his inclination to indulgence, agrees also with what is called duty. He sees then that a system of nature could indeed subsist with such a universal law, although men (like the South Sea islanders) should let their talents rest and resolve to devote their lives merely to idleness, amusement, and propagation of their species—in a word, to enjoyment; but he cannot possibly *will* that this should be a universal law of nature, or be implanted in us as such by a natural instinct. For, as a rational being, he necessarily wills that his faculties be developed, since they serve him, and have been given him, for all sorts of possible purposes.

4. A fourth, who is in prosperity, while he sees that others have to contend with great wretchedness and that he could help them, thinks: What concern is it of mine? Let everyone be as happy as Heaven pleases, or as he can make himself; I will take nothing from him nor even envy him, only I do not wish to contribute anything to his welfare or to his assistance in distress! Now no doubt, if such a mode of thinking were a universal law, the human race might very well subsist, and doubtless even better than in a state in which everyone talks of sympathy and good-will, or even takes care occasionally to put it into practice, but, on the other side, also cheats when he can, betrays the rights of men, or otherwise violates them. But although it is possible that a universal law of nature might exist in accordance with that maxim, it is impossible to *will* that such a principle should have the universal validity of a law of nature. For a will which resolved this would contradict itself, inasmuch as many cases might occur in which one would have need of the love and sympathy of others, and in which, by such a law of nature, sprung from his own will, he would deprive himself of all hope of the aid he desires.

These are a few of the many actual duties, or at least what we regard as such, which obviously fall into two classes on the one principle that we have laid down. We must be *able* to *will* that a maxim of our action should be a universal law. This is the canon of the moral appreciation of the action generally. Some actions are of such a character that their maxim cannot without contradiction be even *conceived* as a universal law of nature, far from it being possible that we should *will* that it *should* be so. In others, this intrinsic impossibility is not found, but still it is impossible to *will* that their maxim should be raised to the universality of a law of nature, since such a will would contradict itself. It is easily seen that the former violate strict or rigorous (inflexible) duty; the latter only laxer (meritorious) duty. Thus it has been completely shown by these examples how all duties depend as regards the nature of the obligation (not the object of the action) on the same principle.

If now we attend to ourselves on occasion of any transgression of duty, we shall find that we in fact do not will that our maxim should be a universal law, for that is impossible for us; on the contrary, we will that the opposite should remain a universal law, only we assume the liberty of making an *exception* in our own favor or (just for this time only) in favor of our inclination. Consequently, if we considered all cases from one and the same point of view, namely, that of reason, we should find a contradiction in our own will, namely, that a certain principle should be objectively necessary as a universal law, and yet subjectively should not be universal, but admit of exceptions. As, however, we at one moment regard our action from the point of view of a will wholly conformed to reason, and then again look at the same action from the point of view of a will affected by inclination, there is not really any contradiction, but an antagonism of inclination to the precept of reason, whereby the universality of the principle is changed into a mere generality, so that the practical principle of reason shall meet the maxim half way. Now, although this cannot be justified in our own impartial judgment, yet it proves that we do really recognize the validity of the categorical imperative and (with all respect for it) only allow ourselves a few exceptions which we think unimportant and forced from us. . . .

## *The Principle of Humanity as an End in Itself*

The will is conceived as a faculty of determining oneself to action *in accordance with the conception of certain laws.* And such a faculty can be found only in rational beings. Now that which serves the will as the objective ground of its self-determination is the *end,* and if this is assigned by reason alone, it must hold for all rational beings. On the other hand, that which merely contains the ground of possibility of the action of which the effect is the end, this is called the *means.* The subjective ground of the desire is the *spring,* the objective ground of the volition is the *motive;* hence the distinction between subjective ends which rest on springs, and objective ends which depend on motives valid for every rational being. Practical principles are *formal* when they abstract from all subjective ends; they are *material* when they assume these, and therefore particular, springs of action. The ends which a rational being proposes to himself at pleasure as *effects* of his actions (material ends) are all only relative, for it is only their relation to the particular desires of the subject that gives them their worth, which therefore cannot furnish principles universal and necessary for all rational beings and for every volition, that is to say, practical laws. Hence all these relative ends can give rise only to hypothetical imperatives.

Supposing, however, that there were something *whose existence* has *in itself* an absolute worth, something which, being *an end in itself,* could be a source of definite laws, then in this and this alone would lie the source of a possible categorical imperative, that is, a practical law.

Now I say: man and generally any rational being *exists* as an end in himself, *not merely as a means* to be arbitrarily used by this or that will, but in all his actions, whether they concern himself or other rational beings, must be always regarded at the same time as an end. All objects of the inclinations have only a conditional worth; for if the inclinations and the wants founded on them did not exist, then their object would be without value. But the inclinations themselves, being sources of want, are so far from having an absolute worth for which they should be desired that, on the contrary, it must be the universal wish of every rational being to be wholly free from them. Thus the worth of any object which is *to be acquired* by our action is always conditional. Beings whose existence depends not on our will but on nature's, have nevertheless, if they are nonrational beings, only a relative value as means, and are therefore called *things;* rational beings, on the contrary, are called *persons,* because their very nature points them out as ends in themselves, that is, as something which must not be used merely as means, and so far therefore restricts freedom of action (and is an object of respect). These, therefore, are not merely subjective ends whose existence has a worth *for us* as an effect of our action, but *objective ends,* that is, things whose existence is an end in itself—an end, moreover, for which no other can be substituted, which they should subserve *merely* as means, for otherwise nothing whatever would possess *absolute worth;* but if all worth were conditioned and therefore contingent, then there would be no supreme practical principle of reason whatever.

If then there is a supreme practical principle or, in respect of the human will, a categorical imperative, it must be one which, being drawn from the conception of that which is necessarily an end for everyone because it is *an end in itself,* constitutes an *objective* principle of will, and can therefore serve as a universal practical law. The foundation of this principle is: *rational nature exists as an end in itself.* Man necessarily conceives his own existence as being so; so far then this is a *subjective* principle of human actions. But every other rational being regards its existence similarly, just on the same rational principle that holds for me, so that it is at the same time an objective principle from which as a supreme practical law all laws of the will must be capable of being deduced. Accordingly the practical imperative will be as follows: *So act as to treat humanity, whether in thine own person or in that of any other, in every case as an end withal, never as means only.* We will now inquire whether this can be practically carried out.

To abide by the previous examples:

*First,* under the head of necessary duty to oneself: He who contemplates suicide should ask himself whether his action can be consistent with the idea of humanity *as an end in itself.* If he destroys himself in order to escape from painful circumstances, he uses a person merely as *a mean* to maintain a tolerable condition up to the end of life. But a man is not a thing, that is to say, something which can be used merely as means, but must in all his actions be always considered as an end in himself. I cannot, therefore, dispose in any way of a man in my own person so as to mutilate him, to damage or kill him. (It belongs to ethics proper to define this principle more precisely, so as to avoid all misunderstanding, for example, as to the amputation of the limbs in order to preserve myself; as to exposing my life to danger with a view to preserve it, etc. This question is therefore omitted here.)

*Secondly,* as regards necessary duties, or those of strict obligation, towards others: He who is thinking of making a lying promise to others will see at once that he would be using another man *merely as a mean,* without the latter containing at the same time the end in himself. For he whom I propose by such a promise to use for my own purposes cannot possibly assent to my mode of acting towards him, and therefore cannot himself contain the end of this action. This violation of the principle of humanity in other men is more obvious if we take in examples of attacks on the freedom and property of others. For then it is clear that he who transgresses the rights of men intends to use the person of others merely as means, without considering that as rational beings they ought always to be esteemed also as ends, that is, as beings who must be capable of containing in themselves the end of the very same action.[6]

---

[6] Let it not be thought that the common: *quod tibi non vis fieri, etc.,* [The Golden Rule, in its so-called negative formulation] could serve here as the rule or principle. For it is only a deduction from the former, though with several limitations; it cannot be a universal law, for it does not contain the principle of duties to oneself, nor of the duties of benevolence to others (for many a one would gladly consent that others should not benefit him, provided only that he might be excused from showing benevolence to them), nor finally that of duties of strict obligation to one another, for on this principle the criminal might argue against the judge who punishes him, and so on.

*Thirdly,* as regards contingent (meritorious) duties to oneself: It is not enough that the action does not violate humanity in our own person as an end in itself, it must also *harmonize with* it. Now there are in humanity capacities of greater perfection which belong to the end that nature has in view in regard to humanity in ourselves as the subject; to neglect these might perhaps be consistent with the *maintenance* of humanity as an end in itself, but not with the *advancement* of this end.

*Fourthly,* as regards meritorious duties towards others: The natural end which all men have is their own happiness. Now humanity might indeed subsist although no one should contribute anything to the happiness of others, provided he did not intentionally withdraw anything from it; but after all, this would only harmonize negatively, not positively, with *humanity as an end in itself,* if everyone does not also endeavor, as far as in him lies, to forward the ends of others. For the ends of any subject which is an end in himself ought as far as possible to be *my* ends also, if that conception is to have its *full* effect with me. . . .

# 13

## *Utilitarianism and Population**

### HENRY SIDGWICK

(1838–1900)

By Utilitarianism is here meant the ethical theory, that the conduct which, under any given circumstances, is objectively right, is that which will produce the greatest amount of happiness on the whole; that is, taking into account all whose happiness is affected by the conduct. . . .

The first doctrine from which it seems necessary to distinguish this, is . . . Egoistic Hedonism. . . . The difference, however, between the propositions (1) that each ought to seek his own happiness, and (2) that each ought to seek the happiness of all, is so obvious and glaring, that instead of dwelling upon it we seem rather called upon to explain how the two ever came to be confounded, or in any way included under one notion. . . . The confusion between these two ethical theories was partly assisted by the confusion with both of the psychological theory that in voluntary actions every agent does, universally or normally, seek his own individual happiness or pleasure. Now there seems to be no *necessary* connexion between this latter proposition and any ethical theory: but in so far as there is a natural tendency to pass from psychological to ethical Hedonism, the transition must be—at least primarily—to the Egoistic phase of the latter. For clearly, from the fact that every one actually does seek his own happiness we cannot conclude, as an immediate and obvious inference, that he ought to seek the happiness of other people. . . .

. . . By Greatest Happiness is meant the greatest possible surplus of pleasure over pain, the pain being conceived as balanced against an equal amount of pleasure, so that the two contrasted amounts annihilate each

*From Henry Sidgwick, *The Methods of Ethics* (London, 1st ed., 1874; 7th ed., 1907), Bk. IV, pp. 411–17. The title of this selection has been supplied by the editor. Compare with selections 9 and 10.

other for purposes of ethical calculation. And of course . . . the assumption is involved that all pleasures included in our calculation are capable of being compared quantitatively with one another and with all pains; that every such feeling has a certain intensive quantity, positive or negative (or, perhaps, zero), in respect of its desirableness, and that this quantity may be to some extent known: so that each may be at least roughly weighed in ideal scales against any other. . . .

Assuming, then, that the average happiness of human beings is a positive quantity, it seems clear that, supposing the average happiness enjoyed remains undiminished, Utilitarianism directs us to make the number enjoying it as great as possible. But if we foresee as possible that an increase in numbers will be accompanied by a decrease in average happiness or *vice versa,* a point arises which has not only never been formally noticed, but which seems to have been substantially overlooked by many Utilitarians. For if we take Utilitarianism to prescribe, as the ultimate end of action, happiness on the whole, and not any individual's happiness, unless considered as an element of the whole, it would follow that, if the additional population enjoy on the whole positive happiness, we ought to weigh the amount of happiness gained by the extra number against the amount lost by the remainder. So that, strictly conceived, the point up to which, on Utilitarian principles, population ought to be encouraged to increase, is not that at which average happiness is the greatest possible,—as appears to be often assumed by political economists of the school of Malthus—but that at which the product formed by multiplying the number of persons living into the amount of average happiness reaches its maximum. . . .

. . . The conclusion just given wears a certain air of absurdity to the view of Common Sense; because its show of exactness is grotesquely incongruous with our consciousness of the inevitable inexactness of all such calculations in actual practice. But, that our practical Utilitarian reasonings must necessarily be rough, is no reason for not making them as accurate as the case admits; and we shall be more likely to succeed in this if we keep before our mind as distinctly as possible the strict type of the calculation that we should have to make, if all the relevant considerations could be estimated with mathematical precision.

There is one more point that remains to be noticed. It is evident that there may be many different ways of distributing the same quantum of happiness among the same number of persons; in order, therefore, that the Utilitarian criterion of right conduct may be as complete as possible, we ought to know which of these ways is to be preferred. This question is often ignored in expositions of Utilitarianism. It has perhaps seemed somewhat idle, as suggesting a purely abstract and theoretical perplexity, that could have no practical exemplification; and no doubt, if all the consequences of actions were capable of being estimated and summed up with mathematical precision, we should probably never find the excess of pleasure over pain exactly equal in the case of two competing alternatives of conduct. But the very indefiniteness of all hedonistic calculations, which was sufficiently shown in Book ii., renders it by no means unlikely that there may be no *cognisable* difference between the quantities of happiness involved in two sets of consequences respectively; the more rough our estimates necessarily are, the less likely we shall be to come to any clear decision between two apparently balanced alternatives. In all such cases, therefore, it becomes practically important to ask whether any mode of distributing a given quantum of happiness is better than any other. Now the Utilitarian formula seems to supply no answer to this question: at least we have to supplement the principle of seeking the greatest happiness on the whole by some principle of Just or Right distribution of this happiness. The principle which most Utilitarians have either tacitly or expressly adopted is that of pure equality—as given in Bentham's formula, "everybody to count for one, and nobody for more than one." And this principle seems the only one which does not need a special justification; for, as we saw, it must be reasonable to treat any one man in the same way as any other, if there be no reason apparent for treating him differently.[1]

[1] It should be observed that the question here is as to the distribution of *Happiness,* not the *means of happiness.* If more happiness on the whole is produced by giving the same means of happiness to B rather than to A, it is an obvious and incontrovertible deduction from the Utilitarian principle that it ought to be given to B, whatever inequality in the distribution of the *means* of happiness this may involve.

# 14

## Critique of the Golden Rule*
## RICHARD WHATELY

### (1787–1863)

### I. The Golden Rule.

That invaluable rule of our Lord's, "To do to others as we would have them do to us," will serve to explain, when rightly understood, the true character of moral instruction. If you were to understand that precept as designed to convey to us the first notions of right and wrong, and to be your sole guide as to what you ought to do and to avoid in your dealings with your neighbor, you would be greatly perplexed. For you would find that a literal compliance with the precept would be sometimes *absurd*, sometimes *wrong*, and sometimes *impossible*. And probably it is through making this mistake that men in general apply the rule so much seldomer than they ought. For the real occasions for its use occur to all of us every day.

Supposing any one should regard this golden rule as designed to answer the purpose of a complete system of morality, and to teach us the difference of right and wrong; then, if he had let his land to a farmer, he might consider that the farmer would be glad to be excused paying any rent for it, since he would himself, if he were the farmer, prefer having the land rent-free; and that, therefore, the rule of doing as he would be done by requires him to give up all his property. So also a shopkeeper might, on the same principle, think that the rule required him to part with his goods under prime cost, or to give them away, and thus to ruin himself. Now such a procedure would be *absurd*.

Again, supposing a jailer who was intrusted with the safe custody of a prisoner should think himself bound to let the man escape, because he

*From Richard Whately, *Introductory Lessons on Morals* (1855), Lesson IV. Compare with selection 15.

himself, if he were a prisoner, would be glad to obtain freedom, he would be guilty of a breach of trust. Such an application of the rule, therefore, would be morally *wrong*.

And again, if you had to decide between two parties who were pleading their cause before you, you might consider that *each* of them wished for a decision in his *own* favor. And how, then, you might ask, would it be possible to apply the rule? since in deciding *for* the one party you could not but decide *against* the other. A literal compliance with the rule, therefore, would be, in such a case, *impossible*.

## II. Application of the Golden Rule.

Now, if you were to put such cases as these before any sensible man, he would at once say that you are to consider, not what you might *wish* in each case, but what you would regard as *fair, right, just, reasonable,* if you were in another person's place. If you were a farmer, although you might feel that you would be very glad to have the land rent-free,—that is, to become the owner of it,—you would not consider that you had any just claim to it, and that you could *fairly expect* the landlord to make you a present of his property. But you would think it reasonable that, if you suffered some great and unexpected loss, from an inundation or any such calamity, he should make an abatement of the rent. And this is what a good landlord generally thinks it right to do, in compliance with the golden rule.

So, also, if you had a cause to be tried, though of course you would *wish* the decision to be in your favor, you would be sensible that all you could *reasonably expect* of the judge would be that he should lay aside all prejudice, and attend impartially and carefully to the evidence, and decide according to the best of his ability. And this—which is what *each* part may fairly claim—is what an upright judge will do. And the like holds good in all the other cases.

## III. Design of the Golden Rule.

You have seen, then, that the golden rule was far from being designed to impart to men the first notions of justice. On the contrary, it *presupposes* that knowledge; and if we had *no* such notions, we could not properly apply the rule. But the real design of it is to put us on our guard against the danger of being blinded by self-interest. A person who has a good general notion of what is just may often be tempted to act unfairly or unkindly towards his neighbors, when his own interest or gratification is concerned, and to overlook the rightful claims of others. When David was guilty of an enormous sin in taking his neighbor's wife, and procuring the death of the husband, he was thinking only of his own gratification, quite forgetful of duty, till his slumbering conscience was roused by the prophet Nathan. On hearing the tale of "the poor man's lamb," his general abhorrence of injustice and cruelty caused him to feel vehement indignation against the supposed offender; but he did not apply his principles to his own case, till the prophet startled him by saying, "Thou art the man!"

And we, if we will make a practice of applying the golden rule, may have a kind of prophet always at hand, to remind us how, and when, to act on our principles of right. We have only to consider, "What should I think were I in the other's place, and he were to do so and so to me? How should I require him to treat me? What could I in fairness claim from him? . . .

# 15

## *Defense of the Golden Rule\**

## MARCUS SINGER
(1926–    )

One of the earliest formulations of the Golden Rule is the Biblical one: "All things whatsoever ye would that men should do unto you, do ye even so unto them." One of its commonest formulations today is: "Do unto others as you would have them do unto you." This last formulation of the Rule is a positive one. It is commonly supposed that there are significant differences between the positive formulation of the Golden Rule and its negative formulation: "Do not do unto others what you would not have them do unto you."

I do not think that this is so. In any case, the negative formulation of the Golden Rule is to be distinguished from its *denial:* "Do *not* do unto others as you would have them do unto you." This is intended to be the outright rejection of the Golden Rule, and not another formulation of it. Another distinction that should be made at the outset is between the Golden Rule and its *Inversion:* "Do unto others as *they* would have you do unto them." A question that arises here is how the Golden Rule is related to its Inversion, and which of them is a sounder precept. One other precept that perhaps should be distinguished is: "Do unto others as they would do unto you," or "Do as you are done by." This is actually a form of the Lex Talionis, and is not likely to be confused with the Golden Rule, though many people have claimed that it ought to be substituted for it. It is not clear to me how this latter claim can consistently be a moral one, if taken as applying universally, but perhaps this is because I am already taking it for

*An abbreviated and revised edition of an essay, "The Golden Rule," by Marcus Singer, which was first published in *Philosophy*, Vol. XXXVIII (October 1963), pp. 293–314. Reprinted here by permission of the editor of *Philosophy*. Compare with selections 5 and 14 and statements 5, 36, and 42.

granted that the Golden Rule somehow, in some submerged manner, formulates a fundamental moral truth.

No one is likely to confuse the Golden Rule with what might be called the Leaden Rule: "Help no one, but, so far as it is to your interest, hurt others." It is, however, a nice question of moral theory why the Golden Rule, rather than its Leaden substitute, has a stronger claim to moral validity. It is another nice question whether the Golden Rule should not be replaced by the rule "Do unto others as you would *not* have them do unto you" (which is not the same as the denial of the Golden Rule), or whether they should not both be rejected altogether.

Despite its name, the Golden Rule has to be understood as a moral principle, and not as a moral rule. That is to say, it does not state of some specifically determined kind of action that it is right or wrong, or that it ought or ought not to be done. It rather sets forth, in abstract fashion, a method or procedure for determining the morality of a line of action, and thus is intended to provide a principle from which, or in accordance with which, more specific or concrete moral rules can be derived. One of the mistakes that has often been made in connection with the Golden Rule is to treat it as though it were a specific directive, having a readily determined application.

## I

Given these preliminary distinctions, we can now embark on our examination of the meaning and validity of the Golden Rule. The method I propose to follow, for the most part, is to consider a number of statements that have been made about it, with the hope that through this consequent sifting of views we may arrive at some closer approximation to the truth about it.

The first statement that I wish to consider is one made just a few years ago by the general counsel of the American Rocket Society. One reason I think it worth considering is that it is so nearly out of this world, and provides, in what it says about the Golden Rule, a neat contrast with its Biblical origins:

> It's one thing to imagine laws suitable for human beings in space—laws regulating the colonizing of other planets, the mining of meteors, and the like. It's something else to imagine laws suitable for beings that are themselves scarcely imaginable. The word I've coined for such a body of laws is "metalaw," which I define as "the law governing the rights of intelligent beings of different natures and existing in an indefinite number of different frameworks of natural laws." The earth is part of a tiny solar

system in a galaxy that contains at least forty billion stars, and there are over forty billion such galaxies in the universe as a whole; the number of planets in the universe capable of sustaining what we would recognise as intelligent life must be enormous. Now, our earthly laws are based roughly on the golden rule and suit us fine, but it would be silly to assume that they would suit any other creatures. I argue that the golden rule would be thoroughly inappropriate to metalaw. Not "Do unto others as you would have them do unto you" but "Do unto others as they would have you do unto them." [1]

This statement is fantastic in at least two ways. One of them is obvious. The other is that it involves an elementary logical error. From absolute ignorance absolutely nothing follows, yet this statement supposes that something does. If the beings mentioned are really "scarcely imaginable," then the laws that should regulate our dealings with them should be "scarcely imaginable" as well, and there is no warrant for supposing that the Golden Rule, in so far as it serves as a basis for "earthly laws," would not serve equally well as a basis for "unearthly laws," unless there is some other reason for supposing it defective. There is certainly no warrant for supposing that the Inversion of the Golden Rule ("Do unto others as they would have you do unto them") would serve as a better basis for such "metalaws," unless there is some other argument to show what its advantages would be, and no such arguments are herein provided. The assumption behind this is that the Golden Rule presupposes some similarity or identity of nature in the beings whose relations it is intended to govern, so that some other rule must serve as the basis for governing the relations among beings whose natures are fundamentally dissimilar. This is an assumption to which I shall return in due course, but first I want to consider why it should be supposed that the Inversion of the Golden Rule has any advantages over it. If we consider its implications, it would certainly not appear so.

Let us suppose that we should do unto others as they would have us do unto them. What sort of conduct would this require of us? Well, for one thing, if you want me to assign to you all of my property, then this rule implies that I should do so, for it requires me to do unto you as you would have me do unto you, and in this case you would have me sign over to you all of my property. If your demands should be increased, and you want me to be your slave for life and do your every bidding, the rule would require me to do this. Such requirements are absurd, and the rule that leads to them can be no better. Under such a rule, no woman's "virtue" would be

---

[1] From an interview with Andrew G. Haley, general counsel of the American Rocket Society, in *The New Yorker,* December 29, 1956, p. 19.

safe from the desires of any importuning male. Indeed, rape would be morally impossible, since no one would have a right to resist. This reasoning leads irresistibly to the conclusion that this "rule" leads to consequences that are absurd and morally wrong. But let us now reverse the application of the rule. The rule actually applies to both parties to the transaction, and not just to me. It applies to everyone alike, for it requires everyone to do unto others as they would have him do unto them. So if I should want you to assign to me all your property, or be my slave for life, then you are required to do so. If $A$ wants you to do $x$, and $B$ wants you to do $y$, and $x$ and $y$ are incompatible with each other, the rule still requires you to do both. The rule therefore leads to impossible results, and is actually impossible to apply. It is tantamount to: "Always do what anyone else wants you to do," which in turn is equivalent to a universal requirement of perfect or absolute altruism, the absurdity of which is so manifest as not to require detailing. Perhaps this is what Kant had in mind when he said: "That one should sacrifice his own happiness, his true wants, in order to promote that of others, would be a self-contradictory maxim if made a universal law."[2] It may be worth noting that Kant concluded from this that what he regarded as the duty to promote the happiness of others is "therefore . . . only indeterminate; it has a certain latitude within which one may be able to do more or less without our being able to assign its limits definitely." Perhaps the Inversion of the Golden Rule is meant to be applied only with certain qualifications, such as "so far as it is not unreasonable or inconvenient or absurd or immoral or impossible." But this would not leave us with much of a principle, or even much of a rule.

The arguments just given show pretty conclusively that the idea that the Inversion of the Golden Rule has certain advantages over the Golden Rule, and should be substituted for it, must be given up, and results only from failure to trace out its implications. But it has still to be determined whether the Golden Rule has itself any great merit. Perhaps it is open to similar criticism. The passage that follows conveys a hint that the Inversion has certain merits lacking in the Golden Rule itself, but I want to examine it mainly for other reasons:

> Consider the Golden Rule, in its positive form which bids us behave in relation to other people in the ways in which we should wish them to behave in relation to us in the same circumstances. It is clear that this rule is not satisfactory as an explicit guide to conduct, as it stands. It is useful as a protest against a line of

[2] Immanuel Kant, Preface to the *Metaphysical Elements of Ethics,* trans. by T. K. Abbott, in *Kant's Theory of Ethics* (6th ed.: London: Longmans, Green & Co., 1909), p. 304.

conduct which simply moves toward a goal regardless of the consequences to other people, but even here it has its limitations. If I am acting not in a private capacity but as a representative (for example as an engine driver or a postman or an army officer or an employee of any kind) my action has to be determined primarily by the conditions of my employment. A person running for a train would naturally wish the engine driver to hold the train back, but the driver has his prescribed duties. Again, even in the sphere of private activities the rule is insufficient. It works well enough in a society where interests are relatively homogeneous and simple. But in a complex society, where there are wide differences of point of view and taste and need, it suggests too strongly that the individual has only to consult his own tastes and needs to discover how he ought to behave toward other people. What I should wish others to do to me is often quite different from what they would wish me to do to them; and the latter is often much more important than the former. At the same time the rule to behave toward others as they would wish you to behave would be equally inadequate, though it does have the merit of stressing the need for an understanding of other people as a basis of our behaviour toward them. Further the rule as it stands gives no hint of the kind of person it is desirable you should be, if you are to be trusted to carry it out. It authorises the quarrelsome person who loves to be provoked, to go about provoking others, and the person who hates friendliness and sympathy, to be cold and unsympathetic in his dealings with others; it authorises the man who loves to find himself in a network of intrigue and sharp dealing, to deal with others habitually in this way.[3]

This passage contains a number of fairly standard criticisms of the Golden Rule: "It authorises the quarrelsome person who loves to be provoked, to go about provoking others," and so on. But the really important point here is the claim that "in a complex society, where there are wide differences of point of view and taste and need, it suggests too strongly that the individual has only to consult his own tastes and needs to discover how he ought to behave toward other people." Here again we have the implication that the Golden Rule presupposes a certain uniformity or similarity of nature. It is quite true that "what I should wish others to do to me is often quite different from what they would wish me to do to them"; it is also quite true that "the latter is often much more important than the former." But this is no argument against the Golden Rule. It is only an argument against the restricted and faulty interpretation of it represented in this passage. It is

[3]L. J. Russell, 'Ideals and Practice', *Philosophy*, vol. XVII (1942), pp. 109–10.

asserted that the Inversion of the Golden Rule has the "merit of stressing the need for an understanding of other people as a basis of our behaviour toward them." The implication here is that the Golden Rule itself does not; but, when it is properly and sensibly interpreted, it does.

To put the point into focus, let us consider the claim made in the following statement by Walter Lippmann:

> The rule that you should do unto others as you would have them do unto you rests on the belief that human nature is uniform. Mr. Bernard Shaw's statement that you should not do unto others what you would have them do unto you, because their tastes may be different, rests on the belief that human nature is not uniform.[4]

Here the presupposition that I have mentioned becomes quite explicit, and leads to the claim that the Golden Rule should be rejected outright. And this claim would be quite reasonable if the Golden Rule did involve this presupposition, because the assumption that human nature is uniform, in the sense that everyone's tastes, interests, needs, and desires are the same, is absurdly and grotesquely false. But it is just because this assumption is so absurdly and grotesquely and obviously false that it ought to be quite obvious that the Golden Rule does not involve or presuppose it. The Golden Rule does not rest on the belief that human nature is uniform, or, in other words, on the belief that human tastes, desires, interests, and needs are all the same; and that this is so is fairly easily shown.

If I am a quarrelsome person who loves to be provoked, does the Golden Rule authorise or require me to go around provoking others, on the ground that I should do unto others as I would have them do unto me? If I love to hear the sound of tom-toms for several hours at a time in the middle of the night, does the Golden Rule enjoin me to inflict this enjoyment on my neighbours? If I am a masochist who would have others torture me, does the Golden Rule require me to do as I would be done by by torturing others? If the Rule did have these consequences, it would certainly be ruled out as an adequate or even as a sane moral principle, since it would require conduct that is obviously immoral, as involving the violation of the rights of others. However, to suppose that the Golden Rule does have these implications is to overlook the distinction, of vital importance in this context, between the words "what" and "as," and seriously to misinterpret its intent. It may be admitted that what others "would wish me to do to," or "for," them is often much more important, as a moral basis for determining how I should act in relation to other people, than "what I should wish others to do" to, or for, me. But the Golden Rule does not deny this.

---

[4] Walter Lippmann, *Public Opinion* (New York: The Macmillan Company, 1922), pp. 121–2.

Let us distinguish between two different statements, and two correspondingly different interpretations, of the Golden Rule: (a) Do unto others *what* you would have them do unto you; and (b) Do unto others *as* you would have them do unto you. I shall call the first of these the *particular* interpretation of the Golden Rule, and the second the *general* interpretation. Now the particular interpretation is open to the various objections that have been made against the Golden Rule, of the sort that I have indicated. The general interpretation, however, is not.

The particular interpretation implies that whatever in particular I would have others do to or for me, I should do to or for them. It is in this particular interpretation that the Rule "authorises the quarrelsome person who loves to be provoked, to go about provoking others, and the person who hates friendliness and sympathy to be cold and unsympathetic in his dealings with others," and so on, and it is evident that there is nothing to be said for it.

The general interpretation, on the other hand, has no such implications. Here what I have to consider is not what in particular I would have others do to or for me, or what particular desires of mine I would have them satisfy. Here what I have to consider is the general ways in which I would have others behave in their treatment of me. And what I would have them do, in abstraction from any of my particular desires, and all that I am entitled to expect them to do, is to take account of my interests, desires, needs, and wishes—which may well be different from theirs—and either satisfy them or else not wilfully frustrate them. If I would have others take account of my interests and wishes in their treatment of me, even though my interests and wishes may differ considerably from their own, then what the Golden Rule in this interpretation requires of me is that I should take account of the interests and wishes of others in my treatment of them. I am to treat others *as* I would have them treat me, that is, on the same principle or standard as I would have them apply in their treatment of me. And the same principle or standard in application to differing circumstances or interests can lead to widely divergent particular results. The Golden Rule, then, is clearly compatible with differences in tastes, interests, wishes, needs, and desires, and does not "rest on the belief that human nature is uniform." Nor does it imply that "the individual has only to consult his own tastes and needs to discover how he ought to behave toward other people." Thus the Rule does not "authorise the quarrelsome person who loves to be provoked, to go about provoking others"—though it may not be easy to get a quarrelsome person to see this. On the contrary, if he is to do as he would be done by, he must take account of and (not ignore but) respect the wishes of people who do not like to be provoked or to engage in quarrels, and restrict his quarrels to those who, like him, enjoy them. Similarly, the person who enjoys hearing the beat of tom-toms in the middle of the night should reflect that the satisfaction of this esoteric desire of his is extremely likely to annoy others, and just as he would not want others to do things that are annoying to him (surely there is something that fits this category—perhaps the blowing of reveille on a bugle after he has fallen asleep), then he ought not to do things that are manifestly annoying to them.

Objections, then, that are conclusive against the particular interpretation of the Golden Rule, are not even so much as relevant to its general interpretation. Of course, the use of the particular word "as" has no great importance by itself, and the principle can be and has been stated with the use of this word without the point I am making having been recognised. Moreover, this particular word need not be used in the statement of the Rule. The important point is to understand the distinction, and to recognise that the statement "do unto others *as* you would have them do unto you" is intended to be equivalent to the principle: One should act in relation to others *on the same principles or standards* that one would have them apply in their treatment of oneself.

Consider the following passage:

> So far are business men from being without moral standards that the majority of them, like the majority of other people, have three. There is first the standard which John Smith applies to his treatment of other people—his competitors, his customers, his employees, and those from whom he purchases his supplies. There is, second, the standard which he expects them to apply to him. Finally there is the standard which he applies to other people's treatment of each other.[5]

The reference here to business men is of course completely immaterial. It occurs only because the book from which the passage is taken is a book on business ethics (written, appropriately enough, by two authors named Sharp and Fox). But the point is made that the "majority of other people," and not just business men, operate with these three different moral standards, and though it may be intended facetiously, it may also be true. It may in fact be the case that the majority of people operate with (or tend to operate with) three different standards. The standard that one uses in judging his own conduct in relation to other people—his treatment of others—will then be different from the standard he uses in judging the conduct of others in relation to himself—their treatment of him—and undoubtedly in both cases the standard is designed to give the advantage to

---

[5]Frank Chapman Sharp and Philip G. Fox, *Business Ethics* (New York: Appleton-Century-Crofts, Inc., 1937), p. 3.

himself, by making his own interest paramount. So presumably one operating on this basis would judge an action right if done by himself or if it is to his advantage, which he would judge wrong if done by someone else or if it is to his disadvantage. It is just this which is condemned by the Golden Rule, which requires that the same standard be applied to an action, no matter who performs it and no matter who benefits by it. It requires, not only that the standard used in judging one's treatment of others be the same as the standard one uses in judging other people's treatment of oneself, but that this same standard also be used in judging other people's treatment of each other, in cases where one's own interests are presumed not to be affected. For whether one's own interests are involved or not makes no moral difference, though it may make a considerable psychological difference or a difference to oneself, and there is no one whose interests are *in general* entitled to a privileged moral position. Perhaps this is what has been intended by those theories that have maintained that one should judge everyone's conduct, including one's own, from the point of view of an "impartial rational spectator." In other words, to judge an action in which one, or one's own interest, is involved, either as the agent performing the action or as the "patient" affected by the action, one should abstract oneself from the situation and consider how one would judge it then. Anyone incapable of making the requisite abstraction is incapable of making a genuine moral judgment—his judgments will all be biased by the pressure of his own concerns. There is no doubt that there are times when all of us are in this way morally incapacitated. But there is also no doubt that not all of us are morally incapacitated all the time.

Thus, even though the situation depicted in the foregoing passage may be widely prevalent, it is condemned by the Golden Rule as immoral, and anyone who applies to another a standard of which he would complain if it were applied to himself has no moral grounds for his complaint. He is being both immoral and illogical. It follows, then, that the Golden Rule formulates a fundamental requirement of justice, that everyone's conduct must be judged by the same standards, and that no one has, in general, any warranted claim to a special or privileged position. It is therefore at the basis of the Principle of Justice, that what is right or wrong for one person must be right or wrong for any similar person in similar circumstances. Stated differently but equivalently: What is right for one person cannot be wrong for another, unless there is some relevant difference in their natures or circumstances.[6]

---

[6] This principle is discussed at length in *Generalization in Ethics* (New York, 1961), chs. II and III and *passim.*

I have just stated that the Golden Rule requires that one apply the same standard in judging the actions of others in relation to oneself as one applies in judging one's own actions, and that this same standard be used in judging the actions of other people in cases where one's own interests are presumably not affected. But now suppose that someone applies to his own conduct a higher and more rigorous standard than he applies to the conduct of others, that instead of demanding more of others than he demands of himself, he demands more of himself than he demands of others. Would this be unjust and ruled out by the Golden Rule? Clearly this is not the sort of case that the Golden Rule is intended to rule out. The sort of case condemned by the Golden Rule is one in which one claims a privilege for himself that he is not willing to grant to others, and not one in which one imposes a burden on himself that he is not willing to impose on others. Such cases are fairly common. There are people who, at least in certain lines of endeavour, are harder on themselves than they are on others. It would clearly be ludicrous to condemn this as immoral. But how should this affect our statement and interpretation of the Golden Rule? As I see it, this way. The sorts of actions that the Golden Rule condemns are those in which one is being unfair to others, by claiming a privilege for himself that he would not be willing to grant to them, without there being any good reason to justify this discrepancy. But the sort of case envisaged here is not one in which one is being unfair to others. We might say that such a person is being "unfair to himself," but this could only be a metaphor. For to be unfair, in the sense in which this implies that one's action is wrong, is literally only to be unfair to others. What this would mean is only that such a person is being foolish, since there is no real need for him to be so hard on himself. But at the same time his actions, and his voluntary assumption of a special burden or sacrifice, may be highly commendable. Only it is not obligatory, and it would not be wrong for anyone not to impose higher standards on himself than he imposes on others—unless these standards are required by the demands of the circumstances or position in which he is placed; but that is another matter. So one in this situation is not violating the Golden Rule as I have stated it. He is not applying a different standard to himself than he applies to the actions of others. He is applying the same standards, only in addition to the common standards that he applies to the actions of everyone, including himself, he applies a higher and more rigorous standard to his own actions, and condemns himself for failures or omissions that he would not condemn others for. This does not violate the requirements of justice or of the Golden Rule, and I see no need to expand or revise my statement of the Rule so as to take explicit account of this situation. The Golden Rule condemns injustice, not heroism; and if there should be competition for the role of hero, then it would be regarded not as a burden but as a privilege. In demanding this role for oneself, one might be unjust, but since this rarely causes any special moral problems, I see no need to consider it.

## II

Let us now consider the ingenious criticisms of the Golden Rule presented by Bishop Whately.[7] Whately concludes that the Golden Rule was "far from being designed to impart to men the first notions of justice. On the contrary, it presupposes that knowledge; and if we had no such notions, we could not properly apply the rule."

This conclusion would appear to conflict with the one arrived at before, that the Golden Rule is the source or at the basis of the Principle of Justice, and would bear examining for this reason alone, apart from the intrinsic interest of the examples used to support it. But disputes about the origin of the sense of justice are futile, and I do not propose to get involved in one. Whately is operating with a moral sense theory, according to which our judgments of what is right and wrong or just and unjust are guided and determined by our moral sense or sense of justice. I shall simply say this. I should not deny for a moment the existence of such a thing as a moral sense, that it is an important thing to have, and that it is an important thing to develop. Too many people unfortunately have no moral sense, and too many others have an undeveloped moral sense. (Just as many people lack a sense of humor.) But it does not follow that one's moral sense or sense of justice is any infallible or even reliable guide to the morality or the justice of an action. On the contrary, principles of justice are required to guide and develop it, and occasionally to correct it. For moral judgments, or judgments of what is just or unjust, must be supported by reasons, and an appeal to one's sense of justice does not provide any reasons. What it provides is a motive to search for and consider moral reasons, a predisposition to acknowledge them, something that one who lacks all moral sense will not and cannot do. Moral sense theories, then, are not and cannot be theories about the nature of the moral standard or of the criteria for distinguishing right from wrong; they are theories about the nature or predisposing basis of moral motivation. Let us not confuse the two.

What I am contending then is that the sense of justice does not itself provide moral guidance, but itself requires moral guidance by a principle or principles of justice. Yet I am not contending that the Golden Rule is by itself sufficient for this. Before going further, however, let us take just a look at what Whately says is "the real design" of the Golden Rule. He says it is

[7]This volume, pp. 112–14.

> to put us on our guard against the danger of being blinded by self-interest. A person who has a good general notion of what is just may often be tempted to act unfairly or unkindly towards his neighbors, when his own interest or gratification is concerned, and to overlook the rightful claims of others. . . .

Therefore, "if we will make a practice of applying the golden rule," we

> may have a kind of prophet always at hand, to remind us how, and when, to act on our principles of right. We have only to consider, 'What should I think were I in the other's place, and he were to do so and so to me? How should I require him to treat me? What could I in fairness claim from him?'

But if this is the sort of question we are to consider, the Golden Rule must be more than just a reminder—it must also be something of a guide. The Golden Rule, in fact, is an instrument of moral education, and a most effective one. If this is so, it must be more than a mere reminder. It must also be something of a teacher.

I propose now, as a possible way out of the dilemma raised here, to go back and examine the examples with which Whately started. *A*, we will suppose, has "let his land to a farmer," *B*. It is claimed that if *A* were to operate on the basis of the Golden Rule, then "he might consider that the farmer would be glad to be excused paying any rent for it, since he would himself, if he were the farmer, prefer having the land rent-free; and . . . therefore the rule of doing as he would be done by requires him to give up all his property." Now "such a procedure would be absurd." But is it the procedure called for by the Golden Rule? I think not. The catch, I think, lies in the phrase: "he himself would, *if he were the farmer,* prefer having the land rent-free." The Golden Rule tells me that I ought to do unto others as I would have them do unto me. It does not tell me that I must imagine myself to *be* another, or that I must imagine myself as constantly shifting back and forth from one role to another. The supposition "if I were he" is not one from which any definite inferences can be drawn, because the supposition itself is so indeterminate. Here "Who's Who?" and "What's What?" become appropriate, but unanswerable, questions. The Golden Rule requires *A* to do unto *B as* he would have *B* do unto him. That is to say, it requires *A* to act towards *B* on the same standard or principle that he would have *B* apply in his treatment of him. No matter what in particular in this situation *B* may actually want—even if *B* should not just want the land rent-free but should also want to be paid for using it—, the Golden Rule does not enjoin *A* to let *B* have the land rent-free, or pay him for using it, because the Golden Rule, when sensibly interpreted, does not require anyone to do for anyone else just those particular things that the other wants to have done. It is only on the particular interpretation of the Golden Rule, which we have already disposed of, that this conclusion can be arrived at, and this would be tantamount to identifying the Golden Rule with its Inversion. The identification, and the result, are both absurd. The rule that we should do unto others as we would have them do unto us does not require us to do unto others *what they* would have us do unto them. Now in its general, sensible, interpretation, the Rule does not require *A* to let *B* have the land rent-free, because, as I have just indicated, it only requires him, in his dealings with *B*, to treat *B* on the same standard as he would have *B* apply in his treatment of him. Such a standard would require only that he charge *B* a reasonable rent, and not that he give up all his property, a conclusion, of course, at which Whately also arrives, but for different reasons.

This conclusion can be reinforced by noticing that the Golden Rule applies not just to *A*, but also to *B*, and if it would require *A* to let *B* have the land rent-free, it would also require *B* to pay a rent that is double or more what he is actually paying, since *B*, if he were the landowner, might reflect that he would want to receive at least twice as much rent for it as was actually asked. Such a conclusion is more than absurd; it is impossible. But it illustrates the consequences of the "if I were he" sort of thinking, shows that this sort of hypothesis is not called for in the application of the Golden Rule, and brings out the necessity of what I have called the general interpretation of the Golden Rule.

This argument has been considerably complicated, and I do not pretend that it is transparently clear. It might help to clarify it if we consider critically Whately's second example, that of the "jailer who was intrusted with the safe custody of a prisoner" and might "think himself bound to let the man escape, because he himself, if he were a prisoner, would be glad to obtain freedom." Let us go directly here to the point of view of the prisoner, who is equally bound by the Golden Rule, and applies similar reasoning by placing himself in the position of the jailer. The prisoner might reflect that he ought not to try to escape, because if he were the jailer, he would want his prisoners to remain in his custody. Of course, thinking of himself now in the position of the jailer, he might apply the Rule further and reflect on what he would want and should consider if he were, as he is, the prisoner. He would probably then arrive at the conclusion the jailer was supposed to have arrived at. But then suppose he reverses roles again? What then? Also, the jailer, after thinking of himself in the position of the prisoner, should then apply the Rule to himself in this position, and reflect that he, if he were the prisoner, should not try to escape, because if he were the jailer he would not want the prisoner to escape, and that therefore, since he is actually the jailer, he should not let the prisoner escape. And each of them could go on and on through further convolutions, but there can be only an arbitrary stopping point. It follows that this way of applying the Golden Rule is illegitimate, since it leads to contradictory results, and can terminate only at the end of an infinite series.

The difficulty of applying the Golden Rule in its particular interpretation is brought out further in Whately's third example, that of the judge: "if you had to decide between two parties who were pleading their cause before you, you might consider that each of them wished for a decision in his own favor. And how, then, you might ask, would it be possible to apply the rule? since in deciding for the one party you could not but decide against the other." This is true, but it does not follow that it is impossible to apply the Rule. It only follows that it is impossible to apply the Rule in its particular interpretation. Let us refer to the judge as $A$, and to the contending parties as $B$ and $C$. Now let us look at this situation from the point of view of $B$, for as I have already remarked, it is not only the judge who is supposed to apply the Rule to his conduct, but everyone else as well. On this method of interpretation, $B$ would reflect that, if he were the judge, he would not want the parties contending before him to place impossible demands upon him, and that he could not possibly decide for both parties. Consequently, he can demand, not that $A$ decide in his favor, but only, as Whately goes on to say, that $A$ decide the case impartially and without bias and in accordance with the relevant law and evidence. The same goes for $C$. Now we could carry this on into further convolutions, and have $B$ place himself in the role of $A$ and then back again in the role of $B$, and so on. We could also have $B$ place himself in the position of $C$, and $C$ place himself in the role of $B$, as, according to this interpretation of the Golden Rule, they are each bound to do. From this point of view, presumably, they should each accede to the claims of the other. And then we could go on to our second and third convolutions, and so on. But since any stopping place must be arbitrary, we might as well stop here. Enough has been said, I think, to show that this interpretation of the Golden Rule is impossible, and that the Rule does not really require anyone to think along the lines of the 'if I were he' sort of hypothesis. For, apart from the extreme indefiniteness of this supposition, the reversal of roles that it requires must go on forever.

I conclude, then, that the Golden Rule does not require anyone to do for another what he thinks he would want himself to do if he were that other. Such an interpretation makes it equivalent to its Inversion. What the Golden Rule requires is that everyone ought to act in his relations with others on the same standards or principles that he would have them apply in their treatment of him, taking account of and respecting, but not necessarily acceding to, their wishes and desires. This is the most that anyone can reasonably ask, but nothing less will suffice. Naturally, the Golden Rule by itself does not unambiguously and definitely determine just what these "standards or principles" should be, but it does *something* towards determining this, and it is not necessary that it do everything.

### III

Whately's main point about the Golden Rule is that it does not "answer the purpose of a complete system of morality," and this is not a point that I am disposed to deny. One very commonly expressed opinion about the Golden Rule is that if only everyone were to act on it then everything would be wonderful. This is merely sentimentalism.

> We sometimes hear it stated . . . that the universal adoption of the Golden Rule would at once settle all industrial disputes and difficulties. But supposing that the principle were accepted in good faith by everybody; it would not at once tell everybody just what to do in all the complexities of his relations with others. When individuals are still uncertain what their real good may be, it does not finally decide matters to tell them to regard the good of others as they would their own. Nor does it mean that whatever in detail we want for ourselves we should strive to give to others.[8]

The various difficulties with the Golden Rule with which I have dealt show that it requires interpretation, and is consequently no substitute for an ethical theory, or other moral ideas, in the light of which it must be interpreted. But my method of dealing with it was also designed to illustrate the method appropriate to and necessary for the criticism and examination of a moral principle, or what is put forward as a moral principle, by determining its implications and testing them in the light of the other moral ideas that we have. If we had no moral beliefs to start with, this method would be impossible. But by the same token, any method would be unnecessary.

[8] John Dewey and James H. Tufts, *Ethics* (New York: Henry Holt and Company, 1908), p. 334 (2nd ed., 1932, pp. 309–10).

# 16

## Outline of a Decision
## Procedure for Ethics*

### JOHN RAWLS
(1921–      )

1.1 The question with which we shall be concerned can be stated as follows: Does there exist a reasonable decision procedure which is sufficiently strong, at least in some cases, to determine the manner in which competing interests should be adjudicated, and, in instances of conflict, one interest given preference over another; and, further, can the existence of this procedure, as well as its reasonableness, be established by rational methods of inquiry? In order to answer both parts of this question in the affirmative, it is necessary to describe a reasonable procedure and then to evidence that it satisfies certain criteria. This I attempt to do beginning at 2.1 below.

1.2 It should be noted that we are concerned here only with the existence of a reasonable method, and not with the problem of how to make it psychologically effective in the settling of disputes. How much allegiance the method is able to gain is irrelevant for our present purposes.

1.3 The original question has been framed the way it is because the objectivity or the subjectivity of moral knowledge turns, not on the question whether ideal value entities exist or whether moral judgments are caused by emotions or whether there is a variety of moral codes the world over, but simply on the question: does there exist a reasonable method for validating and invalidating given or proposed moral rules and those decisions made on the basis of them? For to say of scientific knowledge that it is objective is to say that the propositions expressed therein may be evidenced to be true by a reasonable and reliable method, that is, by the rules and procedures of what we may call "inductive logic"; and, similarly,

*From John Rawls, "Outline of a Decision Procedure for Ethics," *The Philosophical Review*, vol. LX (1951), pp. 177–97. By permission of the author and the editors.

to establish the objectivity of moral rules, and the decisions based upon them, we must exhibit the decision procedure, which can be shown to be both reasonable and reliable, at least in some cases, for deciding between moral rules and lines of conduct consequent to them.

2.1 For the present, we may think of ethics as being more analogous to the study of inductive logic than to any other established inquiry. Just as in inductive logic we are concerned with discovering reasonable criteria which, when we are given a proposition, or theory, together with the empirical evidence for it, will enable us to decide the extent to which we ought to consider it to be true so in ethics we are attempting to find reasonable principles which, when we are given a proposed line of conduct and the situation in which it is to be carried out and the relevant interests which it effects, will enable us to determine whether or not we ought to carry it out and hold it to be just and right.

2.2 There is no way of knowing ahead of time how to find and formulate these reasonable principles. Indeed, we cannot even be certain that they exist, and it is well known that there are no mechanical methods of discovery. In what follows, however, a method will be described, and it remains for the reader to judge for himself to what extent it is, or can be, successful.

2.3 First it is necessary to define a class of competent moral judges as follows: All those persons having to a certain requisite degree each of the following characteristics, which can, if desired, be made more determinate:

(i) A competent moral judge is expected to have a certain requisite degree of intelligence, which may be thought of as that ability which intelligence tests are designed to measure. The degree of this ability required should not be set too high, on the assumption that what we call "moral insight" is the possession of the normally intelligent man as well as of the more brilliant. Therefore I am inclined to say that a competent moral judge need not be more than normally intelligent.

(ii) A competent judge is required to know those things concerning the world about him and those consequences of frequently performed actions, which it is reasonable to expect the average intelligent man to know. Further, a competent judge is expected to know, in all cases whereupon he is called to express his opinion, the peculiar facts of those cases. It should be noted that the kind of knowledge here referred to is to be distinguished from sympathetic knowledge discussed below.

(iii) A competent judge is required to be a reasonable man as this characteristic is evidenced by his satisfying the following tests: First, a reasonable man shows a willingness, if not a desire, to use the criteria of inductive logic in order to determine what is proper for him to believe.

Second, a reasonable man, whenever he is confronted with a moral question, shows a disposition to find reasons for and against the possible lines of conduct which are open to him. Third, a reasonable man exhibits a desire to consider questions with an open mind, and consequently, while he may already have an opinion on some issue, he is always willing to reconsider it in the light of further evidence and reasons which may be presented to him in discussion. Fourth, a reasonable man knows, or tries to know, his own emotional, intellectual, and moral predilections and makes a conscientious effort to take them into account in weighing the merits of any question. He is not unaware of the influences of prejudice and bias even in his most sincere efforts to annul them; nor is he fatalistic about their effect so that he succumbs to them as being those factors which he thinks must sooner or later determine his decision.

(iv) Finally, a competent judge is required to have a sympathetic knowledge of those human interests which, by conflicting in particular cases, give rise to the need to make a moral decision. The presence of this characteristic is evidenced by the following: First, by the person's direct knowledge of those interests gained by experiencing, in his own life, the goods they represent. The more interests which a person can appreciate in terms of his own direct experience, the greater the extent to which he satisfies this first test. Yet it is obvious that no man can know all interests directly, and therefore the second test is that, should a person not be directly acquainted with an interest, his competency as a judge is seen, in part, by his capacity to give that interest an appraisal by means of an imaginative experience of it. This test also requires of a competent judge that he must not consider his own *de facto* preferences as the necessarily valid measure of the actual worth of those interests which come before him, but that he be both able and anxious to determine, by imaginative appreciation, what those interests mean to persons who share them, and to consider them accordingly. Third, a competent judge is required to have the capacity and the desire to lay before himself in imagination all the interests in conflict, together with the relevant facts of the case, and to bestow upon the appraisal of each the same care which he would give to it if that interest were his own. He is required to determine what he would think to be just and unjust if each of the interests were as thoroughly his own as they are in fact those of other persons, and to render his judgment on the case as he feels his sense of justice requires after he has carefully framed in his mind the issues which are to be decided.

2.4 Before considering the next step in the development of the method here adopted, it is necessary to make some comments on the previous remarks. First, the tests for defining and determining the class of competent moral judges are vague; that is, given a group of persons, there would be, in all probability, instances in which we could not decide whether a person is a competent moral judge or not. Yet we do recognize in every day life the pattern of characteristics discussed above; we do think that certain individuals exhibit them to a comparatively pre-eminent degree, and these individuals we call "reasonable" or "impartial"; it is men of their character whom we want to decide any case in which our interests are at stake. Thus, while the foregoing tests are admittedly not precise, they do describe and select a recognized type of person; and those persons who do satisfy them beyond any reasonable doubt, will be called "competent moral judges."

Second, it is important to note that a competent judge has not been defined by what he says in particular cases, nor by what principles he expresses or adopts. Competence is determined solely by the possession of certain characteristics, some of which may be said to be capacities and achievements (intelligence and knowledge), while others may be said to be virtues (thus, the intellectual virtues of reasonableness). It will become clear in later sections why we cannot define a competent judge, at least at the beginning of our inquiry, as one who accepts certain principles. The reason is that we wish to say of some principles for adjudicating interests that one ground for accepting them as reasonable principles is that competent judges seem to apply them intuitively to decide moral issues. Obviously if a competent judge were defined as one who applies those principles, this reasoning would be circular. Thus a competent judge must not be defined in terms of what he says or by what principles he uses.

Third, one should note the kind of characteristics which have been used to define a competent moral judge: namely, those characteristics which, in the light of experience, show themselves as necessary conditions for the reasonable expectation that a given person may come to know something. Thus, we think of intelligence as being such a condition in all types of inquiry; and similarly with knowledge, since the more a man knows, the greater the likelihood of his success in further inquiry. Again, not only is it necessary to have certain abilities and achievements but, to be a good investigator, a person must develop those habits of mind and thought which we may call "intellectual virtues" (cf. 2.3 [iii]). Finally, there are those habits and capacities of thought and imagination which were described in connection with sympathetic knowledge of human interests. Just as intellectual capacities and virtues are found to foster the conditions necessary for successful inquiry of whatever type, so these habits and capacities are believed to be necessary for making fair decisions on moral issues. We may call them the "virtues of moral insight" with the understanding that they do not define either the content or the nature of moral insight, but, assuming it exists, simply represent those habits and capacities which secure the conditions under which we believe it most likely to assert itself effectively. Thus the defining characteristics of a competent judge have not been selected arbitrarily, but in each case there is a reason for choosing them which accords with the purpose of coming to know.

Finally, we can make these remarks clearer if we consider other methods of choosing the class of competent judges. It is one of the marks of an ideology that it violates the above criteria. Ideologies, of whatever type, claim a monopoly of the knowledge of truth and justice for some particular race, or social class, or institutional group, and competence is defined in terms of racial and/or sociological characteristics which have no known connection with coming to know. In the present method care has been exercised to select the class of competent moral judges according to those characteristics which are associated with coming to know something, and not by means of characteristics which are the privileged possession of any race, class, or group, but which can and often do belong, at least to certain degree, to men everywhere.

2.5 The next step in the development of our procedure is to define the class of considered moral judgments, the determining characteristics of which are as follows:

(i) It is required first that the judgment on a case be given under such conditions that the judge is immune from all of the reasonably foreseeable consequences of the judgment. For example, he will not be punished for deciding the case one way rather than another.

(ii) It is required that the conditions be such that the integrity of the judge can be maintained. So far as possible, the judge must not stand to gain in any immediate and personal way by his decision. These two tests are designed to exclude judgments wherein a person must weigh the merit of one of his own interests. The imposition of these conditions is justified on the grounds that fear and partiality are recognized obstructions in the determination of justice.

(iii) It is required that the case, on which the judgment is given, be one in which there is an actual conflict of interests. Thus, all judgments on hypothetical cases are excluded. In addition, it is preferable that the case be not especially difficult and be one that is likely to arise in ordinary life. These restrictions are desirable in order that the judgments in question be made in the effort to settle problems with which men are familiar and whereupon they have had an opportunity to reflect.

(iv) It is required that the judgment be one which has been preceded by a careful inquiry into the facts of the question at issue, and by a fair opportunity for all concerned to state their side of the case. This requirement is justified on the ground that it is only by chance that a just decision can be made without a knowledge of the relevant facts.

(v) It is required that the judgment be felt to be certain by the person making it. This characteristic may be called "certitude" and it is to be sharply distinguished from certainty, which is a logical relation between a proposition, or theory, and its evidence. This test is justified on the ground that it seems more profitable to study those judgments which are felt to be correct than those which seem to be wrong or confused even to those who make them.

(vi) It is required that the judgment be stable, that is, that there be evidence that at other times and at other places competent judges have rendered the same judgment on similar cases, understanding similar cases to be those in which the relevant facts and the competing interests are similar. The stability must hold, by and large, over the class of competent judges and over their judgments at different times. Thus, if on similar cases of a certain type, competent judges decided one way one day, and another the next, or if a third of them decided one way, a third the opposite way, while the remaining third said they did not know how to decide the cases, then none of these judgments would be stable judgments, and therefore none would be considered judgments. These restrictions are justified on the grounds that it seems unreasonable to have any confidence that a judgment is correct if competent persons disagree about it.

(vii) Finally, it is required that the judgment be intuitive with respect to ethical principles, that is, that it should not be determined by a conscious application of principles so far as this may be evidenced by introspection. By the term "intuitive" I do not mean the same as that expressed by the terms "impulsive" and "instinctive." An intuitive judgment may be consequent to a thorough inquiry into the facts of the case, and it may follow a series of reflections on the possible effects of different decisions, and even the application of a common sense rule, e.g., promises ought to be kept. What is required is that the judgment not be determined by a systematic and conscious use of ethical principles. The reason for this restriction will be evident if one keeps in mind the aim of the present inquiry, namely, to describe a decision procedure whereby principles, by means of which we may justify specific moral decisions, may themselves be shown to be justifiable. Now part of this procedure will consist in showing that these principles are implicit in the considered judgments of competent judges. It is clear that if we allowed these judgments to be determined by a conscious and systematic application of these principles, then the method is threatened with circularity. We cannot test a principle honestly by means of judgments wherein it has been consciously and systematically used to determine the decision.

2.6 Up to this point I have defined, first, a class of competent judges and, second, a class of considered judgments. If competent judges are those persons most likely to make correct decisions, then we should take care to abstract those judgments of theirs which, from the conditions and circumstances under which they are made, are most likely to be correct. With the exception of certain requirements, which are needed to prevent circularity, the defining characteristics of considered judgments are such that they select those judgments most likely to be decided by the habits of thought and imagination deemed essential for a competent judge. One can say, then, that those judgments which are relevant for our present purposes are the considered judgments of competent judges as these are made from day to day on the moral issues which continually arise. No other judgments, for reasons previously stated, are of any concern.

3.1 The next step in the present method is as follows: once the class of considered judgments of competent judges has been selected, there remains to discover and formulate a satisfactory explication of the total range of these judgments. This process is understood as being a heuristic device which is likely to yield reasonable and justifiable principles.

3.2 The term "explication" is given meaning somewhat graphically as follows: Consider a group of competent judges making considered judgments in review of a set of cases which would be likely to arise in ordinary life. Then an explication of these judgments is defined to be a set of principles, such that, if any competent man were to apply them intelligently and consistently to the same cases under review, his judgments, made systematically nonintuitive by the explicit and conscious use of the principles, would be, nevertheless, identical, case by case, with the considered judgments of the group of competent judges. The range of an explication is specified by stating precisely those judgments which it is designed to explicate, and any given explication which successfully explicates its specified range is satisfactory.

3.3 The next objective, then, in the development of the present method is to discover and formulate an explication which is satisfactory, by and large, over the total range of the considered judgments of competent moral judges as they are made from day to day in ordinary life, and as they are found embodied in the many dictates of common-sense morality, in various aspects of legal procedure, and so on. If reasonable principles exist for deciding moral questions, there is a presumption that the principles of a satisfactory explication of the total range of the considered judgments of competent judges will at least approximate them. On the basis of this presumption the explication of these judgments is designed to be a heuristic device for discovering reasonable principles. Therefore, while explication is an empirical inquiry, it is felt that it is likely to be a way of finding reasonable and justifiable principles in view of the nature of the class of judgments which make up its range.

3.4 Since the concept of an explication may not be clear, I shall try to clarify it by stating some of the things that an explication is not. First, an explication is not an analysis of the meaning of the ethical terms used in the judgments constituting its range. An explication attempts to do nothing more than that explicitly stated above, and in no way concerns itself with the sense of ethical expressions or with their linguistic meaning.

Second, an explication is not concerned with what people intend to assert when they use ethical expressions or make moral judgments in particular cases.

Third, an explication is not a theory about the actual causes of the considered judgments of competent judges, and this fact, in addition to the restriction to a specified class of judgments, sharply distinguishes it from a psychological or a sociological study of moral judgments. The only sense in which explication, as here defined, is concerned with causes is that a satisfactory explication can be a cause, or could be a cause, of the judgments in its range, i.e., the explicit and conscious adoption of the principles of the explication would yield the same judgments. Since explication is not concerned with the actual causes of judgments, it is immaterial whether the judgments in its range are caused by the intuition of nonnatural ethical characteristics, or by the response of intentional feelings to directly experienced value qualities, or by emotional attitudes which may in turn have been caused by certain specifiable psychological and sociological determinants. Questions about the actual causes, while interesting, are irrelevant from the standpoint of the present method. That such questions are irrelevant is also clear from the fact, previously stated, that the objectivity or subjectivity of moral judgments depends not on their causes, in any of the senses just listed, but solely on whether a reasonable decision procedure exists which is sufficiently strong to decide, at least in some cases, whether a given decision, and the conduct consequent thereto, is reasonable.

Finally, there is only one way of showing an explication to be unsatisfactory, and that is to show that there exist considered judgments of competent judges on specifiable cases for which it either fails to yield any judgments at all or leads one to make judgments inconsistent with them.

Conversely, the only way to show that an explication is satisfactory is to evidence that its explicit and conscious application can be, or could be, a cause of the judgments in its range.

3.5 Having noted some of the things that an explication is not, I consider some positive features thereof. First, an explication must be such that it can be applied intelligently by a competent judge; and since a competent judge is not required to have a special training in logic and mathematics, an explication either must be formulated or formulatable in ordinary language and its principles must be capable of an interpretation which the average competent man can grasp.

Second, an explication must be stated in the form of principles, the reason for this demand lying in the use of explication as a heuristic device. The typical form of a considered judgment is as follows: since $A, B, C, \ldots$, and $M, N, O, \ldots$, are the facts of the case and the interests in conflict, $M$ is to be given preference over $N, O, \ldots$ A considered judgment does not provide any reasons for the decision. It simply states the felt preference in view of the facts of the case and the interests competing therein. The principles of an explication must be general directives, expressible in ordinary language, such that, when applied to specific cases, they yield the preferences expressed in considered judgments.

Finally, an explication, to be completely successful, must be comprehensive; that is, it must explicate, in view of the explication itself (for this proviso, see below, 4.3), all considered judgments; and it is expected to do this with the greatest possible simplicity and elegance. The requirement of simplicity means that, other things being equal, an explication is more or less satisfactory according to the number of principles which it uses; and although this demand is difficult to state precisely, it is clear that nothing is gained if we require a separate principle for each case or for each class of cases.

3.6 The attempt to discover a comprehensive explication may be thought of as the attempt to express the invariant in the considered judgments of competent judges in the sense that, given the wide variety of cases on which considered judgments are made at different times and places, the principles of the explication are such that the conscious and systematic application of them could have been a common factor in the determination of the multiplicity of considered judgments as made on the wide variety of cases. Whether such an explication exists or not, one cannot know at present, and opinions vary; but the belief that such an explication does exist is perhaps a prerequisite for the finding of it, should it exist, for the reason that one who does not so believe is not likely to exert the great effort which is surely required to find it.

4.1 Perhaps the principal aim of ethics is the formulation of justifiable principles which may be used in cases wherein there are conflicting interests to determine which one of them should be given preference. Therefore it remains to consider what is meant by the terms "justifiable principle" and a "rational judgment" in a particular case.

4.2 Consider the simpler question first, namely, what is the test of whether a judgment in a particular case is rational? The answer is that a judgment in a particular case is evidenced to be rational by showing that, given the facts and the conflicting interests of the case, the judgment is capable of being explicated by a justifiable principle (or set of principles). Thus if the explicit and conscious adoption of a justifiable principle (or set of principles) can be, or could have been, the ground of the judgment, or if the judgment expresses that preference which justifiable principles would yield if applied to the case, then the judgment is rational. Clearly the justification of particular judgments, if the above is correct, depends upon the use of justifiable principles. But how do we know whether a principle is justifiable? Four criteria for answering this question are considered below.

4.3 In what follows we shall assume that a satisfactory and comprehensive explication of the considered judgments of competent judges is already known (note proviso under fourth test below). Now consider the question as to what reasons we can have for accepting these principles as justifiable.

The first reason for accepting them has already been touched upon: namely, since the principles explicate the considered judgments of competent judges, and since these judgments are more likely than any other judgments to represent the mature convictions of competent men as they have been worked out under the most favorable existing conditions, the invariant in what we call "moral insight," if it exists, is more likely to be approximated by the principles of a successful explication than by principles which a man might fashion out of his own head. Individual predilections will tend to be canceled out once the explication has included judgments of many persons made on a wide variety of cases. Thus the fact that the principles constitute a comprehensive explication of the considered judgments of competent judges is a reason for accepting them. That this should be so is understandable if we reflect, to take the contrary case, how little confidence we would have in principles which should happen to explicate the judgments of men under strong emotional or physical duress, or of those mentally ill. Hence the type of judgments which make up the range of the explication is the first ground for accepting the principles thereof.

Secondly, the reasonableness of a principle is tested by seeing whether it shows a capacity to become accepted by competent moral judges after they have freely weighed its merits by criticism and open discussion, and after each has thought it over and compared it with his own considered judgments. It is hoped that some principles will exhibit a capacity to win free and willing allegiance and be able to implement a gradual covergence of uncoerced opinion.

Thirdly, the reasonableness of a principle is tested by seeing whether it can function in existing instances of conflicting opinion, and in new cases causing difficulty, to yield a result which, after criticism and discussion, seems to be acceptable to all, or nearly all, competent judges, and to conform to their intuitive notion of a reasonable decision. For example, the problem of punishment has been a troublesome moral issue for some time, and if a principle or set of principles should be formulated which evidenced a capacity to settle this problem to the satisfaction of all, or nearly all, competent judges, then this principle, or set of principles, would meet this test in one possible instance of its application. In general, a principle evidences its reasonableness by being able to resolve moral perplexities which existed at the time of its formulation and which will exist in the future. This test is somewhat analogous to a test which we impose upon an empirical theory: namely, its ability to foresee laws and facts hitherto unknown, and to explain facts and laws hitherto unexplainable.

Finally, the reasonableness of a principle is tested by seeing whether it shows a capacity to hold its own (that is, to continue to be felt reasonable), against a subclass of the considered judgments of competent judges, as this fact may be evidenced by our intuitive conviction that the considered judgments are incorrect rather than the principle, when we confront them with the principle. A principle satisfies this test when a subclass of considered judgments, rather than the principle, is felt to be mistaken when the principle fails to explicate it. For example, it often happens that competent persons, in judging the moral worth of character, blame others in conflict with the rule that a man shall not be morally condemned for the possession of characteristics which would not have been otherwise even if he had so chosen. Frequently, however, when we point out that their judgments conflict with this rule, these persons, upon reflection, will decide that their judgments are incorrect, and acknowledge the principle. To the extent that principles exhibit this capacity to alter what we think to be our considered judgments in cases of conflict, they satisfy the fourth test. It is, of course, desirable, although not essential, that whenever a principle does successfully militate against what is taken to be a considered judgment, some convincing reason can be found to account for the anomaly. We should like to find that the once accepted intuitive conviction is actually caused by a mistaken belief as to a matter of fact of which we were unaware or fostered by what is admittedly a narrow bias of some kind. The rationale behind this fourth test is that while the considered judgments of competent judges are the most likely repository of the working out of men's sense of right and wrong, a more likely one, for example, than that of any particular individual's judgments alone, they may, nevertheless, contain certain deviations, or confusions, which are best discovered by comparing the considered judgments with principles which pass the first three tests and seeing which of the two tends to be felt incorrect in the light of reflection. The previous proviso (3.5) is to be understood in connection with the above discussion of the fourth test.

4.4 A principle is evidenced to be reasonable to the extent that it satisfies jointly all of the foregoing tests. In practice, however, we are wise if we expect less than this. We are not likely to find easily a comprehensive explication which convinces all competent judges, which resolves all existing difficulties, and which, should there be anomalies in the considered judgments themselves, always tends to overcome them. We should expect satisfactory explications of but delimited areas of the considered judgments. Ethics must, like any other discipline, work its way piece by piece.

4.5 It is worthwhile to note that the present method of evidencing the reasonableness of ethical principles is analogous to the method used to establish the reasonableness of the criteria of inductive logic. In the latter study what we attempt to do is to explicate the full variety of our intuitive judgments of credibility which we make in daily life and in science in connection with a proposition, or theory, given the evidence for it. In this way we hope to discover the principles of weighing evidence which are actually used and which seem to be capable of winning the assent of competent investigators. The principles so gained can be tested by seeing how well they can resolve our perplexity about how we ought to evaluate evidence in particular cases, and by how well they can stand up against what appear to be anomalous, but nevertheless settled, ways of appraising evidence, provided these anomalies exist. Thus each test above (4.3) has its parallel, or analogy, in the tests which are applied to inductive criteria. If we make the assumption that men have a capacity for knowing right and wrong, as they have for knowing what is true and false, then the present method is a likely way of developing a procedure for determining when we possess that knowledge; and we should be able to evidence the reasonableness of ethical principles in the same manner that we evidence the reasonableness of inductive criteria. On the other hand, just as the development of science and the method of science evidences the capacity to know what is true and false, so the actual formulation of ethical principles and the method whereby they can be tested, as this formulation is shown in the existence of satisfactory and reasonable explications, will evidence the capacity to know what is right and wrong as well as the validity of the objective distinction between the two. In the next sections I shall state what is designed to be such an explication.

5.1 In daily life we make moral judgments about at least three types of things: the moral worth of persons, the justice of actions, and the value of certain objects and activities. The explication below is designed to explicate our judgments on actions only. It will be necessary to make some preliminary definitions about goods and interests which will not be further discussed.

5.2 The class of things which are termed "goods" is held to fall into three subclasses: (i) good things, which are defined as being any physical objects which have a discernible capacity to satisfy, under specifiable conditions, one or more determinable needs, wants, or likings, e.g., food, clothes, houses. (ii) Good activities, which are defined as any activity which has a discernible capacity to satisfy, under specifiable conditions, one or more determinable needs, wants, or likings, e.g., the pursuit of knowledge, the creating and the contemplating of works of art, social fellowship. (iii) Enabling goods, which are defined as any object, or class of objects, or any activity or set of activities, whose use or exercise under specifiable circumstances tends to foster conditions under which goods of types (i) and (ii) may be produced, appropriated, or exercised.

The term "interest" is understood as follows: an interest is thought to be any need, want, or liking for some good, of any type; and in what follows, we are to think of this need, want, or liking as having been made articulate by means of an express claim before a body of competent judges (not of a legal, but of an ethical, court), and the claim is conceived of as asking for the possession of a good (if a thing), or as seeking the permission to exercise it (if an activity). Thus we may think of a claim as articulating an interest before a forum wherein its merits are to be weighed.

5.3 Next it is necessary to specify the kind of situation in which the problem of the justice of a decision and the action consequent thereto arises. This is done as follows: the problem of justice arises whenever it is the reasonably foreseeable consequence of the satisfaction of two or more claims of two or more persons that those claims, if given title, will interfere and conflict with one another. Hence the problem of the justice of actions, as a theoretical question, is essentially the problem of formulating reasonable principles for determining to which interests of a set of competing interests of two or more persons it is right to give preference.

5.4 It is required, further, to define a just state of affairs as follows:

assuming that the principles just mentioned exist, then a state of affairs is just, if and only if, given the relevant interests in conflict prior to its establishment, those interests which are secured and satisfied within it are those which would be secured and satisfied within it if all those agents, who were instrumental in bringing it about, had intelligently applied those principles in order to determine their decisions and conduct. Otherwise a state of affairs is unjust. It can be seen from this definition that we cannot determine the justness of a situation by examining it at a single moment. We must know what interests were in existence prior to its establishment and in what manner its present characteristics have been determined by human action.

5.5 I shall now give a statement of what are hoped to be satisfactory principles of justice. The reasonableness of these principles is to be tested by the criteria discussed in 4.3. It should be said that the statement below is not intended to be more than provisionary. Little attention has been given to independence, simplicity, or elegance. These are luxuries which can only be had after a fruitful statement of the necessary principles has already been given.

(i) Each claim in a set of conflicting claims shall be evaluated by the same principles. Comment: This principle expresses one aspect of what is customarily meant in the parallel case at law wherein it is said that all men shall be equal before the law. It asserts nothing about the content of the principles, but only that, whatever the principles employed may be, the same ones shall be used for all the interests in conflict, and not one set for one interest, another set for another interest.

(ii) (a) Every claim shall be considered, on first sight, as meriting satisfaction. (b) No claim shall be denied possible satisfaction without a reason. (c) The only acceptable reason for denying a possible satisfaction to a claim, or for modifying it, shall be that its satisfaction has reasonably foreseeable consequences which interfere with the satisfaction of another claim, and the formulation of this rejection or modification is reasonable provided that it can be explicated by this, together with other, principles. Comment: This principle declares that the presumption is always in favor of a claim, and it specifies what kind of reasons are required to rebut this presumption.

(iii) (a) One claim shall not be denied, or modified, for the sake of another unless there is a reasonable expectation that the satisfaction of the one will directly and substantially interfere with the satisfaction of the other. (b) The phrase "reasonable expectation" shall be construed as referring to an expectation based upon beliefs which can be validated by evidence in view of the canons of inductive procedure. (c) The more worthy the claim the greater the tolerance which shall be allowed to its interference, or presumption of interference, with other interests, and vice versa. Comment: This principle may be thought of as a generalization of the so-called "clear and present danger" rule formulated to cover decisions regarding freedom of speech, etc.

(iv) (a) Given a group of competing claims, as many as possible shall be satisfied, so far as the satisfaction of them is consistent with other principles. (b) Before modifying one interest or sacrificing one interest to another, an attempt shall be made to find a way of securing the benefits of both, which, if successful, shall be followed.

(v) (a) If means of any kind are used for the purpose of securing an interest, it shall be reasonably demonstrable that they are designed to secure it. (b) If nonneutral means, that is, means whose employment effect some other interest or interests, are used for the purpose of securing an interest, then the appropriateness of using those means shall be determined by weighing the merits of all the interests effected in accordance with other principles. Comment: The phrase "reasonably demonstrable" is to be construed like the phrase "reasonable expectation" in (iii) (b).

(vi) (a) Claims shall be ordered according to their strength. (b) The strength of a claim depends directly and proportionately on the presence in the bearer of the claim of that characteristic which is relevant for the distribution, or the exercise, of the good. (c) Relevant characteristics are those specifiable needs, wants, and likings which the good thing or activity has a discernible capacity to satisfy under ascertainable conditions. Comment: This principle is designed to order a set of claims for a share in a particular good; and it asserts that relevant characteristics are those needs, wants, or likings whose satisfaction is ordinarily understood to be the purpose of appropriating or exercising a good. Thus, if the competing claims are for a share in a certain amount of food, then the relevant characteristic is the need for food. A test thereof should be devised, and the claims ordered accordingly. A nonrelevant characteristic for claims of this type would be the number of letters in the bearer's last name.

(vii) (a) Given a set of equal claims, as determined by their strength, all shall be satisfied equally, if that is possible. (b) Given a set of equal claims, if it is not possible to satisfy all of them, at least to some extent, then an impartially arbitrary method of choosing those to be satisfied shall be adopted. (c) Given a set of unequal claims, with subsets of equal claims which have been ordered according to (vi), then the claims shall be satisfied in that order; and, within subsets, (vii) (a) shall apply, if that is possible, otherwise (vii) (b). Comment: The term "impartially arbitrary" may be clarified as follows: Imagine a good of such a nature that it is impractical or impossible to divide it, and yet each of a number of persons has an equally strong claim on its possession or exercise. In such a case we would be directed to select one claim as meriting satisfaction by an impartially arbitrary method, e.g., by seeing who draws the highest card. This method is arbitrary because the characteristic of having drawn the highest card is not a relevant characteristic by (vi) (c). Yet the method is impartial because prior to the drawing of the cards each person has an equal chance to acquire in his person the characteristic arbitrarily taken to be relevant.

6.1 The above principles are offered as an explication of the considered judgments of competent judges made in situations involving the problem of the justice of actions. In addition, it is hoped that they will satisfy the tests of reasonableness stated in 4.3. Now it is obviously desirable to give an illustration of at least some of these principles, although space forbids any detailed discussion. The question is, how shall we illustrate them? Shall we use an imaginary example? The following considerations answer this question: just as epistemology is best studied by considering specific instances of intuitively acceptable knowledge, ethics is most profitably pursued by examining carefully instances of what seem to be intuitively acceptable and reasonable moral decisions; and just as the instances suitable for epistemology may often be found in the theories of the well-developed sciences, so instances suitable for ethics can be found in those decisions which seem to represent a well-established result of discussion on the part of moralists, jurists, and other persons who have given thought to the question at issue. Following this suggestion, I shall illustrate several principles by attempting to show that they yield an established result regarding freedom of speech and thought.

6.2 Consider the Inquisition, and recall that this institution justified its activity on the grounds that the teaching of heretics had the consequence of increasing the number of the damned and therefore of substantially interfering with the pre-eminent interests of other men in salvation. The difficulty is that there is no evidence, acceptable to the canons of inductive procedure, to support this belief, and therefore, by (iii), the proceedings of the Inquisition were unjust.

On the other hand, consider a person, or institution, adopting the rule that no one shall believe a proposition unless evidence, acceptable by the canons of inductive procedure, is known to exist as a ground for believing it, and suppose this person, or institution, takes repressive action accordingly. What are we to say of actions consequent to the adoption of this principle? We must hold that they are unjust on the grounds that (ii) is violated, since it is clear that believing propositions for which no evidence yet exists does not necessarily affect the interests of other persons. Consider the following two kinds of cases: First, it is generally recognized that hypotheses, presumed by the investigator to be true, but not known by evidence to be true, play an important part in scientific inquiry, yet no one believes that a scientist who believes such a hypothesis, and who labors to evidence it, is, at the early stage of inquiry, acting unjustly. Second, it is generally recognized that the articles of religious faiths are not usually establishable by evidence acceptable to inductive criteria. Believers themselves are often anxious to grant this point frequently on the grounds that otherwise faith would not be faith. Yet no one, believer or unbeliever, is prepared to maintain that having religious beliefs is unjust, although some may think it mistaken. The having of such beliefs is an interest we respect, and a person is required to evidence his belief only when he proposes to take action on the basis of it which substantially interferes with the interests of other persons.

Thus, applied to the question of freedom of speech, thought, etc., principles (ii) and (iii) seem to yield what is an acceptable, and accepted, rule of justice: namely, each man may believe what he sees fit to believe, but not at the peril of another; and in an action wherein the interests of others are effected, a necessary condition for its being just is that the beliefs on which it is based are evidenced beyond any reasonable doubt.

It should be noted, in the light of this example, that we may think of rules, as opposed to principles, as maxims expressing the results of applying the principles of justice to recognized and frequently occurring types of cases. The justification for following a rule, or appealing to it in ordinary life, consists in showing that it is such a maxim. For brevity, however, we have omitted this intermediate step in discussing justification.

6.3 It is worthwhile to note how a decision with respect to a given set of conflicting interests, under given conditions, can be shown to be unjust. This is done by showing that the decision is not that decision which a competent and intelligent man would make if he used the stated principles of justice to determine his decision on the case, assuming here, for the sake of exposition, that these principles satisfy the tests in 4.3. To show that a given decision conflicts with what a principle would dictate is to give a reason for thinking it is unjust. To show this principle by principle and point by point, is to accumulate reasons against the decision and the conduct consequent thereto, so that, during the course of discussion, a decisive case may be made against it. The procedure is somewhat analogous to evidencing a proposition or theory in the real sciences, except that in moral discussions we try to validate or invalidate decisions and the action consequent thereto, given the circumstances and the interests in conflict (not acts of believing given a proposition or theory and its evidence), and the criteria we use are the principles of justice (and not the rules of inductive logic).

6.4 The manner of describing the decision procedure here advocated may have led the reader to believe that it claims to be a way of discovering justifiable ethical principles. There are, however, no precisely describable methods of discovery, and certainly the finding of a successful explication satisfying the tests of 4.3 will require at least some ingenuity. Therefore it is best to view the exposition as a description of the procedure of justification stated in reverse. Thus if a man were asked to justify his decision on a case, he should proceed as follows: first, he should show that, given the circumstances and the interests in conflict, his decision is capable of being explicated by the principles of justice. Second, he should evidence that these principles satisfy the tests in 4.3. If asked to proceed further, he should remark on the nature of considered judgments and competent judges and urge that one could hardly be expected to prefer judgments made under emotional duress, or in ignorance of the facts by unintelligent or mentally sick persons, and so on. Finally, he should stress that such considerations arise, if the demands for justification are pushed far enough, in validating inductive criteria as well as in justifying ethical principles. Provided an explication exists satisfying the tests in 4.3, moral actions can be justified in a manner analogous to the way in which decisions to believe a proposition, or theory, are justified.

6.5 Two possible objections remain to be considered. First, it may be said that, even if the foregoing decision procedure could be carried out in a particular case, the decision in question still would not be justified. To this I should say that we ought to inquire whether the person making the objection is not expecting too much. Perhaps he expects a justification procedure to show him how the decision is deducible from a synthetic a priori proposition. The answer to a person with such hopes is that they are logically impossible to satisfy and that all we should expect is that moral decisions and ethical principles are capable of the same sort of justification as decisions to believe and inductive criteria. Secondly, it may be said that a set of principles satisfying the tests of 4.3 does not exist. To this I should say that while it is obvious that moral codes and customs have varied in time, and change from place to place, yet when we think of a successful explication as representing the invariant in the considered judgments of competent judges, then the variation of codes and customs is not decisive against the existence of such an explication. Such a question cannot be decided by analysis or by talking about possibilities, but only by exhibiting explications which are capable of satisfying the tests which are properly applied to them. At some future time I hope to be able to offer something more constructive in this direction than the brief remarks in 5.5 and 6.2.

# EDITOR'S AFTERWORD
## *A Moral Checklist?*

The following is part of a column by Ann Landers which appeared on October 5, 1969. Try considering it in the light of the following questions: (1) Is any one of these tests, taken by itself, sufficient to distinguish right from wrong? (2) If so, then are the others necessary? (3) If not, then are these different tests all compatible with one another? (4) If they are not compatible, then how can it be determined which is to be applied? (5) Which ethical theories, if any, can these tests be related to? (6) If none of these tests is sufficient by itself, and if they are incompatible with one another, does it follow that this list of tests is useless? (7) What does follow?

DEAR ANN: In this age of conflicting philosophies, shifting standards, and the emergence of what some choose to call The New Morality, please tell me how a person can differentiate between right and wrong.

Everyday I am beset by new conflicts. I'm frank to admit that I am utterly confused. Can you give me and others some words of guidance?—Dark Side Of The Moon.

DEAR D. S. MOON: Several weeks ago I heard a sermon by the beloved pastor of The Peoples Church of Chicago, Dr. Preston Bradley. He discussed this very subject and in conclusion quoted Dr. Harry Emerson Fosdick's six-point test for deciding right from wrong. I asked Dr. Bradley if he would send me his distilled version and he did so. Here it is:

*One:* Does the course of action you plan to follow seem logical and reasonable? Never mind what anyone else has to say. Does it make sense to you? If it does, it is probably right.

*Two:* Does it pass the test of sportsmanship? In other words, if everyone followed this same course of action would the results be beneficial for all?

*Three:* Where will your plan of action lead? How will it affect others? What will it do to you?

*Four:* Will you think well of yourself when you look back at what you have done?

*Five:* Try to separate yourself from the problem. Pretend, for one moment, it is the problem of the person you most admire. Ask yourself how that person would handle it.

*Six:* Hold up the final decision to the glaring light of publicity. Would you want your family and friends to know what you have done? The decisions we make in the hope that no one will find out are usually wrong.*

*From "Dear Ann," *The Wisconsin State Journal* (Oct. 5, 1969). Reprinted by permission of Ann Landers and Publishers-Hall Syndicate.

# STATEMENTS ON MORALITY
## *Third Series*

*20. It appears to me . . . that the doctrine that it is sometimes right to lie can never be effectively asserted. For our hearers take notice and so make ineffective our subsequent attempts to lie. I recall a sick man who ordered his physician never to tell him the truth in case he should be seriously ill. Picture the state of that sick man's mind when later he hears his physician's reassurances. "Perhaps he doesn't consider this sickness a serious one. Then he will be telling me the truth." How can the sick man know? If he asks the doctor whether he considers the disease serious and gets a negative answer, how is he to interpret that answer? If the doctor did consider the disease serious he would be bound to say "No," and if he did not consider it serious he would also have to say "No." His words have become mere wind. No one can interpret them. His reassuring manner, his smiles, his cheering tones may be true or they may be lies. Who can say?*

R. C. Cabot (1933)

*21. When I lived in Scotland three languages were spoken in my house all day long, and a housemaid came to us from the Lowlands who spoke nothing but Lowland Scotch. She used to ask what was the French for this thing or that, and then what was the Gaelic for it. Having been answered, she invariably asked the further question which of the three words, French, Gaelic, or English,* was the right word. *She remained, to the last, entirely incapable of conceiving how all three could be right.*

Philip Gilbert Hamerton (1875)

*22. In all the world and in all of life there is nothing more important to determine than what is right. Whatever the matter which lies before us calling for consideration, whatever the question asked us or the problem to be solved, there is some settlement of it which will meet the situation and is to be sought as well as various other ways in which it might be fronted which would fail to satisfy the requirements. Otherwise the issue would be unreal or else insoluble; either no consideration would be called for except to clear away our own confusions, or else no consideration we could give would avail us anything. Wherever there is a decision to be made or any deliberation is in point, there is a right determination of the matter in hand which is to be found and adhered to, and other possible commitments which would be wrong and are to be avoided.*

C. I. Lewis (1955)

*23. Anything that must be explained won't be your duty. Duty is very simple and obvious. It is nearly always what you don't* want *to do.*

Elizabeth Taylor (1949)

*24. Instead of saying . . . that whatever is, is right, which would carry with it the conclusion that whatever was, was right, we should say that whatever inevitably tends to be is right, for the right is that which inevitably tends to be under the laws of variation and selection.*

*. . . A new interpretation is put upon the dictum that that is right which is capable of becoming universal. Instead of interpreting this to mean that that is right which we with our present likes and dislikes, approvals and disapprovals, would like to see made universal, we must interpret it to mean that that is right which is capable of making itself universal whether we like it or not, of winning out in the struggle with other conceptions of right, and of forcing itself upon the world by the sure process of selection which . . . is the only method by which progress takes place.*

Thomas Nixon Carver (1915)

*25. From this it is easy to proceed to the Kantian injunction to regard every human being as an end in himself and not as a means.*

*I confess that I rebel at once. If we want conscripts, we march them up to the front with bayonets in their rear to die for a cause in which perhaps they do not believe. The enemy we treat not even as a means but as an obstacle to be abolished, if so it may be. I feel no pangs of conscience over either step, and naturally am slow to accept a theory that seems to be contradicted by practices that I approve.*

Oliver Wendell Holmes, Jr. (1920)

*26. Reverence for life affords me my fundamental principle of morality, namely that good consists in maintaining, assisting and enhancing life, and that to destroy, to harm or to hinder life is evil. Affirmation of the world, that is to say, affirmation of the will-to-live which appears in phenomenal form all around me, is only possible for me in that I give myself out for other life. . . .*

*Ethics thus consists in this, that I experience the same necessity of practising the same reverence for life toward all will-to-live, as toward my own. Therein I have already the needed fundamental principle of morality. It is* good *to maintain and cherish life; it is* evil *to destroy and to check life. . . .*

*The fundamental principle of morality which we seek as a necessity for thought is not . . . a matter only of arranging and deepening current views of good and evil, but also of expanding and extending these. A man is really ethical only when he obeys the constraint laid on him to help all life which he is able to succour, and when he goes out of his way to avoid injuring anything living. He does not ask how far this or that life deserves sympathy as valuable in itself, nor how far it is capable of feeling. To him life as such is sacred. He shatters no ice crystal that sparkles in the sun, tears no leaf from its tree, breaks off no flower, and is careful not to crush any insect as he walks. . . .*

Albert Schweitzer (1923)

# Part III

## Values and Ideals

This part does not really fit neatly into the plan of the book. But there are important questions about values and ideals that are inevitably raised by some of the theories previously presented. What, for example, would an ideal society be like? The selection by Hamerton (17) raises the question whether the notion of an ideal society is a coherent one. It has sometimes been questioned whether ethical principles are at all applicable in an admittedly imperfect society, or whether they are applicable only in an ideal society, and this is the question dealt with by Sidgwick (selection 18). The essay by Acton (selection 20) is one of the few worthwhile discussions to be found of the question whether the end justifies the means —and consequently of the principle, if such it is, that the end justifies the means. (And, it might be asked, if the end doesn't justify the means, then what does?) Selections 21 and 22 (Clutton-Brock and Didion) are by nonphilosophers and (could it be for that reason?) are examples of practical ethics at its best.

There are selections in other parts of the book especially pertinent to the themes of this one; for example, the ones by Griffiths (53), Hook (40), and Perry (41).

# STATEMENTS ON MORALITY
## Fourth Series

*27. The way men live is so far removed from the way they ought to live that anyone who abandons what is for what ought to be pursues his downfall rather than his preservation; for a man who strives after goodness in all his acts is sure to come to ruin, since there are so many men who are not good. Hence it is necessary that a prince who is interested in his survival learn to be other than good, making use of his capacity or refraining from it according to need. . . . Some things which seem virtues would, if followed, lead to one's ruin, and some others which appear vices result in one's greater security and wellbeing.*

Machiavelli (1513)

*28. Whatsoever is the object of any man's appetite or desire; that is it which he for his part calleth* good; *and the object of his hate, and aversion,* evil . . . *For these words of* good, evil, *and* contemptible, *are ever used with relation to the person that useth them: there being nothing, simply and absolutely so; nor any common rule of good and evil, to be taken from the nature of the objects themselves; but from the person of the man. . . .*

Thomas Hobbes (1651)

*29. Would you judge of the lawfulness or unlawfulness of pleasure, take this rule: Whatever weakens your reason, impairs the tenderness of your conscience, obscures your sense of God, takes off your relish for spiritual things—whatever increases the authority of the body over the mind—that thing is sin to you, however innocent it may seem in itself.*

Attributed to Susannah Wesley

*30. One of the obvious facts of human nature is that our unhappiness comes not only from the fact that we cannot have what we want, but very often we are most miserable because we succeed in getting what we thought we wanted. Wisdom, therefore, consists in surveying our various conflicting desires with a view to the attainment of a harmony, or a maximum of happiness. A man may prefer a short but a merry life. Another may prefer suicide. But, if we regard our life as a continuing one, that is, if we have some regard for our own personality, we must integrate all of our desires into one coherent system, so that we can attain self-respect. Just as all of our judgments of perception of nature can be integrated by physical science into a view of the world, so may our judgments of preference be integrated with them into a view of the most desirable mode of life.*

*Ethical issues arise when, in fact, I ask which of a number of possibilities I should choose or approve.*

Morris R. Cohen (1944)

*31. Eric Gill once said that it was a sin to eat inferior ice cream. . . . Mr. Gill was right, and his rightness has nothing to do with calories or ordinary human perversity. It is a moral matter, a matter of intellectual honesty. . . . the purpose of ice cream is simply to give pleasure; no circumstance forces a man to submit himself to a second-best, a third-best, an unpleasing pleasure. To eat ice cream that displeases is to engage in an act which denies its own nature, as surely as a lie denies the nature of the truth. Furthermore, the man who does so has been fretfully conscious of what it was he was doing, and he did it anyway; the act has been willful. How should such a man feel himself in a state of grace?*

Walter Kerr (1962)

# 17

## *The Origin of the Ideal**

### PHILIP GILBERT HAMERTON
### (1834–1894)

The very imperfection of our happiness—an imperfection that we see more clearly after every intellectual advance and that we acknowledge more frankly as we become more honest—impels us to that exercise of the imagination which creates the poem of an ideal felicity.

The process by which this ideal is imaginatively attained is the removal of all that is unpleasant to us in existence, so that we may give ourselves over to the uninterrupted enjoyment of what is agreeable. This may be achieved ideally, but never otherwise. Even for the merely ideal enjoyment of perfect felicity it is perilous to imagine details, as they are sure to be incompatible with each other, after which the scheme of perfect happiness becomes incoherent and the vision fades.

The impossibility of realizing the ideal will be seen at once when we perceive that it is always selfish and personal, it is always the dreamer's own private satisfaction that he has in view. To this he would bend and adapt the convenience of all other beings. In the world of reality this cannot be done; it is easy enough in the world of imagination, so long as the critical faculty remains inactive.

The ideal condition, for each of us, is the pleasantest age of his own life made permanent, without any of the defects that partially spoiled it in the reality. What was the pleasantest age? That would vary in different cases. A likely preference would be for ripe manhood, between thirty-five and forty, and the happiest situation for a man of that age would, according to the most common opinion, be in married life, with a wife still young and charming and merry children around him, his own parents yet living in

*From P. G. Hamerton, *The Quest of Happiness* (1897), ch. 7, pp. 66–75.

cheerful old age, not too far from his bright and beautiful home. I omit for the present all possibly vexatious and irritating details. I allow the supposition that the children are not disappointing through any mental or physical infirmity, that the wife is affectionate and faithful, the old parents neither exacting nor unjust. Still, in this picture of domestic happiness the only persons likely to be entirely satisfied are the husband and the wife. The children do not feel themselves to belong permanently to their home,—the boys are already looking forward to fields of military or civil activity, the little girls are fancying themselves at the head of well-kept and expensive establishments, and the old people, however healthy for their years, find their dignified tranquillity a miserable substitute for the superior energy of their past. Besides these elder and younger relations, we have to consider the feelings of the servants when estimating the happiness of an entire household. The order and cleanliness of the great country house are kept up by the incessant toil of domestics who lead a life of extreme restraint, many of them at a distance from their native place and separated from all their kindred. They are accustomed to their lot in life, and therefore probably not so unhappy as we should be if we suddenly found ourselves compelled to sacrifice every hour of our liberty for bread and to assume the most deferential manners towards the indolent purchasers of our time. Still, it is impossible that a servile existence can be one of ideal happiness, for domestics must constantly feel the lack of that independence which is denied to them. Out of a large household we have therefore, hitherto, only been able to find two persons whose existence could be sufficiently near to the ideal for them to desire its indefinite continuance without change. I need scarcely add that the ideal happiness of the master of the house is no more than a supposition, and a very improbable one. In actual life he would be sure to have a constant succession of vexations, apprehensions, and disappointments, which however philosophically they may be endured are still quite enough to destroy the perfection and the purity of happiness.

The most usual practice, and the most favorable to the pleasures of the imagination, is to transfer the conception of ideal felicity to another state of existence. All the laws of Nature can then be easily repealed, and the dreamer can emancipate himself from reality. He is able to traverse the absolute cold of the interplanetary spaces, or to live for an indefinite length of time in a furnace, like the blazing surface of the sun, without in the least affecting either his visual or his intellectual powers. One of my friends has seriously persuaded himself that after his death he will travel amongst the stupendous mountain scenery of the moon, see the rings of Saturn from the surface of the planet, and explore the mysterious "canals" of Mars. The origin of such dreams as these is obviously nothing but a traveller's instinct, which has been insufficiently gratified in the dreamer's terrestrial existence and which rebels against the natural restrictions that deny us all access to other worlds. He is fond of travelling, and has learned the inconvenience of having a body that requires hotel accommodation and luggage that needs a porter. The traveller's ideal would be to wander through the universe as a pure Intelligence, unembarrassed by any *impedimenta.*

Instead of the traveller's instinct, it may be the social or the artistic instinct that is the origin of the ideal. Suppose it to be the social. The dreamer finds that in actual life he has not so much society as he would like, or that the quality of the conversation does not answer to his ideal of what conversation ought to be. He therefore imagines the Elysian Fields, where he will walk and talk with Socrates and Plato in an eternity of intellectual intercourse. If the artistic instinct is the motive power, the dreamer is probably dissatisfied with the dismal ugliness of some manufacturing town and imagines an ideal city of beauty and light situated in the midst of a lovely landscape and watered by crystal streams.

More commonly still, the conception of ideal happiness has its origin in an imperfectly satisfied state of the affections, and particularly in the profound dissatisfaction that all very affectionate natures experience when they first open their eyes to the hard fact that natural law is not tender, but inexorable. The idealist then imagines a government of the universe as he would like it to be; he imagines an affectionate and sympathetic government of the universe, of all conceptions the most agreeable to humanity, and the one for which, when it is authoritatively expounded and maintained, human beings are the most unfeignedly grateful. The same needs of our affectionate instincts lead us, when we indulge them, to resuscitate in imagination all dead persons, friends or relations, who have at any time been dear to us. We do so in a most irrational and inconsistent manner, but the ideal is too delicate a structure to bear any critical investigation. The most obvious contradiction is that different people resuscitate in their imaginations the same dead person at different and incompatible ages of his life; yet how can he be at the same time what he was to his grandmother, who knew him as a baby, and to his grandson, who knew him only in his age? This, however, only tends to confirm my theory that the ideal is an entirely private indulgence of the imagination, in which each of us fancies to himself a world adapted to his own personal sentiments and tastes. The best evidence of this selfish tendency of the idealizing imagination is, that it so frequently creates for itself a state of things in which the happiness of many others is to be at least partially sacrificed to its own happiness, as when there is an ideal indulgence in the pleasures of successful rivalry or domination.

Ideal dreaming is a habit much more indulged in by some persons than by others, and, in the same person, is far more prevalent at one period of life than at another period. It is common in youth, especially in adolescence, much rarer in active middle life, and frequent again in age, which thinks of existence as it might have been without the unfortunate circumstances that have invariably spoiled it.

The habit of ideal dreaming always presupposes at least some degree of mental culture, however humble, if it be only the religious knowledge of a Russian peasant. It is greatly aided by literary culture of a higher kind, especially by the study of poetry. It is also very much promoted by painting, and still more, perhaps, by music; in a word, by all the higher aesthetic pursuits and pleasures.

The consequence might be, that in an age like ours, when literary and artistic culture has become very common, and all artistic pleasures very accessible, the habit of ideal dreaming would be more prevalent than ever; but this is in a great measure counteracted by the positive tendency of an age which puts men in the closest contact with hard realities, such as industrial work of all kinds and our pressing social questions. Our contemporaries are not impelled so much towards genuine idealism as towards the improvement of what is real, and the desired improvement is usually of a kind that can be effected by intelligence and money. I need hardly observe that there is an essential distinction between these aspirations and the dreams of any genuine idealist. The distinction is that his dreams must always remain dreams, as they are pure poetry, whilst the desires of the practical man are not poetry, but a prosaic conception of what is possible, usually in the form of improved machinery for pleasure or for production,—as a finer and swifter yacht or a larger factory, and, speaking generally, a more elaborate and expensive life, of which a great spending aristocracy sets practically the example. But such an aristocracy, by exhibiting the expensive life as a reality, only proves that it is not an ideal, for a true ideal transcends all possible realities. The only sense in which expensive living can be called an ideal is when it gains a poetry not its own in the imagination of those who long for it as hopelessly beyond their means,—as in the case of some poor poet who fancies all that wealth might be to him if he possessed it. There is a French song about a would-be traveller who longed to visit Carcassonne, but never got there; to him, therefore, Carcassonne remained an ideal city, which it certainly is not to its inhabitants.

# 18

## Ethics and the Ideal Society*

### HENRY SIDGWICK

### (1838–1900)

. . . Some thinkers . . . take a view of Ethical Theory . . . quite different from that just set forth; regarding Theoretical or "Absolute" Ethics as properly an investigation not of what ought to be done here and now, but of what ought to be the rules of behaviour in a society of ideally perfect human beings. Thus the subject-matter of our study would be doubly ideal: as it would not only prescribe what ought to be done as distinct from what is, but what ought to be done in a society that itself *is* not, but only *ought* to be. In this view the conclusions of Theoretical or "Absolute" Ethics would have as indirect and uncertain a relation to the practical problems of actual life as those of Theoretical Politics:—or even more so, as in sober political theory it is commonly only the government and not the governed society that is conceived in an ideal condition. Still the two studies are not unlikely to blend in one theory of ideal social relations;—unless the ideal society is conceived as having no need of government, so that Politics, in the ordinary sense, vanishes altogether.

Those who take this view[1] adduce the analogy of Geometry to show that Ethics ought to deal with ideally perfect human relations, just as

---

*From Henry Sidgwick, *The Methods of Ethics* (7th ed., 1907), Bk. I, ch. 2, sec. 2, pp. 18–22, with some minor omissions. The title of this selection has been supplied by the editor.

[1] In writing this section I had primarily in view the doctrine set forth in Mr. Spencer's *Social Statics.* As Mr. Spencer has restated his view and replied to my arguments in his *Data of Ethics,* it is necessary for me to point out that the first paragraph of this section is not directed against such a view of "Absolute" and "Relative" Ethics as is given in the later treatise—which seems to me to differ materially from the doctrine of *Social Statics.* In *Social Statics* it is maintained not merely—as in the *Data of Ethics*—that Absolute Ethics which "formulates normal conduct in an ideal society" ought to "take precedence of Relative Ethics"; but that Absolute Ethics is the only kind of Ethics with which a philosophical moralist can possibly concern himself. To quote Mr. Spencer's words—"Any proposed system of morals which recognises existing defects, and countenances acts made needful by them, stands self-con-

Geometry treats of ideally straight lines and perfect circles. But the irregular lines which we meet with in experience have spatial relations which
Geometry does not ignore altogether; it can and does ascertain them with a
sufficient degree of accuracy for practical purposes: though of course they
are more complex than those of perfectly straight lines. So in Astronomy, it
would be more convenient for purposes of study if the stars moved in
circles, as was once believed: but the fact that they move not in circles but
in ellipses, and even in imperfect and perturbed ellipses, does not take them
out of the sphere of scientific investigation: by patience and industry we
have learnt how to reduce to principles and calculate even these more
complicated motions. It may be useful for purposes of instruction to assume
that the planets move in perfect ellipses: but what we want, as astronomers,
to know is the actual motion of the stars, and its causes: and similarly as
moralists we naturally inquire what ought to be done in the actual world in
which we live. In neither case can we hope to represent in our general
reasonings the full complexity of the actual considerations: but we endeavour to approximate to it as closely as possible. It is only so that we
really grapple with the question to which mankind generally require an
answer: "What is a man's duty in his present condition?" For it is too
paradoxical to say that the whole duty of man is summed up in the effort to
attain an ideal state of social relations; and unless we say this, we must
determine our duties to existing men in view of existing circumstances: and
this is what the student of Ethics seeks to do in a systematic manner.

The inquiry into the morality of an ideal society can therefore be at
best but a preliminary investigation, after which the step from the ideal to
the actual, in accordance with reason, remains to be taken. We have to ask,
then, how far such a preliminary construction seems desirable. And in
answering this we must distinguish the different methods of Ethics. For it
is generally held by Intuitionists that true morality prescribes absolutely
what is in itself right, under all social conditions; at least as far as determinate duties are concerned: as (*e.g.*) that truth should always be spoken and
promises kept, and "Justice be done, though the sky should fall." And so far

---

demned. . . . Moral law . . . requires as its postulate that human beings be perfect. The
philosophical moralist treats solely of the *straight* man . . . shows in what relationship he
stands to other straight men . . . a problem in which a *crooked* man forms one of the elements,
is insoluble by him." *Social Statics* (chap. i.). Still more definitely is Relative Ethics excluded in
the following passage of the concluding chapter of the same treatise (the italics are
mine):—"It will very likely be urged that, whereas the perfect moral code is confessedly
beyond the fulfilment of imperfect men, some other code is needful for our present guidance
. . . to say that the imperfect man requires a moral code which recognises his imperfection
and allows for it, *seems at first sight reasonable. But it is not really so* . . . a system of morals which
shall recognise man's present imperfections and allow for them *cannot be devised; and would be
useless if it could be devised.*"

as this is held it would seem that there can be no fundamental distinction drawn, in the determination of duty, between the actual state of society and an ideal state: at any rate the general definition of (*e.g.*) Justice will be the same for both, no less than its absolute stringency. Still even an extreme Intuitionist would admit that the details of Justice and other duties will vary with social institutions: and it is a plausible suggestion, that if we can clearly contemplate as a pattern the "absolute" Justice of an ideal community, we shall be better able to attain the merely "relative" Justice that is alone possible under existing conditions. . . .

The question takes a simpler form in the case of the method which proposes as an ultimate end, and supreme standard, Universal Happiness. Here we have merely to ask how far a systematic consideration of the social relations of an ideally happy group of human beings is likely to afford guidance in our efforts to promote human happiness here and now. I shall not at present deny that this task might usefully be included in an exhaustive study of this method. But it can easily be shown that it is involved in serious difficulties.

For as in ordinary deliberation we have to consider what is best under certain conditions of human life, internal or external, so we must do this in contemplating the ideal society. We require to contemplate not so much the end supposed to be attained—which is simply the most pleasant consciousness conceivable, lasting as long and as uninterruptedly as possible—but rather some method of realising it, pursued by human beings; and these, again, must be conceived as existing under conditions not too remote from our own, so that we can at least endeavour to imitate them. And for this we must know how far our present circumstances are modifiable; a very difficult question, as the constructions which have actually been made of such ideal societies show. For example, the *Republic* of Plato seems in many respects sufficiently divergent from the reality, and yet he contemplates war as a permanent unalterable fact, to be provided for in the ideal state, and indeed such provision seems the predominant aim of his construction; whereas the soberest modern Utopia would certainly include the suppression of war. Indeed the ideal will often seem to diverge in diametrically opposite directions from the actual, according to the line of imagined change which we happen to adopt, in our visionary flight from present evils. For example, permanent marriage-unions now cause some unhappiness, because conjugal affection is not always permanent; but they are thought to be necessary, partly to protect men and women from vagaries of passion pernicious to themselves, but chiefly in order to the better rearing of children. Now it may seem to some that in an ideal state of society we could trust more to parental affections, and require less to control the natural play of emotions between the sexes, and that "Free Love" is therefore the ideal; while others would maintain that permanence in conjugal affection is natural and normal, and that any exceptions to this rule must be supposed to disappear as we approximate to the ideal. Again, the happiness enjoyed in our actual society seems much diminished by the unequal distribution of the means of happiness, and the division of mankind into rich and poor. But we can conceive this evil removed in two quite different ways: either by an increased disposition on the part of the rich to redistribute their share, or by such social arrangements as would enable the poor to secure more for themselves. In the one case the ideal involves a great extension and systematisation of the arbitrary and casual almsgiving that now goes on: in the other case, its extinction.

In short, it seems that when we abandon the firm ground of actual society we have an illimitable cloudland surrounding us on all sides, in which we may construct any variety of pattern states; but no definite ideal to which the actual undeniably approximates, as the straight lines and circles of the actual physical world approximate to those of scientific geometry.

It may be said, however, that we can reduce this variety by studying the past history of mankind, as this will enable us to predict to some extent their future manner of existence. But even so it does not appear that we shall gain much definite guidance for our present conduct. For let us make the most favourable suppositions that we can, and such as soar even above the confidence of the most dogmatic of scientific historians. Let us assume that the process of human history is a progress of mankind towards ever greater happiness. Let us assume further that we can not only fix certain limits within which the future social condition of mankind must lie, but even determine in detail the mutual relations of the different elements of the future community, so as to view in clear outline the rules of behaviour, by observing which they will attain the maximum of happiness. It still remains quite doubtful how far it would be desirable for us to imitate these rules in the circumstances in which we now live. For this foreknown social order is *ex hypothesi* only presented as a more advanced stage in our social progress, and not as a type or pattern which we ought to make a struggle to realise approximately at an earlier stage. How far it should be taken as such a pattern, is a question which would still have to be determined, and in the consideration of it the effects of our actions on the existing generation would after all be the most important element.

# 19

## My Station and Its Duties*

### F. H. BRADLEY

(1846–1924)

### I

. . . Although within certain limits I may choose my station according to my own liking, yet I and every one else must have some station with duties pertaining to it, and those duties do not depend on our opinion or liking. Certain circumstances, a certain position, call for a certain course. How I in particular know what my right course is, is a question we shall recur to hereafter—but at present we may take it as an obvious fact that in my station my particular duties are prescribed to me, and I have them whether I wish to or not.

. . . There I realize myself morally, so that not only what ought to be in the world is, but I am what I ought to be, and find so my contentment and satisfaction. If this were not the case, when we consider that the ordinary moral man is self-contented and happy, we should be forced to accuse him of immorality, and we do not do this; we say he most likely might be better, but we do not say that he is bad, or need consider himself so. Why is this? It is because "my station and its duties" teaches us to identify others and ourselves with the station we fill; to consider that as good, and by virtue of that to consider others and ourselves good too. It teaches us that a man who does his work in the world is good, notwithstanding his faults, if his faults do not prevent him from fulfilling his station. It tells us that the heart is an idle abstraction; we are not to think of it, nor must we look at our insides, but at our work and our life, and say to ourselves, Am I fulfilling my appointed function or not? Fulfil it we can, if

*From F. H. Bradley, "My Station and Its Duties," in *Ethical Studies* (Oxford: The Clarendon Press, 1876), pp. 176, 181–83, 189–90, 193–99. The numbering into sections is not in the original. Selections 4, 9, 15, 29, and 38 provide interesting comparisons.

we will: what we have to do is not so much better than the world that we can not do it; the world is there waiting for it; my duties are my rights. On the one hand, I am not likely to be much better than the world asks me to be; on the other hand, if I can take my place in the world I ought not to be discontented. Here we must not be misunderstood; we do not say that the false self, the habits and desires opposed to the good will, are extinguished. Though negated, they never are all of them entirely suppressed, and can not be. Hence we must not say that any man really does fill his station to the full height of his capacity; nor must we say of any man that he can not perform his function better than he does, for we all can do so, and should try to do so. We do not wish to deny what are plain moral facts, nor in any way to slur them over. . . .

## II

Let us now consider our point of view in relation to certain antagonistic ideas; and first against the common error that there is something "right in itself" for me to do, in the sense that either there must be some absolute rule of morality the same for all persons without distinction of times and places, or else that all morality is "relative," and hence no morality. Let us begin by remarking that there is no such fixed code or rule of right. It is abundantly clear that the morality of one time is not that of another time, that the men considered good in one age might in another age not be thought good, and what would be right for us here might be mean and base in another country, and what would be wrong for us here might there be our bounden duty. This is clear fact, which is denied only in the interest of a foregone conclusion. The motive to deny it is the belief that it is fatal to morality. If what is right here is wrong there, then all morality (such is the notion) becomes chance and convention, and so ceases. But "my station and its duties" holds that *unless* morals varied, there could be no morality; that a morality which was *not* relative would be futile, and I should have to ask for something "more relative than this."

Let us explain. We hold that man is φύσει πολιτικός,* that apart from the community he is θεὸς ἢ θήριον,† no man at all. We hold again that the true nature of man, the oneness of homogeneity and specification, is being wrought out in history; in short, we believe in evolution. The process of evolution is the humanizing of the bestial foundation of man's nature by carrying out in it the true idea of man; in other words, by realizing man as an infinite whole. This realization is possible only by the individual's living as member in a higher life, and this higher life is slowly developed in a

*[by nature political—ed.]
†[either a god or a lower animal—ed.]

series of stages. Starting from and on the basis of animal nature, humanity has worked itself out by gradual advances of specification and systematization; and any other progress would, in the world we know, have been impossible. The notion that full-fledged moral ideas fell down from heaven is contrary to all the facts with which we are acquainted. If they had done so, it would have been for their own sake; for by us they certainly could not have been perceived, much less applied. At any given period to know more than he did, man must have been more than he was; for a human being is nothing if he is not the son of his time; and he must realize himself as that, or he will not do it at all. . . .

## III

The next point we come to is the question, How do I get to know in particular what is right and wrong? And here again we find a strangely erroneous preconception. It is thought that moral philosophy has to accomplish this task for us; and the conclusion lies near at hand, that any system which will not do this is worthless. Well, we first remark, and with some confidence, that there cannot be a moral philosophy which will tell us what in particular we are to do, and also that it is not the business of philosophy to do so. All philosophy has to do is "to understand what is," and moral philosophy has to understand morals which exist, not to make them or give directions for making them. Such a notion is simply ludicrous. Philosophy in general has not to anticipate the discoveries of the particular sciences nor the evolution of history; the philosophy of religion has not to make a new religion or teach an old one, but simply to understand the religious consciousness; and aesthetic has not to produce works of fine art, but to theorize the beautiful which it finds; political philosophy has not to play tricks with the state, but to understand it; and ethics has not to make the world moral, but to reduce to theory the morality current in the world. If we want it to do anything more, so much the worse for us; for it can not possibly construct new morality, and, even if it could to any extent codify what exists (a point on which I do not enter), yet it surely is clear that in cases of collision of duties it would not help you to know what to do. Who would go to a learned theologian, as such, in a practical religious difficulty; to a system of aesthetic for suggestions on the handling of an artistic theme; to a physiologist, as such, for a diagnosis and prescription; to a political philosopher in practical politics; or to a psychologist in an intrigue of any kind? All these persons no doubt *might* be the best to go to, but that would not be because they were the best theorists, but because they were more. In short, the view which thinks moral philosophy is to supply us with particular moral prescriptions confuses science with art, and confuses, besides, reflective with intuitive judgement. That which tells us what in particular is right and wrong is not reflection but intuition.[1]

We know what is right in a particular case by what we may call an immediate judgement, or an intuitive subsumption. These phrases are perhaps not very luminous, and the matter of the "intuitive understanding" in general is doubtless difficult, and the special character of moral judgements not easy to define; and I do not say that I am in a position to explain these subjects at all, nor, I think, could any one do so, except at considerable length. But the point that I do wish to establish here is, I think, not at all obscure. The reader has first to recognize that moral judgements are not discursive; next, that nevertheless they do start from and rest on a certain basis; and then if he puts the two together, he will see that they involve what he may call the "intuitive understanding," or by any other name, so long as he keeps in sight the two elements and holds them together.

On the head that moral judgements are not discursive, no one, I think, will wish me to stay long. If the reader attends to the facts he will not want anything else; and if he does not, I confess I can not prove my point. In practical morality no doubt we *may* reflect on our principles, but I think it is not too much to say that we *never* do so, except where we have come upon a difficulty of particular application. If any one thinks that a man's *ordinary* judgement, "this is right or wrong," comes from the having a rule *before* the mind and bringing the particular case under it, he may be right; and I can not try to show that he is wrong. I can only leave it to the reader to judge for himself. We say we "see" and we "feel" in these cases, not we "conclude." We prize the advice of persons who can give us no reasons for what they say. There is a general belief that the having a reason for all your actions is pedantic and absurd. There is a general belief that to try to have reasons for all that you do is sometimes very dangerous. Not only the woman but the man who "deliberates" may be "lost." First thoughts are often the best, and if once you begin to argue with the devil you are in a perilous state. And I think I may add (though I do it in fear) that women in general are remarkable for the fineness of their moral perceptions and the quickness of their judgements, and yet are or (let me save myself by saying) "may be" not remarkable for corresponding discursive ability.

Taking for granted then that our ordinary way of judging in morals is

[1] I must ask the reader here not to think of "Intuitionalism," or of "Organs of the Absolute," or of anything else of the sort. "Intuitive" is used here as the opposite of "reflective" or "discursive," "intuition" as the opposite of "reasoning" or "explicit inferring." If the reader dislike the word, he may substitute "perception" or "sense," if he will; but then he must remember that neither are to exclude the intellectual, the understanding and its implicit judgements and inferences.

not by reflection and explicit reasoning, we have now to point to the other side of the fact, viz. that these judgements are not mere isolated impressions, but stand in an intimate and vital relation to a certain system, which is their basis. Here again we must ask the reader to pause, if in doubt, and consider the facts for himself. Different men, who have lived in different times and countries, judge or would judge a fresh case in morals differently. Why is this? There is probably no "why" before the mind of either when he judges; but *we* perhaps can say, "I know why A said so and B so," because we find some general rule or principle different in each, and in each the basis of the judgement. Different people in the same society may judge points differently, and we sometimes know why. It is because A is struck by one aspect of the case, B by another; and one principle is (not *before*, but) *in* A's mind when he judges, and another in B's. Each has subsumed, but under a different head; the one perhaps justice, the other gratitude. Every man has the morality he has made his own in his mind, and he "sees" or "feels" or "judges" accordingly, though he does not reason explicitly from data to a conclusion.

I think this will be clear to the reader; and so we must say that on their perceptive or intellectual side (and that, the reader must not forget, is the one side that we are considering) our moral judgements are intuitive subsumptions.

To the question, How am I to know what is right? the answer must be, By the αἴσθησις* of the φρόνιμος†; and the φρόνιμος is the man who has identified his will with the moral spirit of the community, and judges accordingly. If an immoral course be suggested to him, he "feels" or "sees" at once that the act is not in harmony with a good will, and he does not do this by saying, "this is a breach of rule A, *therefore*, &c."; but the first thing he is aware of is that he "does not like it"; and what he has done, without being aware of it, is (at least in most cases) to seize the quality of the act, that quality being a general quality. Actions of a particular kind he does not like, and he has instinctively referred the particular act to that kind. What is right is perceived in the same way; courses suggest themselves, and one is approved of, because intuitively judged to be of a certain kind, which kind represents a principle of the good will.

If a man is to know what is right, he should have imbibed by precept, and still more by example, the spirit of his community, its general and special beliefs as to right and wrong, and, with this whole embodied in his mind, should particularize it in any new case, not by a reflective deduction, but by an intuitive subsumption, which does not know that it is a sub-

*[perception—ed.]
†[right-minded person—ed.]

sumption[2]; by a carrying out of the self into a new case, wherein what is before the mind is the case and not the self to be carried out, and where it is indeed the whole that feels and sees, but all that is seen is seen in the form of *this* case, *this* point, *this* instance. Precept is good, but example is better; for by a series of particulars (as such forgotten) we get the general spirit, we identify ourselves on the sides both of will and judgement with the basis, which basis (be it remembered) has not got to be explicit.[3]

There are a number of questions which invite consideration[4] here, but we can not stop. We wished to point out briefly the character of our common moral judgements. This (on the intellectual side) is the way in which they are ordinarily made; and, in the main, there is not much practical difficulty. What is moral *in any particular given case* is seldom

[2] Every act has, of course, many sides, many relations, many "points of view from which it may be regarded," and so many qualities. There are always several principles under which you can bring it, and hence there is not the smallest difficulty in exhibiting it as the realization of either right or wrong. No act in the world is without *some* side capable of being subsumed under a good rule; e.g. theft is economy, care for one's relations, protest against bad institutions, really doing oneself but justice, &c.; and, if all else fails, it probably saves us from something worse, and therefore is good. Cowardice is prudence and a duty, courage rashness and a vice, and so on. The casuist must have little ingenuity, if there is anything he fails to justify or condemn according to his order. And the vice of casuistry is that, attempting to decide the particulars of morality by the deductions of the reflective understanding, it at once degenerates into finding a good reason for what you mean to do. You have principles of all sorts, and the case has all sorts of sides; *which* side is the essential side, and which principle is *the* principle *here,* rests in the end on your mere private choice; and that is determined by heaven knows what. No *reasoning* will tell you which the moral point of view *here* is. Hence the necessary immorality and the ruinous effects of practical casuistry. (Casuistry used not as a guide to conduct, but as a means to the theoretical investigation of moral principles, the casuistry used to discover the principle *from* the fact, and not to deduce the fact from the principle—is, of course, quite another thing.) Our moralists do not like casuistry; but if the current notion that moral philosophy has to tell you what to do is well founded, then casuistry, so far as I can see, at once follows, or should follow.

But the ordinary moral judgement is not discursive. It does not look to the right and left, and, considering the case from all its sides, consciously subsume under one principle. When the case is presented, it fixes on one quality in the act, referring that unconsciously to one principle, in which it feels the whole of itself, and sees that whole in a single side of the act. So far as right and wrong are concerned, it can perceive nothing but *this* quality of *this* case, and anything else it refuses to try to perceive. Practical morality means singlemindedness, the having one idea; it means what in other spheres would be the greatest narrowness. Point out to a man of simple morals that the case has other sides than the one he instinctively fixes on, and he suspects you wish to corrupt him. And so you probably would if you went on. Apart from bad example, the readiest way to debauch the morality of any one is, on the side of principle, to confuse them by forcing them to see in all moral and immoral acts other sides and points of view, which alter the character of each; and, on the side of particulars, to warp their instinctive apprehension through personal affection for yourself or some other individual.

[3] It is worth while in this connexion to refer to the custom some persons have (and find useful) of calling before the mind, when in doubt, a known person of high character and quick judgement, and thinking what they would have done. This no doubt both delivers the mind from private considerations and also is to act in the spirit of the other person (so far as we know it), i.e. from the general basis of his acts (certainly *not* the mere memory of his particular acts, or such memory plus inference).

[4] One of these would be as to how progress in morality is made.

doubtful. Society pronounces beforehand; or, after some one course has been taken, it can say whether it was right or not; though society can not generalize much, and, if asked to reflect, is helpless and becomes incoherent. But I do not say there are no cases where the morally-minded man has to doubt; most certainly such do arise, though not so many as some people think, far fewer than some would be glad to think. A very large number arise from reflection, which wants to act from an explicit principle, and so begins to abstract and divide, and, thus becoming one-sided, makes the relative absolute. Apart from this, however, collisions must take place; and here there is no guide whatever but the intuitive judgement of oneself or others.[5]

This intuition must not be confounded with what is sometimes miscalled "conscience." It is not mere individual opinion or caprice. It presupposes the morality of the community as its basis, and is subject to the approval thereof. Here, if anywhere, the idea of universal and impersonal morality is realized. For the final arbiters are the φρόνιμοι,* persons with a will to do right, and not full of reflections and theories. If they fail you, you must judge for yourself, but practically they seldom do fail you. Their private peculiarities neutralize each other, and the result is an intuition which does not belong merely to this or that man or collection of men. "Conscience" is the antipodes of this. It wants you to have no law but yourself, and to be better than the world. But this intuition tells you that, if you could be as good as your world, you would be better than most likely you are, and that to wish to be better than the world is to be already on the threshold of immorality. . . .

[5]I may remark on this (after Erdmann, and I suppose Plato) that collisions of duties are avoided mostly by each man keeping to his own immediate duties, and not trying to see from the point of view of other stations than his own.

*[right minded persons—ed.]

# 20

## Does the End
## Justify the Means?*

### H. B. ACTON
### (1908–1974)

There are today many people who express their approval of social policies which, in the process of achieving what is held to be a better form of society would, and perhaps do, lead to misery and death for millions. There are many more who, on the ground that by their means a bloody and increasingly devastating war was being brought to a speedy end, have approved the use of weapons which cannot but be indiscriminate in their effects. Those who oppose such policies are accused sometimes of not having the intelligence to see that once the end is chosen it only remains to select the means that will most effectively bring it about, sometimes of overlooking the evils of the existing state of affairs, and sometimes of not really caring about the end that is being aimed at. They for their part are frequently aware that there may be an element of captiousness about their criticisms which would diminish or disappear if they were themselves faced with the responsibilities of office and action. Thus on the one hand there are those who consider that conduct which is wrong when performed from passion or for gain may be right, indeed a duty, when in the service of a worthy cause. On the other hand there are those who, while they may admire the guile of the disinterested cheat, the courage of the self-sacrificing assassin, or the devotion of the unscrupulous public servant, refuse to allow that the conduct they may admire in certain of its aspects is anything but reprehensible from the moral point of view or that the worthiness of a cause

*An Inaugural Lecture originally entitled "Moral Ends and Means," delivered at Bedford College, University of London, on 26th February, 1946. Reprinted from *Philosophical Studies: Essays in Memory of L. Susan Stebbing* (London, 1948), pp. 6–19. Reprinted by courtesy of the Editor of The Aristotelian Society. © 1948 The Aristotelian Society. (The first three paragraphs, which have to do with the occasion and not with the theme, are here omitted.) Compare with statement 15.

justifies departure from the recognised rules of right conduct. Vacillating between these extremes are those who doubt whether worthy causes can or should be promoted by conduct which, apart from these causes, would certainly be regarded as wrong, and yet at the same time recognise that counsels of perfection may be irrevelant or worse in an imperfect world. It is in the context of such problems that the proposition that the end justifies the means is supported or rejected. It is supported by those who feel quite sure that the main thing is to win the worthy cause. It is opposed by those who feel quite sure that the main thing is to play the game whatever the result may be. To the rest it is a source of some bewilderment which, in this lecture, I shall endeavour to lessen.

In the first place it is worth noticing that the proposition "the end justifies the means" is not an ordinary sort of moral proposition like "So and so is a bit mean about money but is honest and kind," or "Such and such would be the right kind of thing to do," or "What he did was quite unjustifiable because he lied deliberately." We often differ about the truth or falsity of propositions like these, but unless we are involved in philo-sophical discussion, we are not in doubt about their meaning. The propo-sition that the end justifies the means differs from these in that it is the result of theorizing about morals. Someone who asserts or denies it is considering, not the goodness or badness of an individual, not the rightness or wrongness of an action, nor even the applicability of a specific moral rule, but rather some alleged relationship between all moral ends and the means to them. He is advancing a moral theory, the acceptance or rejection of which will, it is thought, affect our subsequent moral judgments about people, activities and principles. It is as though someone were to say that pleasure is the only good and then, like Bentham, appeal to this theory in support of some social or political policy. Thus I hope it will be admitted that there is nothing captious or eristic in our proceeding to discuss what is and can be *meant* by saying that the end justifies the means. In doing so we are not raising difficulties about statements that people use adequately in their normal moral concerns. Rather are we endeavouring to get clear about what is in effect a theory propounded to justify courses of action about the rightness or wrongness of which there is legitimate cause for doubt.

The word "end" can mean either an aim being pursued or an aim achieved. On the basis of these different meanings the expression "the end justifies the means" can mean three different things. In the first place it can mean that actions normally considered wrong can be right if performed by someone genuinely *trying* to achieve a good enough end. In the second place it can mean that actions normally considered wrong can be right when performed by someone who *succeeds* in achieving a good enough end at which he genuinely aimed. In the third place it can mean that actions normally considered wrong are right when performed by someone, who, although he did not aim at anything good, in fact brings about a good end. Interpretation (1) would justify the sincere and ruthless idealist whether or not he was successful. Interpretation (2) cautiously reserves justification for the ruthless idealist who is both sincere and successful. Interpretation (3) looks to the result only and would justify whoever brought about the good enough result, whatever he had aimed at.

Interpretation (3), I think, can be dismissed quite briefly. It is conceivable in theory that someone who did not aim at anything good and who performed a series of wicked actions might bring about a highly valuable state of affairs. Should something so unlikely happen, we should congratulate society for its good fortune rather than justify the deeds of the individual in question. It would, indeed, then be possible for this individual, like Napoleon on St. Helena, to claim that his aims had been creditable all along. If his claims were correct, then the case would be that just described as interpretation (2), in which a ruthless idealist is both sincere and successful. If his claims were incorrect, then the fortunate result provides no justification for him. It will thus be sufficient for the proposition "the end justifies the means" to be discussed in terms of interpretation (1) according to which the end justifies the means irrespective of success so long as the aim was genuine, and interpretation (2) according to which the end justifies the means when the good enough end was genuinely sought and was also secured.

Before I pass on to the main discussion of these questions I must mention an argument which might, at first sight, appear to make further examination unnecessary. It may be said that, if someone really believes that the end justifies the means, then, whatever interpretation he may put upon the expression, he is justified in acting in accordance with it and is therefore acting rightly even if he finds it necessary to violate the ordinary moral rules in consequence. This situation, which springs easily both from the scepticism and the sentimentality of the present age, can of course be generalized so as to cover all actions performed by an agent who thinks them right, so that the most atrocious conduct would be right so long as it was performed by someone who thought it was. It is not difficult to see, however, that if we mean anything at all by "rightness" and if we admit that people ought to do what they think right rather than what they do not think right, there may well be a difference between what any given person thinks right and what really is right. If there were no such difference then we could most easily induce right conduct by training people to think that nothing is wrong. Once, therefore, the distinction between what is thought right and what is right is apprehended, it can be seen that we cannot dismiss discussion of the proposition that the end justifies the means in the way just suggested. However sincerely someone may accept it and however conscientiously he may endeavour to carry out its practical implications, we still need to consider whether any clear meaning may be attached to it and whether there is any sense in which it is true. For even though we grant that an individual is justified in doing *anything* he really thinks right, it remains clear that it is better when what is done is both right and thought right, than when it is only thought right. Furthermore, it is only in a rather limited sense that we can regard people as always justified in doing what they think right. For there is also the very fundamental duty of ascertaining what is right in order to be able to do it, and it frequently happens that people fail to do what is right because they have not given adequate attention to the question of what is right in the given circumstances. Now the proposition that the end justifies the means is, as I have already suggested, a rather sophisticated proposition and therefore not to be accepted as a maxim of conduct without due examination.

We cannot, therefore, avoid a frontal approach to the question whether the end justifies the means in sense (1) according to which success is not essential or in sense (2) according to which success is required as well as sincerity. And from what has just been said we can see that when someone is sincere in the sense that he thinks the end good and considers the means he undertakes necessary to achieve it, his conduct may be so far forth justified, even when the end is not achieved or even when the end is not really good at all. But it is also clear that someone whose conduct may be justified in this narrow sense may nevertheless, in a wider sense be acting unjustifiably, if he has not given due thought to the nature of the end, or to the means necessary to achieve it, or to any other relevant circumstances.

Before someone is justified in believing that the end justifies the means and in acting accordingly, he has, in my view, to consider whether the following propositions are all true. (1) We can conceive of states of affairs which we know would be very good if they existed. (2) When such states of affairs have been conceived we ought to try to bring them about. (3) There are some such states of affairs which we know to be so good that, in order to bring them about, it would be right, if necessary, to violate even the most binding of what are normally accepted as moral rules. (4) Situations do arise in which, if the very good state of affairs is to be achieved it *is* necessary for actions to be performed which violate the most binding of what are normally accepted as moral rules. (5) An individual can get knowledge that such a situation exists sufficient to justify him in acting accordingly.

Propositions (4) and (5) have of course been frequently criticized both by preachers and philosophers who have argued that it is highly improbable that the only means of bringing about some very good state of affairs should be actions which, apart from the state of affairs in view, would be regarded as heinous breaches of the moral law; and that it is highly improbable that an individual could be so sure that the good result would follow as to be justified in violating the moral law in question. The line of argument generally employed is to point to historical examples of the failure of such conduct to achieve what was aimed at, as with the Inquisition. Some of these historical moralizings are certainly impressive and it is possible to reinforce them from fairly common experience. On reflection most people will admit that to employ deceit or worse in pursuit of an end, however worthy it may be, frequently leads those who are doubtful whether or not the end is a worthy one, to decide that it is not and to hinder those who are pursuing it. Furthermore, when such reactions are aroused, the consequences become difficult to gauge. Unforeseen situations arise making it seem necessary to embark on still further violations of generally accepted moral rules. Retaliation in kind not infrequently results so that the conflict is heightened and standards lowered. Considerations such as these do, I think, make it unlikely that any very good state of affairs could be brought about by any policy of conduct that subordinated everything to the end to the extent of constantly violating accepted moral rules. Moralists have moreover, extended the argument further and maintained that however creditable the original aim may have been, a course of Machiavellian conduct will inevitably debase the agent and make it improbable that he will continue to pursue it. Psychologists, moreover, may add the observation that self-deception is widespread and that someone who thinks it is often necessary to violate accepted moral rules in the interest of some important end is very probably using the alleged goodness of the end as an excuse for doing the wrong things he wants to do. To these arguments I would add the further suggestion that we get our best founded knowledge of people's aims from what they do rather than from what they say and that therefore it is hard to believe that someone whose conduct frequently diverges from the accepted moral rules really is seeking an acceptable ideal. It is, I suggest, a tacit recognition of this truth that so often engenders opposition to alleged good causes pursued with what is commonly regarded as lack of scruple.

The combined force of these arguments is great and I have no desire to minimize them. It will be seen, however, that they only purport to establish probabilities and relate primarily to *courses* of conduct rather than to some individual breach of a generally accepted moral rule with some great good in view. Nothing that has been said so far shows that it would be wrong to commit some individual crime for the sake of some very good end. What has been shown is that it is most improbable that *courses* of wrong acts will promote any good cause or that anyone could have the knowledge that would justify him in acting on the belief that they would. In order to strengthen the case against the proposition that the end justifies the means we must further discuss what is involved in the use of the word "end." We must, therefore, consider the remaining propositions already mentioned as having to be accepted by someone who is to act on the principle that the end justifies the means viz., (1) that we can conceive of states of affairs which we know would be very good if they existed; (2) that when such states of affairs have been conceived we ought to try to bring them about; and (3) that there are some such states of affairs which we know to be so good that, in order to bring them about, it would be right, if necessary, to violate even the most binding of what are normally accepted as moral rules.

The first of these propositions, viz., that we can conceive of states of affairs that would be very good if they existed, seems innocent enough and fairly obvious. For can we not imagine a state of affairs in which there is no pain or grief or ugliness but rather pleasure, joy and beauty? It is true that we can *talk* in this way, but can we really *conceive* definite states of affairs embodying such characteristics as these, all unmixed? The vague, pallid and depressing nature of most descriptions of heaven suggest that at any rate it is extremely difficult. Hell on the other hand can be most definite and stimulating. The reason for this is, I am afraid, that we are much nearer hell than heaven, and that if we could describe heaven in detail we could also make it, just as we can make hell. The conclusion I draw is that we can easily exaggerate the extent to which good states of affairs can be conceived of. It is more accurate to say that we can conceive better states of affairs than what now exist but that the farther removed from what is is the state of affairs to be conceived, the vaguer it is and the less definitely good it is. That is, we can fairly easily talk sense about something better than what is in certain specific respects, but the farther away from what is that we let our mind wander the nearer it gets to absurdity. Yet it is in favour of remote ends, regarded as ideals determining whole courses of action and even the policies of nations or classes, that the proposition that the end justifies the means is generally invoked.[1]

---

[1] In parenthesis I should like to mention that it has been a merit of Utopian thinkers that they tried to describe in detail the world that was to be striven for. Thus, for example, Fourier: "Mondor's day in summer: Sleep from $10\frac{1}{2}$ in the evening to 3 o'clock in the morning. At $3\frac{1}{2}$, rising, getting ready. At 4, court of public levée, news of the night. At $4\frac{1}{2}$, the délite, first meal, followed by the industrial parade. At $5\frac{1}{2}$, attendance at the hunting group. At 7, attendance at the fishing group. At 8, breakfast, newspapers. At 9, attendance at an agricultural group, under cover. At 10, at mass. At $10\frac{1}{2}$, at the pheasantry group, at $11\frac{1}{2}$

We have now to consider the proposition that when very good states of affairs have been conceived we ought to try to bring them about. If what I have just said is correct, then at any rate we have no duty to engage in the pursuit of any vaguely conceived remote ends. It may, however, be objected at this point that surely it sometimes is someone's duty to leave all and follow some high aim perhaps hitherto unconceived. I admit that it may be, but here again it is important to describe the real state of affairs as concretely as possible. There is no such thing as just following some high aim; any individual has to follow his aim in certain specific ways. Generally these involve talking to other people about it, endeavouring to get their agreement, and forming an association through which the pursuit is organized. Once specific steps of this nature are taken, moral relations are established between all the individuals concerned and between their organization and the rest of society. It may indeed still be argued that the aims of the organization may be so important that they transcend any such specific duties and make it right to avoid performing them. To this I can only reply that such aims must not only be very good indeed, but also clearly conceived, specific, and likely to be attained by certain definitely specified courses of action. The position of John Rosmer in Ibsen's *Rosmersholm* can, I think, be used to illustrate this point. Rosmer, a highly respectable and influential member of the community, whose wife has not long before been found drowned, has changed his political and religious convictions and thinks it is therefore his duty to announce this conversion and engage in politics against the established, conservative elements of the town among whom most of his friends are numbered. He imparts this to the leading local representative of the party he now wishes to adhere to. This expert politician, however, is not nearly so impressed with the new accession to the cause as might have been expected. In the first place he advises silence on the religious issue as a complicating factor that might well diminish the value of Rosmer to his new party. In the second place he sees that the incursion into politics of a man of Rosmer's position and antecedents will lead his opponents to look for mud to throw at him. There are certain very specific lumps of mud that may well be selected, and if Rosmer cannot remove them from his person skilfully and without trace, his accession to the cause might turn out to be more of an embarrassment

---

at the library. At 1, DINNER. At 2½, at the group of cold green-houses. At 4, at the group of exotic plants. At 5, at the group of fishponds. At 6, luncheon, in the fields. At 6½, at the group of merinoes. At 8, at 'Change. At 9, SUPPER, fifth repast. At 9½, court of the arts, ball, theatre, receptions. At 10½, bedtime." (*Selections from the works of Fourier,* translated by Julia Franklin, pp. 167–168). This leaves us in no doubt about what is in store for us, and while we may not ourselves be able to conceive any alternative very good state of affairs, we have no difficulty in deciding whether or not we want to aim at this one.

to it than a help. However convinced Rosmer may be of his own integrity, he may not be able to convey a similar conviction to his political associates and opponents. Once he is in politics what will count is not the real state of his soul but the view of it that circumstances will enable to be presented. John Rosmer, we can say, was living in a vague moral world, not really knowing what his aims were nor what he meant by throwing himself into the new cause. He may have had a picture of some better state of affairs, but he had no definite link connecting him with it and no precise thoughts on the things he next had to do.

This brings us to the last proposition under consideration, viz., that there are states of affairs which we know to be so good that, in order to bring them about, it would be right, if necessary, to violate even the most binding of what are normally accepted as moral rules. I have suggested that this could only conceivably be the case if there were some very definite aim that would be realized by the performance of some definitely specified action or series of actions. These conditions therefore would certainly require the very good state of affairs not to be far in the future and the necessary actions not to be many or too complicated; for the farther into the future the attainment of the end is placed, the greater are the chances of miscalculation or failure. Thus, if the arguments I have used are sound, it would only be in cases where some sufficiently important and definite good is realizable immediately or very soon as the result and only as the result of some single action or short sequence of actions contravening the normally accepted moral rules, that it could reasonably be said that the end justifies the means. I should not be prepared to deny that such cases do sometimes arise, nor that, when they do, violation of some accepted moral rule would, if the end were important enough, be the right course. My point is that they are likely to be rare, and that we are likely to exaggerate their frequency if we conceive of moral behaviour as a pursuit of distant ends.

It is perhaps worth adding that these considerations may be reinforced by three further arguments, all of which indicate how easily we can make misleading abstractions in considering moral ends. (1). When we consider aiming at some end we are prone to overlook concomitants of the end that will come into existence in the very process of achieving it. (2). Furthermore, we sometimes try to consider the end as quite distinct from the specific course of conduct required to bring it about, whereas we should, in conceiving an end, think of it as what follows when such and such actions are undertaken. (3). Again, we sometimes think of ends as if they were the finish of all activity, the final achievement of moral equilibrium, But just as an end is really what follows when such and such actions are undertaken, it is also what necessitates the undertaking of further actions. The probable consequences of achieving an end are therefore factors involved in its assessment. The less clearly such consequences can be envisaged, the less capable are we of assessing the value of the end.

So far in this lecture I have been trying to show that the maxim that the end justifies the means is both intellectually and morally misleading because it leads to vague conceptions of future states of affairs and diverts attention from the nature of the conduct that is our immediate concern. Insufficient time remains in which to consider at all adequately the other question raised at the beginning of the lecture, viz., the contention of those who say that no end can ever be so good as to justify any departure from the recognized rules of right conduct—that, whatever the aim or consequences, no departure from rules of moral conduct is justifiable. I will, however, try to indicate some directions in which this attitude can be criticized.[2]

In the first place, then, I suggest that this is not an attitude that could be maintained consistently in the sphere of private conduct. Let us suppose a doctor who by a series of accidents has been deprived of all means of transport to a patient who must be tended by him if he is not to die. If this unfortunate condition coincided with a London rush hour, it might be the doctor's duty (supposing he is unable to convince a surly and cynical bus queue of his good faith) to try to get on board a bus out of turn or with the exercise of more violence than would normally be right. No one, I think, could seriously maintain that the particular job he was going about did not, in the circumstances, justify departure from certain of the moral equities. It may indeed be objected that in jumping the queue he is not really behaving inequitably at all, but that on the basis of knowledge that he has and they have not he is behaving equitably as between them and his patient. This may well be so. There is no doubt, however, that he is violating a rule to the effect that we should, when there are queues, take our place in them. This rule is rightly abrogated if a human life is at stake— with the agreement of all concerned if they know the facts and are not perverse, or by guile or moderate force if they do not know the facts and cannot be convinced.

Now it seems to me that all definite moral rules, from those which, like the one I have just cited, are not a great deal more than manners or conventions, to the most serious of all, are subject to possible abrogation in

---

[2]It would clearly be possible to argue that, just as the believer in the proposition that the end justifies the means makes a misleading abstraction that leaves out of account the actions leading up to the end, so the extreme stickler for moral rules makes a different sort of misleading abstraction that leaves out of account the end and consequences. Propositions can, however, be true and antithetical without being particularly illuminating, and I think this would be one of that sort.

this way. It is right to keep promises—except in those very exceptional cases when it is not. It is right to tell the truth—except very occasionally when it is our duty to lie. It is right to refrain from killing other people—except on those occasions when killing is not murder. The more trivial the rule, of course, the more subject it is to rightful violation, and hence the rule about keeping place in a queue is one that we should not uphold pedantically. Now if it is said that the man who jumped the disbelieving or callous queue did not break the *real* moral principle involved, which is not that people should keep their places in queues but that they should act with a proper appreciation of the duty they owe to certain special persons as distinct from mere passers-by in the street, then a very different and less definite type of moral rule is being appealed to. It is *always* right to pay the due heed to the moral claims that others have upon us. It is *always* right to act equitably. It is *always* right—to repeat a principle that has already been discussed earlier in the lecture—to do what one believes right rather than not. Such principles, however, are not *definite* moral rules. The principle that we are to tell the truth requires a definite sort of conduct and we generally know when we are not performing it. The principle that we should do what we think right is more general and less informative. To allege exceptions to these less definite moral rules is to betray moral imbecility or to propound villainy. Now it seems likely to me that at any rate some of those who say that it is always wrong to make any exception to any moral rule are confusing these two different sorts. They are so intent in upholding the right that they import into practical moral maxims a necessity that belongs only to the principles that define morality itself. There is plenty of excuse for this since moral philosophers have done little to distinguish the various types of moral statement and to exhibit the fallacies to which confusion of them gives rise.

In the rather simple example I have just made use of, it was seen that departure from some relatively trivial moral rule became the right course when the doctor could not persuade the members of the queue of the real state of affairs or could not move them to the action appropriate to the circumstances. Ruse or violence was justified when negotiations had failed—though in fact negotiations in such a case seldom would fail. Now some analogy to the situations that arise in public life[3] is provided if we suppose that when the doctor addressed the queue about his predicament and showed his stethoscope as evidence of his good faith, several members of the queue stated that they were themselves doctors on similar or even

---

[3] To distinguish public from private life is not easy, as there is a gradual transition from the one to the other. But public life, for moral purposes, includes, besides politics and the state, the life of churches and much of commerce.

more pressing errands and others expressed the opinion that the stethoscope was a dummy or a blind. That is to say, the conduct generally required in public life differs from that normal in private life in that it is confronted with a greater number of existing wrongs, more complicated circumstances, and fewer opportunities for resolving problems by personal approaches.

It was with the manifold existing wrongs in view that Machiavelli wrote: "a man who wishes to act entirely up to his professions of virtue soon meets with what destroys him in so much that is evil."[4] What he should have said is that in so much that is evil, absolute adherence to the practical maxims of private morality would be morally wrong. What matters is not so much, as Machiavelli appears to suggest, that the agent is destroyed as that his conduct is not what the situation requires. It may be, for instance, that in the past a government has given a number of undertakings which subsequent events show to be incompatible. Rules about keeping promises help very little in this situation, where the decision has to be which promise shall be broken. There is no need for me to emphasize the complication of the moral problems of public life. It is worth mentioning, however, that because of this complication the different parties to a dispute will generally have different sets of facts in mind and will consequently urge quite different settlements—a situation which occurs, but is much less common, in private concerns. Again, in public affairs individuals are generally acting as spokesmen or representatives. Therefore their responsibility is different from what it usually is in private matters, and they rightly consider that they are less justified in acting promptly on generous impulses of their own, than if they had been mere private persons.

I am afraid that some people who know enough about politics to have heard of some of its scandals and insufficient about ethics to appreciate that departure from a single maxim of private morality is not the same as departure from the moral standards that really apply to the case in hand, are prone to think that there can be no public morality and that only power can count beyond the personal sphere. The answer to them is, it seems to me, that people are doing different things when they engage in public concerns from what they do in private life, so that it should not be surprising if the specific rules that generally apply to the latter should more often require exceptions when applied to the former. Justice and equity permit of no exceptions in either sphere. They are among the terms that define morality. But they are exhibited in different sorts of rules of conduct in the various levels of behaviour from personal affairs to the relations of states. A comparison of the notions of a promise, a contract, and a treaty is

---

[4] *The Prince,* ch. xv.

instructive in this regard. In the sixteenth century Grotius tried to show how certain public matters, notably war, could be carried out in accordance with the fundamentals of morality. It is, I think, a scandal of twentieth-century thought that the efforts made in this direction are so few and so trivial by comparison with the problems that confront us.

## 21

## *On Irreconcilables**

# ARTHUR CLUTTON-BROCK

(1868-1924)

I suppose there have always been irreconcilables. Diogenes was one, in practice as well as in theory, for he did live in his tub and asked of Alexander only that he would not stand between him and the sunlight. And there were the eremites, Christians and others, who preferred the wilderness to the wickedness of human society. All these we can respect because they did act their rebellion and were thorough and practical rebels. But nowadays we have a kind of irreconcilable who enjoys a theoretic rebellion but suffers no practical discomfort from it—a Diogenes, without a tub and usually with an unearned income, who can find nothing good in the civilization, which secures him so much leisure to abuse it. Him I do not despise—often he is very amusing—but I do resent a little his airs of superiority. During the war he was usually a pacifist. If he went to prison, well and good; his rebellion was practical; and it is clear that, if there were enough of such practical rebels whenever a war broke out, there would soon be no more wars. That is the logic of the pacifist who is ready to suffer for his pacifism; and it makes militarists very angry because they have no answer to it. But there were other irreconcilable pacifists above military age who were not, I think, consistent in their rebellion against society; because, while they abused it for the war which only its permanent iniquities made possible, they continued to enjoy an unearned income which also was made possible only by those iniquities. You may, practically, rebel against war as the particular iniquity which needs most to be resisted at the moment; that is

*From the book *Essays on Life* (pp. 146–53) by A. Clutton-Brock. Published by Methuen & Co. Ltd., London, and E. P. Dutton & Co., Inc. New York (1925) and used with their permission. This is a charming little book, unfortunately little known, which may be recommended to all lovers of good writing and good sense, as well as all lovers of wisdom. Compare with selection 22.

what the C.O. did, and suffered for it; but you have no right to a theoretic and Platonic rebellion against war if you are not also a pacifist where your own private interests are concerned. For the pacifist position, if consistent, is not only against war; it is against every kind of force—against the policeman as well as the soldier; and a well-to-do pacifist ought not to employ the policeman to protect his property. This, you may say, is going too far; but the pacifist, who objects to war on principle, prides himself on going as far as possible. He cannot deny that war may be an attempt to do justice by force; his position is that justice ought never to use force; therefore he ought never to employ a policeman, nor ought he to profit by the existence of the police, even if he finds no occasion to employ them. That is to say, if he has any private property of his own, he ought to give it up; for, as long as he keeps it, he is consenting to the iniquity of our society which employs force so that some people may live on the labour of others.

I am not condemning the theoretic pacifist because he is not entirely consistent in his actions—nobody is. What I do condemn is the satisfaction he gets from the contemplation of his own theoretic consistency, which remains easy because it is theoretic. He lives permanently, I think, in that state of delusion to which we are all subject at times—the delusion that we are spectators and judges of life, whereas, in fact, we are necessarily actors in it. To him our society is a kind of performance which he has paid to watch, and he thinks very poorly of it; he can imagine a much better entertainment and can perhaps even sketch it on paper. But, really, he has paid no money to watch it; nor is he watching it; he is, whether he will or no, playing his own part in it, like all the rest of us; and he has no right to judge and condemn it. If there are iniquities, he is as much responsible for them as most other people; and he cannot escape from that responsibility by feeling angry or superior. The first difficulty of civilization, the chief obstacle to human progress, is the fact that the mass of ordinary, decent, human beings are so busy with their own work, which has to be done, or there would be an end of our society altogether, that they have little energy to consider or promote general reforms. We have more need of intellectual than of material capital—that is to say, of a surplus of mental energy which shall look beyond the needs of the day, shall discover the truth about things, and shall apply it to the common good; but intellectual capital is at present much rarer than material. My quarrel with the theoretic irreconcilable is that he pretends to be an intellectual capitalist; but, if he has any intellectual capital, he wastes it in mere abuse. I do not ask him to sell all that he has and give to the poor; but I do maintain that, if he condemns our society and all who consent to it, he ought, at least, to spend the leisure which that society allows him in a serious attempt to discover a remedy for it. It would be a dull and laborious task, perhaps; but, if he prefers an amusing life, then he gets his amusement from society as it is, and he has no right to abuse it. Above all, he has no right to pride himself upon his theoretic consistency if, in practice, he remains utterly inconsistent.

Perhaps you will say that in all this I am attacking a figment of my own, there are very few of these theoretic irreconcilables, and that they matter very little. But, in fact, we all have a tendency to be theoretic irreconcilables, and our books and newspapers are full of Platonic rebellion. It is one of the ways in which we waste our intellectual capital and our moral energy. We all, for instance, talk about the prevailing ugliness; but we spend little money or thought in trying to mitigate it. The mere talk makes us feel that we have superior taste; and the world is full of people with superior taste, while our streets and our homes remain as ugly as ever. Again, we complain of the state of the press, which indeed is a public danger; but we ourselves read the newspapers we despise; and, while we abuse them, our opinions, our tastes, our whole view of life even, is perverted by them. In theory we are not to be reconciled to the press; in practice it lives on us. We pay ourselves with words and consume our energy in a rebellion which ends in mere irritability.

This irritability produces no change and merely lessens our own happiness. If we would be happier and less confused in our minds, we ought, I think, to ask ourselves what is our real attitude to the present state of society. Do we consent to it, or do we not? Is it to us the best that can be contrived, human beings, including ourselves, being what they are; or is it a damnable corruption and perversion of what should, and might, be? We ought to come to a decision on this point and then act on our decision. I do not say what our decision ought to be; that is a point for each individual, and not an easy one. Our society is full of delightful people and things, and of useful and promising institutions. It may be that it suffers only from the defects of its qualities. But, if that is so, why flatter yourself that you are superior to it? Why rebel in theory when you do not rebel in practice? For, so long as you accept it in action and in fact, you are helping to make it what it is. You are like the shareholder of a railway who complains that it is incompetent and oppressive both to the public and to its own servants, yet continues to draw his dividends. Or you are like that gentleman in Ibsen's play who went about upholding the banner of the Ideal, which meant saying, Ugh! Ugh! to anything that was done. Society is made by what is done, not by saying, Ugh! Ugh! and so long as we get our living by what is done, we ourselves are doing it. If we are uneasy in our consciences about it all, we cannot ease them by saying, Ugh! Ugh! We may get a momentary relief that way, but we cannot attain to happiness. Happiness, when youth is past, comes of a conviction that the order of the universe is rational; and we can attain to that only by behaving rationally ourselves. But theoretic rebellion, with practical submission, is not rational; the two together only make us peevish, and the best we can do with our peevishness is to express it in epigrams, which are like fireworks; they drive no wheels and do not even burn the house down. You may be happy if you decide that society is, on the whole, good, and that you will enjoy it without doing harm to your neighbours—that is the attitude of much delightful comedy. Or you may be happy if you decide that society is bad, and that you will give your life to changing it. But you cannot be happy if the theoretic half of you rebels and the practical part consents; for then your whole life is a makeshift, and your grumbling at society is really a grumbling at yourself for putting up with it. You nag; but the nagging is within you; there is a cat-and-dog life in your own soul, an expense of spirit in a waste of shame; for all the while you are ashamed of yourself for this contrast and conflict between the theoretical and practical parts of you. You may grow used to your shame, but, if you do, you grow used to unhappiness, and that is failure indeed. We all envy, even while we rail at, the great, boisterous, successful men of the world; but they are wiser than we are. They have consented to our society, and they get their strength, their high spirits even, from their consent. We look to see them put to shame and brought to naught; but they are not. They have their own notion of reality and act upon it; hence their energy, whether for good or for evil. We have no right to think ourselves superior to them merely because of an internal conflict which robs us of energy; if we would be superior to them, we must be saints, at one with ourselves, like them, but in the practical refusal of all that they value.

## 22

# On Self-Respect*

## JOAN DIDION
(1934-    )

Once, in a dry season, I wrote in large letters across two pages of a notebook that innocence ends when one is stripped of the delusion that one likes oneself. Although now, some years later, I marvel that a mind on the outs with itself should have nonetheless made painstaking record of its every tremor, I recall with embarrassing clarity the flavor of those particular ashes. It was a matter of misplaced self-respect.

I had not been elected to Phi Beta Kappa. This failure could scarcely have been more predictable or less ambiguous (I simply did not have the grades), but I was unnerved by it; I had somehow thought myself a kind of academic Raskolnikov, curiously exempt from the cause-effect relationships which hampered others. Although even the humorless nineteen-year-old that I was must have recognized that the situation lacked real tragic stature, the day that I did not make Phi Beta Kappa nonetheless marked the end of something, and innocence may well be the word for it. I lost the conviction that lights would always turn green for me, the pleasant certainty that those rather passive virtues which had won me approval as a child automatically guaranteed me not only Phi Beta Kappa keys but happiness, honor, and the love of a good man; lost a certain touching faith in the totem power of good manners, clean hair, and proven competence on the Stanford-Binet scale. To such doubtful amulets had my self-respect been pinned, and I faced myself that day with the nonplused apprehension of someone who has come across a vampire and has no crucifix at hand.

Although to be driven back upon oneself is an uneasy affair at best, rather like trying to cross a border with borrowed credentials, it seems to me

*Reprinted with the permission of Farrar, Straus & Giroux, Inc. from *Slouching Towards Bethlehem* by Joan Didion, Copyright © 1961, 1968 by Joan Didion; and by permission of André Deutsch Ltd., London. Compare with selections 12 and 21.

now the one condition necessary to the beginnings of real self-respect. Most of our platitudes notwithstanding, self-deception remains the most difficult deception. The tricks that work on others count for nothing in that very well-lit back alley where one keeps assignations with oneself: no winning smiles will do here, no prettily drawn lists of good intentions. One shuffles flashily but in vain through one's marked cards—the kindness done for the wrong reason, the apparent triumph which involved no real effort, the seemingly heroic act into which one had been shamed. The dismal fact is that self-respect has nothing to do with the approval of others—who are, after all, deceived easily enough; has nothing to do with reputation, which, as Rhett Butler told Scarlett O'Hara, is something people with courage can do without.

To do without self-respect, on the other hand, is to be an unwilling audience of one to an interminable documentary that details one's failings, both real and imagined, with fresh footage spliced in for every screening. *There's the glass you broke in anger, there's the hurt on X's face; watch now, this next scene, the night Y came back from Houston, see how you muff this one.* To live without self-respect is to lie awake some night, beyond the reach of warm milk, phenobarbital, and the sleeping hand on the coverlet, counting up the sins of commission and omission, the trusts betrayed, the promises subtly broken, the gifts irrevocably wasted through sloth or cowardice or carelessness. However long we postpone it, we eventually lie down alone in that notoriously uncomfortable bed, the one we make ourselves. Whether or not we sleep in it depends, of course, on whether or not we respect ourselves.

To protest that some fairly improbable people, some people who *could not possibly respect themselves,* seem to sleep easily enough is to miss the point entirely, as surely as those people miss it who think that self-respect has necessarily to do with not having safety pins in one's underwear. There is a common superstition that "self-respect" is a kind of charm against snakes, something that keeps those who have it locked in some unblighted Eden, out of strange beds, ambivalent conversations, and trouble in general. It does not at all. It has nothing to do with the face of things, but concerns instead a separate peace, a private reconciliation. Although the careless, suicidal Julian English in *Appointment in Samarra* and the careless, incurably dishonest Jordan Baker in *The Great Gatsby* seem equally improbable candidates for self-respect, Jordan Baker had it, Julian English did not. With that genius for accommodation more often seen in women than in men, Jordan took her own measure, made her own peace, avoided threats to that peace: "I hate careless people," she told Nick Carraway. "It takes two to make an accident."

Like Jordan Baker, people with self-respect have the courage of their mistakes. They know the price of things. If they choose to commit adultery, they do not then go running, in an access of bad conscience, to receive absolution from the wronged parties; nor do they complain unduly of the unfairness, the undeserved embarrassment, of being named co-respondent. In brief, people with self-respect exhibit a certain toughness, a kind of moral nerve; they display what was once called *character,* a quality which, although approved in the abstract, sometimes loses ground to other, more instantly negotiable virtues. The measure of its slipping prestige is that one tends to think of it only in connection with homely children and United States senators who have been defeated, preferably in the primary, for reelection. Nonetheless, character—the willingness to accept responsibility for one's own life—is the source from which self-respect springs.

Self-respect is something that our grandparents, whether or not they had it, knew all about. They had instilled in them, young, a certain discipline, the sense that one lives by doing things one does not particularly want to do, by putting fears and doubts to one side, by weighing immediate comforts against the possibility of larger, even intangible, comforts. It seemed to the nineteenth century admirable, but not remarkable, that Chinese Gordon put on a clean white suit and held Khartoum against the Mahdi; it did not seem unjust that the way to free land in California involved death and difficulty and dirt. In a diary kept during the winter of 1846, an emigrating twelve-year-old named Narcissa Cornwall noted coolly: "Father was busy reading and did not notice that the house was being filled with strange Indians until Mother spoke about it." Even lacking any clue as to what Mother said, one can scarcely fail to be impressed by the entire incident: the father reading, the Indians filing in, the mother choosing the words that would not alarm, the child duly recording the event and noting further that those particular Indians were not, "fortunately for us," hostile. Indians were simply part of the *donnée.*

In one guise or another, Indians always are. Again, it is a question of recognizing that anything worth having has its price. People who respect themselves are willing to accept the risk that the Indians will be hostile, that the venture will go bankrupt, that the liaison may not turn out to be one in which *every day is a holiday because you're married to me.* They are willing to invest something of themselves; they may not play at all, but when they do play, they know the odds.

That kind of self-respect is a discipline, a habit of mind that can never be faked but can be developed, trained, coaxed forth. It was once suggested to me that, as an antidote to crying, I put my head in a paper bag. As it happens, there is a sound physiological reason, something to do with oxygen, for doing exactly that, but the psychological effect alone is incalculable: it is difficult in the extreme to continue fancying oneself Cathy in *Wuthering Heights* with one's head in a Food Fair bag. There is a similar case for all the small disciplines, unimportant in themselves; imagine maintaining any kind of swoon, commiserative or carnal, in a cold shower.

But those small disciplines are valuable only insofar as they represent larger ones. To say that Waterloo was won on the playing fields of Eton is not to say that Napoleon might have been saved by a crash program in cricket; to give formal dinners in the rain forest would be pointless did not the candlelight flickering on the liana call forth deeper, stronger disciplines, values instilled long before. It is a kind of ritual helping us to remember who and what we are. In order to remember it, one must have known it.

To have that sense of one's intrinsic worth which constitutes self-respect is potentially to have everything: the ability to discriminate, to love and to remain indifferent. To lack it is to be locked within oneself, paradoxically incapable of either love or indifference. If we do not respect ourselves, we are on the one hand forced to despise those who have so few resources as to consort with us, so little perception as to remain blind to our fatal weaknesses. On the other, we are peculiarly in thrall to everyone we see, curiously determined to live out—since our self-image is untenable—their false notions of us. We flatter ourselves by thinking this compulsion to please others an attractive trait: a gist for imaginative empathy, evidence of our willingness to give. *Of course* I will play Francesca to your Paolo, Helen Keller to anyone's Annie Sullivan: no expectation is too misplaced, no role too ludicrous. At the mercy of those we cannot but hold in contempt, we play roles doomed to failure before they are begun, each defeat generating fresh despair at the urgency of divining and meeting the next demand made upon us.

It is the phenomenon sometimes called "alienation from self." In its advanced stages, we no longer answer the telephone, because someone might want something; that we could say *no* without drowning in self-reproach is an idea alien to this game. Every encounter demands too much, tears the nerves, drains the will, and the specter of something as small as an unanswered letter arouses such disproportionate guilt that answering it becomes out of the question. To assign unanswered letters their proper weight, to free us from the expectations of others, to give us back to ourselves—there lies the great, the singular power of self-respect. Without it, one eventually discovers the final turn of the screw: one runs away to find oneself, and finds no one at home.

# STATEMENTS ON MORALITY
## *Fifth Series*

*32. The recognition of any end or authority going beyond what is embodied in existing customs, involves some appeal to thought, and moral theory makes this appeal more explicit and more complete. If a child asks why he should tell the truth, and is answered, "because you ought to and that is reason enough"; or, "because it will prove profitable for you to do so"; or "because truth-telling is a condition of mutual communication and common aims," the answer implies a principle which requires only to be made explicit to be full-fledged theory. And when this principle is compared with those employed in other cases to see if they are mutually consistent; and if not, to find a still more fundamental reconciling principle, we have passed over the border into ethical system.*

John Dewey and James Tufts (1908)

*33. The first thing to learn in intercourse with others is non-interference with their own peculiar ways of being happy, provided those ways do not assume to interfere by violence with ours. No one has insight into all the ideals. No one should presume to judge them off-hand. The pretension to dogmatize about them in each other is the root of most human injustices and cruelties, and the trait in human character most likely to make the angels weep.*

William James (1900)

*34. Law, justice, rights, these are all human notions made necessary by human imperfection; and all of them consent to that imperfection. There is a contract, a bargain, implied in all of them; but Christianity tells us to exact no contract or bargain. If we have a duty towards men, it is not because they do their duty towards us; rather the proper aim of the Christian is to rise above the sense of duty, and to do all things from the motive of love, to rise in fact, into a higher state of nature in which he will not need the artifice of duty to guide him.*

A. Clutton-Brock (1925)

*35. In love, as in everything else, Stendhal was not a selfish man (that is to say, a man who seeks to satisfy his desires at whatever cost to others) but an egoist (that is, a man whose primary interest is not in persons or objects outside himself but in his own thoughts and feelings). To a selfish or a proud man, triumph is pleasant and defeat painful, but to an egoist, both are equally interesting, for what matters is not the content of the experience but the fact that it is* his, *and he is always making little experiments with himself and others, less out of desire than out of curiosity to see what will happen.*

W. H. Auden, in *The New Yorker* (1954)

*36. It is not easy—perhaps not even desirable—to judge other people by a consistent standard. Conduct obnoxious, even unbearable, in one person may be readily tolerated in another; apparently indispensable principles of behaviour are in practice relaxed—not always with impunity—in the interest of those whose nature seems to demand an exceptional measure.*

Anthony Powell (1951)

*37. Even in the purely personal realm, Kant's categorical imperative, if taken to mean, Treat every man alike as a human unit, needs to be supplemented by the polar command, Treat every man (including yourself) as unique. Mephistopheles refers to Faust as the doctor, but the Lord calls him by his individual name.*

Morris R. Cohen (1939)

*38. A* right *of private vengeance is an impossibility; for, just so far as the vengeance is private, the individual in executing it is exercising a power not derived from society nor regulated by reference to social good, and such a power is not a right. . . . In a state of things in which private vengeance for hurts inflicted was the universal practice, there could be no rights at all.*

T. H. Green (1882)

*39. In matters of morality most of us are utilitarians: we hold a man responsible for consequences of his acts irrespective of whether what happened is what he intended. For us, good will is not enough.*

Editorial, *Science* (1958)

*40. Kant gives as an illustration of the working of the categorical imperative that it is wrong to borrow money, because if we all tried to do so there would be no money left to borrow.*

Bertrand Russell (1945)

*41. The mistake of the utilitarians was not that they considered consequences, but that they only considered some consequences (namely pleasures), and considered nothing else but consequences. We must also consider the antecedents. Whether I ought to initiate a certain change in a given situation depends upon what that situation is. Whether I ought to pay a sum of money to A or B depends not only upon whether A's or B's possession of it will result in more pleasure, but on whether A or B is my creditor, my government, my parent, my benefactor or a stranger, and upon how they and I have behaved in the past.*

E. F. Carritt (1928)

42.  *But who ever thought, cried Kysarcius, of lying with his grandmother?—The young gentleman, replied Yorick, whom Selden speaks of—who not only thought of it, but justified his intention to his father by the argument drawn from the law of retaliation.—"You lay, Sir, with my mother," said the lad—"why may not I lie with yours?"*

Lawrence Sterne (1767)

43.  *The notion of morals implies some sentiment common to all mankind, which recommends the same object to general approbation, and makes every man, or most men, agree in the same opinion or decision concerning it. It also implies some sentiment, so universal and comprehensive as to extend to all mankind, and render the actions and conduct, even of the persons the most remote, an object of applause or censure, according as they agree or disagree with that rule of right which is established. . . .*

*When a man denominates another his* enemy, *his* rival, *his* antagonist, *his* adversary, *he is understood to speak the language of self-love, and to express sentiments, peculiar to himself, and arising from his particular circumstances and situation. But when he bestows on any man the epithets of* vicious *or* odious *or* depraved, *he then speaks another language, and expresses sentiments, in which he expects all his audience are to concur with him. He must here, therefore, depart from his private and particular situation, and must choose a point of view, common to him with others; he must move some universal principle of the human frame, and touch a string to which all mankind have an accord and symphony.*

David Hume (1751)

# Part IV

## The Varieties of Moral Skepticism

If we think of a moral theory as presenting a moral test—a test for determining the morality of an act or a practice—the question inevitably arises how such a test can be justified. What basis could there be for it? Can it possibly be established as anything other than a personal opinion, bias, or idiosyncrasy, or a consequence of social pressure or mores? Is any such thing as proof or justification or objective judgment possible in ethics at all? The claim that it is not is the chief assertion of the points of view representing moral skepticism, and it is not possible to avoid some consideration of moral skepticism in dealing with the problem of justification and proof in ethics. But moral skepticism is actually not a unitary thing; it comes not as a whole but only in different varieties. For an adequate understanding of it, therefore, one must consider some of these varieties.

In general, any theory that maintains that there can be no such thing as a good and sufficient reason for a moral judgment, that there are no valid or sound moral arguments, that ultimate moral principles cannot be proved, that moral judgments cannot be true or false or correct or incorrect, that morality has no rational basis, or that the difference between right and wrong is merely a matter of taste, opinion, feeling, convention, or tradition is a form of moral skepticism. From this varied listing it is evident that considerations applicable to one form may not be applicable to another.

Three different forms of moral skepticism are presented in the first three selections in this part: 23 (Paulsen), 24 (Ayer), and 25 (Mackie). The piece by Ayer was first published in 1936 and may be taken as no longer representative of its author's views, but it is still one of the most stimulating and also one of the most widely discussed and reprinted pieces in the whole of moral philosophy. The one by Mackie is not so widely known, yet it presents an interesting variant on Ayer's position, and shows that there are many routes to moral skepticism. The selection by Ayer also briefly describes—only to reject—two other forms of skepticism, varieties of what can be called moral subjectivism. On the one (called personal subjectivism), for one to say that something is right or good is to say that one approves of it, oneself. On the other (called social subjectivism), it is to say that one's society approves of it. These are both distinct from the emotive theory, according to which to say that something is right or good is not literally to *say* anything at all, but merely to express emotion.

Like most writers on this subject, Ayer makes no distinction between moral judgments and value judgments, and uses the expressions interchangeably. The selection by Baier (26) argues that value judgments, contrary to what is often supposed, can be empirically verified; his argument is ingenious; the assiduous reader, however, may find that his argument, whether sound or not, has no immediate application to *moral* judgments. (For this distinction, see the General Introduction, pp. 7–8.)

The most widely known and most influential form of moral skepticism is generally called ethical, or cultural, relativism. It is also, in some ways, the most important, for it alone has practical moral implications and generates moral problems. (See Murphy, selection 29, for arguments on this point.) However, the reader should be aware of a common ambiguity in the expression "ethical relativism." It is occasionally used in a wide sense, as equivalent to moral skepticism generally, but here it is used in a more restricted sense, as a variety of moral skepticism. And, of course, there may be more than one variety of ethical relativism.

The last two pieces in this part, by Lundberg (30) and Rudner (31), amount, when taken together, to a debate on the role of science in values and values in science. If Rudner is right, the problems turn out to be very complex indeed, and also more interesting. And it becomes a matter of some importance to determine if he is right. How, then, can we tell?

# STATEMENTS ON MORALITY

## Sixth Series

*44. "Reason" has a perfectly clear and precise meaning. It signifies the choice of the right means to an end that you wish to achieve. It has nothing whatever to do with the choice of ends. But opponents of reason do not realize this, and think that advocates of rationality want reason to dictate ends as well as means. They have no excuse for this view in the writings of rationalists. There is a famous sentence: "Reason is and ought only to be, the slave of the passions." This sentence does not come from the works of Rousseau or Dostoevsky or Sartre. It comes from David Hume. It expresses a view to which I, like every man who attempts to be reasonable, fully subscribe.*

Bertrand Russell (1954)

*45. The truths of morality must in all ages be the same; the praise of its teachers consists in the ability manifested in their development. A satisfactory development of these truths in morals is far more difficult than in other sciences, for the tenure is exceedingly delicate by which faculties imperfect as ours can long retain such objects in steady view; and it is a sagacious observation . . . that our feelings are never in their natural state when, by a forced revocation of them, we can attentively study their aspects. Its fundamental principles are taught by the moral sense, and no advancement of time or knowledge can improve them.*

Ralph Waldo Emerson (1821)

*46. One important service . . . the anthropological school of moralists have undoubtedly performed. They have finally and completely demolished the whole structure of intuitionism. No one with a sense of humor can maintain the existence of moral intuitions as unerring guides after reading such a catalogue of moral variations as is compiled by the anthropological school.*

Thomas Nixon Carver (1915)

*47. As much as it has been disputed wherein virtue consists, or whatever ground for doubt there may be about particulars, yet, in general, there is in reality an universally acknowledged standard of it. It is that, which all ages and countries have made profession of in public; it is that which every man you meet puts on the show of; it is that which the primary and fundamental laws of all civil constitutions over the face of the earth make it their business and endeavor to enforce the practice of upon mankind, namely, justice, veracity, and regard to common good.*

Joseph Butler (1736)

*48. It is now pretty generally accepted by professional philosophers that ultimate ethical principles must be arbitrary. One cannot derive conclusions about what should be merely from accounts of what is the case; one cannot decide how people ought to behave merely from one's knowledge of how they do behave. To arrive at a conclusion in ethics one must have at least one ethical premiss. And so we can go back, indefinitely but not forever. Sooner or later, we must come to at least one ethical premiss which is not deduced but baldly asserted. Here we must be a-rational; neither rational nor irrational, for here there is no room for reason even to go wrong.*

Brian Medlin (1957)

*49. To behave morally is to behave in the way that society approves. When a person obeys the rules and laws of his society, we say that he is* moral *or* good; *when he disobeys, we say that he is* immoral *or* bad. *We must draw another distinction to cover the individual who because of low intelligence or unfamiliarity with the code sometimes violates it. Such a person is called* amoral (*lacking in morals*) *and is not classed as either good or bad.*

Floyd L. Ruch (1941)

*50. I cannot help thinking that a consciousness of the relativity of values, if it became prevalent, would tend to render people more truly social than would a belief that things have intrinsic and unchangeable values, no matter what the attitude of any one to them may be. If we said that goods, including the right distribution of goods, are relative to specific natures, moral warfare would continue, but not with poisoned arrows.*

George Santayana (1913)

*51. Morality is not to be deduced from anything else; the concept of moral obligation is not to be exhibited as a deduction from a system of the universe. On the contrary, the fact that we know what it is to be morally obliged is a moral datum that must be fitted in, if we are so ambitious as to construct a theory of the universe.*

L. Susan Stebbing (1941)

## 23

## *Moral Nihilism* *
# FRIEDRICH PAULSEN
## (1846–1908)

The distinguishing mark of moral nihilism in concrete, individual cases is a complete absence of conscience both in the form of the consciousness of duty as well as of a life ideal. As a theory or argument it denies the validity of all rules of duty or moral laws. It declares: Duty is an empty word; life is a struggle for existence, and in the struggle for existence all means are permissible. Murder, falsehood, violence, are good provided they are successful; they are merely decried as bad by weaklings and gregarious beings, because these are made to suffer by them. Or: Justice and law and religion were invented by despots to enslave the minds of the oppressed; the enlightened man knows that nothing binds him. And just as there are no duties towards others, there can be no duties towards self. So-called ideals are soap-bubbles to delight children, or intended by clever people to delude the fools. Goodness consists in doing and boldly carrying out what our momentary desires demand. Some one has quoted as the motto of an aristocratic Russian: *Je ne crois rien, je ne crains rien, je n'aime rien;* or, Nothing binds me, neither morals nor duty, neither fear nor hope, neither love nor ideals; the free sovereign individual lives in the moment, regardless of the future as well as the past.

Is it possible to refute nihilism; can we prove to any one who reasons thus that he is in the wrong? I do not believe it. We can tell and show him that others feel differently, but he will answer: What do I care? You may find feelings of duty and ideals in yourselves; in me there is nothing of the kind, and I do not regret it either. If we say to him: That is a defect; a

*From Friedrich Paulsen, *A System of Ethics* (1889), Bk. II, ch. 5, sec. 7, translated from the (4th edition) German by Frank Thilly (New York: Charles Scribner's Sons, 1899), pp. 373–77. Some footnotes have been omitted.

human being capable only of momentary pleasures is a contemptible creature, he will reply: I do not agree with you; on the contrary, he is contemptible who has not the courage to do what he pleases, but lets all kinds of imaginary scruples defraud him of the pleasures of the moment.—This position may be logically maintained. We cannot force the nihilist to confess its falseness; this we could do only in case there were some point of agreement between us, a common regard for that which gives life its value. Without this all reasonings are vain, nay, perhaps evil, because they simply confirm the nihilist, who is in love with his opinions and his own astuteness, in his error. The feeling that he cannot be refuted will simply intensify his conviction that he is in the right. Aristotle did not regard the following hint as superfluous: "It is not necessary to examine every problem or every assertion, but only such about which some one is really in doubt who needs instruction and not punishment or sharpened wits;"—a truth of which the age of paradoxes in which we live also needs to be reminded.[1]

It is quite a different question, however, whether nihilism, which cannot be refuted logically, can be consistently applied in practice, and whether any man really feels that only the satisfaction of momentary desires has worth. Perhaps he believes it, but is mistaken about himself and his own will. Perhaps it will be possible to change him by appealing from his understanding to his will: You really do not mean what you say; in you, too, the impulse of self-preservation exists, as more than a desire to satisfy your momentary cravings; in you, too, there is something of an impulse of ideal self-preservation; it manifests itself when you combat and despise whatever you regard as falsehood and sham. The epitaph of Sardanapalus or of the Count Zaehdarm (in Carlyle's *Sartor Resartus*) would not wholly suit you after all. You are not so indifferent to the welfare of others as you yourself say and imagine. Nay, perhaps your belief that customs and the feeling of duty have no influence over you is a delusion. You may really be convinced of it for the time being; under suitable circumstances you would perhaps discover to your surprise that you still have a conscience. I cannot prove this to you; I cannot force the "ought" into you by means of arguments; but perhaps it is in you without your knowing it.

It is just as impossible to force the nihilist by argument to abandon his position as it is logically to refute a man who denies the existence of the sun in the heavens. But this does not mean that nihilism is a valid theory. We cannot prove to the fever-patient that he sees only hallucinations, or to the madman that his fixed ideas are crazy notions. That does not prevent the

[1] Aristotle, *Topics,* I., 11.

former from being sick or the latter from being crazy. An anthropologist, a biological observer of the genus *homo*—let us assume, in order to insure his perfect impartiality, that he has descended from Saturn to the earth, as in Voltaire's *Mikromegas*—would soon convince himself that a man really living according to the principles of moral nihilism was abnormal. He would say: He lacks an organ which is usually present, namely, conscience. And he would add: It seems to be an organ of some importance, for individuals in whom it is lacking invariably perish. And if he were to investigate more closely, he would perhaps find that, as a rule, such abnormal natures at the same time exhibit dangerous perversions of impulse; alcoholism and perverse sexual desires, which are often hereditary, are the usual concomitants or the causes of such perverse feelings and volitions. The usual consequences of the disease, however, he might say, are disgust with life, and suicide.[2] Only in case the abnormal feelings are not the result of organic conditions, but of intellectual error, of half-truths, can the diagnosis be more favorable. Here a more thorough knowledge, based upon wider experience, new problems of life, and advancing age may lead to the removal of the erroneous views and consequently to a change of feeling and volition.

---

[2] Some psychiatrists regard "moral insanity" as a peculiar form of disease. It is characterized by a complete lack of conscience. Krafft-Ebing (*Lehrbuch der Psychiatrie*, II., 65) describes the disease as complete *moral insensibility*. Moral notions and judgments are apprehended by the understanding and the memory, but they have absolutely no feeling-accompaniments, and are therefore wholly incapable of moving the will. "Without interest in anything that is noble and beautiful, dead to all feeling, these unfortunate malformations show a woeful lack of filial and domestic love, of all social instincts, indifference to the weal and woe of their surroundings. They are utterly insensible to the moral approval or disapproval of their fellows, wholly devoid of feelings of conscience and remorse. They do not know what morality means; the law they look upon merely as a police regulation, and the most heinous crime they view about as an ethically sound person would regard the violation of a police ordinance. This defect renders such inferior beings incapable of living permanently in society and makes them fit candidates for the workhouse, insane asylum, or penitentiary.—Besides this lack of ethical, altruistic feelings, they manifest formal affective derangement, great emotional irritability, which in conjunction with the absence of moral feelings impels them to acts of great brutality and cruelty." On the other hand, these patients seem to be unaffected *intellectually*, if we regard formal logical thought, prudence, action according to plan, as decisive. Hallucinations and illusions are absent. Still, intellectual degeneracy is never entirely lacking. "Not only are they ignorant of what is immoral, but they do not even know what is detrimental to their interests. In spite of all evidence of shrewdness they often surprise us by their total disregard of the simplest rules of prudence in their criminal acts. On the formal side, we must especially emphasize the defective way in which they reproduce ideas." Finally, perverse impulses are common in the organic and particularly in the sexual sphere.

# 24

## The Emotive Theory
## of Ethics*

### A. J. AYER
(1910–    )

There is still one objection to be met before we can claim to have justified our view that all synthetic propositions are empirical hypotheses. This objection is based on the common supposition that our speculative knowledge is of two distinct kinds—that which relates to questions of empirical fact, and that which relates to questions of value. It will be said that "statements of value" are genuine synthetic propositions, but that they cannot with any show of justice be represented as hypotheses, which are used to predict the course of our sensations; and, accordingly, that the existence of ethics and aesthetics as branches of speculative knowledge presents an insuperable objection to our radical empiricist thesis.

In face of this objection, it is our business to give an account of "judgements of value" which is both satisfactory in itself and consistent with our general empiricist principles. We shall set ourselves to show that in so far as statements of value are significant, they are ordinary "scientific" statements; and that in so far as they are not scientific, they are not in the literal sense significant, but are simply expressions of emotion which can be neither true nor false. In maintaining this view, we may confine ourselves for the present to the case of ethical statements. What is said about them will be found to apply, *mutatis mutandis,* to the case of aesthetic statements also.[1]

The ordinary system of ethics, as elaborated in the works of ethical philosophers, is very far from being a homogeneous whole. Not only is it

*From A. J. Ayer, *Language, Truth and Logic* (London: Victor Gollancz Ltd, 1936; 2nd ed., 1946), ch. 6. The title of this selection has been supplied by the editor. Compare selection 26 and statement 49.
[1]The argument that follows should be read in conjunction with the Introduction, pp. 20–2 [not reprinted in this collection].

apt to contain pieces of metaphysics, and analyses of non-ethical concepts: its actual ethical contents are themselves of very different kinds. We may divide them, indeed, into four main classes. There are, first of all, propositions which express definitions of ethical terms, or judgements about the legitimacy or possibility of certain definitions. Secondly, there are propositions describing the phenomena of moral experience, and their causes. Thirdly, there are exhortations to moral virtue. And, lastly, there are actual ethical judgements. It is unfortunately the case that the distinction between these four classes, plain as it is, is commonly ignored by ethical philosophers; with the result that it is often very difficult to tell from their works what it is that they are seeking to discover or prove.

In fact, it is easy to see that only the first of our four classes, namely that which comprises the propositions relating to the definitions of ethical terms, can be said to constitute ethical philosophy. The propositions which describe the phenomena of moral experience, and their causes, must be assigned to the science of psychology, or sociology. The exhortations to moral virtue are not propositions at all, but ejaculations or commands which are designed to provoke the reader to action of a certain sort. Accordingly, they do not belong to any branch of philosophy or science. As for the expressions of ethical judgements, we have not yet determined how they should be classified. But inasmuch as they are certainly neither definitions nor comments upon definitions, nor quotations, we may say decisively that they do not belong to ethical philosophy. A strictly philosophical treatise on ethics should therefore make no ethical pronouncements. But it should, by giving an analysis of ethical terms, show what is the category to which all such pronouncements belong. And this is what we are now about to do.

A question which is often discussed by ethical philosophers is whether it is possible to find definitions which would reduce all ethical terms to one or two fundamental terms. But this question, though it undeniably belongs to ethical philosophy, is not relevant to our present enquiry. We are not now concerned to discover which term, within the sphere of ethical terms, is to be taken as fundamental; whether, for example, "good" can be defined in terms of "right" or "right" in terms of "good," or both in terms of "value." What we are interested in is the possibility of reducing the whole sphere of ethical terms to non-ethical terms. We are enquiring whether statements of ethical value can be translated into statements of empirical fact.

That they can be so translated is the contention of those ethical philosophers who are commonly called subjectivists, and of those who are known as utilitarians. For the utilitarian defines the rightness of actions, and the goodness of ends, in terms of the pleasure, or happiness, or satisfaction, to which they give rise; the subjectivist, in terms of the feelings of approval which a certain person, or group of people, has towards them. Each of these types of definition makes moral judgements into a sub-class of psychological or sociological judgements; and for this reason they are very attractive to us. For, if either was correct, it would follow that ethical assertions were not generically different from the factual assertions which are ordinarily contrasted with them; and the account which we have already given of empirical hypotheses would apply to them also.

Nevertheless we shall not adopt either a subjectivist or a utilitarian analysis of ethical terms. We reject the subjectivist view that to call an action right, or a thing good, is to say that it is generally approved of, because it is not self-contradictory to assert that some actions which are generally approved of are not right, or that some things which are generally approved of are not good. And we reject the alternative subjectivist view that a man who asserts that a certain action is right, or that a certain thing is good, is saying that he himself approves of it, on the ground that a man who confessed that he sometimes approved of what was bad or wrong would not be contradicting himself. And a similar argument is fatal to utilitarianism. We cannot agree that to call an action right is to say that of all the actions possible in the circumstances it would cause, or be likely to cause, the greatest happiness, or the greatest balance of pleasure over pain, or the greatest balance of satisfied over unsatisfied desire, because we find that it is not self-contradictory to say that it is sometimes wrong to perform the action which would actually or probably cause the greatest happiness, or the greatest balance of pleasure over pain, or of satisfied over unsatisfied desire. And since it is not self-contradictory to say that some pleasant things are not good, or that some bad things are desired, it cannot be the case that the sentence "$x$ is good" is equivalent to "$x$ is pleasant," or to "$x$ is desired." And to every other variant of utilitarianism with which I am acquainted the same objection can be made. And therefore we should, I think, conclude that the validity of ethical judgements is not determined by the felicific tendencies of actions, any more than by the nature of people's feelings; but that it must be regarded as "absolute" or "intrinsic," and not empirically calculable.

If we say this, we are not, of course, denying that it is possible to invent a language in which all ethical symbols are definable in non-ethical terms, or even that it is desirable to invent such a language and adopt it in place of our own; what we are denying is that the suggested reduction of ethical to non-ethical statements is consistent with the conventions of our actual language. That is, we reject utilitarianism and subjectivism, not as proposals to replace our existing ethical notions by new ones, but as analyses of our existing ethical notions. Our contention is simply that, in our language, sentences which contain normative ethical symbols are not equivalent to sentences which express psychological propositions, or indeed empirical propositions of any kind.

It is advisable here to make it plain that it is only normative ethical symbols, and not descriptive ethical symbols, that are held by us to be indefinable in factual terms. There is a danger of confusing these two types of symbols, because they are commonly constituted by signs of the same sensible form. Thus a complex sign of the form "x is wrong" may constitute a sentence which expresses a moral judgement concerning a certain type of conduct, or it may constitute a sentence which states that a certain type of conduct is repugnant to the moral sense of a particular society. In the latter case, the symbol "wrong" is a descriptive ethical symbol, and the sentence in which it occurs expresses an ordinary sociological proposition; in the former case, the symbol "wrong" is a normative ethical symbol, and the sentence in which it occurs does not, we maintain, express an empirical proposition at all. It is only with normative ethics that we are at present concerned; so that whenever ethical symbols are used in the course of this argument without qualification, they are always to be interpreted as symbols of the normative type.

In admitting that normative ethical concepts are irreducible to empirical concepts, we seem to be leaving the way clear for the "absolutist" view of ethics—that is, the view that statements of value are not controlled by observation, as ordinary empirical propositions are, but only by a mysterious "intellectual intuition." A feature of this theory, which is seldom recognized by its advocates, is that it makes statements of value unverifiable. For it is notorious that what seems intuitively certain to one person may seem doubtful, or even false, to another. So that unless it is possible to provide some criterion by which one may decide between conflicting intuitions, a mere appeal to intuition is worthless as a test of a proposition's validity. But in the case of moral judgements, no such criterion can be given. Some moralists claim to settle the matter by saying that they "know" that their own moral judgements are correct. But such an assertion is of purely psychological interest, and has not the slightest tendency to prove the validity of any moral judgement. For dissentient moralists may equally well "know" that their ethical views are correct. And, as far as subjective certainty goes, there will be nothing to choose between them. When such differences of opinion arise in connection with an ordinary empirical proposition, one may attempt to resolve them by referring to, or actually carrying out, some relevant empirical test. But with regard to ethical statements, there is, on the "absolutist" or "intuitionist" theory, no relevant empirical test. We are therefore justified in saying that on this theory ethical statements are held to be unverifiable. They are, of course, also held to be genuine synthetic propositions.

Considering the use which we have made of the principle that a synthetic proposition is significant only if it is empirically verifiable, it is clear that the acceptance of an "absolutist" theory of ethics would undermine the whole of our main argument. And as we have already rejected the "naturalistic" theories which are commonly supposed to provide the only alternative to "absolutism" in ethics, we seem to have reached a difficult position. We shall meet the difficulty by showing that the correct treatment of ethical statements is afforded by a third theory, which is wholly compatible with our radical empiricism.

We begin by admitting that the fundamental ethical concepts are unanalysable, inasmuch as there is no criterion by which one can test the validity of the judgements in which they occur. So far we are in agreement with the absolutists. But, unlike the absolutists, we are able to give an explanation of this fact about ethical concepts. We say that the reason why they are unanalysable is that they are mere pseudo-concepts. The presence of an ethical symbol in a proposition adds nothing to its factual content. Thus if I say to someone, "You acted wrongly in stealing that money," I am not stating anything more than if I had simply said, "You stole that money." In adding that this action is wrong I am not making any further statement about it. I am simply evincing my moral disapproval of it. It is as if I had said, "You stole that money," in a peculiar tone of horror, or written it with the addition of some special exclamation marks. The tone, or the exclamation marks, adds nothing to the literal meaning of the sentence. It merely serves to show that the expression of it is attended by certain feelings in the speaker.

If now I generalise my previous statement and say, "Stealing money is wrong," I produce a sentence which has no factual meaning—that is, expresses no proposition which can be either true or false. It is as if I had written "Stealing money!!"—where the shape and thickness of the exclamation marks show, by a suitable convention, that a special sort of moral disapproval is the feeling which is being expressed. It is clear that there is nothing said here which can be true or false. Another man may disagree with me about the wrongness of stealing, in the sense that he may not have the same feelings about stealing as I have, and he may quarrel with me on account of my moral sentiments. But he cannot, strictly speaking, contradict me. For in saying that a certain type of action is right or wrong, I am not making any factual statement, not even a statement about my own state of mind. I am merely expressing certain moral sentiments. And the man who is ostensibly contradicting me is merely expressing his moral sentiments. So that there is plainly no sense in asking which of us is in the right. For neither of us is asserting a genuine proposition.

What we have just been saying about the symbol "wrong" applies to all normative ethical symbols. Sometimes they occur in sentences which record ordinary empirical facts besides expressing ethical feeling about those facts: sometimes they occur in sentences which simply express ethical feeling about a certain type of action, or situation, without making any statement of fact. But in every case in which one would commonly be said to be making an ethical judgement, the function of the relevant ethical word is purely "emotive." It is used to express feeling about certain objects, but not to make any assertion about them.

It is worth mentioning that ethical terms do not serve only to express feeling. They are calculated also to arouse feeling, and so to stimulate action. Indeed some of them are used in such a way as to give the sentences in which they occur the effect of commands. Thus the sentence "It is your duty to tell the truth" may be regarded both as the expression of a certain sort of ethical feeling about truthfulness and as the expression of the command "Tell the truth." The sentence "You ought to tell the truth" also involves the command "Tell the truth," but here the tone of the command is less emphatic. In the sentence "It is good to tell the truth" the command has become little more than a suggestion. And thus the "meaning" of the word "good," in its ethical usage, is differentiated from that of the word "duty" or the word "ought." In fact we may define the meaning of the various ethical words in terms both of the different feelings they are ordinarily taken to express, and also the different responses which they are calculated to provoke.

We can now see why it is impossible to find a criterion for determining the validity of ethical judgements. It is not because they have an "absolute" validity which is mysteriously independent of ordinary sense-experience, but because they have no objective validity whatsoever. If a sentence makes no statement at all, there is obviously no sense in asking whether what it says is true or false. And we have seen that sentences which simply express moral judgements do not say anything. They are pure expressions of feeling and as such do not come under the category of truth and falsehood. They are unverifiable for the same reason as a cry of pain or a word of command is unverifiable—because they do not express genuine propositions.

Thus, although our theory of ethics might fairly be said to be radically subjectivist, it differs in a very important respect from the orthodox subjectivist theory. For the orthodox subjectivist does not deny, as we do, that the sentences of a moralizer express genuine propositions. All he denies is that they express propositions of a unique non-empirical character. His own view is that they express propositions about the speaker's feelings. If this were so, ethical judgements clearly would be capable of being true or false. They would be true if the speaker had the relevant feelings, and false if he had not. And this is a matter which is, in principle, empirically verifiable. Furthermore they could be significantly contradicted. For if I say, "Tolerance is a virtue," and someone answers, "You don't approve of it," he would, on the ordinary subjectivist theory, be contradicting me. On our theory, he would not be contradicting me, because, in saying that tolerance was a virtue, I should not be making any statement about my own feelings or about anything else. I should simply be evincing my feelings, which is not at all the same thing as saying that I have them.

The distinction between the expression of feeling and the assertion of feeling is complicated by the fact that the assertion that one has a certain feeling often accompanies the expression of that feeling, and is then, indeed, a factor in the expression of that feeling. Thus I may simultaneously express boredom and say that I am bored, and in that case my utterance of the words, "I am bored," is one of the circumstances which make it true to say that I am expressing or evincing boredom. But I can express boredom without actually saying that I am bored. I can express it by my tone and gestures, while making a statement about something wholly unconnected with it, or by an ejaculation, or without uttering any words at all. So that even if the assertion that one has a certain feeling always involves the expression of that feeling, the expression of a feeling assuredly does not always involve the assertion that one has it. And this is the important point to grasp in considering the distinction between our theory and the ordinary subjectivist theory. For whereas the subjectivist holds that ethical statements actually assert the existence of certain feelings, we hold that ethical statements are expressions and excitants of feeling which do not necessarily involve any assertions.

We have already remarked that the main objection to the ordinary subjectivist theory is that the validity of ethical judgements is not determined by the nature of their author's feelings. And this is an objection which our theory escapes. For it does not imply that the existence of any feelings is a necessary and sufficient condition of the validity of an ethical judgement. It implies, on the contrary, that ethical judgements have no validity.

There is, however, a celebrated argument against subjectivist theories which our theory does not escape. It has been pointed out by Moore that if ethical statements were simply statements about the speaker's feelings, it would be impossible to argue about questions of value.[2] To take a typical example: if a man said that thrift was a virtue, and another replied that it was a vice, they would not, on this theory, be disputing with one another. One would be saying that he approved of thrift, and the other that *he* didn't; and there is no reason why both these statements should not be true. Now Moore held it to be obvious that we do dispute about questions of value, and accordingly concluded that the particular form of subjectivism which he was discussing was false.

It is plain that the conclusion that it is impossible to dispute about questions of value follows from our theory also. For as we hold that such sentences as "Thrift is a virtue" and "Thrift is a vice" do not express propositions at all, we clearly cannot hold that they express incompatible propositions. We must therefore admit that if Moore's argument really refutes the ordinary subjectivist theory, it also refutes ours. But, in fact, we deny that it does refute even the ordinary subjectivist theory. For we hold that one really never does dispute about questions of value.

This may seem, at first sight, to be a very paradoxical assertion. For we certainly do engage in disputes which are ordinarily regarded as disputes about questions of value. But, in all such cases, we find, if we consider the matter closely, that the dispute is not really about a question of value, but about a question of fact. When someone disagrees with us about the moral value of a certain action or type of action, we do admittedly resort to argument in order to win him over to our way of thinking. But we do not attempt to show by our arguments that he has the "wrong" ethical feeling towards a situation whose nature he has correctly apprehended. What we attempt to show is that he is mistaken about the facts of the case. We argue that he has misconceived the agent's motive: or that he has misjudged the effects of the action, or its probable effects in view of the agent's knowledge; or that he has failed to take into account the special circumstances in which the agent was placed. Or else we employ more general arguments about the effects which actions of a certain type tend to produce, or the qualities which are usually manifested in their performance. We do this in the hope that we have only to get our opponent to agree with us about the nature of the empirical facts for him to adopt the same moral attitude towards them as we do. And as the people with whom we argue have generally received the same moral education as ourselves, and live in the same social order, our expectation is usually justified. But if our opponent happens to have undergone a different process of moral "conditioning" from ourselves, so that, even when he acknowledges all the facts, he still disagrees with us

[2] cf. *Philosophical Studies,* "The Nature of Moral Philosophy."

about the moral value of the actions under discussion, then we abandon the attempt to convince him by argument. We say that it is impossible to argue with him because he has a distorted or undeveloped moral sense; which signifies merely that he employs a different set of values from our own. We feel that our own system of values is superior, and therefore speak in such derogatory terms of his. But we cannot bring forward any arguments to show that our system is superior. For our judgement that it is so is itself a judgement of value, and accordingly outside the scope of argument. It is because argument fails us when we come to deal with pure questions of value, as distinct from questions of fact, that we finally resort to mere abuse.

In short, we find that argument is possible on moral questions only if some system of values is presupposed. If our opponent concurs with us in expressing moral disapproval of all actions of a given type *t*, then we may get him to condemn a particular action A, by bringing forward arguments to show that A is of type *t*. For the question whether A does or does not belong to that type is a plain question of fact. Given that a man has certain moral principles, we argue that he must, in order to be consistent, react morally to certain things in a certain way. What we do not and cannot argue about is the validity of these moral principles. We merely praise or condemn them in the light of our own feelings.

If anyone doubts the accuracy of this account of moral disputes, let him try to construct even an imaginary argument on a question of value which does not reduce itself to an argument about a question of logic or about an empirical matter of fact. I am confident that he will not succeed in producing a single example. And if that is the case, he must allow that its involving the impossibility of purely ethical arguments is not, as Moore thought, a ground of objection to our theory, but rather a point in favour of it.

Having upheld our theory against the only criticism which appeared to threaten it, we may now use it to define the nature of all ethical enquiries. We find that ethical philosophy consists simply in saying that ethical concepts are pseudo-concepts and therefore unanalysable. The further task of describing the different feelings that the different ethical terms are used to express, and the different reactions that they customarily provoke, is a task for the psychologist. There cannot be such a thing as ethical science, if by ethical science one means the elaboration of a "true" system of morals. For we have seen that, as ethical judgements are mere expressions of feeling, there can be no way of determining the validity of any ethical system, and, indeed, no sense in asking whether any such system is true. All that one may legitimately enquire in this connection is, What are the moral habits of a given person or group of people, and what causes them to have precisely those habits and feelings? And this enquiry falls wholly within the scope of the existing social sciences.

It appears, then, that ethics, as a branch of knowledge, is nothing more than a department of psychology and sociology. And in case anyone thinks that we are overlooking the existence of casuistry, we may remark that casuistry is not a science, but is a purely analytical investigation of the structure of a given moral system. In other words, it is an exercise in formal logic.

When one comes to pursue the psychological enquiries which constitute ethical science, one is immediately enabled to account for the Kantian and hedonistic theories of morals. For one finds that one of the chief causes of moral behaviour is fear, both conscious and unconscious, of a god's displeasure, and fear of the enmity of society. And this, indeed, is the reason why moral precepts present themselves to some people as "categorical" commands. And one finds, also, that the moral code of a society is partly determined by the beliefs of that society concerning the conditions of its own happiness—or, in other words, that a society tends to encourage or discourage a given type of conduct by the use of moral sanctions according as it appears to promote or detract from the contentment of the society as a whole. And this is the reason why altruism is recommended in most moral codes and egotism condemned. It is from the observation of this connection between morality and happiness that hedonistic or eudæmonistic theories of morals ultimately spring, just as the moral theory of Kant is based on the fact, previously explained, that moral precepts have for some people the force of inexorable commands. As each of these theories ignores the fact which lies at the root of the other, both may be criticized as being onesided; but this is not the main objection to either of them. Their essential defect is that they treat propositions which refer to the causes and attributes of our ethical feelings as if they were definitions of ethical concepts. And thus they fail to recognise that ethical concepts are pseudo-concepts and consequently indefinable. . . .

# 25

---

# A Refutation of Morals*
## JOHN MACKIE
(1917–    )

We all have moral feelings: all of us find that there are human actions
and states of affairs of which we approve and disapprove, and which we
therefore try to encourage and develop or to oppose. (This emotion of
approval is different from liking, one difference being that its object is more
general. If someone stands me a pint, I like it: if someone stands an enemy
of mine a pint, I dislike it: but I should approve of a state of society which
provided free beer all round. So if I hear of someone whom I have never
met and to whom I am personally indifferent being stood a pint, I should
not say that I like it, for I am not directly affected, but I may well approve
of it, because it is an instance of the sort of thing I want to see everywhere.
A thorough distinction of approval from liking and other relations would
require further discussion, but perhaps this will serve to indicate a contrast
between classes with which we are all in fact acquainted. I shall suggest
later a possible source of these generalised emotions.) But most of us do not
merely admit that we have such *feelings*, we think we can also *judge* that
actions and states are right and good, just as we judge about other matters
of fact, that these judgements are either true or false, and that the qualities
with which they deal exist objectively. This view, which almost everyone
holds, may be crudely called "believing in morals." A few sceptics, however,
think that there are only feelings of approval, no objective moral facts. (Of
course the existence of a feeling is an objective fact, but not what is
commonly called a moral fact.) One of their main arguments is that moral
facts would be "queer," in that unlike other facts they cannot be explained

*From John Mackie, "A Refutation of Morals," *The Australasian Journal of Psychology and
Philosophy*, vol. 24 (1946), pp. 77–86, 90, with the first paragraph omitted. Reprinted with
permission of the author and the publisher. Compare with selections 24 and 26.

in terms of arrangements of matter, or logical constructions out of sense-data, or whatever the particular theorist takes to be the general form of real things. This argument is not in itself very strong, or even very plausible, for unless we have good *a priori* grounds for whatever is taken as the basic principle of criticism, the criterion of reality, the mere fact that we seem to observe moral qualities and facts would be a reason for modifying that principle. Their other main argument, which is both older and more convincing, though not logically conclusive, is that although at any one time, in a particular social group, there is fairly complete agreement about what is right, in other classes, other countries, and above all in other periods of history and other cultures, the actual moral judgements or feelings are almost completely different, though perhaps there are a few feelings so natural to man that they are found everywhere. Now feelings may well change with changing conditions, but a judgement about objective fact should be everywhere the same: if we have a faculty of moral perception, it must be an extremely faulty one, liable not only to temporary illusions, as sight is, but to great and lasting error. Of course it may be that every society except our own is mistaken, that savages are morally backward because they lack our illuminating experience of the long-term effects of various kinds of action, and so on. But this complacent view (not indeed very popular now) is shaken by the observation that the variations in moral feelings can be explained much more plausibly not as being due to mistakes, but as reflections of social habits. This moral relativity would be less alarming if we could say that the varying judgements were not ultimate, but were applications to different circumstances of a single principle or a small number of principles, which were everywhere recognised—for example, that whatever produces pleasure is good, that whatever society commands is right, or, at the very least, that we should always do what we believe to be right. But these principles are not commonly laid down first, and the particular judgements deduced from them: rather the particular judgements are made by ordinary people, whereas the principles are later invented by philosophers and manipulated in order to explain them. In any case there is just as little agreement about principles as about particular judgements.

We find on further enquiry that most, perhaps all, actual moral judgements are fairly closely correlated with what we may call social demands: any society or social group has regular ways of working, and, in order to maintain these, requires that its members should act in certain ways: the members—from whatever motive, perhaps mainly habit, which has compelled them to adapt their desires to the established customs—obey these requirements themselves and force their fellows to do so, or at least feel obliged to obey and approve of others obeying. They call "right" and "good" whatever accords with these ways of working. Moreover as the science of social history develops, it is more and more strongly suggested that ways of working and institutions have their own laws of growth, and that the desires or moral views of individuals do not so much control the history of society as arise out of it.

Belief in the objectivity of moral qualities is further undermined when we remark that whenever anyone calls an action or activity or state of affairs right or good (unless he is speaking in an ironical tone or puts these words in inverted commas) he himself either has a feeling of approval, or desires that the action should be done or the activity pursued or the state of affairs come into existence. (Only one of these alternatives is necessary, but they are often found together.)

None of these considerations is conclusive, but each has a certain weight: together they move the moral sceptic (who is often of a scientific and inductive turn of mind, and less devoted than some others to the clear light of intuition or the authority of reason) to conclude that in all probability we do not recognise moral facts, but merely have feelings of approval and disapproval, which arise in general from social demands and therefore vary from one society to another. This view I intend to examine and re-state, and to advance what I regard as decisive arguments for one of its more important aspects.

The simplest formulation of this view is that when someone says "this act is right" he means merely "I approve of this act." The well-known reply simply leaps into the reader's mind: when one person says that an act is right, another that the same act is wrong, they would not on this theory be disagreeing, whereas in fact they think they are. It will not do to say, with Stevenson,[1] that there is a disagreement in attitude, but not in belief: they think, at any rate, that they disagree in belief. Nor does one mean that "society approves of this act," since we frequently meet people who say "I know society approves of this, but it is wrong all the same." But there is no need for argument: direct introspection shows that when we use the terms "right," "good," and the rest, we never intend merely to state that there are feelings of approval. An improved formulation of the sceptical view is that in saying "this is right," and so on, we are not *stating* any approval, but only *expressing* one, that words like "right" and "wrong," "good" and "bad" are to be compared not with "red" and "square" but with exclamations or ejaculations like "ow!", "boo!", and "hurray!" This is certainly nearer the truth, and avoids the previous difficulties, but is, in another way, just as

---

[1] *Ethics and Language*, Chapter I.

unplausible. For we do not think that we are merely ejaculating when we talk in moral terms. If we did, and if someone disagreed with us, we should merely disapprove of his approvals, and either try to coax him into a different emotional attitude, or if he proved obstinate, knock him down. In fact we reason with him. These facts, and the logical tangles that we get into when we try to re-state fairly complex moral situations in the "boo-hurray" language, prove that we think, at least, that we are not merely expressing our emotions but are describing objective facts, and therefore that the meaning of moral terms is not parallel with that of ejaculations. Many refutations of the "boo-hurray" theory have been worked out, but they all depend upon and illustrate the fact that we *think* that we are doing things of quite different sorts when we say "right" and when we say "ow!" Now if philosophy could do no more than elucidate the meaning of the terms of common speech, remove confusions and rationalise the thought of ordinary men, there would be nothing more to be said. Moral terms do mean objective qualities, and everyone who uses them does so because he believes in objective moral facts. But if the very terms of common speech may include errors and confusions within themselves, so that they cannot be used at all without falsity, if, we may add, philosophy may be permitted to enquire into these errors by observing a few facts for itself and founding inductive conclusions on them, the moral sceptic need not be so soon disheartened.

But he must modify his view again, and say that in using moral terms we are as it were objectifying our own feelings, thinking them into qualities existing independently of us. For example, we may see a plant, say a fungus, that fills us with disgust, but instead of stating that we have this feeling, or merely expressing and relieving it by an exclamation, we may ascribe to the fungus a semi-moral quality of foulness, over and above all the qualities that a physical scientist could find in it. Of course, in objectifying our feelings we are also turning them inside out: our feeling about the fungus is one of being disgusted, while the foulness we ascribe to the fungus means that it is disgusting. The supposed objective quality is not simply the feeling itself transferred to an external object, but is something that would inevitably arouse that feeling. (No one would say, "That fungus is foul, but I feel no disgust at it.") The feeling and the supposed quality are related as a seal or stamp and its impression.

This process of objectification is, I think, well known to psychologists and is not new in philosophy. I believe that it resembles what Hume says we do when we manufacture the idea of necessary connection out of our feeling of being compelled, by the association of ideas, to pass from cause to effect, though here the process of turning inside out does not occur.

There are strong influences which might lead us thus to objectify moral feelings. As I have mentioned, our moral judgements seem to arise from approvals borrowed from society, or from some social group, and these are felt by the individual as external to himself. It is for this reason that they are universal in form, applying equally to himself and to others. They are thus formally capable of being objective laws, in contrast to the "selfish" desires of the individual. This generality or universality, which I mentioned as characteristic of the emotion of approval, is reflected in Rousseau's doctrine that the general will and therefore law must be general in their object, and in Kant's criterion of the possibility of universalisation of a moral law. Since we inevitably tend to encourage what we approve of, and to impose it upon others, we want everyone to adopt our approvals, and this will most surely come about if they have only to perceive a genuinely existing objective fact, for what we feel is in general private, what we perceive may be common to all. Suppose that we approve of hard work: then if as well as a feeling of approval in our own minds there were an objective fact like "hard work is good," such that everyone could observe the fact and such that the mere observation would arouse in him a like feeling of approval, and even perhaps stimulate him to work, we should eventually get what we want done: people would work hard. And since what we want does not exist in fact, we naturally construct it in imagination: we objectify our feelings so thoroughly that we completely deceive ourselves. I imagine that this is the reason why our belief in moral objectivity is so firm: we much more readily admit that the foulness of a fungus is an objectification than that the depravity of people who break our windows is. If moral predicates were admitted to be what the moral sceptic says they are, we should never be able to extol a state of affairs as good in any sense which would induce people to bring it about, unless they already wanted it, though we might point out that this state had features which in fact they did desire, though they had not realised this: we should never be able to recommend any course of action, except in such terms as "if you want to be rich, be economical"; nor could we give commands by any moral authority, though we might again advise "if you don't want a bullet through your brains, come quietly"; and we should never be able to lecture anyone on his wickedness—an alarming prospect. The temptations to objectify feelings of approval, and to retain our belief in morals, are clearly strong ones.

This process of objectifying our feelings is, then, neither impossible nor improbable: there is also abundant evidence that it is just what has occurred. It is commonly believed by moralists that good means desirable in a sense such that the mere recognition that a thing is good makes us desire it, and similarly the conclusion of the practical syllogism is both "this is right" and the performance of the action. This is what we should expect if "right" were the objectification of a tendency to compel or command the kind of act so described, and "good" of desire and approval. This is again indicated by the use of the term "value" which is clearly borrowed from spheres like economics where value is created by demand—in fact a quality manufactured in imagination out of the relation of being demanded by someone, the abstraction being the easier because the demand is not essentially that of a single buyer, but of an indeterminate crowd of potential buyers: the analogy with the objectification of moral feelings, aided by their generality, is very plain. Anderson has pointed out (in "The Meaning of Good," published in the Journal for September, 1942) that whenever anyone argues "Y is good, X is a means to Y, therefore X is good" he must be using "good" in an economic sense, as relative to some demand: now this is one of the commonest forms of argument in ordinary moral thought. There is nothing inconsistent in saying that "good" is the objectification of both desire and approval: its meaning is not quite fixed, and approval both is a development from liking and desiring, and attains its end when its object is generally desired. Further evidence is given by the categorical imperative, which looks very much like an abstraction from the commonplace hypothetical imperative, "if you want this, do that," and which may be described as the making objective and so absolute of advice which is properly relative to the condition of the presence of the desire. "Naturalistic" theories of ethics, which seem so absurd to a logician like G. E. Moore, who insists on the objective-quality aspect of moral terms, represent as it were partially successful attempts at objectification. "The good is the desired" and suchlike statements, which recur with remarkable persistence in philosophic history, plainly betray the emotional origin of moral terms. But there is no need to multiply examples: almost every moral term and style of moral thought may be seen to be borrowed from less lofty spheres, and in the course of the transfer objective qualities have appeared where only emotions were previously recognised.

In attempting to give an account of the origin of moral terms in this process of objectification, I do not, of course, claim that it is complete or precise in all respects. It is still open to discussion and correction on empirical grounds. We might go on to consider this process as a psychological process, investigating its causes, its similarities and contrasts with other mental processes, and the steps of which it is made up. We might ask whether "objectification" or some other name is really the most suitable, and also what are the precise motives objectified: we might consider, for example, Westermarck's argument[2] that "ought" normally expresses a conation, is sometimes but not necessarily or essentially imperative, and has its origin in disapproval rather than approval.

My discussion in this paper is intended to open the way for such discussions, not to settle them once and for all. What I am concerned to establish is simply the logical status of moral terms, not the psychological details of their origin; in effect I am asserting only that there are no facts of the form "this is right," that when we use such words the only fact is the existence of some feelings in ourselves or in others or in both, but that in using these terms we are falsely postulating or asserting something of the simple, objective form "this is right."

I am not, of course, disagreeing with the point mentioned several times by Anderson (for example in "The Meaning of Good," p. 120) that "I like this," "I approve of this," "this society approves of this," are all statements of objective fact and would in any particular case be true or false. But they are all of a different form from statements like "this is right," the latter attributing a predicate to a subject, the former asserting a relation between two or more things. When I say that we objectify, I mean that we believe in the truth of statements of the subject-predicate form.

This re-statement does away with the logical difficulties previously encountered by moral scepticism. Nor are there, I think, any non-logical difficulties in the way of our accepting this view, except the persistence of the belief that moral facts are objective. It might be claimed that this firm belief is based on an intuition, but it has no further arguments to support it, and we have indicated social and psychological causes which would produce such a belief even if it had no foundation. However firm the belief may be, therefore, it is not valid evidence for the existence of moral facts. But the true moralist will not be deterred by lack of evidence: he will perhaps be compelled to admit that moral judgements are evolved, historically, by objectification of feelings. But none the less, he will maintain, when evolved they *are* valid. But now we remind him of their variability, their correlation with social demands. Actual moral judgements, en masse, cannot be valid, since they are mutually contradictory: in fact all the evidence suggests that not only are moral judgements derived from feelings, but there are no objective moral facts: the feelings are *all* that exists. We may now legitimately be influenced by the "queerness" of the alleged moral facts, their striking differences from most of the other objects of knowledge and belief. But we must not be over-emphatic. We have only attained

[2] *The Origin and Development of the Moral Ideas,* Chapter VI.

probability. Even when our assumptions and observations are accepted it is still possible that there may be facts of the forms "this act is right," "this activity or state of affairs is good," though our recognition of them is very much confused by desires and approvals. We have seen that a great deal of so-called moral judging is really the objectifying of feelings, but perhaps not all of it is. (This leaves the field open for a positive system of ethics like that upheld by Anderson.) . . .

. . . We may now sum up the progress that we have made. We have discovered how we can state the traditional view of moral sceptics without logical contradiction or denial of the observable facts of moral thinking, by saying that we have only moral feelings, but objectify these and think we are recognising objective facts and qualities. But we were not sure how much of our moral thought was made up of these objectifications, whether there might not be, say, an objective quality of goodness, with which these objectifications have been confused. We have shown that obligation, as we commonly use the term, cannot be an objective fact, but our notion of it must be derived from objectification. The same is true of everything necessarily connected with it, the terms "should," "duty," and "right". Exhortation and recommendation can have no absolute validity when obligation is removed: we can only advise people how to attain what they already desire. With these we place those notions that bear plainly the marks of the process of objectification or of their emotional origin: the notion of value, the notion that goodness, if there is such an objective quality, has any necessary relation to desire, or to happiness and pleasure, since it is through desire that it is connected with these. Also, if there is such a quality, it will be such that we can recognise it without feeling impelled to approve of it or to pursue it. In fact, without going into further detail we may say that there may be an objective quality which we have confused with our objectifications of moral feelings, but if so it has few of the relations and other features that we have been in the habit of associating with goodness. But in any case we have shown that the great mass of what is called moral thought is, not nonsense, but error, the imagining of objective facts and qualities of external things where there exists nothing but our feelings of desire and approval.

## 26

# *Value Judgments* *

## KURT BAIER

(1917-    )

In recent years, there has grown up, both in philosophy and in sociology, a doctrine which has relegated value judgments to the realm of personal idiosyncrasies. On this view, utterances are divided into two kinds, statements of fact and judgments of value. The former occur characteristically in scientific discourse which is concerned to state the facts, to describe and explain the world, to say how things are, were, and will be, or would be in certain conditions, and to say what makes them the way they are. Value judgments, on the other hand, direct our feelings, attitudes, and behavior. Scientific discourse is objective, precise, capable of being true or false, empirically verifiable or the reverse. Value judgments are subjective, vague, ambiguous, unverifiable by the senses. The problem is to show whether, and if so how, statements of fact can be relevant to value judgments. The problem is, to borrow the title of a well-known book, to find "the place of value in a world of facts."

## I. Theoretical and Practical Judgments

More precisely, this widely accepted doctrine maintains that, unlike statements of fact, judgments of value can be neither empirically verified or disproved, nor deduced from any statements of fact. It is plain, however, that there is nothing in the nature of judgment that excludes empirical verification. A man may be a good judge of character, or of distance, or of speed. We say that he is a good judge of these things if he can usually judge

*Reprinted from Kurt Baier: *The Moral Point of View.* © Copyright, 1958 by Cornell University. © Copyright, 1965, by Random House, Inc. Used by permission of Cornell University Press. (This is from ch. 2 of the 1958 edition; ch. 1 of the 1965 edition) Compare selections 24 and 29.

these things correctly. And we say that he has this power if he can get correct results under conditions other than optimum; that is to say, when the pedestrian, reliable methods of verification have not yet been used, as when a person has to judge someone's character after a short acquaintance, or when he has to judge distances without being allowed to use a tape measure, or speeds without a speedometer. Judgment, then, involves giving correct answers under difficult conditions. It involves being able to give correct answers more quickly, in bad light, or without instruments when reliable answers cannot be given without a special skill.

Are there, then, some types of judgment which are not empirically verifiable, perhaps practical or value judgments? Let us first distinguish theoretical and practical judgments. Theoretical judgments are a type of fact-stating claim requiring special talents or skills, such as judging distances, speeds, and chances of success or failure at some enterprise. They differ from meter readings in not being made under optimum conditions, from workings out in not being arrived at by foolproof, easy methods; they differ from guesses, conjectures, or intuitions in being based on a skill or gift, about which we know enough to develop it by practice.

Practical judgments, on the other hand, are judgments with a direct logical bearing on what should be done. Judgments to the effect that something is legal or illegal, just or unjust, good or bad, right or wrong, are directly relevant to answering the question "What shall I do?"

Commands, authoritative decisions, orders, and the like also directly bear on this question. Hence practical judgments have been identified with them. This view reveals a complete misunderstanding of the question "What shall I do?" Its proponents must think that when we ask this question we request to be commanded to do something.

But this is simply not true. Commands are not *essentially* intended for answering questions. They can and will usually be given when no questions have been asked. "Attention," "Bring me the slippers," "Go to bed," may be said out of the blue. They are not essentially replies. In fact, commands are only very exceptionally replies, namely, when children, employees, or subalterns are *asking for orders.*

"What shall I do?" is frequently not asked in order to elicit a command or order. When I come for advice, I do not want to be commanded or ordered about. I do not even want to be requested or begged or pleaded with. I want to know what you think is the best thing for me to do. I need your knowledge, not your authority. I want you to think, to deliberate on my behalf. I want to make use of your intelligence, your experience, your practical wisdom. I don't expect you to take responsibility.

"What shall I do?" may indeed mean "Tell me what to do." But then

I expect you to tell me *what* to do, and not to tell me to do something. The first is answering a question, the second is giving orders. In the first case, "What shall I do?" means "What would you do in my place?" in the second, it means "What are your orders?"

## II. Factual Comparisons and Rankings

I shall now try to show that value judgments, one sort of practical judgment, are empirically verifiable. Note first that they may be either comparisons or rankings—either assertions to the effect that one thing, event, state of affairs, person, or deed is better or worse than, or as good or bad as, another or assertions to the effect that one thing, event, etc., is good, bad, or just average.

Some comparisons and rankings are factual, that is, nonevaluative and empirically verifiable. "This man is taller than that" and "She is a tall girl for her age" are ordinary empirical claims. If we are clear about the logic of empirical comparisons and rankings, we will be in a position to say whether what distinguishes evaluative from nonevaluative comparisons and rankings makes the former unverifiable in principle. It is my contention that the misunderstanding of the logic of empirical comparisons and rankings is, at least partly, responsible for the view that value judgments are not verifiable.

To say that one man is taller than another may be a judgment, for example, when one of them is sitting down and the other standing up. This can be verified by making both stand up, barefoot, back to back. Under these optimum conditions we can see which is the taller or whether they are equally tall. With more experience we learn to make correct claims of this sort even in difficult conditions, as when one has high-heeled shoes, or is sitting down, or is wearing a hat, and so on. Good judgment in this sort of thing is the ability to make correct claims of this kind in other than optimum conditions. We could not say of anyone that he had good judgment unless there were some way of *verifying* his judgments.

Not all comparisons are as simple as this one. Sometimes we compare things in respect of properties which are defined in terms of others. When I say that this house is *bigger* than that, I may base this claim on the possession to a higher degree of one or all of three *other* properties, that is, it is *longer, wider,* or *higher* than the other house. But these are not the only ones. We may also have in mind the possession of *more* rooms, or of *larger* rooms. These properties are the criteria of "being bigger." Criteria are properties, the possession of which to a higher degree (for instance, "smaller") implies the possession of the other property to a higher degree (for instance, "cheaper") or lower degree (for instance, "less comfortable"). In our case we must say that the longer, the wider, the higher it is, the more rooms it has and the larger the rooms are, the bigger is the house.

This case is instructive because it shows how criteria may conflict. We have no way of deciding what we should say if one house were longer and wider but lower, or if it had more but smaller rooms, than the other. We have no way of *compounding* these criteria when they conflict. In such conflict cases, no clear answer can be given to the question "Which is the bigger house?" Yet, there can be no doubt that the claim "This house is bigger than that" is empirical, is capable of empirical verification or disproof. The mere fact that value comparisons may be based on criteria capable of conflicting can, therefore, have no tendency to show that they are not capable of verification.

In ranking something, we are not directly comparing *two* objects, but are concerned with only one. In comparing, we want to know which of *two* objects has a given property to a higher degree. In ranking we want to know *the* degree to which *one* object has the property in question. Nevertheless, rankings too are sorts of comparison, though more complex. When we rank a man as tall, we assign him the highest rank on a three-place scale, tall, medium, short. Knowing the meaning of "tall" involves knowing the logical relationship between being tall, of medium height, and short. One must know the number, names, and order of the places on the scale. One must know that "tall" means "taller than of medium height and short." It is not enough to know that "tall" is the opposite of "short"; for that would not enable us to distinguish between opposites such as "dead" and "alive," which are not capable of degrees, and opposites such as "tall" and "short," which are.

Knowing these things is enough to *understand* rankings, but it is not enough to verify them. For that, we need additional factual information, namely, the *standard* by which the object has been ranked. Every ranking implies such a standard. Though we do not know what the standard is and can, therefore, only understand what is *meant by* the claim "This Pygmy is tall," we could not even understand that claim unless we took *some* standard to be implied. There is, therefore, a sense in which claims such as "This Pygmy is tall," "This man is tall," "This child is tall," "This horse is tall" are all making *the same claim* about different objects, and therefore a sense in which "tall" *means the same* in all these cases. Yet the empirical verification of these claims involves a different factor every time, namely, *the appropriate standard* of tallness.

Remember the differences between criteria and standards. Standards

are implied in all rankings but in no comparison. It would not make sense
to say, "He is tall," "This is hot," and so on unless *some standard of tallness* or
*hotness* were implied. For a tall Pygmy is a short man, and a hot bath would
be merely a warm drink. On the other hand, it does not make sense to ask
by what standard I judge one man taller than another, one drink colder
than another. Criteria may, but need not, be involved in either ranking or
comparing. I simply see that one man is tall, or taller than another. I
simply feel that one bath is hot, or hotter than another. By contrast, "This
cup of tea has a temperature of 60 degrees F." and "This house is bigger
than that" do involve criteria. The criterion of the first is the expansion of
mercury in a thermometer, the criteria of the second are length, width, and
height.

## III. Value Comparisons and Rankings

Still, it will be objected, *value* judgments involve more than criteria and
standards. Let us take a simple case first: "John's was *a faster* mile than
Richard's" and "John's was *a better* mile than Richard's." Do they come to
the same thing? No, "better" is obviously a more general expression than
"faster." In "better ship," "better razor," "better fountain pen," "better
school," "better man," it becomes increasingly less appropriate to replace
"better" by "faster." A man who knows the words "fast" and "mile" must
know that, if the runners have started at the same time, then he who arrives
at the milepost first has run the faster mile. In other words, he must know
the criterion of "running a faster mile." But a man may know the words
"good" and "mile," and yet not know the criterion of "running a *better*
mile." In order to know what is the criterion of "running a *better* mile
than . . ." one must in addition know the purpose of a race. If we know
that races are competitions in which people are trying to run as fast as they
can in order to win, we know what the purpose of races is. It is then also
obvious that we must evaluate miles on the basis of speed.

It might, therefore, be said that "faster mile" is a more objective or
more factual expression than "better mile." If this merely means that the
criterion of "faster mile" is independent of, whereas that of "better mile" is
dependent on, *human purposes,* this is perfectly true. But since in many cases
the purpose, point, or function of something can be quite objectively
determined, the criteria of "better" can, in these cases, also be quite
objectively determined.

Take now a slightly more complicated case: "A is a better miler than
B." Here, too, we are concerned with a competition, though on a some-

what larger scale, as it were. We are here calling someone the winner, not of a particular race, but of a competition made up of many races. Here, too, the purpose of the competition determines the criterion, namely, the number of wins. If A has always won, or won more often than he lost, or has run better times, or run equally good times but more often, or equally often but under more difficult conditions, then he has the greater number of wins, the better record.

Perhaps we are not satisfied to crown the winner merely of past competitions. When we say, "A is a better miler than B," we may have in mind all times, not only the past. We then include his potentialities. In such a case, verification will have to wait for future performances. Many value judgments contain references to the future and cannot, therefore, be "read off" now. Unduly preoccupied with propositions of the form "This chair in front of me is brown," many philosophers have felt that value judgments are not empirically verifiable because the goodness or badness of a thing cannot be "read off," as its brownness can.

No additional difficulties are introduced by value *rankings*. There is, of course, an implied standard, but that is irrelevant, for there were implied standards in the case of factual rankings also. Landy is a superb miler by world standards, I am a bad miler by any standard. But some boys are good milers by college or university or club, though not by world, standards. Obviously, standards of this sort can themselves be ranked as high, medium, or low. The higher the standard, the lower the ranking, and vice versa. A Cambridge IIB is a Tasmanian starred first.

"But," it will be said, "you are forgetting the obvious differences. These value judgments are based essentially on only one criterion: speed. What if there are several?" We have already seen that in factual rankings and comparisons there may be a multiplicity of criteria capable of conflicting with one another. In such a case there may be no clear answer to the question "Which of the two has the required property to a higher degree?" But this has no bearing on empirical verifiability and has nothing to do with the specifically evaluative nature of value comparisons and rankings.

At any rate, there will be an enormous number of cases where value judgments can be verified or disproved. I once bought, from a street vendor, a fountain pen which he described as a Parker 51, imported dutyfree. My friend warned me against buying it. He said it was no good. To cut a long and disappointing story short, it was not a Parker, and it was no good. It did not have a gold nib, or even a proper filling mechanism. When I bought it, I thought it was good, for I tried to write with it and it seemed to work. Later, I discovered that it wasn't any good, for it did not write and could not be filled. It did not satisfy any of the generally recognized criteria of a good fountain pen. There can be no doubt that in this case I *learned from experience,* no doubt that my friend's claim, that the pen was no good, was conclusively verified.

"This does not prove much," it will perhaps be objected. "I possess a Parker 51 and a Waterman. I have had them for many years, and I still do not know which is the better. And it is not as if I had not had the necessary time to try them out. Yet I shall never know." One explanation might be that they are equally good. When, after a long time of using a pen, one cannot discover which is the better, then it may well be that neither *is* better, but that they are equally good.

"But can we be certain whether they are equally good? Or can this never be settled?" It must be admitted that there are some subtleties about the merits of things such as fountain pens about which the average user will never be able to arrive at the truth for himself. I have no record of how often I have had my two pens repaired, nor do I possess the statistics for others; I do not know how well their iridium points have worn or how often I have had to fill the two or how long they will continue to be serviceable and so on. But experts may know; hence experts will be able to tell which is the better pen, even where I cannot. Although value judgments may not always be empirically verifiable by laymen, it is still possible that they can be verified by experts.

## IV. Matters of Opinion and Matters of Taste

"But you know as well as I do," it will be said, "that even experts differ. Some doctors recommend one brand of tooth paste or soap, others another. These things are simply matters of opinion." It is true that some such disagreements are matters of opinion, but not all. That Landy is a better miler than I, that Plato was a greater philosopher than Joad, that cars are now better than they were fifty years ago, that *Hamlet* is a greater play than *A Streetcar Named Desire,* that St. Francis was a better man than Hitler, are not matters of opinion, but are quite indubitably true. Anyone who maintained the opposite would have to be said not to know what he was talking about. That some value judgments are matters of opinion does not have any tendency to show that all are. If all were, then they would indeed be empirically unverifiable. For it is a characteristic of matters of opinion that they are unverifiable, because incurably open issues. But obviously not all value judgments are matters of opinion.

Moreover, many obviously factual issues are also matters of opinion: whether Hitler would have won the war if he had invaded England instead of attacking France; whether Churchill is more of an extrovert than Mussolini was; whether immigration is one of the main causes of inflation in Australia. Some people have been tempted to say that these are value judgments just because they are matters of opinion, that is, not conclusively verifiable or the reverse. Yet this is absurd, for there are other claims of exactly the same sort which are not matters of opinion, but plainly true: that Hitler would have won the war if Russia and America had remained neutral; that Mussolini was more of an extrovert than Kafka; that the higher cost of imports is among the main causes of inflation in Australia.

It is equally absurd to claim that all value judgments are matters of taste. True, when we are engaged in comparing or ranking pictures, cows, clothes, food, or drinks, there comes a point where further talk about the matter is no longer helpful in settling the disagreement. We simply agree to differ. We part peacefully in the knowledge that what separates us is merely a difference in taste. Nevertheless, it is obvious that a 1956 Bentley Continental is a better car than a 1927 Bentley, even if some lovers of vintage cars would rather own the latter. Even in disputes which are so largely matters of taste, such as the quality of a certain meal or someone's cooking, there are claims which are not matters of taste.

## V. Verification and Validation

"But now you have given the show away," our persistent objector will exclaim. "What you have said just now has suddenly illuminated for me that elusive difference between factual and value judgments which so many philosophers have tried to elucidate. You have proved to my satisfaction that value judgments can be transformed into unambiguous and empirically verifiable remarks. But in doing so, you have also shown, without meaning to, that by this transformation they become, *eo ipso,* something else. They not only come to *mean* something different, they become utterances of a different sort, they cease to be guides to behavior. They no longer provide reasons for us to do one thing rather than another. When we have made a value judgment unambiguous and verifiable, we have turned it into a factual judgment. It then no longer *guides us,* it merely describes something."

This objection is based on an important truth, but it is stated in a confused and misleading manner. The truth contained in it is this. Value judgments and factual claims serve different purposes. In factual comparisons and rankings, our normal purpose is to characterize something, to say to what degree it has certain properties. The idea is to enable someone else to identify it, or to establish laws about it, that is, correlations of some of its properties with others, or correlations between variations in some of its properties and variations in others. With evaluative comparisons and rankings, our purpose is different, however. We are not concerned to characterize a thing, so that people can identify it or can establish laws, but to give rational guidance. We are concerned not merely and not even primarily with the nature of the thing in question, but also with how well a thing of this nature can minister to our wants, desires, aims, needs, aspirations, ideals, and the like.

This has an important corollary. In the case of factual comparisons and rankings, a change in the criteria is of no great consequence. Of course, such a change might give rise to misunderstandings, if one party is unaware of it. You may be using "being bigger than . . ." with the same criteria as "having a greater volume than . . ." whereas I may be using it with the ordinary criteria. We may then appear to disagree about the size of a given house, whereas we have merely misunderstood each other's claims. When I say, "Smith's house is bigger than Gordon's," I base this on the fact that Smith's house has more rooms, but when you say, "No, they are equally big," you base it on the fact that they have the same volume. When this difference between us is brought to light, however, our disagreement vanishes, for it is of no consequence in which of these two ways we use the expression "bigger than. . . ."

But where value judgments are concerned, the discovery that we have been using different criteria does not end the disagreement. The real disagreement may only begin here. For while in nonevaluative comparisons and rankings we are simply concerned to state the degree to which a given thing satisfies given criteria, in value judgments we are concerned to say more. When, in nonevaluative judgments, we change the criteria, we are simply making a different nonevaluative claim, we are simply asserting the possession of a different property. In value judgments this is not so. Here we are concerned not merely to say something about the properties of the thing, but something about the *appropriateness* of certain lines of behavior in relation to a thing with such properties. Nothing follows about the appropriateness or otherwise of someone's behavior from saying either that the first house is bigger than the second or that it has a greater volume. Something does follow from saying that the first house is better than the second. It follows that, other things being equal, it would be contrary to reason to buy the second and in accordance with reason to buy the first. Hence a change of the criteria in the case of evaluative comparisons and rankings would *amount to giving different advice*. When we change criteria in factual comparisons and rankings, we are merely making different remarks about the things in question; hence people using different criteria *cannot* contradict each other, for they are no longer talking "on the same plane." When we use different criteria in value judgments, we *can* contradict each other, for we are still "talking on the same plane": we are saying that one thing is *better or worse than* another, that is, that there is a good reason for doing one thing rather than the other.

Value judgments, therefore, give rise to an additional question, which cannot arise in the case of factual ones, namely, "Are these the *right* criteria?"

The characteristic disagreement *in value,* as opposed to disagreements about fact, is the disagreement about the rightness of the criteria employed in ascertaining the "value" or "goodness" of the thing in question. Let us then distinguish between *verification* and *validation.* We have seen that value judgments can be verified just like factual claims, but that in value judgments we make claims that give rise to a further question, namely, whether the criteria employed are the right ones. Factual judgments are decisively confirmed if they are empirically verified. Value judgments, on the other hand, must be not only verified but also validated. It is not enough to show that, *if* certain criteria *are* employed, then a thing must be said to have a certain degree of "goodness"; we must also show that these criteria *ought* to be employed.

We can now return to our objection, which was, it will be remembered, that if a given remark is rendered empirically verifiable and unambiguous, then it (logically) cannot be a value judgment. This is completely wrong. The question of the verifiability, and unambiguousness of a remark is quite independent of its being either evaluative or factual. Both evaluative and factual claims may be empirically verifiable or the reverse, and comparatively unambiguous or ambiguous. It is not true that, of their nature, factual remarks are characterized by empirical verifiability and unambiguity, whereas value judgments are characterized by empirical unverifiability and ambiguity. That a remark is evaluative does not entail that it is in principle unverifiable or the opposite, comparatively ambiguous, and vague. It does mean, however, that we can ask the question whether the criteria employed in verifying it are the right or the wrong ones, whereas this question cannot (literally) be asked when we are talking about nonevaluative comparisons and rankings.

## VI. The Technique of Validation

"All right," my imaginary opponent will reply, "value judgments *are* verifiable. But this is an empty triumph. What people meant to say was, of course, that they are incapable of what you now call validation. Value judgments differ from factual statements in just this, that they *require* to be validated, and that this is impossible, at least objectively. For to say that they are *valid* is to make another value judgment. And this in turn will require criteria and they in turn will have to be validated, and so on ad infinitum."

I do not wish to belittle the difficulties involved in validating value judgments, but there must be something wrong with this argument. For could anyone deny that "Landy is the best miler in the world today" is capable of both verification and validation? Could anyone deny that, at any rate, the criteria mentioned for comparing and ranking milers are the right ones? Surely, Landy's record-breaking mile *is* the best mile ever run so far. Surely, the criterion, speed, is the right criterion to apply. Although it would not be true to say, literally, that "the best mile" *means* "the fastest mile," yet since winning a race is running faster than any other competitor, speed is the proper criterion to use. Surely, here we have both verification and validation.

And what is true of this case is also true of all cases involving purposes. Roughly speaking, the proper criteria for evaluating cars, fountain pens, milers, and so on are determined by the purpose of the thing, activity, or enterprise in question. Knowing the purpose of the car enables us to see that speed, comfort, safety, and the like are proper criteria.

"But how are we enabled to *see* all this? How, for instance, do we know the purpose of cars? Is that something to know, anyway? Is it not something that *we give to* these things? And don't different people give different purposes to their cars? What purpose a car has is for its owner to decide, and to decide at will." It will be granted that we all know what cars are. And the fact that I know what a car is implies that I know the purpose of cars. For knowledge of what a car is, is more than the ability to recognize a car when it is parked in the street or in deserted country lanes or when it stands in a garage or in a showroom. The ability to do that amounts only to a knowledge of what cars look like. A Melanesian recently arrived in Melbourne and observing cars parked at night is told, in reply to his question, "These things are cars." This may be enough to enable him correctly to pick out cars. But even so he cannot be said to know what cars are, if he thinks that they are shelters for adolescents to pet in. He could not be said to know *the* purpose of cars, even though he has correctly guessed one of the purposes for which they can be and frequently are used by joy-riders.

Knowing the purpose of cars by itself is not enough to derive the appropriateness of criteria such as safety, comfort, or reliability. They can be derived from the purpose of cars only if taken together with a great many other more general human aims. Safety is a criterion not simply because cars have the purpose of serving as means of transportation, but because we want to live unhurt as long as possible. Of course, as I said before, if instead of them we wanted other things, then the criteria of excellence in cars would be different. It is, however, a plain fact that we do want these things. There is nothing arbitrary, subjective, personal about it. It would be absurd to claim that this was a matter of taste, opinion, personal preference, an idiosyncrasy, or what have you. On the contrary, anyone who claims that safety, reliability, comfort, and the like are *not* appropriate criteria of excellence in cars simply does not know what he is talking about, or is a little crazy, to say the least.

The real difficulty, however, does not lie in establishing that some criteria are objectively valid, but in drawing the line between those capable of objective validation and the others and, furthermore, where there are several criteria, in establishing which are the more important ones, and how much more important.

One way of extending the range of the capacity for objective validation is to narrow the basis of comparison. Instead of comparing or ranking cars, we may compare and rank racing cars or station wagons. Then the more specific purpose of the car determines objectively a narrower range and a clearer hierarchy of the criteria. Obviously speed is more important in a racing car than in a bus, and being able to carry a pay load is more important in a utility car than in a sports car. This method has corresponding disadvantages. It prevents me from saying that the Austin Healey is better than the Fargo, for one is a sports car, the other a truck. But this is not a very serious drawback, since there is little point in comparing the two anyway.

If we *insist* on comparing them, we can still do so by ranking each one on a scale appropriate to *it* and by comparing the respective ranks. Suppose the Austin Healey is an excellent sports car and the Fargo merely an average truck; then we can say that the Austin Healey is better than the Fargo, even though they have not been *directly* compared. What has been compared is merely the respective rank in their respective scales. What standards are appropriate for the ranking would depend on the purpose for which such a comparison was made.

Another thing we might do is to draw up a list of all criteria relevant to any type of car. We could then rank cars on the basis of each criterion, leaving it to everyone to determine for himself which criteria he regards as most important. In such a case only the selection of the criteria and the ranking for each are objective. No computation of all the partial rankings

232 / KURT BAIER

for the purpose of arriving at an over-all ranking or comparison is here attempted. The over-all rankings must be made by each individual on the basis of *his own* special purposes or aims. They are to that extent personal, but not purely subjective, since mistakes are possible even then: anyone having the same special purposes must obtain the same over-all ranking, *unless he has made a mistake.*

Alternatively, one might decide to compute such partial rankings conventionally. One might decide to rank, not on a three-place scale, good, average, bad, but on a numerical, say, ten-place scale. One has then made computation possible. The ranking is conventional, because all criteria are given the same importance. This sort of thing is done in the so-called score charts in motor journals. The person testing the car in question has a list of all the criteria he will consider, for example, Styling, Bodywork, Interior, Instruments, Comfort, Driving Position, and so on. For all these criteria, the road tester gives a rank by using one of the ordinary "grading labels," for example, attractive, well finished, neat, easy to read, good, excellent, good for short driver, and so forth. But he also gives a corresponding conventional number, say, 4, 4, 4, 4, 4, 5, 4. These numbers can be added up and provide an *over-all* evaluation. If we compare each ranking, and the over-all ranking, with the ranking for the average, we get a fairly clear idea of how good the car in question is.

I take it as established, then, that there are value judgments which can be empirically verified and also validated.

# 27

## *Cultural Relativism* *

## RUTH BENEDICT

### (1887–1948)

1. The diversity of cultures can be endlessly documented. A field of human behaviour may be ignored in some societies until it barely exists; it may even be in some cases unimagined. Or it may almost monopolize the whole organized behaviour of the society, and the most alien situations be manipulated only in its terms. Traits having no intrinsic relation one with the other, and historically independent, merge and become inextricable, providing the occasion for behaviour that has no counterpart in regions that do not make these identifications. It is a corollary of this that standards, no matter in what aspect of behaviour, range in different cultures from the positive to the negative pole. We might suppose that in the matter of taking life all peoples would agree in condemnation. On the contrary, in a matter of homicide, it may be held that one is blameless if diplomatic relations have been severed between neighbouring countries, or that one kills by custom his first two children, or that a husband has right of life and death over his wife, or that it is the duty of the child to kill his parents before they are old. . . . (p. 45)

The three cultures of Zuñi, of Dobu, and of the Kwakiutl are not merely heterogeneous assortments of acts and beliefs. They have each certain goals toward which their behaviour is directed and which their institutions further. They differ from one another not only because one trait is present here and absent there, and because another trait is found in two regions in two different forms. They differ still more because they are oriented as wholes in different directions. They are travelling along differ-

*From Ruth Benedict, *Patterns of Culture* (Boston: Houghton Mifflin, 1934; London: Routledge & Kegan Paul, Ltd., 1935). Reprinted by permission of the publishers and The Benedict Estate. Page references are given in the text. The title of this selection was supplied by the editor.

ent roads in pursuit of different ends, and these ends and these means in one society cannot be judged in terms of those of another society, because essentially they are incommensurable. . . . (p. 223)

2. The Dobuans amply deserve the character they are given by their neighbours. They are lawless and treacherous. Every man's hand is against every other man. . . . The social forms which obtain in Dobu put a premium upon ill-will and treachery and make of them the recognized virtues of their society. . . . (p. 131) Jealousy . . . suspicion . . . fierce exclusiveness of ownership . . . are characteristic of Dobu. . . . All existence is cut-throat competition, and every advantage is gained at the expense of a defeated rival. . . . (p. 141) The good man, the successful man, is he who has cheated another of his place. . . . (p. 142)

The Dobuan . . . is dour, prudish, and passionate, consumed with jealousy and suspicion and resentment. Every moment of prosperity he conceives himself to have wrung from a malicious world by a conflict in which he has worsted his opponent. The good man is the one who has many such conflicts to his credit, as anyone can see from the fact that he has survived with a measure of prosperity. It is taken for granted that he has thieved, killed children and his close associates by sorcery, cheated whenever he dared. . . . The bad man, on the other hand, is the one who has been injured in fortune or in limb by the conflicts in which others have gained their supremacy. The deformed man is always a bad man. He carries his defeat in his body for all to see. . . . (pp. 168–69) Treacherous conflict . . . is the ethical ideal in Dobu. . . . (p. 170) Anything that one can get away with is respected. . . . (p. 169)

. . . The Dobuan islands . . . are rocky volcanic upcroppings that harbour only scanty pockets of soil and allow little fishing. Population presses hard upon the possible resources. . . . (p. 130) Food is never sufficient in Dobu, and everyone goes hungry for the last few months before planting if he is to have the requisite yams for seed. . . . (p. 140)

3. The Puritan divines of New England in the eighteenth century were the last persons whom contemporary opinion in the colonies regarded as psychopathic. Few prestige groups in any culture have been allowed such complete intellectual and emotional dictatorship as they were. They were the voice of God. Yet to a modern observer it is they, not the confused and tormented women they put to death as witches, who were the psychoneurotics of Puritan New England. A sense of guilt as extreme as they portrayed and demanded both in their own conversion experiences and in those of their converts is found in a slightly saner civilization only in

institutions for mental diseases. They admitted no salvation without a conviction of sin that prostrated the victim, sometimes for years, with remorse and terrible anguish. It was the duty of the minister to put the fear of hell into the heart of even the youngest child, and to exact of every convert emotional acceptance of his damnation if God saw fit to damn him. It does not matter where we turn among the records of New England Puritan churches of this period, whether to those dealing with witches or with unsaved children not yet in their teens or with such themes as damnation and predestination, we are faced with the fact that the group of people who carried out to the greatest extreme and in the fullest honour the cultural doctrine of the moment are by the slightly altered standards of our generation the victims of intolerable aberrations. From the point of view of a comparative psychiatry they fall in the category of the abnormal.

In our own generation extreme forms of ego-gratification are culturally supported in a similar fashion. Arrogant and unbridled egoists as family men, as officers of the law and in business, have been again and again portrayed by novelists and dramatists, and they are familiar in every community. Like the behaviour of Puritan divines, their courses of action are often more asocial than those of the inmates of penitentiaries. In terms of the suffering and frustration that they spread about them there is probably no comparison. There is very possibly at least as great a degree of mental warping. Yet they are entrusted with positions of great influence and importance and are as a rule fathers of families. Their impress both upon their own children and upon the structure of our society is indelible. They are not described in our manuals of psychiatry because they are supported by every tenet of our civilization. They are sure of themselves in real life in a way that is possible only to those who are oriented to the points of the compass laid down in their own culture. Nevertheless a future psychiatry may well ransack our novels and letters and public records for illumination upon a type of abnormality to which it would not otherwise give credence. In every society it is among this very group of the culturally encouraged and fortified that some of the most extreme types of human behaviour are fostered.

Social thinking at the present time has no more important task before it than that of taking adequate account of cultural relativity. . . . The recognition of cultural relativity carries with it its own values, which need not be those of the absolutist philosophies. It challenges customary opinions and causes those who have been bred to them acute discomfort. It rouses pessimism because it throws old formulas into confusion, not because it contains anything intrinsically difficult. As soon as the new opinion is embraced as customary belief, it will be another trusted bulwark of the good life. We shall arrive then at a more realistic social faith, accepting as grounds of hope and as new bases for tolerance the coexisting and equally valid patterns of life which mankind has created for itself from the raw materials of existence. (pp. 276–78)

The truth of the matter is rather that the possible human institutions and motives are legion, on every plane of cultural simplicity or complexity, and that wisdom consists in a greatly increased tolerance toward their divergencies. No man can thoroughly participate in any culture unless he has been brought up and has lived according to its forms, but he can grant to other cultures the same significance to their participants which he recognizes in his own. (p. 37)

4. There is . . . one difficult exercise to which we may accustom ourselves as we become increasingly culture-conscious. We may train ourselves to pass judgment upon the dominant traits of our own civilization. . . .

Appraisal of our own dominant traits has so far waited till the trait in question was no longer a living issue. . . . Yet the dominant traits of our civilization need special scrutiny. We need to realize that they are compulsive, not in proportion as they are basic and essential in human behaviour, but rather in the degree to which they are local and overgrown in our own culture. The one way of life which the Dobuan regards as basic in human nature is one that is fundamentally treacherous and safeguarded with morbid fears. The Kwakiutl similarly cannot see life except as a series of rivalry situations, wherein success is measured by the humiliation of one's fellows. Their belief is based on the importance of these modes of life in their civilizations. But the importance of an institution in a culture gives no direct indication of its usefulness or its inevitability. The argument is suspect, and any cultural control which we may be able to exercise will depend upon the degree to which we can evaluate objectively the favoured and passionately fostered traits of our Western civilization. (pp. 249–50)

War is, we have been forced to admit even in the face of its huge place in our own civilization, an asocial trait. In the chaos following the World War all the wartime arguments that expounded its fostering of courage, of altruism, of spiritual values, give out a false and offensive ring. War in our own civilization is as good an illustration as one can take of the destructive lengths to which the development of a culturally selected trait may go. If we justify war, it is because all peoples always justify the traits of which they find themselves possessed, not because war will bear an objective examination of its merits. . . . (p. 32)

The complexity of the problem of social values is exceptionally clear in Kwakiutl culture. The chief motive that the institutions of the Kwakiutl rely upon and which they share in great measure with modern society is the motive of rivalry. Rivalry is a struggle that is not centred upon the real objects of the activity but upon outdoing a competitor. The attention is no longer directed toward providing adequately for a family or toward owning goods that can be utilized or enjoyed, but toward outdistancing one's neighbours and owning more than anyone else. Everything else is lost sight of in the one great aim of victory. Rivalry does not, like competition, keep its eyes upon the original activity; whether making a basket or selling shoes, it creates an artificial situation: the game of showing that one can win out over others.

Rivalry is notoriously wasteful. It ranks low in the scale of human values. It is a tyranny from which, once it is encouraged in any culture, no man may free himself. . . . (pp. 246–47)

# 28

## *Ethical Relativity* *

### EDWARD WESTERMARCK
#### (1862–1939)

1. . . . Neither the attempts of moral philosophers or theologians to prove the objective validity of moral judgments, nor the common sense assumption to the same effect, give us any right at all to accept such a validity as a fact. . . .

. . . In my opinion the predicates of all moral judgments, all moral concepts, are ultimately based on emotions, and . . . as is very commonly admitted, no objectivity can come from an emotion. It is of course true or not that we in a given moment have a certain emotion; but in no other sense can the antithesis of true and false be applied to it. The belief that gives rise to an emotion, the cognitive basis of it, is either true or false; in the latter case the emotion may be said to be felt "by mistake"—as when a person is frightened by some object in the dark which he takes for a ghost, or is indignant with a person to whom he imputes a wrong that has been committed by somebody else; but this does not alter the nature of the emotion itself. . . . (p. 60)

. . . Moral values are not absolute but relative to the emotions they express. (p. 289)

2. . . . Ethical subjectivism, instead of being a danger, is more likely to be an advantage to morality. Could it be brought home to people that there is no absolute standard in morality, they would perhaps be on the one hand more tolerant and on the other hand more critical in their judgments.

*From Edward Westermarck, *Ethical Relativity* (London: Routledge & Kegan Paul, Ltd., 1932). Page references are given in the text. These extracts are designed merely to bring out a point of view, not to represent the philosophy of the author. The point of view brought out is discussed in selection 29.

Emotions depend on cognitions and are apt to vary according as the cognitions vary; hence a theory which leads to an examination of the psychological and historical origin of people's moral opinions should be more useful than a theory which postulates moral truths enunciated by self-evident intuitions that are unchangeable. In every society the traditional notions as to what is good or bad, obligatory or indifferent, are commonly accepted by the majority of people without further reflection. By tracing them to their source it will be found that not a few of these notions have their origin in ignorance and superstition or in sentimental likes or dislikes, to which a scrutinizing judge can attach little importance; and, on the other hand, he must condemn many an act or omission which public opinion, out of thoughtlessness, treats with indifference. It will, moreover, appear that moral estimates often survive the causes from which they sprang. And what unprejudiced person can help changing his views if he be persuaded that they have no foundation in existing facts? . . . (pp. 59–60)

# 29

## *Ethical Relativism* \*

## ARTHUR E. MURPHY

### (1901–1962)

*The Negations of Moral Positivism.* The type of ethical theory that goes by the name of "relativism" is frequently not admitted by its advocates to be an ethical theory at all. Its defenders are in many cases aggressively "plain" men who profess with pride their incapacity to understand what "philosophers" are talking about when they deal with moral issues. As men of "facts," with a proper scorn for "abstractions," and a recently acquired technique of "semantic" criticism with which to dispose of them, the relativists seem to themselves to be in a far sounder position than the philosophers. Yet they do make statements, supposed to be true and well-substantiated, about the nature and validity of moral judgments, and they do use the conclusions which these statements seem to them to justify as the basis of a distinctive type of moralizing in which they frequently and fervently indulge. Thus they employ their supposed discovery that no moral judgment is *really* anything more than the expression of the bias of the person who utters it as a basis for the claim that no moralist has a "right" to impose his own biases on others, and vigorously condemn those who violate this maxim of their moral doctrine. We are therefore entitled, I think, to conclude that they have at least a theory about the nature of moral conduct and the validity of moral judgment which has (or is supposed to have) an important bearing on the further direction of such conduct in so far as it is enlightened and instructed by the acceptance of the theory. This, for our purposes, is what it means to have an ethical theory.

\*From A. E. Murphy, *The Uses of Reason* (New York: Macmillan, 1943), Part II, ch. ii, pp. 140–45, 153–54, 154–64. Reprinted with the kind consent of Dr. Frederick Ginascol, executor of the Murphy estate. The title of this selection has been supplied by the editor. Compare selections 3, 24, and 28.

We do not ask them to accept the term, but we can fairly ask them to understand the implications of what, as both analysts and lay preachers, they are doing, and to justify its commitments.

An ethical relativist is, in general, a theorist who holds that so-called "moral judgments" are nothing more than verbal expressions of the attitude, preference or bias of those who utter them. Any claim they make—or appear to make—to any further cogency or warrant than that which they possess as such expressions is incapable of any sort of "objective" substantiation, and ought to be rejected. The preference expressed may be that of the individual merely, or of "the group." In the latter case it acquires an added social sanction but no added moral validity—unless moral validity is "positivistically" identified with social sanction, and thus deprived of any independent significance. *For* the individual or the group in question such a preference possesses the urgency which inheres in any *de facto* drive or interest. *For* the objective observer the occurrence of such preferences is a fact to be observed and, where possible, correlated with other observable phenomena. *For* individuals or groups with opposing preferences, it is a factor to be taken account of in cases of actual or potential conflict. So much is sheer, positive, matter of fact. From that point on the relativist is likely to become somewhat incoherent, though by no means inarticulate, and to moralize in a manner not easy to reconcile with the primary negations on which his theory is based. It is these negations, however, which are distinctive of his theory. What are the grounds for them, and to what, if consistently accepted, would they commit us?

The two chief considerations which underlie and are supposed to justify the theory of ethical relativism are those derived from "positivism" as a theory of scientific method and from the observation of the diversity and incompatibility of existing moral codes. Since the chief evidence on this latter point is borrowed from the broad area now marked out as the province of sociology, it will be convenient to speak of "sociological relativism" here, as a source of the ethical relativism we are to examine. We shall examine these two sorts of consideration in some detail.

The term "positivism" has a two-fold significance. It stands, in the first place, for a theory of scientific method which proclaims the emancipation of the sciences from metaphysics and their right to develop such categories of explanation and description as their own subject-matter and methods of inquiry demand, without regard for the requirements of the "ultimate reality" of the metaphysicians. Whatever may be true of such reality in its absolute or final nature, the facts which a physicist or a biologist will properly take account of are those which can be tested by his own well-authenticated methods of inquiry, and whatever is not thus testable is outside the province of his scientific concern. In this phase of its development, positivism, as we saw in Part I, is a positive contribution to a right understanding of the nature and validity of scientific inquiry. Its anti-metaphysical emphasis is a quite natural protest against the confusion (still persisting in some quarters), which ensues when independent inquiry into the structure of the physical world is hampered by preconceptions about what "the real" must be and what, in consequence, the physical world must "really" be, even though it cannot, by scientific investigation, be found out to be anything of the sort. The elimination of this sort of consideration from the evaluation of scientific truth has, on the whole, contributed to the progress of the sciences.

There is, however, another side to the positivist doctrine which it is less easy to accept. The methods of inquiry which have proved their worth in physics and biology tend to take on, in the minds of their more devoted users, a canonical authority comparable to that which metaphysics possessed in an earlier age. Just as nothing was once "intelligible" which did not conform to the canons of a teleological metaphysics, so today nothing is held to make sense in advanced circles which violates a rule of verifiability which "the scientist" follows in his experimental research. Applied to the study of moral behavior, this means that nothing is to be accredited as "objective" which cannot be identified by criteria guaranteed as "scientific" through their use in the sciences which have become in our time, as were the doctrines of Aristotle in the thirteenth century, the model for intellectually respectable thinking about the world.

It must be apparent, I think, that positivism in this latter use bears about the same relationship to the liberating insights of its scientific ancestors, as do the Daughters of the American Revolution to their revolutionary progenitors. Each has indeed an honorable lineage and a great inheritance, but each seems at times to suffer from spiritual pride and intellectual inflexibility. One good custom can indeed corrupt a world, and one set of ideas, however excellent and liberating in its original use, can become a barrier to further inquiry when it is set up as the measure to which all further truth, however different the context in which it is acquired, must approximate. It might have been the case that moral inquiry could proceed successfully with categories borrowed from physics or biology. It was certainly an experiment worth trying, and all honor is due to the experimenters of the eighteenth century who tried it. And if there are experimenters prepared to try it again, they are entitled to a respectful hearing. What is not legitimate, however, is the attempt of the positivists to settle the question *in advance*, by stipulating that only what would be pertinent to physics or biology can count as "objective" in morals. It is as easy to prove in this way that what is not verifiable by "positive" methods has no "objective" status, as it was to prove that what did not satisfy metaphysical criteria for Real Being or Existence was, on the terms set by such criteria, infected with non-Being. The method is essentially the same in each case. In neither is the result achieved by its use a contribution to our understanding of the specific subject-matter of moral inquiry.

The transition from methodological positivism to ethical relativism is easily made. Men judge that some actions are "right," others "wrong"; that some proposed ends are "good," and others "bad." If such judgments are to claim "objective" validity, the positivist argues, a method must be specified for determining which are true and which false. Apart from such specification, judgments of this kind will have to be denied any theoretical sense, though they can be understood as expressing the attitudes or emotions of those who utter them. Not just *any* method, however, will do. The sciences have their own methods of testing statements that purport to supply information concerning matters of fact. The operations that are performed in verifying such statements are *real*, not merely verbal, operations, and the experiences in which they eventuate are objective, authentic, real. If the statements which express moral judgments are to stand critical inspection, it should be possible to verify them in a similar way. If no such verification is available we must—if we properly value "intellectual honesty"—refuse to accept such statements, or "pseudo-statements," as more than emotively expressive but intellectually groundless utterances of "ultimately" arbitrary preferences.

In fact, it is alleged, no such verification *is* available. Scientific method reports what is, not what ought to be; it can discover social pressures, but not moral obligations; it verifies statements about the desired, and the most efficient means for securing it, not about the desirable in any further sense. Hence, if we accept with intellectual honesty the results of critical analysis, we shall be obliged to admit that, as far as reputable examination can determine, so-called obligations are just social pressures, and ostensible value judgments the verbal front for arbitrary bias and demands. . . .

Are moral judgments "verifiable," or are they not? This seems to be a plain question, and we can give it a plain, though not a simple, answer. If "verification" means proof or disproof by reference to agreement or disagreement with observed matters of fact, the answer is that they cannot. For such reference, while essential, is simply not sufficient to determine the moral worth of actions. We need also to know the relevance of facts thus ascertained to ideals whose cognitive authority is not that of an *is* but of what ought to be, as this concerns, not scientific curiosity, but a rightly directed will or purpose. If "scientific method" is identified with the procedures by which matters of fact are ascertained, then practical reason is not reducible to scientific method, though it depends at every turn on information which the sciences supply. And if nothing is to be called "objective" which cannot be substantiated by "scientific method" in this sense, then the conclusions of practical reason about, for example, the worth of freedom are not "objective," for they are not thus substantiated. So far we agree with the positivist. We further agree in holding that what you get if you try to measure the correctness of moral judgments by these standards is nonsense.

All this, however, says very little, and says it in a misleading way. For while moral judgments cannot be verified, like the predictions of physics, they can be substantiated, and it is extremely important that they should be. And while the method of their substantiation is not "scientific," it is and ought to be rational, in a sense in which what is reasonably grounded is distinguished from that which is biased, arbitrary and unsound. And while, again, the conclusions thus reached are not "objective" as physically measurable, they are publicly justifiable within a community whose common concerns they bring to reasonable expression and adjudication, and it is essential to their validity that they should be so. Thus understood, they are not nonsense, and neither are they *merely* verbal manipulations of uncriticizable biases. It is precisely their function to criticize such biases reasonably, and in their fulfilment of this function they further the work of reason in conduct by the only methods that would be sensible or appropriate to this purpose. The outcome of this process when stated will, of course, be words, and so "verbal." But it will be words used to express and to produce moral enlightenment on issues of profound human importance. . . .

*Sociological Relativity and Ethical Relativism.* A second main source of contemporary relativism is the observed relativity of existing moral codes to the habits, interests and conditions of life of the societies in which they are accepted. Since these codes are different and conflicting, and since each *seems* valid to those who adopt it, the conclusion has been drawn that each is "right" from its own standpoint and none "really" right in any further or more absolute sense. It is further held that a recognition of this relativity of standards will make for tolerance, since it makes plain the natural and social basis of all morality and deprives the advocates of any particular doctrine of authority over the preferences and beliefs of others. This view has enjoyed wide popularity in recent years, and will merit critical examination. The problem is precisely one of determining the moral relevance of "facts" whose factual status is not in question, but whose significance for the evaluation of conduct has been variously interpreted. Social scientists of various persuasions have in recent years brought in additional evidence of what, in a general way, we already knew—that the actual standards by which men in different groups and societies distinguish right and wrong are different, that what is considered obligatory in one group may be regarded as indifferent or even be condemned in another, and hence that terms of moral praise and blame, in their actual usage, at least, have no unequivocal meaning apart from the folkways and group-approvals of the societies in which they are employed. Hence it has become fashionable, as a mark of critical caution, to enclose terms like "good" and "bad" in quotation marks, in order to indicate that it is what is *called* good in a particular social group that is under discussion. No commitment is so far made as to whether what is thus *called* good is "really" so or not, in any further or normative sense, and where the purpose is simply to describe the actual diversity of social standards, no such commitment is required. There may be dispute concerning the extent of this diversity and the reality of "underlying" uniformities that show that "human nature" after all is really the same everywhere, and at all times. So far as this is a factual question and not a dispute about the inner "realities" of a common humanity which underlies observable behavior but is only dimly discernible in it, the answer to it is to be sought in anthropological investigation. And while the evidence is still incomplete, there is enough of it at hand to indicate that the diversity in moral standards is so great that no man could act rightly according to any specific moral code that has ever gained wide acceptance without offending against some of the precepts of other codes which are felt to be no less binding for those who accept them. Hence in this sense what is right for one is wrong for the other, and there is no common standard, acknowledged by both, in terms of which this difference can be adjudicated.

Such is the factual situation, what is its moral relevance? How should the knowledge that existing criteria of good conduct are thus relative and variable affect our judgments of what in fact *is* right and wrong, when we are not merely describing and cataloguing such judgments but making them for ourselves? So long as we remain on the descriptive level no such problem arises, and a scientist who is content to leave the matter there has no need to be concerned about it. But when—and if—he goes on to moralize about it, we have a right to demand that he do so responsibly and with some regard for the requirements of practical reason. Suppose our moral standards are thus relative: what of it? The usual answer of the relativist has been that this discovery ought to make us more tolerant of the opinions and actions of those who differ from us. They are "right" by their standards, as we are by ours, and where such standards differ, what right have we to claim that *our* "good" is the right one and theirs simply wrong? Thus E. Westermarck, whose compendious researches into the variety of moral codes have added considerably to our information on this matter, does not hesitate to pass from social variety to ethical relativity, and to claim a considerable moral advantage for the position thus reached. "Could it be brought home to people that there is no absolute standard in morality, they would perhaps be on the one hand more tolerant and on the other hand more critical in their judgments. Emotions depend on cognitions and are apt to vary according as the cognitions vary; hence a theory which leads to an examination of the psychological and historical origin of people's moral opinions should be more useful than a theory which postulates moral truths enunciated by self-evident intuitions that are unchangeable."[1]

This may prove to be a sound observation, but, if so, it is as a judgment about the way in which people *ought* to feel, not as a description of the way in which they uniformly or even usually *do* feel under such conditions. No one has stressed the relativity of moral ideas to particular races and cultures more than have the Nazi prophets of Aryan superiority. The Germans are a peculiar people, and their morality a peculiar morality, which lesser breeds will "naturally" fail to appreciate. There is no absolute standard of morality for all people, but one code for the masters and another for those they are peculiarly fitted to rule. It is by no means the case that stress on this doctrine has led in fact to tolerance of the views of others or to greater self-criticism in Nazi circles. Nor is there any reason in the fact of a diversity of standards why it should. The knowledge of one's moral peculiarity may serve as well to feed national pride as to induce humility and self-criticism. The descriptive scientist can catalogue such differences, but it is not within his province to judge that one response is reasonable, proper and appropriate and the other not, unless this judgment is made by reference to some standard which he accepts as right and proper, not only for himself, but for those who disagree with him as well, since it is here of the rightness of their response that he is judging.

There is, then, no reason whatever for accepting the "fact" of social relativity as a justification for tolerance or a ground for condemning the most intolerant and arbitrary of moral judgments until the moral relevance of this fact has been made out by reference to a standard of enlightenment, fairness and benevolence to which such judgment ought to conform, a standard to whose authority the would-be moralist commits himself in

[1] E. Westermarck, *Ethical Relativity*, p. 59 [pp. 238–39 this volume].

judging and which he applies to the conduct of those who differ from him as well. Short of this he would simply be recording the autobiographical observation that the discovery of social relativity did in fact affect him in this particular way. This would be of interest, no doubt, to his friends and associates, but it could have no more bearing on the justification of tolerance than the quite different effect a similar doctrine has had on Hitler's Dr. Rosenberg. Whatever the ground for moral tolerance may be, it cannot possibly be a refusal to take the responsibility for making moral judgments, for it is only in terms of such moral judgment that tolerance—or anything else—can be justified. It would be well if those who claim to make such judgments with the authority of "science," but refuse to take the responsibility for them which only an adequate moral theory could warrant, would understand this.

*The Good of Tolerance.* Yet there clearly is a moral insight which the relativists have been trying to express through their insistence on the diversity of accepted codes of conduct and the importance of taking account of such diversities when we are tempted to impose our own opinions on those who differ from us in their valuations. The trouble is that they have been prevented by their theory as to the nature and validation of moral judgment from stating this insight clearly and defensibly. The straightforward questions to ask, surely, would be: What *good* is tolerance? What is there in the end sought which justifies the measures recommended to attain it? And how is the existing diversity of moral standards relevant to the attainment of this good? These, however, are questions of practical reason, of the organization of interests and purposes around ideal ends rightly judged to be worth achieving, and of the obligations reasonable men will acknowledge as co-workers for this achievement. But the relativist is committed in advance to a refusal to deal with moral issues on a moral basis. He dare not make moral judgments except by disguising them as statements of existing matters of fact. Since the whole point in adducing the variety of codes and customs as a ground for tolerance is to provide a *reason* for one course of conduct and a basis for the condemnation of its intolerant opposite, the result of this procedure can only be confusion.

The results of this confusion are of practical importance. They reflect upon the very genuine good the relativists are interested in defending the dubiety which attaches to their mistaken ethical theory, and thus weaken a case that should be made as strong as possible. For there are and will continue to be men interested in discrediting the worth of tolerance as a human ideal who will know how to use such weakness and confusion among "liberals" in a very effective way. And indeed, if no better sense is to be made of the good of tolerance than the relativists have made, its opponents have a strong case against it. Thus Professor Pegis, in criticizing "a dangerous and indeed tragic conception of tolerant objectivity"[2] which he believes to be widespread among modern educators, identifies such "tolerance" with the view that, for example, political ideas cannot be rationally defended and are finally nothing more than preferences and pleasing prejudices. This he takes to be a kind of skepticism about the foundations of rational morality, and he quite plausibly maintains that such "tolerance" is not a secure basis for the case for human freedom. "The very thing which we wish to maintain, liberty, is the very thing which intellectual skepticism can be guaranteed to ruin. It is surely a poor liberty to allow men the right to be the victims of their own inability to know true principles with finality and to act in their light with deliberateness; and it is a poor democracy which must build upon such an inability."[3]

In fact, of course, the case for tolerance, and for secular freedom in education, has a very different foundation than this. The good of tolerance is a spiritual good. We respect the right of others to make up their own minds and their right to express freely convictions thus arrived at, not because we think these opinions are as likely to be right as our own, or that there is no genuine basis for discriminating right from wrong with respect to them, but because we think it important that the convictions should be their own, and freely arrived at, and that they should accept the responsibility for them. The freedom of the mind that is worth having is not an indefinite suspension of judgment, on the ground that there is so much disagreement on these matters that no opinion can really claim any rational cogency. It is a freedom for each man to make up his own mind, in the light of the best he knows, and with a decent respect for the right of others to come to a similar decision for themselves. It is grounded not on what we cannot make up our minds about but on what we can—the preeminent worth of human personality and of the freedom of inquiry and of speech which are its essential preconditions.

The liberty which, in this country, guarantees to every man the right to make up his mind on basic issues, the issues of religion among them, is not at all a poor sort of liberty, nor the democracy that for one hundred and fifty years has maintained it a poor sort of democracy. Yet both liberty and democracy are constantly open to attack, both from avowed enemies and professed friends, who burn with self-righteous indignation at the political toleration of beliefs which contravene their own, and seek to substitute indoctrination for inquiry and responsible judgment as the ideal

[2] Anton C. Pegis, "In Search of Man," in *Science, Philosophy and Religion,* Vol. I, p. 352.
[3] *Ibid.,* p. 355.

to which our educational system should approximate. It is not indifference or skepticism but reasonably grounded conviction of the worth of freedom of thought and of conscience which leads us to reject such claims. It is to be hoped that those who have recently been so active in denouncing the false ideal of tolerance which they view with alarm, will be equally zealous in defending the true ideal of tolerance, with its political and educational implications, against the attacks, both secular and ecclesiastical, which are being and will be made upon it.[4]

There is another difficulty which impedes an adequate understanding of the worth of tolerance, and here, too, the doctrines of ethical relativism have played their part in the ensuing confusion. The problem here is not as to the worth of tolerance, but about its application. Each man may properly judge for himself, it is said, but what "right" has he to claim that what seems right to him is right for others as well? After all, they are right from their point of view, as he is from his own, and to claim that his opinion has any validity as against theirs, or is more than an expression of his own bias, preference or point of view is to be "intolerant," and hence unjust. Thus we seem to return to the position of ethical relativism, and this time in the name of equity and fair dealing. For to assume that one's own moral judgment was better than that of others, or had a prior right to general acceptance, would be to claim a special privilege for oneself and to violate the principle of equality to which all sound morality is committed.

This sort of view had a considerable vogue among college students a few years ago. To all questions about right and wrong they would pose the counter question, "Who's to judge?" with the conviction that for any one party to a dispute to claim that privilege, so long as there were others who disagreed with him, was so obviously dogmatic, arbitrary and unfair as to merit no further consideration. *By what right* does any man set himself up in the privileged role of judge of the actions of others? Here again "tolerance" emerges as a refusal to make moral judgments on the high moral ground that those who do so are committing the morally blameworthy sin of intolerance, or of dogmatism, in a situation in which their *right* to judge cannot be defended.

It is obvious, I think, that those who assume this position are not themselves refusing to make moral judgments, but are making them in a peculiarly confused and whimsical way. For, once more, it is only by reference to a standard of what is right, just and appropriate that a distinction can sensibly be made between moral judgments *rightly* condemned as "arbitrary," and "dogmatic," and those which are just and

---

[4] I have discussed this issue more fully in an article, "Sectarian Absolutes and Faith in Democracy," in *The Humanist*, October, 1941.

reasonable. If all are condemned alike by the very fact of being moral judgments there is no sense left in the condemnation nor, for that matter, in the good of tolerance to which this disintegrating liberalism remains incongruously addicted. The reasonable answer to the query, "Who's to judge?" is surely this: in a community of free men each must judge for himself, but he must judge responsibly, that is to say, *not* arbitrarily or merely in his own behalf, but with respect for principles which hold for all alike. It is only for and in respect to such judgment that the distinction between what is arbitrary and what is just and reasonable makes sense, or has any sort of moral significance. The individual who judges thus—and only so is he a moral agent—is not claiming a privilege which he refuses to accord to others as well. He is accepting a responsibility and exercising a moral function that he cannot honestly avoid, though he may through carelessness, confusion, or mere indifference disavow it. This disavowal, however, where and in so far as it occurs, is not to be dignified as scientific objectivity or moral enlightenment. It is an evidence of failure to see in what the nature of tolerance consists, or to make sense of its claims and commitments.

The failure to see this point is, of course, the outcome of the prior failure to distinguish the standpoint of practical reason from that of mere bias, preference or special interest. It would indeed be arbitrary and unjust to claim that one's own "point of view," considered simply as a personal bias or idiosyncrasy, was entitled to greater public credence or authority than that of anyone else. But the only standpoint from which this verdict of "injustice" makes sense is that of a rational moral judgment which itself purports to be more than a bias, preference or idiosyncrasy, and to be valid not only for the individual who makes it, but for all men who can rightly understand and estimate the merits of the case. In making such a judgment a responsible moral agent *ought* to take full account of existing diversities of code, custom and point of view, and to respect the *right* of others to follow their own bent and genius on all cases in which such diversity is compatible with the essential conditions under which a community of shared purpose and mutual respect can actually exist. To impose any narrower conditions and thus *arbitrarily* to exclude from the moral community those who in fact have the capacity and the will to share in it is illiberal, intolerant and morally wrong. Nor should any of us be overeager in condemning the motives of others when he is not in a position to understand them. The commandment "judge not" is, in its context, one of the most excellent of moral judgments. But once more, the decision that such liberality is morally excellent makes sense only with respect to a standard which the judger acknowledges as valid not only for himself, but for all who share in the community whose moral structure that standard defines. To try to moralize in the name of such a standard—to speak of "rights," and "justice" and a "tolerance" which right and justice enjoin—without accepting its commitments is not to be peculiarly mentally and morally enlightened. It is to be mentally and morally confused and irresponsible on fundamental issues.

There is, then, no honest way for the moralist, however "relativistic" his preconceptions, to escape the responsibility which moral judgment entails. We can raise the dictates of conscience to the level of the best we know. We can use the fact of sociological relativity as a valid reminder that our own initial moral preferences are likely to be parochial and one-sided and that they need the closest rational scrutiny we can give them. But when all proper self-examination has been made, we must judge of the right as we see it, and we cannot see it with any other eyes than our own or judge it with any minds but the minds we have. To have a mind of one's own is part of the peculiarity and the dignity of being human, and we shall gain nothing humanly worth having by denying it. . . .

# 30

## Science and Ethics*

### GEORGE A. LUNDBERG

(1895–1966)

Closely related to the aspect of science and ethics discussed above are the following:

1. It is pointed out, as scientists have always recognized, that (*a*) scientific method has its own ethics and that (*b*) every scientist indulges in evaluating (1) what problems to investigate and (2) what data are relevant to his problem. These considerations are taken to prove that scientific methods themselves call for evaluation, and therefore, it is implied, scientific conclusions are also ethical. To this reasoning there is a twofold answer: (1) Not all evaluation is ethical. There are no ethical questions involved in the statement that one object is heavier than another, although this is unquestionably an evaluation of two objects with respect to weight. (2) The scientific rules or mores against suppressing evidence and corrupting experiments are not themselves arrived at or tested by the scientific operations which resulted, for example, in the conclusion that one object is heavier than another. Likewise, a scientific conclusion that one tribe is technologically more highly developed than another carries with it no intrinsic ethical evaluation whatever regarding technological development. Scientific mores, like all others, are arrived at from experience and tested as to their value as means to desired ends. The end of science is a certain kind of understanding, but that end is not determined or imposed on us by scientific methods. It is *taken* because man's wants and interests are what they are. Man's wants and interests are what they are, as we have said, because of his whole evolutionary history in the world in which he has

*From George A. Lundberg, "Alleged Obstacles to Social Science," *The Scientific Monthly*, vol. LXX, no. 5 (May 1950), Sect. III, pp. 304–305. Reprinted by permission of the editors of *Scientific Monthly*. The title of this selection has been supplied by the editor. Compare with selection 31.

lived. All his characteristics, including his so-called inherent ones—habits, culture (including science), taste, wants, and goals—are the result of this life history.

It will be noted that we include science among the influences that have made man what he is. The role of social science among all the other factors influencing man's social behavior has thus far been small. It could become very important. But, as we have seen, scientific conclusions will always be in the form of a conditional statement: "If the spark [and all the other necessary and sufficient conditions], then the explosion." Such a statement can never carry any ethical implications regarding the social desirability of explosions.

Now the scientist, as a member of a community, is likely to have ethical views also on the latter subject. This has misled some writers into declaring that since the scientist is also a human being and a member of a community, with definite ideas about the goodness or badness of various kinds of explosions, it is specious to separate his total behavior into (*a*) his role as scientist and (*b*) his role as citizen. Yet, clearly, we make such separations in all other lines of activity, including the professions. The physician is expected to treat patients he dislikes or whom he believes are a social menace with the same care that he treats his other patients. An actor wins applause for the excellence of his enactment of the villain's role, not because of his personal approval or disapproval of the character portrayed. The latter question is recognized as a separate issue of relevance in other contexts. Exactly the same is true of the scientist. He has performed his full function as a scientist when he has clearly depicted the consequences of a proposed type of behavior, as, for example, when he has accurately predicted an explosion. His applause or abhorrence of the explosion is not part of his scientific conclusion or function.

2. Another error regarding the relation of science and ethics lies in mistaking hypotheses, which are always present in scientific work, for ethical value judgments. Arnold Rose has said, for example, that "a statement of the type of solution sought is a value premise" (*op. cit., American J. Sociol.*). But the hypotheses of science are never statements of "conclusions sought" in the sense of conclusions *desired* by the scientist. A hypothesis disproved is a scientific contribution just as truly as one proved. The only kind of solution sought in science is confirmation *or* refutation of a hypothesis. It is probably true, unfortunately, that many social scientists today do regard their hypotheses as conclusions to be proved by appropriately selected data and reasoning rather than as questions to be impartially (scientifically) tested.

3. The persistence of the old dichotomy of "voluntary" and "invol-

untary" behavior further confuses the subject here under consideration. Traditionally, ethics is assumed to be concerned only with so-called voluntary behavior. The questions that have arisen in this connection are, in fact, the basis for the emergence of the value problem and ethics as a separate problem. Given a certain frame of reference, it can doubtless be logically held that only voluntary behavior is subject to ethical evaluation. This position has the further advantage that, by defining voluntary behavior in such a way as to exclude all behavior of the inanimate world and of nearly all the animals below man, the foundation is laid for the great dualistic systems of thought which find it necessary to deal with man in a different framework from the rest of nature. In the scientific orientation, voluntary behavior, to the extent that the category is used at all, becomes merely that behavior which is characterized by delayed response and which is mediated by symbolic (language) mechanisms. As such, voluntary behavior is subject to the same kind of systematic study as any other action.

That is, science circumvents the whole argument about free will by simply leaving this metaphysical issue alone and pointing out that the "free will" behavior, including the observed will of God himself, is just as subject to statistical study and prediction as any other kind of behavior. In the same way, science circumvents the problem which is perhaps chiefly responsible for the persistence of ethics as a separate field of thought, namely, the principle that man is morally responsible only for his voluntary behavior. This view is, of course, also enshrined in our criminal law, which rests squarely on medieval theology rather than on science. Science simply observes that nature holds man (and other animals) accountable for their involuntary as well as their voluntary behavior. That is, the poison man takes by mistake kills him just as certainly as that he takes deliberately. The "insane" (i.e., identifiable under present definitions of insanity) criminal is apprehended and incarcerated as is the "voluntary" criminal. It is true that radically different treatment is accorded the two, but both treatments have the primary purpose of protecting the community and rehabilitating (curing, reforming) the criminal. Except as a detail in the diagnosis and treatment of the case, therefore, the question of voluntary versus other behavior turns out to be irrelevant as far as the possibility of scientific study, social accountability, and free will is concerned.

The traditional viewpoint regarding voluntary behavior, however, still crops up as an interesting hangover in the discussion of the value problem by social scientists. First, there is the reluctant concession that "where human behavior is compulsive and unthinking, it probably lends itself to statements of invariable relationship. Such behavior would encompass infant development, mental pathology, crowd behavior, and perhaps other very limited areas of social study" (Rose. *Amer. Sociol. Rev.*, 1945, August, 560). The implication is that "thinking," "reasonable," and "normal" behavior is less subject to scientific study. Again, it is held that behavior that results from an organism's interpretations of stimuli is of quite a different order as far as scientific study is concerned as compared with behavior consisting of reactions "directly to stimuli" (Rose. *Amer. J. Sociol.*, 1948, November, 233), whatever that may mean. The fact is, I take it, that any response whatsoever is necessarily a reaction to the stimulus as interpreted and defined by the sensory equipment of the responding organism in whatever state of conditioning it may be. The elaborateness of the "interpretation" will, of course, vary according to the nature and development of the nervous system, including its conditionings and so-called apperceptive mass. That is to say, the interpretation and definition of the stimulus-situation to which an organism responds will vary according to the species, individual capacities, and the past responses, especially in the case of organisms capable of responding to symbols and their own symbolic constructs, memories, anticipations, predictions, etc. The "apperceptive mass" of traditional psychology is surely nothing more than the traces left in matter, organic or inorganic, by its previous behavior. That is, the tendency of a wire or a paper to bend more easily in a place where it has been previously bent is as much the "apperceptive mass" or particular "interpretation" of these respective substances as is the modification of human responses by education or conditioning of whatever sort. (See N. Rasvesky: Learning as a Property of Physical Systems. *J. Gen. Psychol.*, 1931, 5, 207–29.)

There appears, therefore, to be no ground whatever for injecting considerations of "interpretation," "definition of the situation," "apperceptive mass," "situation as a whole," etc., into a discussion of the applicability of the usual methods of natural science to human social behavior. These terms merely describe in greater detail the history and nature of the response and do not change the basic fact that, in any event, science observes and records the significant response regardless of the fact that some responses consist of simple reflexes, whereas others are highly mediated by conditioning, training, and symbolic mechanisms. Those differences are of interest from other points of view. But the present uses of these considerations in the social sciences constitute little more than a smoke screen of verbiage under cover of which it is hoped to reserve for social scientists certain privileges of a nonscientific character which are denied to other scientists. One of these privileges is that of injecting ethical judgments into generalizations about behavior and claiming that these judgments, as well as the generalizations, are arrived at by scientific methods.

## 31

*Value Judgments in Science**

# RICHARD RUDNER

(1921–    )

An important underlying point in the three preceding articles is the manner in which, if at all, value judgments impinge on the process of validating scientific hypotheses and theories.

I think that such validations do *essentially* involve the making of value judgments in a typically ethical sense. And I emphasize *essentially* to indicate my feeling that not only do scientists, as a matter of psychological fact, make value judgments in the course of such validations—since as human beings they are so constituted as to make this virtually unavoidable—but also that the making of such judgments is *logically* involved in the validation of scientific hypotheses; and consequently that an adequate logical reconstruction of this process would entail the statement that a value judgment is a requisite step in the process.

My reasons for believing this may be set forth briefly, but before presenting them I should like to distinguish my thesis as clearly as I can from apparently similar ones that have traditionally been offered.

Traditionally, the involvement of value judgments (in some typically ethical sense) in science has ordinarily been argued on three grounds: (i) Our having a science at all, or, at any rate, our voluntary engagement in such activities, in itself presupposes a value judgment. (ii) To be able to select among alternative problems, or, at any rate, among alternative foci of his interests, the scientist must make a value judgment. (iii) The scientist cannot escape his quite human self. He is a "mass of predilections," and

*From Richard Rudner, "Remarks on Value Judgments in Scientific Validation," *The Scientific Monthly,* vol. 79, no. 3 (September 1954), pp. 151–53. Reprinted by permission of the author and the editors. As the selection itself suggests, it is one of four articles comprising a symposium on "Reasons for the acceptance of scientific theories." The essay has been somewhat revised by the author for its inclusion in this collection. The title of this selection has been supplied by the editor. Compare with selection 30.

these predilections must inevitably influence all his activities—not except-ing his scientific ones. These traditional arguments have never seemed entirely compelling, and the responses that some empirically oriented philosophers and some scientists have made to them have been telling. The responses have generally had the following import.

(i) If it is necessary to make a value decision to have a science before we can have one, then this decision is literally prescientific and has not, therefore, been shown to be any part of the *procedures of science.*

(ii) Similarly, the decision that one problem is more worth while as a focus of attention than another is an extraproblematic decision and forms no part of the procedures involved in scientifically dealing with the prob-lem *decided* upon. Since it is these procedures that constitute the method of science, the value judgment has not thus been shown to be involved in the scientific method as such.

(iii) With respect to the presence of our predilections in the laboratory, most empirically oriented philosophers and scientists agree that this is "unfortunately" the case; but, they hasten to add, if science is to progress toward objectivity, the influence of our personal feelings or biases on experimental results must be minimized. We must try not to let our personal idiosyncrasies affect our scientific work. The perfect scientist—the scientist *qua* scientist—does not allow this kind of value judgment to influence his work. However much he may find doing so unavoidable, *qua* father, *qua* lover, *qua* member of society, *qua* grouch, *when* he does so he is not behaving *qua* scientist. Consequently, a logical reconstruction of the scientific method would not need, on this account, to include a reference to the making of value judgments. From such considerations it would seem that the traditional arguments for the involvement of value judgments in science lack decisiveness. *But I think a different and somewhat stronger argument for the involvement of value judgments can be made.*

I assume that no analysis of what constitutes the method of science would be satisfactory unless it comprised some assertion to the effect that the scientist validates—that is, accepts or rejects—hypotheses. But if this is so, then clearly the scientist does make value judgments. Since no scientific hypothesis is ever completely verified, in rational acceptance of a hypothe-sis on the basis of evidence, the scientist must make the decision that the evidence is *sufficiently* strong or that the probability is *sufficiently* high to warrant the acceptance of the hypothesis. Obviously, our decision with regard to the evidence and how strong is "strong enough" is going to be a function of the *importance,* in the typically ethical sense, of making a mistake in accepting or rejecting the hypothesis. Thus, to take a crude but easily manageable example, if the hypothesis under consideration stated that a toxic ingredient of a drug was not present in lethal quantity, then we would require a relatively high degree of confirmation or high level of significance or confidence before accepting the hypothesis—for the consequences of making a mistake here are exceedingly grave by our moral standards. In contrast, if our hypothesis stated that, on the basis of some sample, a certain lot of machine-stamped belt buckles was not defective, the "degree of confidence" we would require would be relatively lower. *How sure we must be before we accept a hypothesis depends on how serious a mistake would be.*

The examples I have chosen are from scientific inferences in industrial quality control. But the point is clearly quite general in application. It would be interesting and instructive, for example, to know how high a degree of probability the Manhattan Project scientists demanded for the hypothesis that no uncontrollable pervasive chain reaction would occur before they proceeded with the first atomic bomb detonation or even first activated the Chicago pile above a critical level. It would be equally interesting and instructive to know how they decided that the chosen probability value (if one was chosen) was high enough rather than one that was higher; on the other hand, it is conceivable that the problem, in this form, was not brought to consciousness at all.

In general, then, before we can accept any hypothesis, the value decision must be made in the light of the seriousness of a mistake, and the degree of probability must be *high enough* or the evidence must be *strong enough* to warrant its acceptance.

Some empiricists, confronted with the foregoing considerations, agree that *acceptance* or *rejection* of hypotheses essentially involves value judgments, but they are nonetheless loathe to accept the conclusion; instead they have denied the premise that it is the business of the scientist *qua* scientist to validate hypotheses or theories. They have argued that the scientist's task is *only to determine the strength of the evidence* for a hypothesis and not, as scientist, to accept or reject the hypothesis.

But a little reflection shows that the plausibility of this as an objection is doubtful. The determination that the degree of confirmation is, say, $p$ or that the strength of the evidence is such and such, which is on this view the indispensable task of the scientist *qua* scientist, is clearly nothing more than *the acceptance, by the scientist, of the hypothesis that the degree of confidence is $p$ or that the strength of the evidence is such and such;* and, as these men have conceded, acceptance of hypotheses does require value decisions.

If the major point I have tried to establish is correct, then we are confronted with a first-order crisis in science and methodology. The positive horror with which most scientists and philosophers of science view the intrusion of value considerations into science is wholly understandable.

Memories of the conflict, now abated but to a certain extent still continuing, between science and, for example, the dominant religions and obscurantist cults over the intrusion of religious value considerations into the domain of scientific inquiry are strong in many reflective scientists. The traditional search for objectivity exemplifies science's pursuit of one of its most precious ideals. But, for the scientist to close his eyes to the fact that scientific method *intrinsically* requires the making of value decisions, and for him to push out of his consciousness the fact that he does make them, can in no way bring him closer to the ideal of objectivity. To refuse to pay attention to the value decisions that *must* be made, to make them intuitively, unconsciously, and haphazardly, is to leave an essential aspect of scientific method scientifically out of control.

What seems necessary (and no more than the sketchiest indications of the problem can be given here) is nothing less than a radical reworking of the ideal of scientific objectivity. The naive conception of the scientist as one who is cold-blooded, emotionless, impersonal, and passive, mirroring the world perfectly in the highly polished lenses of his steel-rimmed glasses is no longer, if it ever was, adequate.

What is proposed here is that objectivity for science lies at least in becoming precise about what value judgments are being made and might have been made in a given inquiry—and, stated in the most challenging form, what value decisions ought to be made.

# Part V

---

# Casuistry and Conflict

Let us suppose, if only for the sake of argument, that some first or fundamental or ultimate principle of morality can somehow be proved or justified or established—or even that we simply adopt one and try to proceed from there. Now what possible relevance can this principle have to concrete problems of morality? This question, about the very possibility of practical ethics, is the question underlying this part. "General propositions do not decide concrete cases," Justice Holmes once stated, enunciating a general proposition which has ever since, judging from the number of times it is quoted, been taken as somehow decisive in deciding the concrete question of how general principles are relevant to concrete cases.[1]

On the standard definition of "casuistry" it is the science of the application of general ethical principles to particular cases of conscience or conduct, or perhaps the process of application itself. But the term also has come to acquire the derogatory sense of the fallacious or dishonest application of such principles, so that it has come to be regarded by many as synonymous with sophistry, "destroying, by distinctions and exceptions, all morality."[2] Yet there is no reason why "casuistry" *must* mean the same as "sophistry"; a casuist need not be a sophist. There are two different words; let there be two different meanings. At any rate, the issues concerning casuistry are sufficiently important and interesting to warrant separate treatment—though the student should be made aware that this

---

[1] In *Lochner* v. *New York,* 198 U.S. (1905) 45 at 74; reprinted in *The Mind and Faith of Justice Holmes,* ed. by Max Lerner (Boston: Little, Brown & Co., 1943), p. 149.

[2] This phrase is attributed to Lord Bolingbroke, in *The Shorter Oxford English Dictionary* entry under "casuistry."

is not a topic usually dealt with in ethics texts or anthologies. Included in this part are a number of contrasting and conflicting positions on the possibility, utility, and desirability of casuistry—and even its morality. Can general rules or principles be used to resolve any concrete question of conduct? Can they be used to resolve any moral conflicts or disagreements? Should they be so used? How can disagreements on these rules or principles or standards themselves be resolved? And how *should* they be resolved? Such questions are dealt with, in varying and conflicting ways, by the various selections in this part.

# STATEMENTS ON MORALITY
## Seventh Series

*52. No man lives without jostling and being jostled; in all ways he has to elbow himself through the world, giving and receiving offence. His life is a battle, in so far as it is an entity at all.*

Thomas Carlyle (1838)

*53. The great difficulty of the moral life is that our knowledge of right conduct, as embodied in the Decalogue, the Sermon on the Mount, or the Analects of Confucius, is abstract—like the articles of a constitution. The concrete application of the rules cannot help being difficult because we find ourselves in complex situations in which we usually are required to act on the spur of the moment. The Constitution states that a man may not be deprived of property without due process of law. What is "due process"? To answer this there are millions of words defining circumstances which the courts have studied at leisure. A comparable question in ethics cannot be similarly studied and defined to fit every case. For example: should one tell the truth, regardless of consequences? Ask any intelligent, responsible person you know and he or she will say: "It depends. Some consequences should be disregarded. Others not." Just so.*

Jacques Barzun (1954)

*54. It is well known that when people who stand for one value die, those who stand for an opposing value are happy. When Hitler was in power his death was freely wished for—and undoubtedly prayed for—by many Jews. Other examples could easily be cited. If these are the facts, it is irrational to behave as though everyone shared the same values and goals in life.*

Thomas Szasz (1960)

*55. In one sense indeed Morality depends upon Law. . . . Law supplies the definitions of some of the terms which morality employs; and without these definitions, moral rules would be indefinite, unmeaning and inapplicable. Morality says, You shall not seek or covet another man's property: Law defines what is another man's property. Morality says, You shall not desire her who is another man's wife: Law determines whether she be his wife. Morality says, Willingly obey and wisely rule, according to your station in society: Law determines what your station is. In this way, certainly, our moral precepts depend for their actual import on law.*

William Whewell (1854)

56. *We all acknowledge that, in matters of conduct, there is a definite standard of right and wrong. But although this abstract standard of morals is recognised as supreme and indefeasible, yet even here there are many concrete cases and questions about which good men might well feel a difficulty as to the right course of conduct to pursue. Aristotle long ago pointed out that in such cases the only criterion is the judgment of the right-thinking man, of the man whose habitual right conduct has endowed him with a right judgment. The same idea is expressed in more spiritual fashion by the canon of the Gospel, "If any man will do His will, he shall know of the doctrine." It is true that a perversion of this doctrine has given rise to the so-called science of casuistry, and casuistry has no good repute among right-thinking men. But there is a sound casuistry as well as an unsound; and no man can be said to have had a very wide ethical experience if his own conscience has never been confronted with a concrete conflict between right and wrong in the abstract.*

Anonymous (1915)

57. *It will be agreed on all hands that no number of moral rules will save us from exercising intuition; for a rule can only be general, but an act must be particular, so it will always be necessary to satisfy ourselves that an act comes under the rule, and for this no rule can be given.*

E. F. Carritt (1928)

58. *In passing moral judgments as we all sooner or later inevitably do in regard to legal and other human arrangements, we generally oscillate between the appeal to self-evident principles and the appeal to the obvious demands of the specific situation before us. This seems a highly unsatisfactory procedure to those who feel that certainty must be found in one or the other terminus, else all our moral judgments fail for lack of an assured support. . . .*

*. . . Such oscillation is under certain logical precautions and scientific systematization the only proper procedure . . . to trust rigid principles regardless of specific consequences makes for inhuman absolutism, while to rely on nothing but the feeling of the moment leads to brutal anarchy. Consider the ethical atomists who think that life breaks itself up into a number of separate autonomous situations, each immediately revealing its own good or proper solution to our conscience, intuition, or intuitive reason,*

*intelligence or common sense. When these moralists are confronted by a challenge to any of their particular judgments, they generally adduce some reason or at least cite an analogous case, thus involving explicitly or implicitly an appeal to some determining principle more abstract and wider than the specific case before them. On the other hand, those who rely on principles to decide specific cases do, and have to, defend these principles by showing that they lead to the proper consequences.*

Morris R. Cohen (1940)

# 32

## A Problem of Conduct*

### JEAN-PAUL SARTRE
(1905–    )

To give you an example which will enable you to understand forlorn-ness better, I shall cite the case of one of my students who came to see me under the following circumstances: his father was on bad terms with his mother, and, moreover, was inclined to be a collaborationist; his older brother had been killed in the German offensive of 1940, and the young man, with somewhat immature but generous feelings, wanted to avenge him. His mother lived alone with him, very much upset by the half-treason of her husband and the death of her older son; the boy was her only consolation.

The boy was faced with the choice of leaving for England and joining the Free French Forces—that is, leaving his mother behind—or remaining with his mother and helping her to carry on. He was fully aware that the woman lived only for him and that his going-off—and perhaps his death—would plunge her into despair. He was also aware that every act that he did for his mother's sake was a sure thing, in the sense that it was helping her to carry on, whereas every effort he made toward going off and fighting was an uncertain move which might run aground and prove completely useless; for example, on his way to England he might, while passing through Spain, be detained indefinitely in a Spanish camp; he might reach England or Algiers and be stuck in an office at a desk job. As a result, he was faced with two very different kinds of action: one, concrete, immediate, but concerning only one individual; the other concerned an incomparably vaster group, a national collectivity, but for that very reason

*From Jean-Paul Sartre, *Existentialism,* translated by Bernard Frechtmann (New York: Philosophical Library, 1947), pp. 28–31. The title of this selection has been supplied by the editor.

was dubious, and might be interrupted en route. And, at the same time, he was wavering between two kinds of ethics. On the one hand, an ethics of sympathy, of personal devotion; on the other, a broader ethics, but one whose efficacy was more dubious. He had to choose between the two.

Who could help him choose? Christian doctrine? No. Christian doctrine says, "Be charitable, love your neighbor, take the more rugged path, etc., etc." But which is the more rugged path? Whom should he love as a brother? The fighting man or his mother? Which does the greater good, the vague act of fighting in a group, or the concrete one of helping a particular human being to go on living? Who can decide *a priori?* Nobody. No book of ethics can tell him. The Kantian ethics says, "Never treat any person as a means, but as an end." Very well, if I stay with my mother, I'll treat her as an end and not as a means; but by virtue of this very fact, I'm running the risk of treating the people around me who are fighting, as means; and, conversely, if I go to join those who are fighting, I'll be treating them as an end, and, by doing that, I run the risk of treating my mother as a means.

If values are vague, and if they are always too broad for the concrete and specific case that we are considering, the only thing left for us is to trust our instincts. That's what this young man tried to do; and when I saw him, he said, "In the end, feeling is what counts. I ought to choose whichever pushes me in one direction. If I feel that I love my mother enough to sacrifice everything else for her—my desire for vengeance, for action, for adventure—then I'll stay with her. If, on the contrary, I feel that my love for my mother isn't enough, I'll leave." . . .

# 33

## *Casuistry and Morality**

# WILLIAM WHEWELL
## (1794–1866)

In the early Christian writers, though there is much on the subject of *Morality,* there is little or nothing which can properly be called *Moral Philosophy.* Moral questions are in those writings based almost entirely on the commands and doctrines of Scripture. Yet even in these cases, there enter necessarily into the discussion the general principles of morality which are universal in the human breast, and which must aid Christians in understanding, reconciling and applying the precepts of Scripture morality. Along with the *precepts* also, the *examples* contained in Scripture necessarily attract notice; and especially cases in which persons represented as the objects of divine favour are related to have performed actions which were, or seem at first sight to have been, at variance with the general rules of ordinary morality. The discussion of such cases led at an early period to a kind of Christian Casuistry. It would be easy to say of this, as is so often said of Casuistry in general, that it is a perverted and dangerous morality; but it may also be said of this, as may likewise be said of Casuistry in general, that it consists of attempts to answer questions which inevitably force themselves upon men's minds, which are not answered to the satisfaction of any thoughtful person by calling them perverted and dangerous, and to which answers really moral and Christian, in some form or other, must exist and ought to be pointed out by Christian teachers. If it be asked, for instance, whether Jacob did right, or was excusable, in personating his brother Esau, the proper answer may possibly be that he was; or that he was not; or that his action is no example for us; or that it is not to have common rules applied to it, being part of a special scheme of divine

*From William Whewell, *Lectures on the History of Moral Philosophy* (London, 2nd ed., 1862), Additional Lectures, pp. 78–79. The title of this selection has been supplied by the editor.

government; or that we do unwisely to seek to define a class of actions which are excusable though wrong:—or we might probably find other answers which might possibly be given: but it cannot be a matter of indifference to us which of those answers are more and which are less conformable to Christian truth, and fitted to promote Christian morality in those who ask the question and look for the answer as a part of their moral guidance. The condemnation of Casuistry applied to such cases should at least be put in an intelligible and temperate and definite form; and when this is done, such condemnation becomes itself a portion of Casuistry: of Casuistry in a good sense: meaning thereby an answer to the question, *What ought we to do in given cases:*—a question which can hardly be held to be a part of a perverse and dangerous morality; for if we are to have moral rules at all, we must include among them such questions as this. Nor can any generalities, such as a prohibition of all fraud, a reverent estimate of the plans of Providence, a contemplation of Scripture narratives for edification, be of much use to us, if we are not allowed to endeavour to make such injunctions consistent with each other. . . .

# 34

## A Critique of Casuistry*

### F. H. BRADLEY
(1846–1924)

The popular belief in logic endows it with ability to test all reasonings offered it. In a given case of given premises the logician is thought to be a spiritual Director who, if he can not supply, at least tests right and wrong. Thus, if logic is no art which provides us with arguments, yet, once give it the premises, and it is both the art of extracting conclusions and of assaying all those which amateurs have extracted without its authority. But, understood in this sense, logic has no existence, for there is and there can be no art of reasoning. Logic has to lay down a general theory of reasoning, which is true in general and in the abstract. But when it goes beyond that, it ceases to be a science, it ceases to be logic, and it becomes, what too much of it has already become, an effete chimæra which cries out for burial.

It should not lie alone. There is another false science more unlovely in life and more unpleasant in decay, from which I myself should be loath to divide it. Just as Logic has been perverted into the art of reasoning, so Ethics has been perverted into the art of morality. They are twin delusions we shall consign, if we are wise, to a common grave.

But I would not grudge Casuistry a Christian burial. I should be glad to see it dead and done with on any terms; and then, if all the truth must be spoken, in its later years it has suffered much wrong. That it became odious beyond parallel and in parts most filthy, is not to be denied; but it ill becomes the parents of a monster, who have begotten it and nourished it, to cry out when it follows the laws of its nature. And, if I am to say what I

---

*From F. H. Bradley, *The Principles of Logic* (Oxford: The Clarendon Press, 1883; 2nd ed., 1922), vol. I, pp. 268–71. Reprinted by permission of The Clarendon Press, Oxford. The title of this selection has been supplied by the editor. Compare with selections 9, 13, 16, and 19.

think, I must express my conviction that it is not only the Catholic priest, but it also is our Utilitarian moralist, who embraces the delusion which has borne such a progeny. If you believe, as our Utilitarian believes, that the philosopher should know the reason why each action is to be judged moral or immoral; if you believe that he at least should guide his action reflectively by an ethical code, which provides an universal rule and canon for every possible case, and should enlighten his more uninitiated fellows, then it seems to me you have wedded the mistake from which this offensive offspring has issued. It may be true that the office of professional confessor has made necessary a completer codification of offences, and has joined doctrinal vagaries to ethical blunders. We may allow that it was the lust for spiritual tyranny which choked the last whisper of the unsanctified conscience. It may be true that, in his effort theoretically to exhaust the possibilities of human depravity, the celibate priest dwelt with curious refinement on the morbid subject of sexual transgression. But unless his principle is wholly unsound I confess that I can hardly find fault with his practice; for if there is to be an art and a code of morality, I do not see how we can narrow its scope beforehand. The field is not limited by our dislikes, and whoever works at the disgusting parts, is surely deserving not of blame but of gratitude. Hence if the Utilitarian has declined to follow the priest, he has also declined to follow his own principles; he has stopped short not from logical reasons but from psychological causes.

It is natural to think that logic has to tell us how we are to reason from special premises; and it is natural to think that ethics must inform us how we are to act in particular cases. Our uncritical logic and our uncritical ethics naturally assume these doctrines as self-evident. But the mistake, if natural, is in both cases palpable. Unless you artificially limit the facts, then models of reasoning can not be procured, since you would need in the end an infinitude of schemes to parallel the infinitude of possible relations. And a code of morality is no less impossible. To anticipate the conclusion in each special case you would have to anticipate all possible cases; for the particular condition which makes *this* conduct right here and wrong elsewhere, will fall outside the abstractions of the code. You are thus committed to a dilemma: at a certain point you must cease to profess to go right by rule, or else, anticipating all possible combinations of circumstances, you must succeed in manufacturing countless major premises. The second alternative is in the first place illusory, since the principle is really got *from* the intuition, and in the next place it is impossible, since the number of principles will be limitless and endless. But if you accept the first alternative, and admit that only in certain cases it is possible to deduce the conclusion from a principle, you have given up the hope of your "practical reason," and denied the axiom from which you set out.

The syllogistic logic possesses one merit. If its basis is mistaken and its conclusion false, at least it has not stopped short of its goal. In *Barbara Celarent* its code is perfected, and it has carried out the purpose with which it began. We can not say so much of the Casuistry of Hedonism. The confident dogmatism of its setting-out has been lost in vagueness and in hesitation. It flies to ambiguities it does not venture to analyze, and sighs faintly to a Deity which it dares not invoke. But if the principle of our most fashionable Ethics is true, then an art of Casuistry and a Science of Sin are the goal of that Ethics, and the non-recognition of this evident result, if creditable to the heart, does no honour to the head. If the popular moralist will not declare for a thorough-going Casuistry, if he retires in confusion from the breath of its impurity, he should at least take courage to put away the principles which have given it life. We may apply to him as he stands a saying of Strauss, "He partly does not know what he wants, and partly does not want what he knows."

# 35

---

## Casuistry the Goal of
## Ethical Investigation*

### G. E. MOORE
(1873–1958)

. . . We may be told that Casuistry differs from Ethics, in that it is
much more detailed and particular, Ethics much more general. But it is
most important to notice that Casuistry does not deal with anything that is
absolutely particular—particular in the only sense in which a perfectly
precise line can be drawn between it and what is general. It is not particular
in the sense just noticed, the sense in which this book is a particular book,
and A's friend's advice particular advice. Casuistry may indeed be *more*
particular and Ethics *more* general; but that means that they differ only in
degree and not in kind. And this is universally true of "particular" and
"general," when used in this common, but inaccurate, sense. So far as
Ethics allows itself to give lists of virtues or even to name constituents of the
Ideal, it is indistinguishable from Casuistry. Both alike deal with what is
general, in the sense in which physics and chemistry deal with what is
general. Just as chemistry aims at discovering what are the properties of
oxygen, *wherever it occurs,* and not only of this or that particular specimen of
oxygen; so Casuistry aims at discovering what actions are good, *whenever
they occur.* In this respect Ethics and Casuistry alike are to be classed with
such sciences as physics, chemistry and physiology, in their absolute
distinction from those of which history and geography are instances. And it
is to be noted that, owing to their detailed nature, casuistical investigations
are actually nearer to physics and to chemistry than are the investigations
usually assigned to Ethics. For just as physics cannot rest content with the
discovery that light is propagated by waves of ether, but must go on to
discover the particular nature of the ether-waves corresponding to each

*From G. E. Moore, *Principia Ethica,* Cambridge University Press (1903), pp. 4–5. Reprinted by permission. The title of this selection has been supplied by the editor.

several colour; so Casuistry, not content with the general law that charity is a virtue must attempt to discover the relative merits of every different form of charity. Casuistry forms, therefore, part of the ideal of ethical science: Ethics cannot be complete without it. The defects of Casuistry are not defects of principle; no objection can be taken to its aim and object. It has failed only because it is far too difficult a subject to be treated adequately in our present state of knowledge. The casuist has been unable to distinguish, in the cases which he treats, those elements upon which their value depends. Hence he often thinks two cases to be alike in respect of value, when in reality they are alike only in some other respect. It is to mistakes of this kind that the pernicious influence of such investigations has been due. For Casuistry is the goal of ethical investigation. It cannot be safely attempted at the beginning of our studies, but only at the end. . . .

# 36

## The Possibility of Casuistry*

### HASTINGS RASHDALL
(1858–1928)

Many of the objections commonly urged against the possibility of Casuistry seem, indeed, to turn upon easily demonstrated mistakes, confusions, or exaggerations. It is urged that the complexity of life is so great that no two cases of conduct resemble one another, and that therefore each case must be considered on its own merits. If this means that there are no general principles in Ethics at all, the objection is one which has been already dealt with, and which is not open to those who have accepted our ethical method. If it means merely that, besides features which the case has in common with other cases, it has features peculiar to itself, that is true; and it is true equally of every medical case—a consideration which does not prevent Medical Science and medical books from being of the utmost utility. No two cases are exactly alike, but they may be alike in all relevant particulars; or if not alike, the difference can be allowed for in the treatment of the particular case—an allowance which may itself be covered by some more or less definable general principle. The existence of Medical Science and medical books does not dispense with the need for the trained tact of the Physician, or even (in some cases) with the exercise of common sense by the patient. The argument would only tend to show that the trained Casuist must be as important as his Science. Then it is urged that, though the detailed consideration of ethical questions is possible, it is morally unwholesome and undesirable. The objection seems to be largely based upon the concentration of attention upon one or two particular departments of Morality, in which no doubt the objection has some force;

*From Hastings Rashdall, *The Theory of Good and Evil* (Oxford: The Clarendon Press, 1907; 2nd ed., 1924), vol. II, pp. 428–29, 443–44. By permission of The Clarendon Press, Oxford. The title has been somewhat modified.

276 / HASTINGS RASHDALL

though the medical analogy might still allow the apologist of Casuistry to plead that the task, though disagreeable and not without moral peril, has to be faced on certain occasions and by certain persons. But the most serious misconception which seems to be at the bottom of the objection lies in the assumption that Casuistry necessarily deals with detailed particular cases—either cases which have actually occurred or which may occur, envisaged in all the wealth and variety of circumstance which belongs to actual life. This is a complete misunderstanding. Casuistry deals with classes of cases. And there is no difference in principle between such discussions as we find in the pages of so comparatively uncasuistical a Moralist as Green—discussions, for instance, as to the grounds for asserting the principle of monogamous marriage or as to the conditions under which political rebellion is justifiable—and the kind of cases which fill the pages of the professed theological Casuists, Roman Catholic, Puritan, or Anglican. At most the difference is merely one in the degree of particularity to which the discussion is carried. Even if we admitted that objections exist to the detailed anticipation of those strange and abnormal difficulties which seldom occur, and in which the true solution depends upon such a delicate estimate of circumstances that the actual case will never be exactly the anticipated case, there would still be room for a Casuistry which should deal with the difficulties which do arise every day—the question when if ever it is right to tell a lie, what constitutes a just price or a just wage, what constitutes commercial Morality, the morality of gambling, the legitimacy of field sports or of Vivisection, and the like. And in these questions there would seem to be room both for the casuistical writer and for the trained judgement of the expert in that Science. . . .

. . . Most of the objections brought against Casuistry, whether in its theological or its purely philosophical form, affect mainly the scientific consideration of individual, and especially of abnormal and exceptional, problems in conduct. The most, it seems to me, that Moral Philosophy can do for such cases is to produce, in conjunction with other studies and influences, a habit of mind favourable to their reasonable consideration. We may quite well deprecate the discussion of such abnormal cases by anticipation, and may even admit that when they do occur in actual practice a healthy instinct will decide them better than theoretical subtlety.. But the assailant of Casuistry usually talks as if on the general questions of conduct—on those general questions of which each man has to settle a good many for himself one way or another every day between the time he gets up in the morning and the time he goes to bed at night—he talks (I say) as if on such questions as these there was a general consensus, at least among sensible and well-meaning people. Such an assumption seems to me the very shallowest of delusions. Directly we leave words and come to things, the consensus disappears. It is merely the vagueness of language that seems to sanction its existence. People are agreed, no doubt, as to the wrongness of murder. But that is only because murder means killing, except where killing is justifiable. As to the immorality of killing in war, or by means of punishment, or to reduce population, or by way of Euthanasia, there is no consensus at all. No doubt, in these questions of merely negative Morality there is an approximate consensus among the great majority. But come to positive precepts. There, again, we find a consensus as to copy-book headings, such as "Be truthful, be honest, be charitable, be temperate." There is a consensus as to virtues; there is none as to duties. "Be temperate." Yes. But there are many ways of being temperate. It is possible to eat and drink wealth equivalent to one pound, or even five pounds, a day without positively injuring one's constitution; and it is possible also to live on a shilling a day, or with practice on a great deal less. Which course am I to adopt, my income and position being so-and-so? I ought to give money to Charity; but how much? I ought to provide for the future; but how much? I ought to devote myself to my profession; but how much time should I give to my pupils? I ought to research; but how ought I to divide my time between research, teaching, and amusement, or more general social duties? It is no use to say that an exact determination of such questions is impossible. There is scarcely a consensus as to the barest outline of an answer. It is on these general questions of conduct, which can never be escaped, rather than in the discussion of abnormal complications of individual circumstance, that the practical application of clearly thought out ethical principles seems likely to be most fruitful.

## 37

## *Casuistry* \*

# RICHARD TAYLOR
(1919–    )

If there is a true morality, embodying true general principles of right and wrong, then it ought to be possible to apply them to particular actions to see whether such actions do or do not possess the moral quality of rightness. Thus, if among the various alternative actions open to one, the *right* action will be the one that will, more than any of the others, promote the greatest happiness for the greatest number, then we can determine which is the right action by seeing, as best we can, which has that tendency. Or on the other hand, if a right action is one that is prompted by duty, and it is one's duty always to so act that one could will the maxim of his action to be a universal law for all rational beings, then again, one can determine whether his action is right by seeing whether it is so motivated; and so on.

This is the procedure of *casuistry*, which can be defined as the determination of the moral quality of particular actions by the subsumption of them under true general rules or principles of morality. It is almost invariably the approach most persons take to moral problems, whether they know the name for it or not, and most moralists seem to presuppose its legitimacy. Most moral philosophers seem to think it extremely important to find and enunciate some ultimate principle of moral rightness, the implication being that such a principle can then be used as a criterion for the moral praiseworthiness or blameworthiness of particular actions.

Here I am going to show that such a procedure is quite impossible, and that the customary approach to moral decisions is, therefore, fundamentally mistaken. What are appealed to as moral principles are usually

*Reprinted with permission of Macmillan Publishing Co., Inc. from *Good and Evil: A New Direction* (ch. 12, pp. 161–77) by Richard Taylor. Copyright © 1970 by Richard Taylor. Compare with, among others, selections 15 and 16 and statement 58.

rationalizations for courses of action decided on quite independently of any such principle. Casuistry is, in fact, always a putting of the cart before the horse, for the general principles in terms of which men try to justify their conduct are themselves only justified by the assumed rightness of that conduct itself. There seems to be no exception to this. It becomes perfectly evident when we discover that in case of a clear conflict between a given course of action that seems wholly right and proper on its own merits and some principle that we had hitherto thought to be true and unexceptionable, it is the principle that is modified or abandoned, rather than the action itself.

More particularly, we shall see that:

1. There is no general moral principle declaring a certain kind of action to be always right or always wrong that cannot be shown to have an exception, even in the eyes of those who declare their allegiance to that principle.

2. Such an exception to the principle cannot (obviously) be made on the basis of the principle itself and must, therefore, be made either (a) on the basis of some still higher principle, or (b) on some other ground.

3. It cannot be made on the basis of some still higher principle, for such a principle will itself, under (1), admit of exceptions, even in the eyes of those who uphold it.

4. Exceptions to general principles are, therefore, made on some other ground, and that is what I shall call ordinary human feeling.

5. Because such ordinary human feeling is, therefore, what finally settles the matter anyway, the moral principle was superfluous from the outset, contributing nothing to the judgment of whether a given course of action is right or wrong.

That, somewhat formally stated, is the thesis, and it now needs to be filled out and made clear.

## The Futility of Justifying Conduct

In the meantime, the importance of this claim should be well understood. For if what I am saying is correct, it follows that the usual, typical, and normal approach to questions of morality is basically wrong. When a man appears, perhaps to himself as well as to others, to have given a moral justification for a certain course of conduct by showing that it accords with some general principle of rightness, he has in fact done nothing of the sort. The principle to which he appeals is itself in need of justification, and (here is the rub) nothing under the sun can possibly justify that principle unless the course of action in question is itself seen to be right independently of that principle. When one appeals to a moral principle in justification of his decision, he only succeeds in changing the subject; he in no way justifies anything. He changes the subject to the principle itself, which now comes under scrutiny, and if, as is typical, this principle is "justified" by still another principle, then he only manages to change the subject still another time. This, I believe, is the basic reason why discussions of morality are so invariably inconclusive and no one's mind is really changed about anything. They involve a perpetual jump from one subject to another, getting further and further away from the issue originally raised, without hope of settling anything. We can also find here the basis for a very common illusion about moral problems: namely, that the answers to moral problems are very difficult to reach. Indeed they are, if they are sought in this way, for *that* kind of answer does not even exist. Still, people simply assume that the only allowable moral justification of an action must be in terms of some moral principle, and plenty of philosophers reinforce this assumption. Moral discussion therefore weaves tortuously from principle to principle, going about in circles, getting increasingly remote from the issue at hand, in a vain search for "the answer." Insofar as the answer exists at all, however, it lies right under one's nose, in the very action itself, and cannot possibly exist anywhere else. It is as if a man were to set forth from his cottage in search of his son, getting farther and farther away and still with nothing but misleading clues, until he finally gave up and came home to find the youngster in bed.

## Samples of Casuistry

Let us consider some typical examples of casuistry.

*Sample 1.* A man of military age decides to resist a summons to serve; he will go to jail first, or perhaps flee the country. Why? "Because killing is wrong" (the appeal to a principle). Does he mean *all* killing is wrong—for that is what the principle seems to assert—such that one may not innocently swat a mosquito that is biting him, for example? This he dismisses as pettifogging. Obviously, what he is talking about is killing *people*. This is what is wrong, and because serving in war might oblige him to do it, he will, in obedience to his conscience, resist serving. (Here, it will be noted, "conscience" comes into the picture and plainly means nothing more than allegiance to a principle.) So the principle—and it is a slightly new one—is that it is always, without exception, wrong to kill any *man*. Then one may not drive a car, even with due care, over any considerable distance on crowded highways, or build great bridges or tunnels for human convenience, or fly in airplanes, because all such activities clearly risk life, and in fact take great tolls of it each day? This he again dismisses as petti-fogging—he was not talking of that sort of thing. What he meant was the *deliberate* taking of human life—shooting at people, and that sort of thing. That is what is morally wrong, and is always so. So the principle, it must not be overlooked, has been changed still again. At this point the discussion can go in either of two directions, each of which will, in its own way, get us a bit further from the question at hand. First, one can seek a definition of "deliberate," which will conveniently serve to rule out what the man wants to rule out while preserving what he wants to preserve—a definition, for example, that will enable one to say that driving down crowded highways is not deliberate, whereas marching off to boot camp, the alternative being jail, is. Or secondly, one can skip all that and look at the new principle here. Suppose we go in the second direction. Here someone will say, "What if a madman is approaching your wife and children with a knife, bent on cutting them to pieces, and you can only stop him by shooting at him?" Or, perhaps, "What if your wife were pregnant, but in such a way that her life could only be preserved by an abortion?" Or other cases of that sort that are, of course, proposed as the *deliberate* taking of human life. Now the challenge is to modify the principle still once more, thus producing what is really a new principle—and so on and on. But here is the thing to note: At every stage of this attempted justification, a moral principle, already enunciated, is modified for the obvious purpose of *ruling out* those cases to which it *does not apply*. And why does it "not apply" to these? Not, obvi-ously, because they do not in fact fall under it, for they do. If killing is wrong (period), then killing a mosquito is wrong. The principle is thought not to apply to these cases because they are *not* considered morally wrong. It is thought to be no sin to kill a mosquito, drive a car with due care, or (perhaps) even permit an abortion in some circumstance. The principle was not *meant* to cover things of this sort. What it was *meant* to cover is the thing with which we began: going off to war. But now look at what has hap-pened. It is assumed that we already know, without appealing to any principle, that certain things are *not wrong*. Moreover, someone seems to be assuming, before he even has any principle to justify it, that something *is* wrong, and the only job then is to tailor some principle to show why it is wrong. This is the whole course of the discussion. Something is just assumed to be wrong and other things not wrong, quite independently of any principles of right and wrong, and then the whole discussion is aimed at finding some principle that will *fit* what is thus already assumed. This is not the justification of anything. It is at best a game of definition, and at worst, pure rationalization.

At this point the question should honestly be faced: If we already know that certain things are *not* wrong, and if someone thinks he already knows that something, not agreed to by others, *is* wrong, then just how are these things known? Not, obviously, by the light of any moral principles, for no principles were suggested, and certainly none were needed, for the former, and every principle proposed for the latter was immediately proved to be inadequate. Indeed, what the whole discussion turned on was not the justification of any course of action in the light of some principle, but the very opposite; that is, the justification of the principle itself by whatever modifications and amendments seemed required, in the light of various actions antecedently thought to be right or wrong.

*Sample 2.* This time we shall start, not with some proposed course of action, but with a moral principle that is thought to be fairly secure. We shall then see what happens to the principle when the attempt is made to apply it to difficult cases. Here the point will be to illustrate how a principle, which is supposed to provide the very criterion of right and wrong, is admitted to have exceptions, even by those sworn to uphold that principle. If this is so, then it will show that some criterion *other* than the principle is the one that is really at work.

Let the principle then be the commandment "Thou shalt not kill." Let us grant at once that what is intended by this principle is that one may not, without moral guilt, deliberately and with premeditation take the life of another human being, and furthermore that no considerations of practical advantages to others can morally justify such an act.

Now it is pretty clear that such a principle, if rigidly adhered to, is going to have some very real and large consequences in some situation. Let us consider, then, a hospital administered by a church that is sworn to uphold that commandment—not merely to respect it, in the sense of paying lip service to it, but actually to decide difficult cases by applying the principle without any exception. In such a hospital no nurse or physician will intentionally administer to any patient any substance that might precipitate or hasten that patient's death. Now if a medication seems called for that might, admittedly, shorten life, but it is administered for some other purpose—for the alleviation of pain, for example—then such a course is perhaps not forbidden, because the purpose or intention of the medication is not to hasten death, but rather, to alleviate pain, which is a permissible end. What is forbidden is the deliberate hastening of death, even though the interests of others and even those of the patient might greatly be served by such action. One could not, for example, take the life of a patient in order to relieve the work load of the nurses. And of course a terminal disease will provide no exception. If a patient is clearly approaching death day by day, and there is no hope whatsoever of reversing this course, then his family might, indeed, wish profoundly that the disease and its suffering might not be prolonged. But if such a wish is expressed as a request that his life be shortened, it cannot be honored, and the moral justification for refusal will be the principle: One may not deliberately take the life of another, even if the interests of others would greatly be served by such action. In short, murder is wrong. And finally, of course, abortion of pregnancy is ruled out on the same principle. Even though the pregnancy may have resulted from rape or from incest, or there may be clear evidence that it is seriously abnormal, such that the resulting birth will be grossly deformed, the prohibition of murder will be followed. A child, although unborn, is already human. It does not await the light of day or the first drawing of breath to become a human being, although of course it is not fully developed. The rule thus becomes, in such cases, that one may not deliberately take the life of the child, even though the interests of others—of the mother herself, for example—would be greatly enhanced by that step.

The principle appears, then, to admit of no exception. It can be applied in all situations, and what is forbidden will stand out very clearly as morally wrong. One will, accordingly, have a *moral* justification for his conduct whenever it falls under that principle, and the principle is adhered to.

So it seems, but now let us look again. Suppose the hospital is subjected to aerial bombardment; is one not permitted to shoot back? Well, it will be said, this (obviously) puts the whole thing into a new dimension. The principle was not meant (note) to condemn war, as such, nor was it meant (note again) to apply to every case of self-defense, or the defense of things one is sworn to protect. Now it will be noted that already exceptions are being made, but what must be particularly noted is that they are *not* made on the basis of that principle. How can they be, when they are exceptions to the principle? What has happened here is that a certain course of action is assumed to be permissible, quite apart from this or any other principle, and it is then simply declared that the principle was not *meant* to rule it out. Of what final use, then, was the principle anyway? And may not one then declare, with equal justification (and lack of it), that the principle was not meant to rule out abortion or euthanasia either?

Let us, then, stay within the dimension in which the principle is declared to have no exception, the relatively narrow dimension involving only the care of persons consigned to hospital treatment. We suppose a case of ectopic pregnancy, in which the embryo becomes lodged, and begins to develop, within the fallopian tube. Now in such cases the foetus cannot develop and be born; it will inevitably die and abort itself, sooner or later.

In the meantime, however, there is grave danger to the mother, for she is exceedingly likely to perish unless an abortion is performed promptly. *Now* what shall we do in the light of the principle that one may not deliberately take the life of another, even though this would greatly serve the interests of others, or in the light of the more particular principle, that one may not take the life of the unborn child?

The course of action actually taken in such cases is, of course, abortion, although this was allowed to become a policy only after the most tortuous casuistry of theologians, who were confronted with the impossible task of maintaining the authority of a principle while declaring that it does not always apply. What actually determines that this type of case constitutes an exception to the principle is no moral principle at all, even though one could perhaps be contrived. It is nothing but ordinary common sense and human feeling. If the result of doing nothing is going to be the loss of *two* lives, whereas one life can be saved by taking the other, soon destined to be lost anyway, then one needs no moral principle to discover the course of action to take. Common sense produces its verdict, and no moral principle whatever, from whatever source it may issue, overrules it. On the contrary, as soon as the principle is discovered to conflict with what is so plainly seen to be not wrong, then it is the principle that yields. If one then contrives some still "higher" principle that will reconcile the contradiction between moral principle and common sense, then he does not, as he may imagine, preserve moral principles after all; he only conceals his rejection of them.

*Sample 3.* I shall now render two descriptions of the same case. The first description will be a general one, in which a series of events is correctly described, but not in detail. The second will simply fill in the details.

The general description is this: A man came into possession of a very small human being. He nurtured it for a time, with great devotion and care, but then after a while discovered that it was developing quite abnormally, whereupon he deliberately destroyed it.

Now, with only that before us, let us ask: Did the man commit a murder? Did he do something morally wrong? Is seems quite clear that, if the description of what happened is true, the first answer is Yes, and most persons would be inclined to answer the other in the same way. Now why? Because the action fits the definition of murder, and there is a general moral principle that murder is morally wrong.

The more detailed description of the same set of events is this: A medical researcher succeeded in fertilizing a human ovum in his laboratory, in a dish. The ovum began to develop, in a quite normal way, and this development proceeded for a considerable time, upward of three weeks, at which time serious abnormality became quite apparent under magnification. The researcher then flushed the contents of the dish into the sink.

*Now* the answers to our two questions are not so apparent. Hardly anyone will say that a murder was committed, and hence a moral wrong, even though some might object to such an experiment being undertaken to begin with, which is of course another question altogether.

What is significant, however, is the reasoning by which men are now apt to counter their original verdict. It was not, they say, really a human being at all. It was not large enough. Or it was not conceived in a natural way. Or it did not look like the usual human being. Or it had not yet begun to draw breath, or to move, or whatnot. But here the thing to note is that an effort is being made to *define a term* (*human*) in such a way as to preserve the second verdict of innocence of murder, without in any way appearing to unsettle the moral principle that gave rise to the first verdict. (It is perhaps worth noting that, even in the first very general description, it was conceded that the human being was "very small," and nothing was said concerning whether it was or was not normally conceived or how it looked to the eye.) Surely it would be more honest to put the matter like this: Technically, a living human being, although a minute one, was deliberately destroyed; hence, technically, a murder was committed, according to a perfectly good definition of murder. Under these bizarre circumstances, however, murder is not really wrong, notwithstanding the moral principle.

The other approach, involving finding a definition of human that will enable us to arrive at what is for all practical purposes the same conclusion while still appearing to preserve the moral law, is the one most persons feel somehow obliged to pursue, and it is not hard to see why. It is simply assumed that the moral principle has got to be true, and that no exception should be granted. One thus feels compelled to find some way of describing the exception, so that it will not be an exception.

It will not work, however, as can be seen from the following. Let us suppose that the abnormality is discovered a bit later on. Suppose that this child, conceived in a dish, develops fairly normally for about three hundred days and then begins to draw breath. It turns out to be a boy, and a few months later the first tooth appears, a few months after that he begins to walk, and to say a few words—"daddy" and that sort of thing. But *then,* at that still undeveloped stage, abnormality is discovered—one ear is found to be very distorted, and he appears deaf in that ear. So at that point, being still very small, he is destroyed. *Now* who will say he was not "really" a human being—that he was too small, or not conceived in a natural way, or did not look (quite) like normal human beings? Here, surely, our original verdict still stands. A murder was done, and the size, shape, manner of conception, and so on, of whoever was killed are quite plainly irrelevant. They were as irrelevant before. A human life was taken in either case, even though, in neither case, was it a life that was fully developed. But in the first case this was not, as then seemed quite obvious, morally wrong. Of course some would, at this point, revise this verdict and conclude that even this was murder *and hence wrong* after all. This shows how desperately one wants to cling to a moral principle, at whatever cost.

## The Significance of These Examples

Now it is important not to lose sight of the philosophical issue these examples were meant to exhibit. What we are concerned with is not whether it is sometimes morally permissible to take human life. We are not discussing the morality of war, abortion, or the like. In fact, the issue before us now is no moral one at all. It is a purely philosophical one, expressed in the claim that there is no moral principle, whatever it might be, that will not be admitted to have some exception, even by those sworn to uphold it. Such an exception is made, it appears, not on the basis of the principle itself, which is plainly impossible, nor on the basis of any other principle, but on the basis of common sense or ordinary human feeling. More specifically, it is made in the light of the practical consequences of one's actions, and how these affect the deepest interests of those involved. Nor is this to propose still another criterion or morality: namely, that an action is right if its consequences are good. No such claim has been made. On the contrary, I have suggested that there is *no* principle, generality, or rule whatever that will guide one to the "right" action. Even to put matters in those terms—in terms of what is the right as opposed to the wrong action—is to invite all over again an exercise in casuistry, and it is the entire enterprise of moral casuistry, on whatever terms it is conducted, that is declared to be impossible. The very nature of such an approach precludes its ever giving any knowledge of what is right or what is wrong, for it must at every step presuppose that we already know this, at least in certain clear and "obvious" cases.

## The Function of Principles

From this it of course does not follow that moral rules and principles have no function or use, or that they should be scorned. It only follows that they cannot be used in the way that is so often attempted: to grind out "answers" to moral problems. It is not merely that, when so used, they work badly; they do not work for that purpose at all. The question of whether a given course of conduct is or is not morally right—that is, does or does not conform to a moral principle—is not, contrary to what is generally supposed, the basic question at all. It cannot be, because it cannot be answered. One can find, quite easily, whether a given action does or does not conform to a rule; but this never, by itself, tells one whether the action is morally right, wrong, or indifferent. The principle itself can find no justification except in the rightness of the actions that fall under it, and when tested in that way, no such principle is unexceptionably true. We must always, in any case, first find what we should do, and after that see whether this does or does not agree with any principle. The principle, accordingly, can never tell us what we should do. If we did not somehow know that already, we would have no way whatever of knowing what principles to embrace.

Moral principles are nothing but conventions, but they have the real and enormous value to life that conventions in general possess. They help men to get where they want to go. Without them social life would be impossible, and hence any kind of life that is distinctively human. Their justification is, therefore, a practical one and has nothing to do with moral considerations in the abstract. The moment such a principle ceases to have that value, the moment its application produces more evil than good, then it ceases to have any significance at all and ought to be scorned. Nothing is achieved, other than those dexterous feats of intellectual dishonesty called casuistry, by paying homage to the principle while redefining all the terms necessary to abate its effects. It is far simpler and more honest to declare: Here the principle ceases to work; let us cast it from view; we owe it nothing, and it is not going to coerce us.

The purely practical basis and the justification of rules of conduct are very obvious in the case of those that have not been so hallowed by age as to acquire in our minds the status of moral principles. Rules governing the movement of vehicular traffic are good examples. There is, for example, no ultimate moral principle from which it can be derived that cars should proceed on the right lane rather than the left of the highway. Countries that follow the opposite practice are not censured in our eyes. All that matters is that there be *a* rule, and the reason it matters is very obvious. General adherence to the rule enables people, quite literally, to get where they want to go. The rule minimizes hindrances, obstacles, and danger. It is for this reason, and this reason only, that it ought to be followed; its practical justification is its moral justification, and the whole of it. When, accordingly, circumstances arise such that adherence to the rule would cause more harm than good, its whole basis is swept away and it ought then to be disregarded. This is recognized by all in the case of an ambulance, under certain conditions, on an urgent mission. The driver of such a vehicle would be a fool who deemed it an unexceptionable principle to drive always in the manner prescribed by the rule, even though it was obvious that, in some situations, this would produce great harm. He would be no less a fool if he cast about for some higher principle to justify every departure from it. The only "principle" involved is a practical concern for human welfare. It is the only justification for the rule to begin with, and no other justification is required for departing from it, provided such a justification for the departure actually exists.

The case is no different with what men have come to think of as *moral* rules and principles, except that these are much older, have acquired the venerability bestowed by time, and have for the most part become embodied in religion. The rules against murder, adultery, bigamy, and so on have an obvious practical basis. Like traffic rules, they enable men to get where they want to go, with the minimum of hindrance and danger, although in not so literal a sense. "Enabling men to get where they want to go" means, here, enabling them to fulfill their various aims and purposes in such a way as to hinder as little as possible the pursuits of others. All such rules prohibit certain ends, or the means to them, in order that other more widespread and important pursuits may flourish. The general utility of the rule against murder, for instance, is too obvious to belabor. The utility of the prohibition of adultery and bigamy is hardly less obvious. Such rules tend, although not infallibly, to protect home life, in which most men have a deep interest, as well as the interests of children. As with all rules, however, they do not always work. Adherence to them can sometimes produce more harm than good and in such circumstances the basis for adherence evaporates. It is probably the reluctance to face this fact that has led men to suppose that such rules have some origin other than practical utility. It is, once one has become accustomed to it, easier to follow the rule than to depart from it. It gives one a sense of security and innocence and relieves him of the necessity to think or to make difficult decisions. Men accordingly invent other sources for the rules, saying, for example, that they are delivered by God, or that they are derived from some eternal Moral Law.

Does a wise man, then, deal lightly with rules and conventions, following or departing from them as he pleases? Surely not. A general adherence to rules that is not slavish, unthinking, and mechanical, even in situations in which there seems to be no practical point to it, is perhaps a virtue, although certainly a minor one. It is by such general adherence to rules, just because they are rules, that social life is made regular and predictable, and this is itself a considerable source of security. If the members of any group know what the rules are and in general comply with them, then human relationships are enlivened and relieved of friction and uncertainties. This does not imply, however, that rules, even though one chooses to view them as principles of morality, are to be respected for their own sake and adhered to mechanically; for it always remains possible that the violation of a rule on a given occasion—the violation, if one likes, of a "fixed" moral principle—will still produce more good than harm. Putting the matter graphically, a man should really think twice before committing a murder, just as one should think twice before going through a red light. A man of very dull understanding might take this to mean that murder is considered to be no more significant than a traffic violation, but one of more sense will not fail to see its true meaning. The rules involved here have, certainly, not the same importance, but the justification of both is identical, and in neither case does that justification always hold.

There is a strong tendency in men, particularly in those who think a great deal, to prize consistency above ordinary human goodness. Such persons are apt to extend consistency beyond thought and opinion to conduct itself, and then, almost before one realizes what has happened, one finds them *equating* human goodness with consistency of behavior—that is, with acting on principles. It is in such a mind that casuistry flourishes, in spite of its inherent defects. Moral principles can become, in such a mind, veritable tyrants, guiding one into courses of conduct in which no fine conscience or good sense can find the slightest merit. The actions of such a man have in their favor only this, that they are *consistent* with the rest of his actions, or in other words, that they fall under some rule. But clearly, it is perfectly possible for a truly good man to pursue one course of conduct one day and the very opposite course the next, enhancing the goodness in the world both times. It is hardly a justification for any action that it resembles one that was done yesterday, or indeed, that it resembles those one has done all his life. Suppose one were to say, "Yes, I can see that what I am about to do might be a bit cruel on this occasion, if one puts it in those terms; still, there *is* the moral principle to consider, and it clearly obliges me to act in this way." Surely one does not detect here any expression of human goodness. One detects only consistency.[1] Worse than this, such devotion to moral principle easily provides rationalization and excuse for conduct that

---

[1] Compare Mark Twain's remark: "I am persuaded that the world has been tricked into adopting some false and most pernicious notions about consistency—and to such a degree that the average man has turned the rights and wrongs of things entirely around, and is proud to be 'consistent,' unchanging, immovable, fossilized, where it should be his humiliation that he is so." *The Complete Essays of Mark Twain.* Charles Neider, ed. (Garden City, N.Y.: Doubleday & Co., 1963), p. 583.

290 / RICHARD TAYLOR

one could not, without the principle, possibly approve. More than one abominable cruelty has been committed in obedience to the most high-sounding principle, more than one vicious truth has been uttered out of respect for veracity, and plenty of men have been needlessly punished for breaking rules that needed breaking. A decent and sensitive man does not, in any case, imagine that the sweet and considerate things he does stand in need of the guild stamp of any moral principle. Their goodness is apparent in the actions themselves; or if it is not, then no moral rule will bring it to light. On the contrary, when a man is found justifying his conduct by citing principles and rules, it is not unreasonable to suspect that he is excusing himself—that he is doing what would never occur to any really decent person—and then making it look all right by its conformity to principle. Moral principles, if conscientiously applied, sometimes enable one to get through life with the minimum risk of censure, but by themselves they tend to deaden rather than enliven the heart. Even though they sometimes serve to minimize evils, if not applied too rigorously, they rarely give birth to genuine goodness.

# 38

## The Application to Practice*

## JOHN LAIRD
### (1887–1946)

. . . What has to be justified in any given case is action, and actions are always particular events, actual particulars when they are actual, possible particulars when we consider only what might be done. To be sure, the detail of all practice is as good as infinite, and there is multitudinous variety between particular actions of the same general type. Despite this, it is essential for us to consider the manner, extent, and security of moral guidance in respect to particular deeds.

This is the subject sometimes called casuistry, an art which, according to Mr. Bradley,[1] is "unlovely in life and unpleasant in decay, from which I myself should be loath to divide it," and, according to Mr. Moore,[2] is "the goal of ethical investigation." The first of these judgments appears to be rather a condemnation of certain casuists than a reflection upon their art, and the second to applaud a goal that can seldom, perhaps, be reached. Even if our ethical studies, however, have to remain imperfectly casuistical (either from the nature of things, or on account of our invincible ignorance) they might still give important instruction concerning actual doing, and there does not seem to be the slightest reason why the scrutiny of particular actions should necessarily suggest evasion, or have to peer into matters which a healthy, blunt, ignorant reaction is content to ignore. In short, Mr. Bradley seems to be wrong—or merely a-weary of the *Ductor Dubitantium* and its fellows. It is surely neither offensive nor peculiar to suppose that Omniscience Itself knows the right in its very letters and in its commas, or

*From John Laird, *A Study in Moral Theory* (London: George Allen & Unwin Ltd., 1926), pp. 62–63.
[1]*Principles of Logic*, p. 247. [p. 270 this volume.]
[2]*Principia Ethica*, p. 5. [p. 274 this volume.]

that certain duties (such as the "perfect obligation" of paying one's debts) may be precise to a farthing. In any case, vituperation is needless. Casuistry may, indeed, be dull; but in principle it is void of offence. There *is* an art of morals, for morality includes wise living; and this is an art. This art, moreover, must apply to particular actions. . . .

# 39

## The Use of Moral Principles*

### JOHN LAIRD

### (1887–1946)

1. It would be generally agreed that if some particular moral obligation is our duty, that is, is the decisive moral obligation in some particular case, and if that duty is also completely determinate (like debt-paying, the keeping of a clear promise, or the telling of the simple truth), then the moral agent has only to apply his general rule and he will know, in detail, how to act. It is also argued, however, that much of our duty is far more intricate, and that the niceties of the particular case must very often be decided by trained moral perception and not by the juridical application, *in foro conscientiae,* of general rules. As in the natural world so in the moral. Perception acquaints us with what is individual, or else individuality escapes us. Logic and general rules are too abstract for this office. But moral problems are problems of life itself, and moral principles also are too abstract to insinuate themselves into the particularity of life and change.

It is safest to express this view in Greek, ἐν τῇ αἰσθήσει ἡ κρίσις. The English of it, "the decision rests with perception," is far too ambiguous and far too disputable to be comforting; but we might perhaps admit that most decisions, moral or non-moral, require gumption.

(*a*) We need perception to inform us that there *is* a particular case, i.e. that the instance exists and that its actual nature is such and such. This inevitable circumstance, however, tells us only that we have to deal with actual situations, and not that the things we ought to do about them, our moral obligations regarding them, are themselves perceptual.

Moral situations deal with human factors, and very largely with the minds of men. Much of the relevant "perception," indeed, includes the

*From John Laird, *An Enquiry into Moral Notions* (London: George Allen & Unwin Ltd., 1935), pp. 156–62. The title of this selection has been supplied by the editor.

sympathetic understanding of our fellows and, some would boldly add, a sort of "sympathy" with ourselves. Such sympathy may reasonably be classed with perception, although, as the phrase "sympathetic under-standing" shows, thinking has something to do with it also. M. Bergson would say that although "intuition" (i.e. perception) and intelligence commingle in nearly all human activities they are utterly distinct in their nature, and he would add that "intuition" must preponderate in all the affairs of life. He and his followers prefer to speak of *two* moralities, the one of rule, conservatism, and intellectual principle, the other of romance, of aspiration, and of sympathy with the imponderables in all human doings.

The interest and importance of such contentions should be beyond dispute. I submit, however, that what they prove is the delicacy of our acquaintance with psychical matter of fact, and not the impotence of moral principles arising out of these delicate facts.

(*b*) Everyone agrees that the art of expressing principles in their full generality and without irrelevance is an expert's business requiring special training. Most competent people argue logically about the matters in which they are competent, but they would be very unwise if they attempted to formulate their views in correct logical dress without a logician's special training. Consequently there is only the appearance of paradox in Lord Mansfield's advice to the colonial governor who had gumption but had had no legal training, namely, to give his decisions boldly because they were almost sure to be right, but not to give his reasons since he would then become the experts' prey. The expression of moral principles is the business of moralists, not of honest men; but an honest man grasps and follows moral principles whether or not he has had practice in moral conveyancing.

(*c*) Another suggestion sometimes made is that although morality is not simply a type of skill, it is always a sort of practical efficiency. Practical efficiency, however, can never afford to proceed merely by rule, and we are reminded of the difference (in old-fashioned warfare) between the type of general who directed his troops by trained perception on the battlefield, and the type of general who relied upon his recollection of manuals of the military art. The former type of general, it is suggested, always won.

What this argument really proves, however, is the importance of *quick* thinking on the battlefield. If perception is contrasted with thinking, it is likewise contrasted with quick thinking. The quick-thinking general's decisions become the delight of subsequent military critics, who find no difficulty in naming the eternal principles of warfare he employed.

(*d*) The suggestions may be made that perception should supplement the indeterminateness of many moral obligations, and again that although all moral obligations are matters of general principle, there may be no sufficient principle to decide the *conflicts* between obligations, so that, where such a conflict exists, the decision should be left to perception. Both these matters will be discussed more fully later. For the present it may be sufficient to deal with them summarily. Regarding the first it would have to be proved that whatever is left indeterminate in the obligation is moral at all. If the obligation, for example, is to give an adequate subscription to the local hospital, it may be morally indifferent whether the actual subscription is ten pounds or ten guineas. Regarding the second it seems preposterous to argue that any mysterious faculty of divination is competent to reconcile or to override warring principles, and it is entirely arbitrary to call such a faculty "perception."

The point of substance regarding all such arguments is surely that any moral decision, if valid, is implicitly general. If a given moral being has a certain obligation in a certain situation, *every* moral being would have the same obligation unless his situation differed in some morally relevant way. This statement may be a truism; but even truisms cannot be neglected without serious risk. The penalty for neglecting this particular truism is the necessity for a prolonged debate that has no justification except the neglect of the truism.

2. Moral obligations, therefore, are general in their very nature. An unprincipled moral obligation is a contradiction in terms. This truism, however, does not settle the debatable ethical question concerning the extent to which such obligations give specific practical guidance.

Our obligations are practical, that is to say deal with men's rightful practice, and practice consists of particular, completely determinate actions. Again, morality should not compete with anything else. We may indeed admire and in certain ways commend wicked conduct. "A villain, but with something great about him," "A scamp, but a pleasing scamp," are quite defensible statements; but if an action is definitely wrong in the moral way, it is definitely unjustifiable whether or not certain of its features evoke admiration.

Hence it is sometimes inferred that "casuistry" in the sense of determinate application to particular cases is the goal of ethics, and that moral principles are woolly or negligible if they do not determine our particular actions in detail. This consequence, however, is peculiarly disputable. To apply to particular cases is one thing, to determine such cases in all their detail is quite another thing, and the alleged consequence would not follow even on a thoroughly legalistic view of ethics. Scottish lawyers, for instance, distinguish between ordinances, regulations, and cases. Regulations must conform to their governing ordinances, but are seldom simple deductions from the ordinances. The ordinances apply to but do not exhaust the regulations. The particular cases, again, must conform to the regulations, but few regulations exhaust the actual complexity of their instances.

Accordingly, if objections to such "casuistry" are well founded, they should not be based on the view that casuistry is all too legal to be ethically sound. Case-morality may indeed be a poor sort of ethical method, and good moral laws may be extracted with difficulty from hard moral cases. It may further be true that no official of any ecclesiastical or other such body is a good judge of other men's morals, and that there should be no such thing as an extra-legal judiciary with powers of absolution and of penance. Such attempts at moral administration, again, may be abused in the way that is incident to positive law. There are few rules that can never be used for purposes of obstruction or of evasion, and tutiorism, probabilism, and probabiliorism—that is to say clinging to rules for safety's sake, relying on one favourable authority, or upon a bare majority of authorities—may deserve some of the hard things that are said of them by persons who do not realize the difficulties of any honest priest whose professional office involves the giving of spiritual advice.

Nevertheless, *abusus non tollit usum.** Casuistry, in the general sense of the application of ethical principles to particular cases is surely quite unexceptionable, and hard cases should at least put moralists upon their mettle. A general charge of over-minuteness, again, is entirely worthless unless it is possible to explain with clarity where and why over-minuteness occurs. If the wrangles of Catholic doctors regarding what is or is not "water" for baptism, or the disputes of Jews and Scotch Presbyterians regarding sabbatarianism have a ludicrous appearance, it is necessary to give a reason why such squabbles have nothing to do with principles and are not the inevitable consequence of taking principles seriously and attempting to live seriously by them.

In general, it seems clear that moral obligations do apply to practice and that such application is a matter of ordinary logical deduction. If, however (to follow the legal analogy already suggested), all moral principles are of the nature of general ordinances rather than of specific regulations, they may well give decisive but incomplete guidance in practice, and the degree of specific guidance they afford may very well differ in different instances and classes of instances.

Some such distinction seems inevitable. Thus industry may be a moral obligation (and commonly is so unless the cause is bad). And negligence may be culpable. Neither industry nor any other moral quality, however, will, for example, tell a doctor what to do, that is to say, make a correct

---

*[Roughly: the misuse of a principle does not destroy its use.]

diagnosis and prescribe with skill. In short, medicine or any other useful art is *not* a kind of applied ethics, and in so far as it should be morally governed, the government permits great local autonomy. The separation of hygiene, medicine, eugenics, economics, civics, and politics from ethics is indeed one of the principal lessons modern man has learned. He should not model his moral code upon the Book of Leviticus. Yet if these discoveries (as we believe) enfranchize ethics instead of banishing it, the charter of emancipation should be able to state its reasons. Again, since few (if any) actions have no moral bearing (at least remote), and since so many of them have a bearing upon health, economics, and the like, it seems inevitable that the general line of division between moral and extra-moral specification of conduct should be of the type we have described.

Moral principles, then, are general, applicable to practice, and (we hold) superior to all others in the sense that *de jure* they do not compete with any others, although they frankly admit that other principles are and should be practical guides. If moral principles, besides being clear and clearly applicable, fully determine the essentials of any given action there is nothing more to be said. The truthful witness of our former illustration may have but to answer "Yes." In that case his duty is completely determinate. His duty, however, may be to give an elaborate narrative, and there may be many alternative ways of conveying a true impression regarding the subject of his examination. On the whole, however, the obligation of veracity is a clear instance of a determinate obligation.

On the other hand, many moral obligations are much less determinate. Generosity, for example, is such an obligation, but there is considerable latitude regarding the time, the type, the subject, and other relevant particulars of the generous act. It would be a complete mistake, however, to infer that generosity is less of a duty than veracity because it is, in these ways, less determinate. The "latitude" in question is not a sign of weakness in the obligation. Instead it indicates a certain width of range in place of a narrow restriction; and the same type of difference might occur within a single class of obligation. For example, the promise, "I shall visit you one of these days in your nursing home," is not less of a promise, or less binding than the promise, "I shall visit you next Thursday at 2:45 in your nursing home"; but it is much less determinate. . . .

# Part VI

## Conflict, War, and Morality

Given the existence of moral strife and controversies, how can they best be settled? Can they be settled at all? The selection by Hook (40) contains, among other things, the quite radical suggestion that what is morally right or wrong—the moral rights and duties of the various parties to an actual controversy or conflict—can be determined, and morally ought to be determined, by a process of negotiation, bargaining, or compromise.

The alternative to this process is war, the other main topic of this part. War can be regarded in at least two morally relevant ways. It is a means— and sometimes a very effective means—of settling disputes. Of course, war does not always bring about this result, and very often war itself has to be terminated by some form of negotiation process. But it by no means follows that war never works. It very often does; and very often after a war, or a series of wars, the relative positions of the parties, and their rights and duties with respect to one another, are drastically changed, sometimes irreversibly. Yet war is also an institution of society and must, accordingly, answer some deep-seated needs and satisfy some presumably permanent and important purposes. Unless we recognize this, there can be no reasonable hope of ever ending war. This is the theme developed in James's essay on this topic (43). It is, deservedly, a classic piece, and very far from being out-dated.

A further question that arises in this connection is whether the principles of morality applicable to the actions of individual persons are applicable to the actions of states or nations or corporate groups. It has, indeed, been questioned, in a way that must be taken seriously, whether any moral principles at all are applicable to the actions of states or nations. Henry Sidgwick (42) has something of interest to say on this, but his remarks cannot be taken as the last word on the subject. This is an area of ethics greatly in need of further reflection, refinement, and analysis. (See statements 15, by Tawney, and 59, by Lecky.) So is the area explored in the selection by Perry (41), which has intriguing connections with the selection by Hook (40) and the materials in Parts II (on theories and tests) and V (on casuistry). It also has connections, in what it says about love, to selection 53, by Griffiths, at the end of Part VII.

# STATEMENTS ON MORALITY
## Eighth Series

*59. In the affairs of private life the distinction between right and wrong is usually very clear, but it is not so in public affairs. Even the moral aspects of political acts can seldom be rightly estimated without the exercise of a large, judicial, and comprehensive judgment, and the spirit which should actuate a statesman should be rather that of a high-minded and honourable man of the world than that of a theologian, or a lawyer, or an abstract moralist.*

W. E. H. Lecky (1899)

*60. It is not what a man outwardly has or wants that constitutes the happiness or misery of him. Nakedness, hunger, distress of all kinds, death itself have been cheerfully suffered, when the heart is right. It is the feeling of* injustice *that is insupportable to all men. . . . No man can bear it, or ought to bear it. . . . It is not the outward pain of injustice; that, were it even the flaying of the back with knotted scourges, the severing of the head with guillotines, is comparatively a small matter. The real smart is the soul's pain and stigma, the hurt inflicted on the moral self. The rudest clown must draw himself up into attitude of battle, and resistance to the death, if such be offered him. He cannot live under it; his own soul aloud, and all the Universe with silent continual beckonings, says, It cannot be.*

Thomas Carlyle (1839)

*61. There have been long ages in the history of the world when social life has been languid and impoverished, and yet there has been no revolt of which literature gives any record. Custom will reconcile men and women to conditions that they would find intolerable if they came fresh to them. For custom has a magic that takes the sting out of injustice, making it seem rather the decree of heaven than the sin of man. Thus the spell that custom casts on the imagination is the greatest conservative force in the world, a force so strong that it will keep life in institutions which have long ceased to serve, or even to remember, the purpose that brought them into use. As life follows its circle of unbroken routine no fierce questions are asked about facts and conditions that seem part of everyday experience, the face of a familiar world. When, therefore, society is passing through changes that destroy the life of custom, the statesman who seeks, in Bacon's words, to command man's will and not merely his deeds and services, has a specially difficult task, for those changes bring into men's minds the dreaded questions that have been sleeping beneath the surface of habit.*

J. L. and Barbara Hammond (1930)

62. *It is not mere inequality . . . that can be a reproach to the aristocratic or theistic ideal. Could each person fulfil his own nature the most striking differences in endowment and fortune would trouble nobody's dreams. The true reproach to which aristocracy and theism are open is the thwarting of those unequal natures and the consequent suffering imposed on them all. Injustice in this world is not something comparative; the wrong is deep, clear, and absolute in each private fate. A bruised child wailing in the street, his small world for the moment utterly black and cruel before him, does not fetch his unhappiness from sophisticated comparisons or irrational envy; nor can any compensations and celestial harmonies supervening later ever expunge or justify that moment's bitterness. The pain may be whistled away and forgotten; the mind may be rendered by it only a little harder, a little coarser, a little more secretive and sullen and familiar with unrightable wrong. But ignoring that pain will not prevent its having existed; it must remain for ever to trouble God's omniscience and be a part of that hell which the creation too truly involves.*

George Santayana (1905)

63. *Somehow, our sense of justice never turns in its sleep till long after the sense of injustice in others has been thoroughly aroused; nor is it ever up and doing till those others have begun to make themselves thoroughly disagreeable, and not even then will it be up and doing more than is urgently required of it by our convenience at the moment.*

Max Beerbohm (1921)

# 40

## Moral Conflicts*
### SIDNEY HOOK
(1902–       )

What, then, do I mean by the tragic sense of life and what is its relevance to pragmatism? I mean by the tragic sense a very simple thing which is rooted in the very nature of the moral experience and the phenomenon of moral choice. Every genuine experience of moral doubt and perplexity in which we ask: "What should I do?" takes place in a situation where good conflicts with good. If we already know what is evil the moral inquiry is over, or it never really begins. "The worse or evil," says Dewey, "is the rejected good" but until we reject it, the situation is one in which apparent good opposes apparent good. "All the serious perplexities of life come back to the genuine difficulty of forming a judgment as to the values of a situation: they come back to a conflict of goods." No matter how we resolve the opposition some good will be sacrificed, some interest, whose immediate craving for satisfaction may be every whit as intense and authentic as its fellows, will be modified, frustrated or even suppressed. Where the goods involved are of a relatively low order, like decisions about what to eat, where to live, where to go, the choice is unimportant except to the mind of a child. There are small tragedies as there are small deaths. At any level the conflict of values must become momentous to oneself or others to convey adequately the tragic quality. Where the choice is between goods that are complex in structure and consequential for the future, the tragic quality of the moral dilemma emerges more clearly. And when it involves basic choices of love, friendship, vocations, the quality becomes poignant.

*From Professor Hook's Presidential Address to the Eastern Division of the American Philosophical Association, entitled "Pragmatism and the Tragic Sense of Life," December 1959. Reprinted from *Proceedings and Addresses of the American Philosophical Association*, vol. 33 (The Antioch Press, 1960), pp. 13–20, 23–25, by permission of the author. Compare selection 41.

The very nature of the self as expressed in habits, dispositions and character is to some extent altered by these decisions. If, as Hobbes observes, "Hell is truth seen too late," all of us must live in it. No matter how justified in smug retrospect our moral decisions seem to have been, only the unimaginative will fail to see the possible selves we have sacrificed to become what we are. Grant that all regrets are vain, that any other choice would have been equally or more regretted, the selves we might have been are eloquent witnesses of values we failed to enjoy. If we have played it safe and made our existence apparently secure, the fascinating experience of a life of adventure and experience can never be ours, and every thought of a good fight missed will be accompanied by a pang. It is a poor spirit William James reminds us who does not sense the chagrin of the tardy Crillon, who arriving when the battle is over is greeted by Henry IV with the words: "Hang yourself, brave Crillon! We fought at Arques, and you were not there!" On the other hand, if we have scorned to put down our roots, hugged our liberty tightly to ourselves by refusing to give hostages to fortune, become crusaders or martyrs for lost causes, we have thrust from ourselves the warmth of sustained affection, and the comforting regularities which can best heal the bruised spirit.

There is a conflict not only between the good and the good but between the good and the right where the good is a generic term for all the values in a situation and the right for all the obligations. The *concepts* of good and right are irreducible to each other in ordinary use. We are often convinced we must fulfill a certain duty even when we are far from convinced to the same degree that the action or the rule it exemplifies will achieve the greatest good. The "good" is related to the reflective satisfaction of an interest: "the right" to the fulfillment of a binding demand or rule of the community. There is no moral problem when in doing the right thing we can see that it *also* leads to the greatest good or when striving for the greatest good conforms to our sense of what is right. But the acute ethical problems arise when in the pursuit of the good we do things which appear not to be right, as e.g., when in order to avoid the dangers of war a nation repudiates its treaty obligations or when in order to win a war non-combatants are punished who are in no way responsible for the actions of others. They also arise when in doing what is right our actions result in evil consequences, as e.g., when a dangerous criminal, set free on a legal technicality, kills again or when the refusal to surrender to the unjust claims of an aggressor results in wholesale slaughter. Many have been the attempts made to escape the antinomies between the right and the good by defining the good as the object of right or the right merely as the means to the good. All have failed. To act upon the right no matter what its consequences for human weal or woe seems inhuman, at times insane. The thirst for righteousness has too often been an angry thirst satisfied if at all by long draughts of blood. On the other hand, the attempt to do good by *any* means no matter how unjust, is subhuman and usually irrational.

As compared to traditional ethical doctrines, ideal utilitarianism reaches farthest in our quest for an adequate ethics but in the end it, too, must be rejected. And it was the pragmatist and pluralist, William James, long before Pritchard and Ross, who indicated why in the famous question he asked: "If the hypothesis were offered us of a world in which Messrs. Fourier's and Bellamy's and Morris' Utopia should all be outdone, and millions be kept permanently happy on the one simple condition that a certain lost soul on the far off edge of things should lead a life of lonely torture, what except a specifical and independent sort of emotion can it be which would make us immediately feel . . . how hideous a thing would be its enjoyment when deliberately accepted as the fruit of such a bargain?" The situation is unaltered if we recognize that there are other goods besides happiness and that justice is itself a good, because in that case the conflict breaks out again between good and good. In this connection I would venture the statement that it is the failure to see the radical pluralism in the nature of the goods which are reckoned in the consequences of an action which accounts both for Moore's view that it is self-evident that it can *never* be right knowingly to approve an action that would make the world as a whole worse than some alternative action and for Kant's view that there are some duties that it would *always* be right to perform, even if the consequences of the action resulted in a worse world or in no world at all. No specific rule can be laid down as absolutely binding in advance either way. Nothing can take the place of intelligence; the better or the lesser evil in each situation can be best defined as the object of reflective choice. Even the decision in the stock illustration of the text-books whether to execute an innocent man or turn him over to be tortured in order to save the community from destruction—would depend upon a complex of circumstances. It is perfectly conceivable that an unjust act will sometimes produce the greater good or the lesser evil. It is sometimes necessary to burn down a house to save a village. Although when applied to human beings the logic seems damnable, few are prepared to take the position of Kant in those agonizing moral predicaments that are not uncommon in history, especially the history of oppressed minority peoples, in which the survival of the group can be purchased only at the price of the pain, degradation and death of the innocent. No matter how we choose, we must either betray the ideal of the greater good or the ideal of right or justice. In this lies the agony of the choice.

Many have been the attempts to escape the guilt of that choice. I cite one from the past. During the Middle Ages Maimonides writing on the Laws of the Torah to guide his people discusses what a community is to do when it is beset by enemies who demand the life of one man with the threat to kill all if he be not turned over to them. Maimonides teaches that they are to refuse to turn over any man even if all must die in consequence, except if their enemies call out the name of a specific person. I had heard this teaching defended on the ground that if the community itself had to make the decision who was to die, it would be taking the guilt of an innocent man's death upon itself, which is impermissible. But if the enemy names the man, then he can be turned over because the guilt and sin fall now on *their* heads. By this miserable evasion it was thought that the tragic choice could be avoided. But it turns out that Maimonides has been misread. What Maimonides really taught is that only if the name of the person who has been called out is of one already under the death sentence for his crimes should he be surrendered. But never an innocent man. "Never," however, is a long time. It is problematic whether the Jews would have survived if they had always abided by Maimonides' injunction.

If anything, human beings are more readily inclined to sacrifice the right to the good than the good to the right especially in revolutionary situations which have developed because of grievances too long unmet. It can easily be shown that it was Lenin's conception of Communist ethics which implicitly defined the right action as consisting in doing *anything*— literally anything that would bring victory in the class struggle—which explains the transformation of a whole generation of idealists into hangmen. In fact the health of the revolution whether in the times of Robespierre or Castro never really requires the holocaust of victims offered up to it. But no revolution including our own has ever been achieved without injustice to someone. However the conflict between the principles of right and the values of good be theoretically resolved, in every concrete situation it leads to some abridgement of principle or some diminution of value.

The most dramatic of all moral conflicts is not between good and good, or between good and right, but between right and right. This in its starkest form is the theme of Sophoclean tragedy but the primary locus of the tragic situation is not in a play but in life, in law, and in history. Innocence in personal matters consists in overlooking the conflict of moral duties and obligations. Innocence in political matters, the characteristic of ritualistic liberalism, consists in failing to see the conflicts of rights in our Bill of Rights and the necessity of their intelligent adjustment. In our own country we have witnessed again and again the antinomy of rights revealed in divided loyalties, in the conflict between allegiance to the laws of the state and allegiance to what is called divine law or natural law or the dictates of conscience. On the international scene it is expressed in the conflict of incompatible national claims, each with *some* measure of justification, as in the Israeli-Arab impasse.

One of the noteworthy features of moral intuitionism as illustrated in the doctrines of Ross is this recognition that *prima facie* duties conflict and that every important moral act exhibits at the same time characteristics which tend to make it both *prima facie* right and *prima facie* wrong so that although we may claim certainty about these *prima facie* duties, any particular moral judgment or action is at best only probable or contingent. As Ross says, "There is therefore much truth in the description of the right act as a fortunate act." From this the conclusion to be drawn, it seems to me, is that the most important *prima facie* duty of all in a situation requiring moral decision is that of *conscientiousness,* or reflective assessment of all the relevant factors involved, and the searching exploration of our own hearts to determine what we sincerely want, whether we really wish to do what is right in a situation or to get our own scheming way come what may. As much if not more evil results from confusion of our purposes and ignorance of our motives than from ruthless and clear-eyed resolve to ignore everyone's interests but one's own. This emphasis on the importance of reflective inquiry into the features of the situation which bear on the rightness of an action seems to me to be more important than Ross' conception or interpretation of the intuitive apprehension of our *prima facie* duties. It is easier to doubt that we have this faculty of infallible intuition than that our intelligence has the power to discover our conflicts and mediate between them.

Irony is compounded with tragedy in the fact that many of the rights we presently enjoy we owe to our ancestors who in the process of winning them for us deprived others of their rights. In some regions of the world the very ground on which people stand was expropriated by force and fraud from others by their ancestors. Yet as a rule it would be a new injustice to seek to redress the original injustice by depriving those of their possessions who hold present title to them. Every just demand for reparations against an aggressor country is an unjust demand on the descendants of its citizens who as infants were not responsible for the deeds of aggression. That is why history is the arena of the profoundest moral conflicts in which some legitimate right has always been sacrificed, sometimes on the altars of the God of War.

The Christian and especially the Buddhist ethics of purity which seeks to transcend this conflict and avoid guilt by refusal to violate anyone's right in such situations, can only do so by withdrawing from the plane of the ethical altogether. This may succeed in God's eyes but not in man's. The Buddhist saint or any other who out of respect for the right to life of man or beast refuses ever to use force, or to kill, even when this is the only method, as it sometimes is, that will save multitudes from suffering and death, makes himself responsible for the greater evil, all the more so because he claims to be acting out of compassion. He cannot avoid guilt whether we regard him as more than man or less than man. No more than we does he escape the tragic decision.

There are three generic approaches to the tragic conflicts of life. The first approach is that of history. The second is that of love. The third is that of creative intelligence in quest for ways of mediation which I call here the pragmatic.

The approach of history is best typified by Hegel precisely because he tries to put a gloss of reason over the terrible events which constitute so much of the historical process. Its upshot is woefully inept to its intent. It suggests not only that whatever cause wins and *however* it wins, is more just than the cause which is defeated, but that the loser is the more wicked and not merely the weaker. Further, it calls into question the very fact of tragic conflict from which it so perceptively starts. No one has seen more profoundly into the nature of the tragic situation than Hegel and its stark clash of equally legitimate rights. But his solution, expressed in Schiller's dictum *Die Weltgeschichte ist das Weltgericht,* * as Hegel develops it, makes the philosophy of history a theodicy. It thereby vulgarizes tragedy. For it attempts to console man with a dialectical proof that his agony and defeat are not really evils but necessary elements in the goodness of the whole. The position is essentially religious. No monotheistic religion which conceives of God as both omnipotent and benevolent, no metaphysics which asserts that the world is rational, necessary and good has any room for genuine tragedy.

The approach of love is incomplete and ambiguous. It is incomplete because if love is more than a feeling of diffused sympathy but is expressed in action no *man* can love everyone or identify himself with every interest. Empirically love has produced as much disunity as unity in the world—not only in Troy but in Jerusalem. Injustice is often born of love, not only of self-love but of love of some rather than others. Love is not only incomplete but ambiguous. There are various kinds of love and the actions to which they lead may be incompatible. An order of distinction is required. A man's love for his family must be discriminatory: his love of mankind not. He cannot love both in the same way without denying one or the other. The quality of love is altered with the range of its generalization. In one sense

*[The history of the world is the judgment of the world.]

love always shows a bias which reinforces some conflicting interest; in another it gives all conflicting values its blessing without indicating any specific mode of action by which conflict can be mediated. Love may enable a person to live with the burden of guilt which he assumes when he sacrifices one right to another. But it is no guide to social conflict as the last two thousand years have shown. Because the Lord loves man equally nothing follows logically about the equality of man before the Law. "The *Agape* quality of love," says Tillich, "sees man as God sees him." But what *man* can tell us how *God* sees man? "Agape," continues Tillich, "loves in everybody and through everybody love itself." Karl Barth speaks more simply and intelligibly, and with a basic brutality which is the clue to his crude neutralism, when he claims that such love has no bearing whatever for the organization of any human society.

Finally there is the method of creative intelligence. It, too, tries to make it possible for men to live with the tragic conflict of goods and rights and duties, to mediate not by arbitrary fiat but through informed and responsible decision. Whoever uses this method must find his way among all the conflicting claims. He must therefore give each one of them and the interests it represents tongue or voice. Every claimant therefore has a right to be heard. The hope is that as much as possible of each claim may be incorporated in some inclusive or shared interest which is accepted because the alternatives are less satisfactory. To this end we investigate every relevant feature about it, the conditions under which it emerged, its proximate causes and consequences, the costs of gratifying it, the available alternatives and *their* costs. Every mediation entails some sacrifice. The quest for the unique good of the situation, for what is to be done here and now, may point to what is better than anything else available but what it points to is also a lesser evil. It is a lesser evil whether found in a compromise or in moderating the demand of a just claim or in learning to live peacefully with one's differences on the same general principle which tells us that a divorce is better for all parties concerned than a murder. In every case the rules, the wisdom, the lessons of the past are to be applied but they have presumptive, not final, validity because they may be challenged by new presumptions. "The pragmatic import of the logic of individualized situations," says Dewey, "is to transfer the attention of theory from preoccupation with general conceptions to the problem of developing effective methods of inquiry," and applying them. It is a logic which does not preach solutions but explores the suggestions which emerge from the analyses of problems. Its categorical imperative is to inquire, to reason together, to seek in every crisis the creative devices and inventions that will not only make life fuller and richer but tragedy bearable. William James makes essentially the same point as Dewey in the language of ideals. Since in the struggles between ideals "victory and defeat there must be, the victory to be philosophically prayed for is that of the more inclusive side—of the side which even in the hour of triumph will to some degree do *justice* to the ideals in which the vanquished interests lay. . . ." But prayer is not enough. He goes on: "*Invent some manner* of realizing your own ideals which will also satisfy the alien demands—that and that only is the path of peace." To which we must add, provided there is a reciprocal will to peace in the matter. And even then, your own or the alien demands or both must be curtailed. . . .

To the meliorist the recognition of the gamut of tragic possibilities is what feeds his desire to find some method of negotiating conflicts of value by intelligence rather than war, or brute force. But this is not as simple as it sounds. There is no substitute for intelligence. But intelligence may not be enough. It may not be enough because of limitations of our knowledge, because of the limited reach of our powers of control. It may not be enough because of the recalcitrance of will—not merely the recalcitrance of will to act upon goods already known and not in dispute, but because of unwillingness to find out what the maximizing good in the situation is. And although we are seeking to settle conflicts of value by the use of intelligence rather than by force, is it not true that sometimes intelligence requires the use of force?

Let us take this last question first. Faced by a momentous conflict of values in which some value must give away if the situation is to be resolved, the rational approach is to find some encompassing value on the basis of some shared interest. This, as we have seen, involves willingness to negotiate—to negotiate honestly. The grim fact, however, is that there is sometimes no desire to reason, no wish to negotiate except as a holding action to accumulate strategic power, nothing but the reliance of one party or the other upon brute force even when other alternatives may exist. In such cases the moral onus rests clearly upon those who invoke force. Their victory no more establishes their claim to be right than a vandal's destruction of a scientists' instruments of inquiry has any bearing on the validity of his assertions, evidence for or against which, could have been gathered by the instrument destroyed. The intelligent use of force to *prevent* or crush the use of force where a healthy democratic process, equitable laws and traditions and customs of freedom make it possible to vent differences in a rational and orderly way, is therefore justifiable even if on prudential grounds one may forego such action. This means that tolerance always has limits—it cannot tolerate what is itself actively intolerant.

There is a tendency in modern philosophical thought which, in rejecting too sweeping claims for the role of intelligence in human affairs, settles for too little even when it does not embrace a wholesale skepticism. Of course, a man may know what is right and not do it just as he may know what is true and not publicly assert it. In neither case is this a ground for maintaining that we cannot know what action is more justified than another or what assertion is more warranted than another. The *refusal* to follow a rational method, to give good reasons is one thing: the claim that there are different rational methods, different *kinds* of good reasons each with its own built-in modes of validity, is something else again—and to me unintelligible. To be sure, the acceptance of rational method is not enough. Men must have some non-rational element in common. Hume is on unquestionably solid ground in asserting that reason must always *serve* a human need, interest or passion. But his mistake outweighed his insight when he contended that rational method could only be a servant or slave of what it served and that needs, interests and passions could not be changed or transformed by the use of intelligence. In our flights into space if we encounter other sentient creatures capable of communicating with us, it is more likely that their logical and mathematical judgment will be the same as ours than their ethical judgments, because we can more readily conceive creatures of different needs than of different minds.

At any rate the world we live in is one in which men do not share all their needs and interests and yet it is one in which they have sufficient needs and interests in common to make possible their further extension, and to give intelligence a purchase, so to speak, in its inquiry.

The most difficult of all situations is one in which even the common use of methods of inquiry seem to lead to conclusions which are incompatible with each other although each is objectively justified. There is always an open possibility of ultimate disagreement no matter how far and long we pursue rational inquiry. We can conceive it happening. In such situations we must resign ourselves to living with our differences. Otherwise we must fight or surrender. But it is simply a non sequitur to maintain that because no guarantee can be given that there will not be ultimate disagreement, penultimate agreements cannot be validly reached and justified.

In any case we cannot in advance determine the limits of reason or intelligence in *human* affairs. So long as we don't know where it lies, it is sensible to press on, at the same time devising the means to curb the effects of the refusal to reason when it manifests itself. Above all, we must avoid oversimplifying the choice of evils and encouraging the hope that to be unreasonable will pay dividends.

We are moving into another period of history in which freedom once more is being readied for sacrifice on the altars of survival. The Munichmen of the spirit are at work again. The stakes are now for the entire world.

Our task as philosophers is not to heed partisan and excited calls for action, but rather to think through the problems of freedom and survival afresh. In a famous pronouncement two years ago Bertrand Russell declared that if the Kremlin refused to accept reasonable proposals of disarmament, the West should disarm unilaterally "even if it means the horrors of Communist domination." Although he no longer believes this, there are many others who do. I know that common sense is at a discount in philosophy but in ethics it should not be lightly disregarded. A position like this obviously can have only one effect, viz., to encourage the intransigence of those who wish to destroy the free world without which there cannot be a free philosophy. You cannot negotiate successfully by proclaiming in advance that you will capitulate if the other side persists in being unreasonable. Our alternatives are not limited to surrender and extinction of freedom, on the one hand, and war and the danger of human extermination on the other. There are other alternatives to be explored—all tragic in their costs but not equally extreme. The very willingness, if necessary, to go down fighting in defence of freedom may be the greatest force for peace when facing an opponent who makes a fetish of historical survival. On pragmatic grounds, the willingness to act on a position like Kant's *fiat justitia, pereat mundus* * may sometimes—I repeat—sometimes—be the best way of preserving a just and free world—just as the best way of saving one's life is sometimes to be prepared to lose it. The uneasy peace we currently enjoy as a result of "the balance of terror" is tragic. But it may turn out that it is less so than any feasible alternative today. If it endures long enough and it becomes clear to the enemies of freedom that they cannot themselves survive war, they may accept the moral equivalents of war in the making. The pragmatic program is always to find moral equivalents for the expression of natural inpulses which threaten the structure of our values.

*[Let justice be done, though the heavens fall.]

## 41

# Conflict, Harmony, and Justice*

## RALPH BARTON PERRY

(1876–1957)

*1. Conflict between Persons.* Having defined the sense in which a harmonious personality is superior to a state of inner conflict, we have now to consider the more notable case of the superiority of a harmonious society to a state of conflict between persons. The problem is vividly presented by a striking passage in James's essay on "The Moral Philosopher and the Moral Life":

> If the hypothesis were offered us of a world in which Messrs. Fourier's and Bellamy's and Morris's utopias should be all out-done, and millions kept permanently happy on the one simple condition that a certain lost soul on the far-off edge of things should lead a life of lonely torture, what except a specifical and independent sort of emotion can it be which would make us immediately feel, even though an impulse arose within us to clutch at the happiness so offered, how hideous a thing would be its enjoyment when deliberately accepted as the fruit of such a bargain?[1]

The "specific and independent emotion" which inspired the writer of this paragraph, and which affects us so poignantly when we read it, is a distinctly modern and occidental sentiment,—the legitimate offspring of Christianity and democracy. There was a time when the European conscience would not even have been disturbed by the thought that a single favored individual, or a small caste of the *élite*, should enjoy happiness

---

*Reprinted by permission of the publishers from Ralph Barton Perry, *General Theory of Value* (pp. 669–82), Cambridge, Mass.: Harvard University Press, Copyright, 1926, by the President and Fellows of Harvard College; 1954 by Ralph Barton Perry. The title of this selection has been supplied by the editor. Compare selections 9, 12, 40, and 43.
[1] *Will to Believe, and other Essays,* 1898, p. 188.

through the misery of millions of lost souls. The new conscience not only requires that the majority shall be admitted to happiness, but that no man shall be excluded from it. It is as though one were to feel that the feast cannot begin until every one is seated at the table, and that joy cannot be unalloyed without a sense of universal participation.

In creating this fictitious case the author was for the moment concerned to show that there is a moral sentiment *sui generis,* which cannot be reduced to the memory or expectation of private pleasures. A historian of the age in which we live would doubtless record the fact that there are persons with consciences so tender that they cannot be happy unless they believe that everybody is happy. Is this the end of the matter? Have we here to do only with a peculiar hypersensitiveness, like the fear of cats or the vertigo felt in high places? Shall we merely enter it in our clinical catalogue of human experience? Or shall we *credit* this species of conscience as possessed of moral insight? Does it contain some judgment of comparative value that is *true,* in the light of fact and reason?

We have first to note the unmistakable presence of judgment. When I imagine the situation, I not only feel pity for the lost soul and disgust at the millions who are willing to be happy at his expense, but I experience the firm conviction that the happiness of a million somehow fails utterly to compensate or even to mitigate the torture of one. I feel that my feeling has nothing to do with it, and that the situation would not be materially altered if I were to become careless about lost souls and less squeamish about tainted happiness. The conviction is all the more explicit because it involves the rejection of a plausible alternative. It would seem that the happiness of the millions *ought* so far to outweigh the torture of the lost soul as to reduce the latter to a negligible quantity. One *ought* to comment favorably on the thrifty expedient by which so much good is purchased at so small a price. But no such judgment occurs. On the contrary, the evil of the one seems unrelieved, and even aggravated, by the fact that it is a cause of the good of the many.

That this judgment is justified, there is, in the light of the foregoing analysis of comparative value, good reason to believe. As co-exclusive, the claims of the lost soul and of the happy millions are incommensurable. They may be assumed to be of equal intensity,—their preferences are opposed and therefore incomparable. To declare the good of the millions to be greater than the evil of the one would ignore this incomparability, and would assume on the part of unit-persons an equality of extensive magnitude to which it is impossible to give any meaning. We must not be misled into supposing that because the good of the millions is neither greater than nor less than the good of the one, the two goods are therefore equal. The supposition of the equal extensive magnitude of persons may arise from this confusion, since conflict most commonly occurs between two unit-persons, each of whose claims is deemed to be "as good as" that of the other. But since the situation is not affected by adding persons to either side of the equation, it is evident that the relation is not one of equality at all, but of incomparability. The evil of the lost soul is pure, stark, unmitigated and unrelieved.

    *2. The Postulate of Concurrence.* There is, then, no solution of the problem through a comparative judgment *between* the lost soul and the happy millions. Is there *no* comparative judgment which will point a solution? The sentiment which James describes suggests, if it does not embody, such a judgment. What is the active impulse that the situation arouses in us? The answer seems clear. We are impelled to go out to that lonely sufferer and *bring him in.* We ask those seated at the table to move up so that the uninvited guest may find a place at the table, or appeal to the fortunate so to alter or moderate their claims as to make them consistent with those of the unfortunate. At the same time we appeal to the newcomer to adjust his claims to those of the group with whom he is now associated. In order that all may be seated it may be necessary that some one shall take the foot of the table or accept a smaller portion than the rest. We find no injustice provided this less privileged person accepts his share of his own volition. We persuade him to *concur,* pointing out that unless he or some one in his place will accept some abatement of his original claims there cannot be room for all. We have found a solution when, and only when, the wills of all are so attuned that each is content with a situation in which provision is made for all.

    Whatever may be true of the decision of war, a *solution* of conflict is to be found only in a "peace without victory"; that is, when those who formerly protested now concur. The most familiar application of this principle is to the political conflict between a majority and a minority. So long as there is disagreement in respect of preference, the conflict can never be resolved by a measurement of numbers; or, if the conflict is so resolved, the outcome is the triumph of the stronger but not of the better cause. The *justification* of the majority lies not in its numerical superiority, but in a *general willingness to abide by* the will of the majority. If it were so agreed in advance, the will of two-thirds, or of a plurality (even when a minority) would be just as sacred.[2] It is becoming more and more apparent that the

---

[2] It is this recognition of the need of agreement that underlies the theory of popular sovereignty, and that has led to the introduction of fictions such as Rousseau's "general will" (*Contrat Social,* Bk. I, Ch. 1–3), to provide for such agreement when actual wills disagree.

settlement of international differences appeals to the same principle. The innumerable conferences which have followed the war are evidently based on the assumption that by discussion the interests of all parties can somehow be satisfied, the only guarantee of peace being a constructive plan which provides for all, and in the support of which all are positively united.

The practical recognition of the same principle in every-day life appears in the appeal to some existing agreement, or in the effort to obtain concurrence, whenever it is desired to settle an issue on the basis of right rather than of force. Indeed, to raise between man and man the question, "What is the good way?" is to invite attention to common facts in the expectation of seeing alike; or is a joint undertaking by agreement, to find something that can be agreed on.

In all spheres there is a sense of guilt in the presence of discord. Even the most chauvinistic nation wants to be generally accepted in the role to which it assigns itself, as the champion of culture or civilization. Even a policy of isolation seeks (for example, in the United States) to justify itself as an experiment in free institutions, a refuge for the oppressed, or a model for the political regeneration of the world. There is scarcely any form of individual or party self-assertion that does not excuse itself as for the general good, and so make at least some slight effort to obtain the willing consent even of those whom it injures. All of these rationalizations, even when they are uncandid or little more than conciliatory gestures, nevertheless testify to an admission in principle that a conflict of interest can be *solved* only when the conflicting parties are brought into agreement.

In seeking such a solution we virtually employ the principle of inclusiveness, as that has already been applied to the case of personal conflict, and as it is more or less consciously adopted in all moral reasoning. It is evident that a situation in which both the one and the millions were happy *would be* better. We do not attempt to compare the weight of the majority and minority interests with one another, or balance one man's loss against a million's gain. We acknowledge that there are amounts or degrees of value associated with each party, between which it is impossible to discriminate because they are incommensurable. We fall back on the principle that just as the fulfilment of an interest is better than its defeat, whatever the intensity or grade of the interest, so a situation which fulfils that interest will, other things being equal, be better than a situation which defeats it. By the same token, the fulfilment of any given interest together with the fulfilment of a second interest, will be better than the fulfilment of either interest together with the defeat of the other.

*3. The Independence of Persons.* Just how does such a harmonious integration take place? What relation between the constituent persons does it involve? When we raise this question we meet at once with the fundamental difference between personal and social integration, which consists in the fact that the principle of subordination is operative in the one and inoperative in the other. The relation of dependence in which one interest derives its motive power from another, or loses its motive power when opposed by another, is a relation which is internal to a person, and does not obtain *between* persons.[3]

In order that we may view the matter as precisely as possible, let us put ourselves successively in the place of the millions, of the lost soul and of a disinterested observer. As one of the millions, I justify the defeat of the lost soul on the ground that it is a means to my own success. In this way evil seems to have been transmuted into good. I may positively delight in the lost soul's pain—and not from malice, but from the enthusiastic anticipation of my own pleasure. I prudently subordinate my natural sympathies, and contrive that my feelings towards the sufferer shall be dictated entirely by my ulterior desire.[4] But if I now transfer myself to the position of the lost soul, I find that in fact the evil has not been removed at all. As lost soul I dislike my pain with a heartiness that is not in the least diminished by the fact that it ministers to the pleasure of millions of mankind. On the contrary, I now desire such limitation of the pleasures of the balance of mankind as shall relieve my pain. I see their loss as my gain.

If now I ascend to the judge's bench and review my previous partisanship I see that in each case I made the same rather stupid blunder of supposing that I could subordinate the interest of another person simply by subordinating my *own* interest *in* that interest. I enjoyed the illusion of converting evil into good because I took it for granted that when I had ceased to shrink from the other man's pain, he had ceased also; or that when I *treated* his interest as a means to my end, his interest had *become* a means to my end. I now see from my neutral vantage-point that the other man's interest is not in the slightest degree affected by the subordination of my interest in it. I can subordinate one of my interests to another, and so can he; but neither of us can by so doing in the least diminish the independence of the other's interest. I may be tempted as a neutral observer to commit the same error from my new station. I may find the triumph of one of the rival parties more to *my* liking, or I may even find their very rivalry a

---

[3]For a fuller statement of the argument, cf. §§ 188 ff. This is what Professor Goblot has in mind when he says that two ends, in order to be compared, must be subsumed under an "ulterior and superior end."—E. Goblot, *Traité de la Logique*, 1922, pp. 370–371. Cf. Ch. XVII, *passim*, on "Les Jugements de Valeur." Such a verdict cannot be rendered by *any* third or ulterior interest, but only by a third interest which is related to the others as end to means, and which must, therefore, be an end of the same person.

[4]I adopt Nietzsche's counsel of "hardness," not from a desire to hurt, but lest I be diverted from my main purpose.

means of satisfying my dramatic interest, and thus seem to achieve a condition of pure goodness. But, here again, all that I have done is to reduce my interests one to another without in the least altering the rival interests themselves.

The Kantian dictum, "So act as to treat humanity, whether in thine own person or in that of any other, in every case as an end withal, never as a means only," [5] may be interpreted as an appeal to empirical fact. The ultimate purposes of persons remain ultimate regardless of how other persons treat them. By supposing that the interests of other persons are no more than the uses which they have for us, we are led to *ignore* their independence, but we do not in any way negate it. All independent personal ends are *absolutely* independent.

It is the absence of this relation of dependence or subordination between persons that prevents their fusion or synthesis in a person of a higher order. The essential error of Durkheim's and other like philosophies is, as we have seen, the transposition to the social relation of a mode of composition that applies only to the several interests of one and the same organic subject.[6] It is impossible by the direct application of the method of subordination to secure a harmonious society. We must, therefore, in this case place our whole reliance on that second method of integration, the method of love or benevolence, whose application in a limited sense we have already noted in the case of personal integration.

What we require is a *personal* integration that shall be *socially qualified,* or that shall guarantee a harmonious fulfilment of all interests. The first step towards such a solution is to suppose any given person $M$ to be governed by the purpose of universal benevolence within a community of two persons, $M$ and $N$. Such a will effects an adjustment between the two persons in so far as $M$'s love of $N$, being benevolent, is mediated by a judgment regarding $N$'s interest. But $N$'s interest itself still remains outside the unity, and cannot be said to have been absorbed by the new integration.[7] The next step is to secure a like purpose in $N$, and the final step is so to modify the benevolence of $M$ and $N$ as to bring them into agreement.

---

[5] *Metaphysic of Morals,* trans. by T. K. Abbott, *Kant's Theory of Ethics,* 1883, p. 47. [This volume, p. 107.]

[6] Cf., Ch. XVI, Sect. I. Durkheim speaks of a "synthesis" of individual persons comprised within a qualitatively distinct social person. Cf. *Bulletin de la Soc. Française de la Philos.,* 1906, pp. 128–129.

[7] Even the most sympathetic spectator could not supersede the interests of those to whom his sympathy was addressed, because of the fallibility of his judgment. A pure lover of mankind might still find himself in conflict with mankind; and the harmony of his humanity would not preclude a conflict among the men who were its objects. Nevertheless such a love, sometimes imputed to parent, ruler or God, prefigures that harmony which is fully achieved only when it is confirmed by all parties.

The resulting situation will be freed of all possibility of conflict, since neither $M$ nor now $N$ has any interest contrary to the dominant benevolent purpose which they share. Finally, let us add $O$, $P$, $Q$, etc., until all persons are comprised within one community each member of which wills only what is consistent with the wills of all the rest. Such a will is personal in its seat, and in the mode of its composition; while it is social in its object, and in its distribution. Let us now examine this solution more in detail.

*4. Harmony through Universal Love.* In order to understand the harmonizing effect of love it is necessary to define this attitude strictly. Love means, as we have seen, a favorable interest in the satisfaction of a second interest. In the present context it is assumed that the second interest is the interest of a second person. Love begins and ends abroad. That "charity begins at home" is one of those many proverbs which have been coined by the devil to flatter human weakness. Love is, in the next place, essentially *indulgent;* it coincides with, and supports, the interest which is its object. The success or defeat of the loving interest will be a function of what is judged to be the success or defeat of the loved interest. Other-love, in this sense, may be directed to any one, or to the whole system, of the second person's interests. Where love is directed to the whole person it may oppose one of that person's particular interests, in so far as the person is imperfectly integrated. Where a person suffers from internal conflict, another's love may side with the integral self against the insubordinate element; but if love is to be indulgent, there must already be such an integral self in some form or stage of development. Love, in other words, is an interested support of another's preexisting and independently existing interest.[8]

There are several common meanings of love which this definition excludes. In the first place, love is neither approving nor censorious. It does not prescribe the object of the loved interest, but desires that that interest shall have its object *whatever* that object. Suppose a son to desire fame; then the father's desire for the son's fame, if founded on the father's admiration of fame, is not love; nor is it love if the father desires that the son shall substitute for fame some other object, such as knowledge, which he, the father, prefers. Action towards another dictated by the agent's belief that he knows better what is good for the other than does the other himself, may be praiseworthy, but it is not love.[9] The true quality of love is to be found in

---

[8] This does not preclude the possibility that the loved one may be momentarily unaware of his interest, and need to be reminded of it; but only that the interest must really be his, and not merely one felt in his behalf by somebody else.

[9] It was patriotism and not love for the Alsatians which dictated Treitschke's judgment that "we Germans, who know both Germany and France, know better what is for the good of the Alsatians than do those unhappy people themselves" (quoted from H. W. C. Davis, *The Political Thought of Treitschke,* 1915, p. 112).

that sensitive imagination which can find its way into the secret sources of a man's joy and sorrow.[10] Similarly, censoriousness, though it may be just, is not love. Love does not rebuke the sinner, or rejoice in his merited punishment; but grieves for him, and seeks to *bring him in*, as the shepherd seeks his lost sheep. Love, like Thomson's "Hound of Heaven," follows its object relentlessly into every corner of the universe and refuses to be offended or repelled.

The support of another's interest that springs from a sense of plenitude and power, or that looks to bind the other in gratitude, is not love. Nor is it love when an appetite feeds upon another individual, even though the other be of the same species. So-called sex-love may be as unloving as cannibalism. Finally, love must have an object other than itself. To love another's love of oneself, supposing oneself to consist only in love of the other, would be meaningless, even though it occurs in poetry and fiction. The circle must be broken at some point by an interest directed to an object, in order that there may be something for love to indulge. What seems to be circular love is the gratification afforded to each of two individuals by the presence of the other. Other-love finds itself most purely embodied in parental love, for the very reason that it is commonly one-sided or unreciprocated. Reciprocity adds to the intensity of love, but tends to impair its purity through introducing an element of sensuous gratification or of self-reference.

Love in the present sense consists essentially, then, in an activity which supports the interested activity of another person; seeking to promote that other person's achievement of what he desires, or enjoyment of what he likes. Universal love would be such a disposition on the part of one person towards all persons. If it is psychologically possible (in the sense of the general capacity of human nature) towards one, it is psychologically possible towards two or more; or towards all members of a class, such as the family, the nation, mankind, or sentient creatures. This attitude of general kindly interest, or of amiability, has its negative form, as in Lincoln's maxim, "with malice toward none, with charity for all"; and its positive form, as in good Samaritanism and humanity. A personal integration dominated by such a purpose is known in the tradition of moral philosophy as 'good will'.

*5. The Conflicts of Benevolence.* Such a universal love, felt by any person for all mankind, including himself, defines a system of objects which is better than any personal system which lacks this benevolent purpose. The

[10]Cf. W. James, "On a Certain Blindness in Human Beings," *Talks with Teachers*, etc., 1899.

man who loves his neighbor as himself loves more inclusively than the neighbor who does not reciprocate. This is true only because the latter is a partial constituent of the former. While in this sense unselfishness takes precedence of selfishness,[11] it is not justified in *overriding* the latter. We cannot say that the triumph of unselfishness and defeat of selfishness, is better than the triumph of selfishness and defeat of unselfishness; because the defeat of selfishness would imply the defeat of that unselfishness which embraces it. We can only say that the triumph of both which is implied in the triumph of unselfishness, is better than the triumph of one which is implied in the triumph of selfishness.[12] Love is not satisfied by the suffering of the sinner even when it is merited, but only by his repentance and participation in the general happiness.

Unfortunately, however, the good will of one person does not necessarily accord with the good will of another person. It is doubtless true that a great part of social conflict can be attributed to a difference of ultimate purpose. A will which incorporates interests $a$, $b$, and $c$ differs from a will which incorporates $a$, $b$, $c$, and $d$, and the solution then lies in modifying the first will by the incorporation of $d$. This situation is commonly obscured by the supposition that $d$ is already incorporated, when the first will has an interest in the subject of $d$, but not in his interest; as when the father's interest in his son is supposed to embrace the son's interests, when it really embraces only a certain state or condition of the son. Often the situation is candidly recognized, as when a nation may assert itself against the larger interest of mankind and claim on its own behalf a finality which it does not really possess. Different integrations of interests will have different objects, and it is absurd to suppose, as has been claimed in behalf of the doctrine of *laissez-faire,* that there is any preëstablished harmony between self-interest and social-interest. They may partially coincide, or accidentally and momentarily agree, but sooner or later they will differ, *because their premises differ.* The only way in which self-interest and social-interest can be made to agree in principle, or necessarily, is to subsume the interests of the self under an interest in society.

Although social conflict can often, perhaps usually, be resolved by

---

[11] Selfishness meaning not self-love, but the *absence* of other-love.

[12] This principle has an important bearing on jurisprudence and on the relation of man to lower forms of life. Punishment involves the deliberate inflicting of pain or some other form of evil on the guilty man, and does defeat his interest. This can be rationalized ultimately only provided the guilty man can be said to have agreed to suffer the penalty of his transgression. This would be the correct interpretation of the Socratic maxim that virtue can do no evil, or that it is impossible to justify an act in terms of evil consequences. Where, as in the case of the *use* of animals, or the punishment of the defiant transgressor, the interest of the second party is ignored, the relation becomes one which cannot be moralized, but can be defended only in terms of the interest of the stronger.

showing that one of the conflicting wills embraces the other and is therefore better, or entitled to precedence, this does not fully meet the difficulties. The supreme tragedy of life is the conflict of good wills, or the opposition of the integral interests of two equally well-intentioned persons. Two men may love mankind equally and yet be brought into antagonism with one another by the very earnestness of their benevolence. How is this possible? It arises obviously from the fact that the same constituent interests, where some are present and others represented, may be differently mediated and integrated. To present the fact in the simplest form, suppose three persons, $L$, $M$ and $N$, to love one another in accordance with the Golden Rule. Suppose each to be interested in the interests of the other two as well as in his own, and suppose the complexus of interests in each person to assume the form of a unified purpose or plan of life, with an order of precedence among all the interests involved. It is entirely possible that three different and opposing purposes should emerge, since in $L$'s purpose $M$ and $N$ are represented only through $L$'s benevolence, while $L$ and $N$ are so represented in $M$, and $L$ and $M$ in $N$. These differences are likely to involve other differences of angle, of distance, and of judgment as to the causal relations of means to ends. It follows that such differences will be mitigated by the perfecting of sympathy or understanding, and by the substitution of common truth for diverse error. The way to secure a just solution is to seek a benevolent purpose on which all can unite. In such a purpose the effects of bias will neutralize and cancel one another. The purpose of which it can be said that it most perfectly incorporates the interests of all three is the *common plan* adopted by $L$, $M$ and $N$, after the discussion of the three benevolent plans initially proposed by $L$, $M$ and $N$ severally. All parties will be disposed to harmony because of being benevolent, and when agreement is desired the chief obstacle to its attainment is already overcome.

These are, however, questions of moral education and of social reconstruction. The important thing is to recognize not only that an agreement of good wills is possible and may be methodically cultivated, but that such an agreement is better than anything else, and may properly be adopted as a standard and end.

This conclusion is perhaps not far from the meaning of Kant's famous rendering of the 'categorical imperative': "Act on that maxim whereby thou canst at the same time will that it should become a universal law." [13] The defect in this formula as it stands, lies in the term "canst," which seems to appeal to a psychological capacity, and to suggest a subjective criterion

---

[13] *Metaphysic of Morals,* trans. by T. K. Abbott, *Kant's Theory of Ethics.* 1889, p. 38. [This volume, p. 102.]

of right conduct. There is, as a matter of fact, *no* maxim that *cannot* be willed to become universal law. Amended in accordance with the conclusions already reached, Kant's imperative would read, "Cultivate that kind of will that is qualified to bring harmony through its universal adoption." A will meeting this requirement will be first of all a benevolent will; and beyond that a conciliatory will, disposed by experience and discussion to the adoption of a common plan.

## 42

# Principles of International Morality*

## HENRY SIDGWICK
### (1838–1900)

. . . It is sometimes frankly affirmed, and more often implied, in discussions on the principles of foreign policy, that a State is not properly subject—as an individual is commonly held to be—to any restraint of duty limiting the pursuit of its own interest: that its own interest is, necessarily and properly, its paramount end; and that when we affirm that it is bound to conform to any rules of international duty we can only mean, or ought only to mean, that such conformity will—on the whole and in the long run if not immediately—be conducive to its national interests. In my view all such statements are essentially immoral. For a State, as for an individual, the ultimate end and standard of right conduct is the happiness of all who are affected by its actions. It is of course true, for an individual no less than for a State—as the leading utilitarian moralists have repeatedly and emphatically affirmed—that the general happiness is usually best promoted by a concentration of effort on more limited ends. As Austin puts it—"The principle of general utility imperiously demands that [every individual person] commonly shall attend to his own rather than to the interests of others: that he shall not habitually neglect that which he knows accurately in order that he may habitually pursue that which he knows imperfectly." But—as the same writer is careful to add—"the principle of utility does demand of us that we shall never pursue our own peculiar good by means which are inconsistent with the general good": accordingly, in the exceptional cases in which the interest of the part conflicts with the interest of the whole, the interest of the part—be it individual or State—must necessarily

*From Henry Sidgwick, *The Elements of Politics* (London: Macmillan and Co., 1891; 3rd ed., 1908), ch. 18, pp. 298–301, with a few words omitted. The title of this selection has been supplied by the editor. Compare with selections 9, 13, and 44.

give way. On this point of principle no compromise is possible, no hesitation admissable, no appeal to experience relevant: the principle does not profess to prescribe what states and individuals have done, but to prescribe what they ought to do. At the same time, I think it important not to exaggerate the divergence between the private interest of any particular State and the general interest of the community of nations. I conceive that it will be usually the interest of any particular State to conform to what we have laid down as the rules of international duty, so long as it has a reasonable expectation of similar conformity on the part of its neighbours;—at any rate in dealing with civilised, coherent, and well-ordered States, in whose case conquest could not be justified in the interest of the conquered State as a means of getting rid of the evils of disorder; or in the interest of humanity at large as a means of substituting a higher civilisation for a lower. And so far as the past conduct of any foreign State shows that reciprocal fulfilment of international duty cannot reasonably be expected from it, any State that may have to deal with it must, I conceive, be allowed in the interest of humanity, the extension of the right of self-protection which its own interests would prompt it to claim. From any point of view, it must be held right for a State to anticipate an attack which it has reasonable grounds for regarding as imminent, to meet wiles with wiles, as well as force with force, and in extreme cases to stamp out incurable international brigandage even by the severe measure of annihilating the independent existence of the offending State.

Again, it seems to be plain that, in its own interest, no less than in that of humanity at large, a State should incur some risk of sacrifice in order to avoid war, by accepting arbitration on all points of minor importance, or negotiation if an impartial arbiter cannot be found; and that it should make it a point of international policy to aim at improving the machinery of arbitration.

It is a different question whether it is the right policy to run the risk of war in order to prevent high-handed aggression by another State against a third. . . . For any State to embark in a career of international knight-errantry, and send its armies about to take part in remote quarrels with which it had no special concern, would be hardly more conducive to the interests of the civilised world than it would be to those of the supposed quixotic community. Still, where the assailant is clearly in the wrong, it would seem to be the ultimate interest, on the whole, as well as the duty, of any powerful neighbouring State—even if its own more obvious interests are not directly threatened—to manifest a general readiness to co-operate in forcible suppression of the wrong. Indeed, unless we suppose that the mere exercise of superior force is kept under some check by the fear of the intervention of other States against palpable injustice, war between States decidedly unequal in strength will hardly retain its moral character at all: to treat it, even so far as I have done, as a sanction against the breach of international duty would be solemn trifling. And I think that co-operation to prevent wanton breaches of international peace is the best mode of preparing the way for the ultimate federation of civilised States, to which I look forward. But in the present stage of civilisation, it would, I think, be a mistake to try to prevent wars altogether in this way. We may hope to put down by it palpable and high-handed aggression; but it is not applicable where there is a conflict of reasonable claims, too vague and doubtful to be clearly settled by general consent, and at the same time too serious to be submitted to arbitration. . . .

# 43

## The Moral Equivalent
## of War*

### WILLIAM JAMES
### (1842–1910)

The war against war is going to be no holiday excursion or camping party. The military feelings are too deeply grounded to abdicate their place among our ideals until better substitutes are offered than the glory and shame that come to nations as well as to individuals from the ups and downs of politics and the vicissitudes of trade. There is something highly paradoxical in the modern man's relation to war. Ask all our millions, north and south, whether they would vote now (were such a thing possible) to have our war for the Union expunged from history, and the record of a peaceful transition to the present time substituted for that of its marches and battles, and probably hardly a handful of eccentrics would say yes. Those ancestors, those efforts, those memories and legends, are the most ideal part of what we now own together, a sacred spiritual possession worth more than all the blood poured out. Yet ask those same people whether they would be willing in cold blood to start another civil war now to gain another similar possession, and not one man or women would vote for the proposition. In modern eyes, precious though wars may be, they must not be waged solely for the sake of the ideal harvest. Only when forced upon one, only when an enemy's injustice leaves us no alternative, is a war now thought permissible.

It was not thus in ancient times. The earlier men were hunting men, and to hunt a neighboring tribe, kill the males, loot the village and possess the females, was the most profitable, as well as the most exciting, way of living. Thus were the more martial tribes selected, and in chiefs and peoples a pure pugnacity and love of glory came to mingle with the more fundamental appetite for plunder.

*An essay of 1910. Reprinted here from William James, *Memories and Studies* (New York: Longmans, Green, and Co., 1911).

Modern war is so expensive that we feel trade to be a better avenue to plunder; but modern man inherits all the innate pugnacity and all the love of glory of his ancestors. Showing war's irrationality and horror is of no effect upon him. The horrors make the fascination. War is the *strong* life; it is life *in extremis;* war-taxes are the only ones men never hesitate to pay, as the budgets of all nations show us.

History is a bath of blood. The Iliad is one long recital of how Diomedes and Ajax, Sarpedon and Hector *killed.* No detail of the wounds they made is spared us, and the Greek mind fed upon the story. Greek history is a panorama of jingoism and imperialism—war for war's sake, all the citizens being warriors. It is horrible reading, because of the irrationality of it all—save for the purpose of making "history"—and the history is that of the utter ruin of a civilization in intellectual respects perhaps the highest the earth has ever seen.

Those wars were purely piratical. Pride, gold, women, slaves, excitement, were their only motives. In the Peloponnesian war for example, the Athenians ask the inhabitants of Melos (the island where the "Venus of Milo" was found), hitherto neutral, to own their lordship. The envoys meet, and hold a debate which Thucydides gives in full, and which, for sweet reasonableness of form, would have satisfied Matthew Arnold. "The powerful exact what they can," said the Athenians, "and the weak grant what they must." When the Meleans say that sooner than be slaves they will appeal to the gods, the Athenians reply: "Of the gods we believe and of men we know that, by a law of their nature, wherever they can rule they will. This law was not made by us, and we are not the first to have acted upon it; we did but inherit it, and we know that you and all mankind, if you were as strong as we are, would do as we do. So much for the gods; we have told you why we expect to stand as high in their good opinion as you." Well, the Meleans still refused, and their town was taken. "The Athenians," Thucydides quietly says, "thereupon put to death all who were of military age and made slaves of the women and children. They then colonized the island, sending thither five hundred settlers of their own."

Alexander's career was piracy pure and simple, nothing but an orgy of power and plunder, made romantic by the character of the hero. There was no rational principle in it, and the moment he died his generals and governors attacked one another. The cruelty of those times is incredible. When Rome finally conquered Greece, Paulus Æmilius was told by the Roman Senate to reward his soldiers for their toil by "giving" them the old kingdom of Epirus. They sacked seventy cities and carried off a hundred and fifty thousand inhabitants as slaves. How many they killed I know not; but in Etolia they killed all the senators, five hundred and fifty in number.

Brutus was "the noblest Roman of them all," but to reanimate his soldiers on the eve of Philippi he similarly promises to give them the cities of Sparta and Thessalonica to ravage, if they win the fight.

Such was the gory nurse that trained societies to cohesiveness. We inherit the warlike type; and for most of the capacities of heroism that the human race is full of we have to thank this cruel history. Dead men tell no tales, and if there were any tribes of other type than this they have left no survivors. Our ancestors have bred pugnacity into our bone and marrow, and thousands of years of peace won't breed it out of us. The popular imagination fairly fattens on the thought of wars. Let public opinion once reach a certain fighting pitch, and no ruler can withstand it. In the Boer war both governments began with bluff but couldn't stay there, the military tension was too much for them. In 1898 our people had read the word "war" in letters three inches high for three months in every newspaper. The pliant politician McKinley was swept away by their eagerness, and our squalid war with Spain became a necessity.

At the present day, civilized opinion is a curious mental mixture. The military instincts and ideals are as strong as ever, but are confronted by reflective criticisms which sorely curb their ancient freedom. Innumerable writers are showing up the bestial side of military service. Pure loot and mastery seem no longer morally avowable motives, and pretexts must be found for attributing them solely to the enemy. England and we, our army and navy authorities repeat without ceasing, arm solely for "peace," Germany and Japan it is who are bent on loot and glory. "Peace" in military mouths to-day is a synonym for "war expected." The word has become a pure provocative, and no government wishing peace sincerely should allow it ever to be printed in a newspaper. Every up-to-date dictionary should say that "peace" and "war" mean the same thing, now *in posse,* now *in actu.* It may even reasonably be said that the intensely sharp competitive *preparation* for war by the nations *is the real war,* permanent, unceasing; and that the battles are only a sort of public verification of the mastery gained during the "peace"-interval.

It is plain that on this subject civilized man has developed a sort of double personality. If we take European nations, no legitimate interest of any one of them would seem to justify the tremendous destructions which a war to compass it would necessarily entail. It would seem as though common sense and reason ought to find a way to reach agreement in every conflict of honest interests. I myself think it our bounden duty to believe in such international rationality as possible. But, as things stand, I see how desperately hard it is to bring the peace-party and the war-party together, and I believe that the difficulty is due to certain deficiencies in the program of pacificism which set the militarist imagination strongly, and to a certain extent justifiably, against it. In the whole discussion both sides are on imaginative and sentimental ground. It is but one utopia against another, and everything one says must be abstract and hypothetical. Subject to this criticism and caution, I will try to characterize in abstract strokes the opposite imaginative forces, and point out what to my own very fallible mind seems the best utopian hypothesis, the most promising line of conciliation.

In my remarks, pacificist though I am, I will refuse to speak of the bestial side of the war-*régime* (already done justice to by many writers) and consider only the higher aspects of militaristic sentiment. Patriotism no one thinks discreditable; nor does any one deny that war is the romance of history. But inordinate ambitions are the soul of every patriotism, and the possibility of violent death the soul of all romance. The militarily patriotic and romantic-minded everywhere, and especially the professional military class, refuse to admit for a moment that war may be a transitory phenomenon in social evolution. The notion of a sheep's paradise like that revolts, they say, our higher imagination. Where then would be the steeps of life? If war had ever stopped, we should have to re-invent it, on this view, to redeem life from flat degeneration.

Reflective apologists for war at the present day all take it religiously. It is a sort of sacrament. Its profits are to the vanquished as well as to the victor; and quite apart from any question of profit, it is an absolute good, we are told, for it is human nature at its highest dynamic. Its "horrors" are a cheap price to pay for rescue from the only alternative supposed, of a world of clerks and teachers, of co-education and zo-ophily, of "consumer's leagues" and "associated charities," of industrialism unlimited, and feminism unabashed. No scorn, no hardness, no valor any more! Fie upon such a cattleyard of a planet!

So far as the central essence of this feeling goes, no healthy minded person, it seems to me, can help to some degree partaking of it. Militarism is the great preserver of our ideals of hardihood, and human life with no use for hardihood would be contemptible. Without risks or prizes for the darer, history would be insipid indeed; and there is a type of military character which every one feels that the race should never cease to breed, for every one is sensitive to its superiority. The duty is incumbent on mankind, of keeping military characters in stock—of keeping them, if not for use, then as ends in themselves and as pure pieces of perfection,—so that Roosevelt's weaklings and mollycoddles may not end by making everything else disappear from the face of nature.

This natural sort of feeling forms, I think, the innermost soul of army-writings. Without any exception known to me, militarist authors take a highly mystical view of their subject, and regard war as a biological or sociological necessity, uncontrolled by ordinary psychological checks and motives. When the time of development is ripe the war must come, reason or no reason, for the justifications pleaded are invariably fictitious. War is, in short, a permanent human *obligation.* General Homer Lea, in his recent book "The Valor of Ignorance," plants himself squarely on this ground. Readiness for war is for him the essence of nationality, and ability in it the supreme measure of the health of nations.

Nations, General Lea says, are never stationary—they must necessarily expand or shrink, according to their vitality or decrepitude. Japan now is culminating; and by the fatal law in question it is impossible that her statesmen should not long since have entered, with extraordinary foresight, upon a vast policy of conquest—the game in which the first moves were her wars with China and Russia and her treaty with England, and of which the final objective is the capture of the Philippines, the Hawaiian Islands, Alaska, and the whole of our Coast west of the Sierra Passes. This will give Japan what her ineluctable vocation as a state absolutely forces her to claim, the possession of the entire Pacific Ocean; and to oppose these deep designs we Americans have, according to our author, nothing but our conceit, our ignorance, our commercialism, our corruption, and our feminism. General Lea makes a minute technical comparison of the military strength which we at present could oppose to the strength of Japan, and concludes that the islands, Alaska, Oregon, and Southern California, would fall almost without resistance, that San Francisco must surrender in a fortnight to a Japanese investment, that in three or four months the war would be over, and our republic, unable to regain what it had heedlessly neglected to protect sufficiently, would then "disintegrate," until perhaps some Caesar should arise to weld us again into a nation.

A dismal forecast indeed! Yet not unplausible, if the mentality of Japan's statesmen be of the Caesarian type of which history shows so many examples, and which is all that General Lea seems able to imagine. But there is no reason to think that women can no longer be the mothers of Napoleonic or Alexandrian characters; and if these come in Japan and find their opportunity, just such surprises as "The Valor of Ignorance" paints may lurk in ambush for us. Ignorant as we still are of the innermost recesses of Japanese mentality, we may be foolhardy to disregard such possibilities.

Other militarists are more complex and more moral in their considerations. The "Philosophie des Krieges," by S. R. Steinmetz is a good example. War, according to this author, is an ordeal instituted by God, who weighs the nations in its balance. It is the essential form of the State, and the only function in which peoples can employ all their powers at once and convergently. No victory is possible save as the resultant of a totality of virtues, no defeat for which some vice or weakness is not responsible. Fidelity, cohesiveness, tenacity, heroism, conscience, education, inventiveness, economy, wealth, physical health and vigor—there isn't a moral or intellectual point of superiority that doesn't tell, when God holds his assizes and hurls the peoples upon one another. *Die Weltgeschichte ist das Weltgericht;*\* and Dr. Steinmetz does not believe that in the long run chance and luck play any part in apportioning the issues.

The virtues that prevail, it must be noted, are virtues anyhow, superiorities that count in peaceful as well as in military competition; but the strain on them, being infinitely intenser in the latter case, makes war infinitely more searching as a trial. No ordeal is comparable to its winnowings. Its dread hammer is the welder of men into cohesive states, and nowhere but in such states can human nature adequately develop its capacity. The only alternative is "degeneration."

Dr. Steinmetz is a conscientious thinker, and his book, short as it is, takes much into account. Its upshot can, it seems to me, be summed up in Simon Patten's word, that mankind was nursed in pain and fear, and that the transition to a "pleasure-economy" may be fatal to a being wielding no powers of defence against its disintegrative influences. If we speak of the *fear of emancipation from the fear-régime,* we put the whole situation into a single phrase; fear regarding ourselves now taking the place of the ancient fear of the enemy.

Turn the fear over as I will in my mind, it all seems to lead back to two unwillingnesses of the imagination, one aesthetic, and the other moral; unwillingness, first to envisage a future in which army-life, with its many elements of charm, shall be forever impossible, and in which the destinies of peoples shall nevermore be decided quickly, thrillingly, and tragically, by force, but only gradually and insipidly by "evolution"; and, secondly, unwillingness to see the supreme theatre of human strenuousness closed, and the splendid military aptitudes of men doomed to keep always in a state of latency and never show themselves in action. These insistent unwillingnesses, no less than other aesthetic and ethical insistencies, have, it seems to me, to be listened to and respected. One cannot meet them effectively by mere counter-insistency on war's expensiveness and horror. The horror makes the thrill; and when the question is of getting the extremest and supremest out of human nature, talk of expense sounds ignominious. The weakness of so much merely negative criticism is evi-

---

\*[The history of the world is the judgment of the world.]

dent—pacificism makes no converts from the military party. The military party denies neither the bestiality nor the horror, nor the expense; it only says that these things tell but half the story. It only says that war is *worth* them; that, taking human nature as a whole, its wars are its best protection against its weaker and more cowardly self, and that mankind cannot *afford* to adopt a peace-economy.

Pacificists ought to enter more deeply into the aesthetical and ethical point of view of their opponents. Do that first in any controversy, says J. J. Chapman, *then move the point,* and your opponent will follow. So long as antimilitarists propose no substitute for war's disciplinary function, no *moral equivalent* of war, analogous, as one might say, to the mechanical equivalent of heat, so long they fail to realize the full inwardness of the situation. And as a rule they do fail. The duties, penalties, and sanctions pictured in the utopias they paint are all too weak and tame to touch the military-minded. Tolstoi's pacificism is the only exception to this rule, for it is profoundly pessimistic as regards all this world's values, and makes the fear of the Lord furnish the moral spur provided elsewhere by the fear of the enemy. But our socialistic peace-advocates all believe absolutely in this world's values; and instead of the fear of the Lord and the fear of the enemy, the only fear they reckon with is the fear of poverty if one be lazy. This weakness pervades all the socialistic literature with which I am acquainted. Even in Lowes Dickinson's exquisite dialogue,[1] high wages and short hours are the only forces invoked for overcoming man's distaste for repulsive kinds of labor. Meanwhile men at large still live as they always have lived, under a pain-and-fear economy—for those of us who live in an ease-economy are but an island in the stormy ocean—and the whole atmosphere of present-day utopian literature tastes mawkish and dishwatery to people who still keep a sense for life's more bitter flavors. It suggests, in truth, ubiquitous inferiority.

Inferiority is always with us, and merciless scorn of it is the keynote of the military temper. "Dogs, would you live forever?" shouted Frederick the Great. "Yes," say our utopians, "let us live forever, and raise our level gradually." The best thing about our "inferiors" to-day is that they are as tough as nails, and physically and morally almost as insensitive. Utopianism would see them soft and squeamish, while militarism would keep their callousness, but transfigure it into a meritorious characteristic, needed by "the service," and redeemed by that from the suspicion of inferiority. All the qualities of a man acquire dignity when he knows that the service of the collectivity that owns him needs them. If proud of the collectivity, his own

[1] "Justice and Liberty," N.Y., 1909.

pride rises in proportion. No collectivity is like an army for nourishing such pride; but it has to be confessed that the only sentiment which the image of pacific cosmopolitan industrialism is capable of arousing in countless worthy breasts is shame at the idea of belonging to *such* a collectivity. It is obvious that the United States of America as they exist to-day impress a mind like General Lea's as so much human blubber. Where is the sharpness and precipitousness, the contempt for life, whether one's own, or another's? Where is the savage "yes" and "no," the unconditional duty? Where is the conscription? Where is the blood-tax? Where is anything that one feels honored by belonging to?

Having said thus much in preparation, I will now confess my own utopia. I devoutly believe in the reign of peace and in the gradual advent of some sort of a socialistic equilibrium. The fatalistic view of the war-function is to me nonsense, for I know that war-making is due to definite motives and subject to prudential checks and reasonable criticisms, just like any other form of enterprise. And when whole nations are the armies, and the science of destruction vies in intellectual refinement with the sciences of production, I see that war becomes absurd and impossible from its own monstrosity. Extravagant ambitions will have to be replaced by reasonable claims, and nations must make common cause against them. I see no reason why all this should not apply to yellow as well as to white countries, and I look forward to a future when acts of war shall be formally outlawed as between civilized peoples.

All these beliefs of mine put me squarely into the anti-militarist party. But I do not believe that peace either ought to be or will be permanent on this globe, unless the states pacifically organized preserve some of the old elements of army-discipline. A permanently successful peace-economy cannot be a simple pleasure-economy. In the more or less socialistic future towards which mankind seems drifting we must still subject ourselves collectively to those severities which answer to our real position upon this only partly hospitable globe. We must make new energies and hardihoods continue the manliness to which the military mind so faithfully clings. Martial virtues must be the enduring cement; intrepidity, contempt of softness, surrender of private interest, obedience to command, must still remain the rock upon which states are built—unless, indeed, we wish for dangerous reactions against commonwealths fit only for contempt, and liable to invite attack whenever a centre of crystallization for military-minded enterprise gets formed anywhere in their neighborhood.

The war-party is assuredly right in affirming and reaffirming that the martial virtues, although originally gained by the race through war, are absolute and permanent human goods. Patriotic pride and ambition in their military form are, after all, only specifications of a more general competitive passion. They are its first form, but that is no reason for supposing them to be its last form. Men now are proud of belonging to a conquering nation, and without a murmur they lay down their persons and their wealth, if by so doing they may fend off subjection. But who can be sure that *other aspects of one's country* may not, with time and education and suggestion enough, come to be regarded with similarly effective feelings of pride and shame? Why should men not some day feel that it is worth a blood-tax to belong to a collectivity superior in *any* ideal respect? Why should they not blush with indignant shame if the community that owns them is vile in any way whatsoever? Individuals, daily more numerous, now feel this civic passion. It is only a question of blowing on the spark till the whole population gets incandescent, and on the ruins of the old morals of military honor, a stable system of morals of civic honor builds itself up. What the whole community comes to believe in grasps the individual as in a vise. The war-function has grasped us so far; but constructive interests may some day seem no less imperative, and impose on the individual a hardly lighter burden.

Let me illustrate my idea more concretely. There is nothing to make one indignant in the mere fact that life is hard, that men should toil and suffer pain. The planetary conditions once for all are such, and we can stand it. But that so many men, by mere accidents of birth and opportunity, should have a life of *nothing else* but toil and pain and hardness and inferiority imposed upon them, should have *no* vacation, while others natively no more deserving never get any taste of this campaigning life at all,—*this* is capable of arousing indignation in reflective minds. It may end by seeming shameful to all of us that some of us have nothing but campaigning, and others nothing but unmanly ease. If now—and this is my idea—there were, instead of military conscription a conscription of the whole youthful population to form for a certain number of years a part of the army enlisted against *Nature*, the injustice would tend to be evened out, and numerous other goods to the commonwealth would follow. The military ideals of hardihood and discipline would be wrought into the growing fibre of the people; no one would remain blind as the luxurious classes now are blind, to man's relations to the globe he lives on, and to the permanently sour and hard foundations of his higher life. To coal and iron mines, to freight trains, to fishing fleets in December, to dishwashing, clothes-washing, and window-washing, to road-building and tunnel-making, to foundries and stoke-holes, and to the frames of skyscrapers, would our gilded youths be drafted off, according to their choice, to get the childishness knocked out of them, and to come back into society with healthier sympathies and soberer ideas. They would have paid their blood-tax, done their own part in the immemorial human warfare against nature; they would tread the earth more proudly, the women would value them more highly, they would be better fathers and teachers of the following generation.

Such a conscription, with the state of public opinion that would have required it, and the many moral fruits it would bear, would preserve in the midst of a pacific civilization the manly virtues which the military party is so afraid of seeing disappear in peace. We should get toughness without callousness, authority with as little criminal cruelty as possible, and painful work done cheerily because the duty is temporary, and threatens not, as now, to degrade the whole remainder of one's life. I spoke of the "moral equivalent" of war. So far, war has been the only force that can discipline a whole community, and until an equivalent discipline is organized, I believe that war must have its way. But I have no serious doubt that the ordinary prides and shames of social man, once developed to a certain intensity, are capable of organizing such a moral equivalent as I have sketched, or some other just as effective for preserving manliness of type. It is but a question of time, of skilful propagandism, and of opinion-making men seizing historic opportunities.

The martial type of character can be bred without war. Strenuous honor and disinterestedness abound elsewhere. Priests and medical men are in a fashion educated to it, and we should all feel some degree of it imperative if we were conscious of our work as an obligatory service to the state. We should be *owned,* as soldiers are by the army, and our pride would rise accordingly. We could be poor, then, without humiliation, as army officers now are. The only thing needed henceforward is to inflame the civic temper as past history has inflamed the military temper. H. G. Wells, as usual, sees the centre of the situation. "In many ways," he says, "military organization is the most peaceful of activities. When the contemporary man steps from the street, of clamorous insincere advertisement, push, adulteration, underselling and intermittent employment into the barrack-yard, he steps on to a higher social plane, into an atmosphere of service and cooperation and of infinitely more honorable emulations. Here at least men are not flung out of employment to degenerate because there is no imme-diate work for them to do. They are fed and drilled and trained for better services. Here at least a man is supposed to win promotion by self-forget-fulness and not by self-seeking. And beside the feeble and irregular en-dowment of research by commercialism, its little shortsighted snatches at profit by innovation and scientific economy, see how remarkable is the steady and rapid development of method and appliances in naval and military affairs! Nothing is more striking than to compare the progress of civil conveniences which has been left almost entirely to the trader, to the progress in military apparatus during the last few decades. The house-appliances of to-day for example, are little better than they were fifty years ago. A house of to-day is still almost as ill-ventilated, badly heated by wasteful fires, clumsily arranged and furnished as the house of 1858. Houses a couple of hundred years old are still satisfactory places of residence, so little have our standards risen. But the rifle or battleship of fifty years ago was beyond all comparison inferior to those we possess; in power, in speed, in convenience alike. No one has a use now for such superannuated things."[2]

Wells adds[3] that he thinks that the conceptions of order and discipline, the tradition of service and devotion, of physical fitness, unstinted exertion, and universal responsibility, which universal military duty is now teaching European nations, will remain a permanent acquisition, when the last ammunition has been used in the fireworks that celebrate the final peace. I believe as he does. It would be simply preposterous if the only force that could work ideals of honor and standards of efficiency into English or American natures should be the fear of being killed by the Germans or the Japanese. Great indeed is Fear; but it is not, as our military enthusiasts believe and try to make us believe, the only stimulus known for awakening the higher ranges of men's spiritual energy. The amount of alteration in public opinion which my utopia postulates is vastly less than the difference between the mentality of those black warriors who pursued Stanley's party on the Congo with their cannibal war-cry of "Meat! Meat!" and that of the "general-staff" of any civilized nation. History has seen the latter interval bridged over: the former one can be bridged over much more easily.

[2]"First and Last Things," 1908, p. 215.
[3]"First and Last Things," 1908, p. 226.

# 44

## Morality in War*

### ADLAI E. STEVENSON

(1900–1965)

War is one of the oldest institutions. It is deeply imbedded in the traditions, the folkways, the literature, even the values of almost all countries. It has engaged countless talented men and produced countless national heroes. At the same time, civilized men and women for centuries past have abhorred the immorality of organized killing of men by men.

Yet, let us confess at once, to our common shame, that this deep sense of revulsion has not averted wars, nor shortened one by a day.

While I do not say that all wars have been started for unworthy purposes, let us also confess, morality to the side, that almost all past wars have served to promote what was conceived to be the national or princely or religious interests of those who fought them—or at least those who won them.

For in past wars, there have been winners as well as losers, the victors and the vanquished, the decorated and the dead. In the end, valuable real estate and other riches have changed hands. Thrones have been won, regimes transferred, rule extended, religions and ideologies imposed, empires gained and lost, aggressions halted or advanced.

Thus wars in the past have sometimes been a means of settling international disputes, of changing political control, of inducing social transformation and even of stimulating science and technology.

And I suppose that on moral grounds it is only a difference of degree whether millions are killed or only thousands, whether the victims include children in the debris of a big city building or only young men lying on a battlefield in the countryside.

*From a statement to the Political Committee of the United Nations, November 15, 1961; reprinted in *Looking Outward* (New York: Harper & Row, 1963), pp. 40–42. The title of this selection has been supplied by the editor.

Nor has war been a very efficient way of settling disputes. Yesterday's enemies are today's friends. First, the victor pays for destruction of his enemy, then for reconstruction of his friend.

But war in the future would differ fundamentally from war in the past, not in degree but in kind. It is this which seems so difficult to grasp. Thermonuclear war cannot serve anyone's national interest—no matter how moral or immoral that interest may be, no matter how just or unjust, no matter how noble or ignoble, regardless of the nation's ideology, faith or social system.

It is no satisfaction to suggest that the issue of morality in war thus has become academic. Yet this is the fact and perhaps it will serve to clarify the dialogue of war and peace. For we can now free our collective conscience of nice ethical distinctions, and face the stark, amoral fact that war has ceased to be practical, that no nation can contemplate resort to modern war except in defense against intolerable exaction or aggression. Therefore we must abolish war to save our collective skins. For as long as this nuclear death dance continues, millions—tens of millions—perhaps hundreds of millions—are living on borrowed time.

I suggested that war is such an ancient institution, so deeply entrenched in tradition, that it requires a strenuous intellectual effort to imagine a world free from war. So it does. But I submit that the alternative effort is to imagine a world at the end of another war; when great areas and great places have been turned into radioactive wasteland; when millions upon millions of people are already dead, while debris from those great mushroom clouds drifts ghoulishly over the living; when great parts of our institutions, ideologies, faiths and beliefs, even our art and literature, lie mashed in the smoke and rubble of material destruction.

I submit that however difficult the vision of a world *without war* may be, it is not only a happier, but an easier vision to imagine than one of a world *after war*. In any event, we must choose between them. . . .

# Part VII

## Institutional Ethics

The previous two parts deal in an abstract and theoretical way with the questions whether and how moral principles and rules are applicable to concrete cases and how moral theory is relevant to moral practice. This is no substitute for the actual application, however, though such abstract discussion may clear away some of the theoretical hindrances to reasonable application to practice. Thus we come to the present part, dealing with what I have called institutional ethics. This is the section of the book devoted most clearly and distinctly to questions of practical ethics. Yet even here theoretical issues cannot be wholly avoided, nor is it desirable that they should be.

It was said before that war is an institution of society (p. 299; see also selection 44). But what exactly is a social institution, how does this claim better enable us to understand war, and what has this to do with practical ethics?

1

An institution is not the same as an organization, nor is it the same as an association, though a number of organizations and associations are also institutions. "Cricket, five-o'clock tea, the House of Lords, Eton, the Workhouse, a hospital, the National Gallery, marriage, capital punishment, the Law Courts," to cite a list presented by Fowler, "are all institutions."[1] That is true, but they are, many of them, institutions of quite different kinds, and in quite different senses of the term, and the fact that most of the

---

[1] H. W. Fowler, *A Dictionary of Modern English Usage* (Oxford: Clarendon Press, 1926), p. 278.

ones listed exist only in Britain should help to bring this out. The term "institution" is one of those special terms whose importance is matched only by its ambiguity and the complexity of its conception.

I shall here present only some preliminary remarks on the matter, designed to help the reader see his way through this part of the book and perhaps also through some part of the subject.

An institution can be thought of as (1) a relatively permanent system of social relations organized around (that is, for the protection or attainment of) some social need or value, or (2) a recognized and organized way of meeting a social need or desire or of satisfying a social purpose.

These two definitions, though very similar, are nonetheless different. But what they both do is bring out the conception of an institution as an abstraction, as a complex of rules defining rights and duties, roles, privileges, immunities, responsibilities, and services, and this is the subject dealt with in institutional ethics. Neither the University of Wisconsin nor the First National Bank nor the New York Times is an institution in the sense intended. They are all, to be sure, institutions, but in some other sense of the term or on some other conception of an institution. They are *concrete embodiments* of the institutions of the university, banking (or finance), and the press. Similar statements can be made about cricket, the House of Lords, and the other institutions listed above, even though it may not always be possible to specify the abstract institution that some more concrete institution is a concrete embodiment of. In fact, there need not, actually, even be an abstract institution corresponding to every more concrete one.

In other words, the sense of "social institution" relevant to this subject is the sense in which property, punishment, marriage, the family, industry, advertising, religion, and contracts or promising are institutions. Even here, there are differences amongst the institutions noted that may or may not correspond to differences of meaning and may or may not correspond to differences in the relevant and appropriate criteria of evaluation. For example, though the family is an association of persons, property is not, even though it necessarily involves relations among persons.

2

Two fundamental institutions of society, and, it so happens, two of the most controversial, are property and punishment. It may be worth noting that each traditionally corresponds to a branch of justice. Property corresponds to distributive justice; and punishment, to what has been called retributive justice (not the so-called retributive theory of punishment, which is something else entirely).

The selections by Paley (46 and 48) bring out the application of his theological utilitarianism to punishment and to property. Bentham is usually thought of in connection with punishment, since that is one of the main concerns of his voluminous writings; there is special interest, then, in selection 49, which brings out how Bentham would apply the principle of utility to the idea of property. Kant's theory of punishment is criticized in the selection by Willoughby (47), in which some other theories of punishment, mostly utilitarian, are also distinguished and discussed; this selection is especially useful for the succinct account it gives of the various theories that have been traditionally advanced and acknowledged as having some plausibility. The selection by Spencer (50)—once so popular, now so rarely read—shows how Spencer applies the "law of equal freedom," his first principle of morals—"Every man has freedom to all that he wills, provided he infringes not the equal freedom of any other man"—to determine the right of property.

Thus what we have in Part VII is an application of the theories of Part II, or similar theories, to these basic institutions. This is not altogether so. The selection by Tawney (51) cannot be related in any obvious manner to anything presented previously (though it may, of course, have relations that are not obvious). Similarly with the selection by Mayer (52). The one by Griffiths (53), though greatly influenced by Kant, is not obviously derivative from any theory previously discussed. It is of special value for what it says about love, ends in themselves, and, preeminently, institutions: "Institutions cannot logically be unless they are conceived as such-and-such"; and what an institution is "is how it is conceived." That it is an attempt to determine the essential nature of the university—also an institution—is an added value.

Is it reasonable to expect an ethical theory, without any modifications or adjustments, to be applicable not only to the actions of individual persons but also to institutions? This is one of the unanswered questions of ethics, until recently rarely asked. Can general principles be formulated and established that will apply to institutions in a way analogous to the relatively familiar way in which general principles can be applied to the actions of individual persons? In what respects does, or should, the existence of an institution bear on the understanding and the judgment of an action? From a judgment about the morality of an institution as such, what, if anything, follows about the morality of an action falling under, or constituted by, the institution? These are all questions of institutional ethics, and the selections included herein should provide some stimulus to clearer and more fruitful thought on the matter.

# STATEMENTS ON MORALITY
## Ninth Series

*64. An appeal to principles is the condition of any considerable reconstruction of society, because social institutions are the visible expression of the scale of moral values which rules the minds of individuals, and it is impossible to alter institutions without altering that valuation.*

R. H. Tawney (1920)

*65. It is possible to measure progress because of the persistence throughout the whole course of human history of certain identical interests and purposes. When such an interest or purpose is sufficiently broad in its scope, and gets itself permanently embodied, it is called an* institution. *Thus* government *embodies the need of the general regulation of interests within the social community.* Education *is due to the individual's prolonged period of helplessness and dependence, and the need of assimilating him to the order of his time.* Science *is man's knowledge of the ways of nature in detail, when this is recorded, organized, and preserved as a permanent utility answering to the permanent need of adaptation. And* religion *expresses in outer form the human need of reckoning with the final day of judgment, of establishing right relations with the powers that underly and overrule the proximate sphere of life. There is no limited number of institutions, but these are notable examples. Government, education, science, and religion are fixed moral necessities. They arise out of those conditions of life which are general and constant. Hence each has a history coextensive with the history of society itself. And since the function of each remains identical throughout, the adequacy with which at any given time it fulfils that function may be taken as a measure of civilization.*

Ralph Barton Perry (1909)

66. *War is at the present time the most purposeful of our social institutions; and we shall make no progress towards its elimination until we recognise, and provide for, the essential social function which it performs. If we are to find a substitute for war, we must be clear about the function of war in our time.*

E. H. Carr (1942)

67. *The justice of the punishment depends on the justice of the general system of rights; not merely on the propriety with reference to social well-being of maintaining this or that particular right which the crime punished violates, but on the question whether the social organisation in which a criminal has lived and acted is one that has given him a fair chance of not being a criminal.*

T. H. Green (1882)

68. *It is not the business of government to make men virtuous or religious, or to preserve the fool from the consequences of his own folly. Governments should be repressive no further than is necessary to secure liberty by protecting the equal rights of each from aggression on the part of others. . . . Out of the principle that it is the proper end and purpose of government to secure the natural rights and equal liberty of the individual, grows the principle that it is the business of government to do for the mass of individuals those things which cannot be done, or cannot be so well done, by individual action.*

Henry George (1883)

69. *The institution of private property is to be justified on four main interconnected grounds.*

*First, the possession of property is a right of the individual—a legitimate aspiration which human beings as such are naturally entitled to pursue as a means of developing their personalities.*

*Second, private property is the natural right and safeguard of the family, which is itself the natural unit of society and is and ought to be the foundation of the whole fabric of civilised society.*

*Third, private property is to the interest of the community since the desire to obtain it provides an incentive for work which is morally legitimate, and at the same time sufficiently material to operate on natures which in most of us contain certain elements not entirely spiritual or unselfseeking.*

*Fourth, private property—including some large fortunes—is the natural bulwark of liberty because it ensures that economic power is not entirely in the hands of the State.*

Quintin Hogg (1947)

70. *If promising and property are both of them institutions, promising would appear to be the more fundamental, and even if we grant that human society is conceivable without property, we may well question whether it is conceivable without*

*promising. For would not such a society be one in which no arrangements of any sort could be made which depended upon co-operation between individuals who were not continually in one another's presence? If plans and projects are to be undertaken parts of which have to be carried out by different people at different times and places, they must assure one another that they can each go on with their own part of it, and it is by means of promises that this is done.*

H. B. Acton (1970)

# 45

## *Institutions and Obligations* *
## ALAN GEWIRTH
### (1912–    )

## Institutional Obligations

One important concept of obligation is logically tied to the concepts of an institution and a rule. An institution is a standardized arrangement whereby persons jointly pursue or participate in some purposive activity which is socially approved on the ground of its value for society. This arrangement may be solely functional in that it is concerned only with the purposive activity itself, or it may also be organizational in that it is concerned as well with structured groupings of persons associated for pursuing and regulating the activity.[1] Thus if education, religion, and buying and selling are institutions in the functional sense, the corresponding organizational institutions are, among others, schools, churches, and corporations. Indeed, we sometimes refer to the latter groups as "organized education," "organized religion," and the like; and we sometimes ask whether a given (organizational) institution has lost its function. In any case, institutions are constituted by rules which define what men are required to do if they are to participate in the respective functions or activities; and these requirements are the obligations which men have qua such participants. Thus, in virtue of the requirements set by the rules constitutive of the institutions mentioned above, men have obligations to

*The main portion (pp. 56–74) of an essay entitled "Obligation: Political, Legal, Moral." Reprinted from *Political and Legal Obligation: Nomos XII,* edited by J. Roland Pennock and John W. Chapman (New York: Atherton Press, 1970), pp. 55–88. Copyright © 1970 by Atherton Press, Inc. Reprinted by permission of Lieber-Atherton, Incorporated. Compare with selections 15 and 53.

[1] See such discussions of institutions as B. Malinowski, *A Scientific Theory of Culture and Other Essays* (Chapel Hill: University of North Carolina Press, 1944), pp. 52 ff.; S. F. Nadel, *The Foundations of Social Anthropology* (London: Cohen and West, 1958), pp. 107 ff.

teach, to pray or worship, to pay for what they buy, and the like, just as, in connection with such other institutions as promising and marriage, we speak of the obligations persons have to keep their promises and to be faithful to their spouses. I shall refer to such requirements as *institutional obligations.*

It follows from this that institutional obligations are "objective" in that persons who are to participate in institutions must take on the corresponding obligations. This "must" is not moral but logical. It is analogous to the requirements for participating in rule-governed games: if one is to play tennis, for example, then one must hit the ball with one's racket, not with one's bare hands, and so forth. This logical status of institutional obligations should not be obscured by the reference to "purpose" or "function" in the definition of an institution, nor by the fact that institutional obligations operate as constraints or demands on individuals, tying them to performances of acts of certain kinds even in the face of contrary inclinations. Despite these features, the relation of the purpose or function of an institution to its institutional obligations is not primarily a contingent one of end to means but rather is a conceptual one of a definition to its logical components or logical consequences. It is not that action in accordance with institutional obligations comprises the most efficient means to achieving the purpose or goal of some institution, but rather that the obligations are logically required by the very concept of that institution as contained in its constitutive rules. It is in this logical sense that we may say that institutional obligations rest (logically) on reasons which consist in the function or purpose and the corresponding constitutive rules of the institution in question.

Institutions may, of course, change, so that at certain points it may be unclear just what are their constitutive rules and corresponding obligations. Consider, for example, the various changes in religious practices, or in American marriage as depicted in the Kinsey reports. This flexibility does not, however, affect the logical relation indicated above between institutions and obligations. For at such transitional periods questions arise as to whether it is still the same institution, or indeed whether it is then an institution at all, since the aspects of standardization and of social approval are sharply reduced. It remains the case, then, that so long as an institution is defined by constitutive rules, the relation between it and its corresponding obligations is a logical one.

It must also be noted, however, that there is nothing in the concept of an institution, as such, which necessitates either that participation in it be voluntary, or that all participants in it have rights correlative with their obligations, or that the obligations involve equal sacrifices on the part of all. For example, Negro slavery in the Southern United States, sometimes described by its adherents as "the peculiar institution," was an institution in the sense defined above. But while it imposed extreme obligations on the slave, the obligations of the master were minimal, and were in any case sharply curtailed by his ownership relation to the slave.[2] Other examples of such one-sided institutions are suttee, apartheid, the Inquisition, and the jus primae noctis.*

The use of the word "obligation" in connection with such institutions may be challenged. It may be contended that "obligation," like "ought," presupposes both "can" and "may not," so that it is illegitimate to speak of a person's having obligations where he has not freely accepted the requirement or status in question and where he is not free to refrain from fulfilling it except at a prohibitive price. Thus it may be urged that the slave, like a man accosted by a gunman, was *obliged* to accede but not that he had an *obligation* to do so. In this connection, however, it is important to note not only the distinction between institutional and moral obligations (to be discussed below), but also the distinction between institutionalized and noninstitutionalized relationships. Since a gunman's domination of his victim, unlike the master's domination of his slave, is not part of a standardized, socially approved arrangement, it does not have the aspects of alleged justification and of formal, stabilized allocation of responsibility that underlie the use of "obligation" to describe the institutional relationship.[3]

## Descriptive and Prescriptive Obligation-Statements

The consideration of such institutions suggests the following consequence: one may, with full consistency, describe and even participate in an institution and fulfill its obligations, without holding that one *ought* to fulfill those obligations. To put it schematically, from "*A* has an obligation to do *x*" there does not logically follow "*A* ought to do *x*."[4] The reason why it does not follow is that the obligation-statement may be a purely descriptive

---

[2] See K. M. Stampp, *The Peculiar Institution: Slavery in the Ante-Bellum South* (New York: Alfred A. Knopf, 1956), pp. 192 ff.; S. M. Elkins, *Slavery: A Problem in American Institutional and Intellectual Life* (New York: Grosset and Dunlap Universal Library, 1963), pp. 52 ff.

*[The right of the first night.]

[3] See, for example, Stampp, *Institution, op. cit.,* p. 206. The slave codes of each slave state "held slaves, as thinking beings, morally responsible and punishable for misdemeanors and felonies."

[4] Such logical disconnection between "obligation" and "ought" has been emphasized, among others, by H. L. A. Hart. See "Are There any Natural Rights?" *Philosophical Review,* 64 (April 1955), 186; *The Concept of Law* (Oxford: Clarendon Press, 1961), p. 83. Hart does not, however, tie this point to institutional obligations.

one about what is required by some institution; but the person making the statement may not himself accept the institution or its purposes as right or justified. He may therefore admit that the obligation does in fact exist as part of an institution and yet deny that the obligation ought to be carried out.[5]

We must therefore distinguish between *descriptive* and *prescriptive* obligation-statements. Both kinds of statement as uttered by a speaker $S$ may have the form, "$A$ has an obligation (or is under an obligation) to do $x$." In its descriptive sense, however, the statement is used by $S$ to indicate that $A$'s doing $x$ is required by certain institutional rules, but $S$ does not himself endorse or advocate $A$'s doing $x$. There are two possibilities here. One is that $S$ in general accepts the relevant institution and its requirements but holds that in this particular case the requirement should not be fulfilled because it conflicts with a more important obligation. The other possibility is that $S$ does not accept the relevant institution at all. As an example of the first case $S$, while recognizing that $A$ has the obligation to repay on a certain date a sum of money he borrowed, may yet hold that $A$ ought not to repay the money on that date because he needs it to buy medicine for his sick child. As an example of the second case $S$, while recognizing that $A$, a South African black person, has certain obligations under apartheid, may yet hold vigorously that the obligations ought not to be fulfilled.

In its prescriptive sense, on the other hand, the obligation-statement is used by $S$ to endorse or advocate $A$'s doing $x$; and insofar as $S$ regards $A$'s doing $x$ as a requirement deriving from the rule of some institution, $S$ endorses that rule and institution as well. He may, indeed, endorse the act because of the rule; but then his attitude toward the rule is not merely a descriptive or reportive one but rather one of advocacy or endorsement. In addition, however, $S$ may use the statement to endorse $A$'s doing $x$ without regard to the act's being required by an institutional rule. For example, he may say to $A$, with solemn emphasis, "It was your moral obligation to come to that poor man's rescue when he was being attacked; in failing to do so,

---

[5] See the use of "obligation" in such passages as: "In the British West Indies the achievement of manumission merely involved a release from the obligation to serve a special master. It did not carry with it any new rights . . ." (F. Tannenbaum, *Slave and Citizen: The Negro in the Americas* [New York: Vintage Books, 1946], pp. 93–94).

"The existing Hindoo written law, which is a mixed body of religious, moral, and legal ordinances, is pre-eminently distinguished by the strictness with which it maintains a number of obligations plainly traceable to the ancient despotism of the Family . . ." (H. S. Maine, *Lectures on the Early History of Institutions* [London: John Murray, 1875], pp. 322–23).

"A Henry County, Alabama, landlord required two Negro laborers to sign the following contract before giving them employment: 'That said Laborers shall not attach themselves, belong to, or in any way perform any of the obligations required of what is known as the Loyal League Society . . .'" (K. M. Stampp, *The Era of Reconstruction, 1865–1877* [New York: Vintage Books, 1967], p. 204).

you fell down on your obligation." Here, "obligation" is used as equivalent to "ought," in the sense of what one was required to do as determined by strong justifying reasons.

The failure to take account of this distinction between prescriptive and descriptive obligation-statements has led some philosophers to hold that the correct use of "obligation" is exclusively restricted to what I have called institutional obligations.[6] This view, however, overlooks the fact that "obligation" may be used in a prescriptive way which lacks the tentativeness or conditionalness characteristic of the concept of an institutional obligation as such. To restrict "obligation" to the institutional context is to make unintelligible both its connection with "obligatory" and the features which are common to descriptive and prescriptive, institutional and moral uses of "obligation." What all uses of "obligation" have in common is the idea of a practical (or task-setting) requirement based on some general alleged justifying reason which can be understood as such, even if not accepted as successfully justificatory, by those who are subject to the requirement. This reason may be some institution with its purpose and rules; but the reason may also consist in quite different considerations, including moral ones.

## Tentative and Determinative Obligations

The distinction between prescriptive and descriptive obligation-statements leads us to recognize a related distinction between what I shall call *tentative* and *determinative* obligations. A tentative obligation is one that obtains only within a context which has not itself yet received successful justification; it hence does not determine what one's "real" obligations are, that is, what is justifiably required of one, or what one ought to do. A determinative obligation, on the other hand, determines what is justifiably required of one, what one ought to do. Unlike a tentative obligation, it is already justified, and hence does not need to await justification (or dis-

[6]For a useful corrective, see R. B. Brandt's distinction between "paradigm" and "extended" uses in "The Concepts of Obligation and Duty," *Mind,* 73 (July 1964), 384 ff. The failure to note the distinction between descriptive and prescriptive obligation-statements underlies many attempts to deduce a moral ought-statement from a factual is-statement. Such attempts begin from premises which are descriptive obligation-statements (is-statements) to the effect that some person has an institutional obligation; they conclude with a prescriptive obligation-statement to the effect that he ought to fulfill that obligation. This conclusion is a *non sequitur* because it contains an endorsement of the institutional obligation, whereas the premise according to the argument as presented contains no such endorsement. For a recent noteworthy instance of this attempt, see J. R. Searle, "How To Derive 'Ought' from 'Is,'" *Philosophical Review,* 73 (January 1964), 43–58; see also the critique by A. Flew, "On Not Deriving 'Ought' from 'Is,'" *Analysis,* 28 (1964). For a related attempt in connection with the justification of legal obligation, see note 14 below [not included in this volume].

justification) from some further set of considerations. Determinative obligations, in turn, are of two kinds, *prima facie* and *conclusive*. A prima facie obligation is one that ought to be fulfilled unless some other determinative or justificatory obligation has a higher priority in the particular case in question. A conclusive obligation is one where this question of competing priority either does not arise or has already been resolved in favor of the obligation in question; hence, a conclusive obligation determines what one ought to do, decisively and without further question.

In these terms, what is the status of institutional obligations? While a full answer to this question must wait on an explicit discussion of the criteria of justification, the following preliminary considerations can be presented here. We may distinguish two aspects of any institution, its form and its content. Its form is what it has in common with any institution, as indicated by the definition of an institution given above. Its content is the specific kind of institution that it is. Now in respect of its form, the relevant question is: If we consider an institutional obligation simply qua institutional, is it a tentative or a determinative obligation? To answer this question, we must ask another: Do institutions, as such, perform justifiable functions in society? Let us assume that there may be both institutionalized and noninstitutionalized ways of pursuing or participating in the same purposive activities and let us assume also, for the present context, that those activities are themselves justified ones. Does the fact of their being institutionalized itself contribute an important element relevant to justification? One obvious answer to this question is that since the aspect of standardization common to all institutions involves acting in accordance with rules, this provides an important stabilizing element. On the other hand, such stabilization may operate to reduce or even remove spontaneity and innovation, so that an activity which was itself a justified one might be diminished rather than augmented in relevant valuable respects by the fact of institutionalization. We must add to this the consideration that the contents of institutions may themselves be unjustifiable or evil, and a stabilized evil is still an evil. I conclude, then, that institutional obligations, as such, are only tentative, not determinative: the mere fact that an obligation derives from some institution does not, as such, determine what one ought to do. In other words, institutions with their rules and obligations are not, as such, self-justifying; if their obligations are to determine what is justifiably required of persons, the institutions must be justifiable by other considerations.

This question of the justification of institutions may take two different forms. One is the general question: Why should there be such an institution at all? Another is the specific question: Granted that there should be such an institution, why should it involve such and such a particular arrangement, have such and such a particular rule? Whether there is any point to asking the specific question depends on whether or not the general institution admits of variation. In the case of promising, for example, it seems that only one arrangement is possible: that one keep one's promises. But in the case of marriage, defined in general terms as the contractually established and socially recognized cohabitation of persons of opposite sex, many arrangements are possible, such as monogamy, polygamy, polyandry, endogamy, exogamy, and so forth. Both forms of the question of justification can be construed as questions about second-order obligations. For both forms ask, in the terms presented above, why is there a determinative obligation to have the obligations which, simply as deriving from some institution, are tentative. The determinative obligation derives from reasons which justify that one fulfill the institutional obligations.

## Moral Reasons

An obvious move at this point is to say that these justifying reasons must be moral ones. Now I think this is true; but it is important to be clear about its meaning and status in order to avoid question-begging assumptions. For one thing, men have often tried to justify institutions and their rules and obligations by an appeal to such considerations as the national interest, or the interests of some race, class, or other group, or tradition, or religion, and so forth. Are all, or any, of these considerations moral ones? If we answer in the affirmative, then to call a reason a moral one will mean merely that it is any reason appealed to in justification of an institution, so that the assertion that institutions must be justified by moral reasons will be an unilluminating tautology. In addition, the question will still remain as to why *such* reasons should be accepted as succeeding in the task of justification. If, on the other hand, we say that considerations like those listed above are not moral ones, then the question will remain as to what we mean by the considerations or reasons that we do call moral, and why these should be accorded greater justificatory weight over the others and over institutional obligations generally.

To deal with these questions we must first note that "moral" can be used either in a descriptive sense (in which it is opposed to "nonmoral") or in an evaluative sense (in which it is opposed to "immoral"). Initially, I shall be concerned with the former sense. Now nonmoral rules as well as moral ones may be practical or "action-guiding"; but two differences between them have been held to be especially important. One difference is "formal": a person who upholds a rule or a reason as a moral one regards it as supremely authoritative or of overriding importance, such that it should, in his view, take precedence over all other rules or reasons. The other difference is "material": a person who upholds a rule or a reason as a moral one regards it as being affected with a social interest, in that it bears importantly on furthering the welfare of persons other than himself.[7]

Now there is, of course, no assurance that these two differentiating criteria will always coincide. But even if we were to take them jointly as the criteria of the moral as opposed to the nonmoral, it would still remain the case that considerations of the national interest and the others mentioned above could qualify as moral reasons. Hence, if we hold that institutions must be justified by moral reasons, these considerations would, so far, pass muster as such reasons. There would still remain, then, the question of how we are to choose among them: Which of these moral reasons is morally right or justified?

There is a further difficulty in our project of justifying institutions by moral reasons. It may be contended that morality is itself an institution parallel to such other institutions as law and religion, in that it is a very extensive, socially endorsed arrangement for participating in and regulating a broad range of purposive activities. On this view, moral obligations would themselves be a kind of institutional obligation, and moral obligation-statements, far from representing justificatory reasons superior to those of institutions, would themselves be conditional upon one's acceptance of an institution, morality. Moreover, just as specific legal or religious rules may or may not be accepted as right or justified, so too with specific moral rules.

Now it is true that there are and have been different "positive" or "conventional" moralities in the sense of informal systems of social regulation. But it is also true that these moralities can themselves be evaluated in respect of their moral rightness. This might be interpreted as meaning simply that one code of positive morality is used to evaluate another. Such an interpretation, however, would still leave open the question of which of these positive moralities is right or justified. What this shows is that the concept of morality in the sense of moral rightness is distinct from the concept of morality in the sense of what is upheld as supremely authoritative and welfare-furthering by the rules of one or another institution of positive morality. It is to the former concept, and not to the latter, that

---

[7] See W. K. Frankena, "Recent Conceptions of Morality," in H. N. Castaneda and G. Nakhnikian, eds., *Morality and the Language of Conduct* (Detroit: Wayne State University Press, 1963), pp. 1–24; N. Cooper, "Two Concepts of Morality, *Philosophy,* 41 (January 1966), 19 ff. I have discussed the relation between moral and nonmoral "oughts" in "Must One Play the Moral Language Game?" *American Philosophical Quarterly,* 7 (April 1970).

appeal is made when the question concerns the evaluation and justification of institutions, including those of the various positive moralities.

By what kinds of considerations of moral rightness, then, are institutions and their rules and obligations to be justified? Let us put the question in the negative: How do we show (or try to show) that an institution is not justified? That is, how do we criticize institutions? We do so, I suggest, by appealing to one or more of three main kinds of consideration: first, that the institution does no good, or does harm, or does more harm than good; second, that even if the institution does good, it is at others' expense, or is wrongly discriminatory, so that the goods which the institution fosters or the harms which it removes are distributed unjustly or unfairly; third, that even if the institution does good and distributes that good fairly, still the institution and its obligations were imposed on the persons subject to them without those persons' consenting or participating in the decision. These three considerations involve reasons, respectively, of welfare, justice, and freedom. The first two considerations are substantive ones bearing on the content of institutional obligations, whereas the third consideration is a procedural one: it concerns the decision-making process whereby men came to be subject to the institution with its rules and obligations.

## The Inherent Rationality of Moral Reasons

Many questions may, of course, be raised about each of these considerations and about the relations between them. But first I must supplement the above a posteriori approach with an a priori one. The reason for this is that the a posteriori approach still leaves unanswered the question of why these considerations should be accepted as the ones that are to be used in evaluating institutions. After all, the considerations have competitors, such as the national interest and the other grounds mentioned above. What must be shown, then, is that the considerations of freedom, welfare, and justice, as adumbrated above, are superior to their competitors in terms of rightness.

Let us try to make this point more precise. As we have seen, institutional obligations, as such, are not self-justifying, since when the question is raised whether they ought to be fulfilled it must be answered by an appeal to considerations other than the fact that they derive from an institution. Now we seem to have seen the same thing in relation to the competing basic reasons or principles of moral obligation-statements. The question, then, is whether there are any moral principles which are self-justifying. Since moral principles are advanced as basic reasons, another way to put this question is whether any moral principles are inherently rational. For if a principle is inherently rational, then it needs no further reason to justify it and is hence self-justifying.

But what does it mean for a principle to be inherently rational? One traditional answer has been that the principle must be self-evident, in the sense of being seen to be true or correct by immediate inspection or intuition. Such a criterion, however, is open to well-known and well-founded charges of psychologism and dogmatism. The "inherent rationality" which is here in question must be understood in a logical rather than in a psychological sense. Now a necessary condition of all rationality is freedom from self-contradiction. If a principle is self-contradictory, then, entirely apart from any other considerations, it is inherently irrational and self-disjustifying, since it can be shown to refute itself: it denies what it affirms. If, on the other hand, a principle is such that its denial is self-contradictory, then it is inherently rational and self-justifying, since its denial refutes itself, so that the original principle must stand unchallenged by any reasons that may be brought against it.

Can any moral principle be shown to be inherently rational in this sense? The most famous example of such an attempt is Kant's categorical imperative, according to which the test of the rightness of a moral rule or maxim is that when generalized it not be self-contradictory. This test, however, has important difficulties; it would not, for example, rule out the maxim that deformed children should be left unprotected to die. I wish to sketch here an argument for a somewhat different principle. Thus far I have discussed rationality in the logical sense of freedom from self-contradiction: this is the formal requirement of rationality. There is also, however, a material requirement, in that reason takes account of the necessary features of one's subject matter. Now the subject matter of morality is, primarily, human action. When human agents act, they do not merely engage in bodily movements; their action has certain necessary features which may be summarized as voluntariness and purposiveness. For insofar as men are agents, they initiate and control their movements (voluntariness) in the light of their intentions and purposes (purposiveness). This is why human agents can be held responsible both for their acts and for the consequences of the acts.

These features of voluntariness and purposiveness are the maximally general, constitutive conditions of all human action. I shall refer to them as the *categorial rules* of action, since they descriptively pertain to the category of human action as such, and not merely to one kind of act as against another. Whenever a human agent acts, he necessarily applies to himself these categorial rules: that is, he necessarily acts voluntarily and purposively.

Now suppose one person (the agent) acts on another (the recipient). I shall refer to this situation as a *transaction*. In transactions, the agent may or may not apply to his recipient the same categorial rules that he applies to himself. That is, while the agent necessarily acts voluntarily and purposively, he may act toward his recipient in such a way that the latter does or does not himself participate in the transaction voluntarily and purposively. If the recipient's participation is not voluntary, this means that the agent has coerced him; if it is not purposive, this means that the agent has harmed him, in that the recipient's own purposes or aims have not been considered or have been frustrated by the agent's action.

It is at this point that the formal aspect of rationality makes connection with the material aspect. If the agent does not apply to his recipient the same categorial rules that he applies to himself—that is, if the agent coerces or harms his recipient—then the agent contradicts himself. For since the recipient, as a potential or prospective agent, is similar to the agent in respect of the categorial rules of action, the agent would be in the position of saying that what is right for him—to participate voluntarily and purposively in their joint transaction—is not right for a relevantly similar person. And this is self-contradictory. Hence, on pain of self-contradiction, the agent logically must accept a principle which may be stated as follows: Apply to your recipient the same categorial rules of action that you apply to yourself. I shall call this the *Principle of Categorial Consistency* (*PCC*), since it combines the formal consideration of consistency with the material consideration of the categorial rules of action. The *PCC* fulfills the requirement mentioned above, that the principle of moral rightness must be inherently rational or self-justifying.[8]

It will be noted that the *PCC* contains the same three components as emerged in my brief a posteriori discussion above of how we justify and criticize institutions. We may now put those components in terms of obligation. According to the *PCC*, men have three basic moral obligations: they must refrain from coercing other persons (freedom); they must refrain from harming other persons (welfare); and they must be impartial as between themselves and other persons when the latter's freedom and welfare are at stake (justice). Indeed, the *PCC* as a whole may be explicated in terms of justice, in that it requires an agent to respect his recipient's freedom and welfare as well as his own. As I have stated them, these

[8] I have presented this argument in somewhat more detail in "Categorial Consistency in Ethics," *Philosophical Quarterly,* 17 (October 1967), 289 ff. For a discussion of the related question of whether the "criterion of relevant similarities" can be so individualized that its application is restricted to a single person, see my "The Non-trivializability of Universalizability," *Australasian Journal of Philosophy,* 47 (August 1969). In my forthcoming book, *Reason and Morality,* I attempt a full-scale development of the whole argument.

obligations are, of course, quite general. The important point, however, is that while their specific application in various contexts must inevitably involve many complexities, this application can nevertheless be made, so that it can be ascertained whether or not the criteria set by the obligations are fulfilled. Because these obligations have been justified by reasons which are inherently rational, they are not only determinative of what men ought to do but are the basis of all other determinative obligations. Hence, if the tentative obligations deriving from institutions are to be determinative, they must meet the criteria set by the *PCC*.

The basis of these determinative moral obligations differs, in respects which are both theoretically and practically important, from that espoused in a pervasive tradition of moral and legal philosophy. This tradition upholds the following interrelated theses: that moral obligations must be "self-imposed";[9] that the only legitimate way to indicate the content of one's moral obligations is to say that one ought to do what one thinks right ("subjective obligation"), not what is right ("objective obligation");[10] that what one ought to do, including whether one ought to obey a law, must be determined by one's own conscience. These theses are often put into a context of "agent morality" rather than "act morality." The former is concerned primarily with the moral goodness of the agent, including the quality of his motivations and their relation to his character, while act morality is concerned rather with the moral rightness of external acts themselves, including within "acts" the agent's intention, his knowledge of relevant circumstances, and his ability to control what he does in the light of his intention and knowledge.[11]

[9] See, e.g., P. H. Nowell-Smith, *Ethics* (Baltimore: Penguin Books, 1954), p. 210: "The feature which distinguishes moral obligations from all others is that they are self-imposed." This position goes back in modern times at least to Hobbes. See *Leviathan*, ch. 21, ed. M. Oakeshott (Oxford: Basil Blackwell, n.d.), p. 141: ". . . there being no obligation on any man, which ariseth not from some act of his own; for all men equally, are by nature free." The idea that obligations are "self-imposed" is highly ambiguous, it can mean at least three different things: (a) one has no moral obligations until one performs voluntary acts toward other persons; (b) whether one has moral obligations depends on one's voluntary agreements with or promises to other persons; (c) whether one has a moral obligation (including the content of the obligation) depends on whether one accepts it as an obligation, and not merely on what one says or does to other persons.

[10] See H. D. Thoreau, *Civil Disobedience*, in *Selected Writings on Nature and Liberty*, O. Cargill, ed. (Indianapolis: Bobbs-Merrill, 1952), p. 11: "The only obligation which I have a right to assume is to do at any time what I think right." On the distinction between "subjective" and "objective" obligation, see A. C. Ewing, *The Definition of Good* (New York: The Macmillan Co., 1947), pp. 118 ff., and K. Baier, *The Moral Point of View* (Ithaca, N.Y.: Cornell University Press, 1958), pp. 143 ff.

[11] For a good discussion of this distinction, see J. Laird, "Act Ethics and Agent Ethics," *Mind*, 55 (April 1946), 113–132. I have discussed the bearing of the tradition discussed in the text on the relation between legal and moral obligation, in "Some Misconceptions of the Relation between Law and Morality," *Proceedings of the Seventh Inter-American Congress of Philosophy* (Quebec: Les Presses de l'Université Laval, 1967), I, 208, 222.

The *PCC* is directly concerned with act morality rather than with agent morality, although it can also be used to evaluate in part the agent's moral character. According to the *PCC,* an agent has basic moral obligations toward his recipient whether the agent agrees to have them or not, and they are obligations to do what is right as determined by the *PCC.* The appeal to conscience leaves unanswered the question whether there are any moral reasons or criteria for the guidance of conscience itself. If there are no such reasons, then there is an obvious danger of arbitrariness and anarchy. But if there are such reasons, then conscience is at most a secondary rather than a primary determinant of moral obligation, since conscience must itself conform to these reasons if it is to be morally right.

The two interrelated ideas of the self-imposition of moral obligations and guidance by one's own conscience are somewhat similar to the freedom criterion adduced above as a component of the *PCC:* that if transactions are to be morally right, then their recipients must participate in them voluntarily. The similarity arises especially when we think of institutions as imposing obligations; for the freedom criterion requires that those who are subject to such obligations accept them freely. Even in this case, however, there are some important differences. The freedom criterion of the *PCC* is advanced not as a definition of moral obligation but rather as a basic theorem about moral obligation, which must itself be proved. Moreover, the freedom criterion, of itself, sets prima facie rather than conclusive moral obligations; as a procedural criterion, it must be supplemented by the substantive criteria of welfare and justice. Hence, whereas exclusive reliance on conscience as the determinant of moral obligations might be used (and has been used) to justify harmful and unjust acts and institutions, this is not the case with the freedom criterion. While the individual's conscience must be respected, then, because of its relation to his freedom and its importance to his feelings, it should not of itself determine the content of moral obligations.

Another aspect of the basic moral obligations must be briefly considered at this point. It may be objected that the welfare criterion as stated above, requiring merely that one refrain from harming other persons, is too negative, for one might fulfill it by sheer inaction or passivity, and this would make no positive contribution to welfare. The justice criterion, however, puts this point in proper perspective. Specifically, two replies must be made to the objection. First, to refrain from harming other persons requires action rather than inaction whenever one's voluntary or deliberate inaction is harmful to others. The "duty to rescue" is an obvious example of this, but there are also many other such cases in a mass society of interdependent persons.[12] Second, to put the welfare criterion in positive terms, as the obligation to do good or to advance the welfare or interests of other persons, would yield an unmanageable proliferation of obligations. The moral obligation to obey the law is sometimes upheld by such a criterion: law ought to be obeyed because it does great good. But this argument would similarly go to prove that men have a moral obligation to support garden clubs, madrigal-singing groups, and the like. If it were replied that the law does more good than any of these, this would subject the obligation to obey the law to a calculus which would jeopardize the stability often alleged as a chief argument for obeying the law. Some of the familiar problems of utilitarianism involved in this issue will be touched on below in connection with legal obligation.[13]

## The Moral Justification of Institutions

Let us now consider how the *PCC*'s criteria of moral obligation are to be applied in ascertaining whether an institution's obligations are determinative of what men ought to do. To begin, we must note that while the *PCC*'s criteria refer directly to how an agent, a human individual, is to act toward his recipients, there is also a sense in which an institution is an agent. For it operates by imposing obligations on the persons who participate in it, so that the latter are in the position of recipients of the institution's operations. If this seems too metaphorical, however, the same point can be made in terms of human agents. For although many institutions are

[12] See G. A. Coe, "What Is Violence?" In M. Q. Sibley, ed., *The Quiet Battle* (New York: Doubleday, 1963), p. 48: "For mere non-intercourse, mere refusal to buy and sell, can produce hunger and death just as surely as an embargo by means of warships. . . . For certainly, given the present interdependence of men, we can weaken, distort, and destroy the bodies of our fellows by merely doing nothing." Cf. from a different perspective, the comments of A. Tunc, "The Volunteer and the Good Samaritan," in J. M. Ratcliffe, ed., *The Good Samaritan and the Law* (New York: Doubleday, 1966), pp. 45–46: "From a philosophical point of view, it does not appear possible to distinguish between the man who does something and the man who allows something to be done, when he can interfere. Such a distinction would disregard the liberty of man, his freedom of choice, his creative power, his 'engagement' in the world and among other men. A stone does not bear any liability if a murder is committed beside it; a man does. By his decision not to interfere or to intervene, he participates in the murder." In order to keep clear the distinction between the morally obligatory and moral athleticism or supererogation, this position would have to specify many factual matters about knowledge, ability, and consequences. Nevertheless, when properly interpreted, the position does indicate an important positive application of the welfare and justice criteria.

[13] It is not always easy, of course, to distinguish among refraining from harm, preventing harm, and doing good. Formally, it may be said that all cases of preventing harm are cases of doing good, although not conversely. Also, when one is able to prevent harm to other persons and is aware of this, to refrain from harming them requires that one prevent that harm. Further qualifications are needed, however, especially concerning the cost aspects of "able."

the results of organic growth rather than of human contrivance, each institution has persons who profit from it or who at least uphold it. Hence, they can be asked the questions set by the *PCC*'s criteria. It must also be noted that individuals and groups often act on other persons in accordance with the rules of institutions. Hence, we can ask whether these actions are in accord with the criteria set by the *PCC*. This is to ask whether the tentative obligations which derive tautologically from the constitutive rules of an institution are also determinative or moral obligations. The application of the *PCC* to test the moral justification of institutions, then, may be made from two different perspectives: from that of the institution as agent and from that of the persons who participate in the institution as agents. Let us consider each of these in turn.

From the first perspective, the following questions set by the *PCC* are addressed to an institution or to its upholders: Was the institution freely accepted by the persons subject to it? Would its absence be harmful to their interests or welfare? Does it respect the freedom and welfare of all equally? If these questions are answered in the affirmative, they establish that the institution's obligations are determinative, whereas if they are answered in the negative, then the institution's obligations remain only tentative. But what if one question is answered in the affirmative and another in the negative? With respect to the freedom and welfare criteria which enter, respectively, into the first two questions, one of their underlying assumptions, based on the categorial structure of human action as sketched above, is that men in acting voluntarily intend to fulfill their own purposes and hence to obtain something that seems good to them. In this broad sense, which is the one that figures in the *PCC*, there is no conflict between what men freely choose to do and their interests or welfare, except insofar as the latter may involve means to what men want rather than the wants themselves as ends. As for the justice criterion which enters into the third question above, this may well conflict with the freedom and welfare criteria, in that an institution may be unequal or discriminatory in its relation to persons' freedom and welfare. In such a case, however, it is important to ask whether the inequality is instrumental or final, that is, whether the inequality is used as a means toward increasing freedom and welfare to a point where they come closer to equality for all who are affected or whether, on the contrary, the inequality is accepted as an end of the institution. In the former case, the institution's obligations are determinative; in the latter case, they are not.

Let us now turn to the other perspective from which the *PCC* is to be applied to institutions, that of the individuals who act in accordance with the institutions. Whereas from the first perspective all the individuals who participate in an institution were regarded as recipients of the institution's operations, from this second perspective some of these participants are agents and others recipients, each fulfilling the role set for him by the institution's rules. In this perspective, the specific questions set by the *PCC* are addressed to the agents: Do they, in fulfilling their institutional obligations, coerce or harm other persons or favor the freedom and welfare of some persons at the expense of others? If the answer to any part of this complex question is affirmative, then the persons involved have no prima facie determinative or moral obligation to fulfill their institutional obligations. The significance of this prima facie qualification is related to the reason for distinguishing between the institutional and individual perspectives in asking the questions set by the *PCC*. For it is possible that institutions satisfy the requirements of the *PCC* while individuals who act in accordance with those institutions do not. For example, insofar as a teacher gives a failing grade to a college student, the teacher may be said to harm the student and to act on him against his will; but in so doing, the teacher is acting in accordance with institutional rules (for example, the rules of the college) which are themselves accepted by, and are beneficial to, the students as a whole insofar as they are involved in the functioning of the institution. Hence, the relation of the *PCC* to the acts of individuals and to institutional rules must be put as follows. The obligations which the *PCC* sets for the particular acts of individuals are prima facie rather than conclusive, in that any particular act must be in accord with the *PCC* unless the act is in accord with an institutional rule which is itself in accord with the *PCC*.

The above paragraphs provide, of course, only a very general sketch of the criteria involved in the moral justification of institutions. A fuller account would have to analyze in much greater detail both the criteria themselves and the complex ways in which they may or may not be satisfied by various institutions. Apart from the fact that I attempt such an analysis elsewhere (see note 8), I have tried at least to suggest the logical basis and the general features of the relevant criteria. . . .

# 46

## *Of Crimes and Punishments**

## WILLIAM PALEY

### (1743–1805)

The proper end of human punishment is, not the satisfaction of justice, but the prevention of crimes. By the satisfaction of justice, I mean the retribution of so much pain for so much guilt; which is the dispensation we expect at the hand of God, and which we are accustomed to consider as the order of things that perfect justice dictates and requires. In what sense, or whether with truth in any sense, justice may be said to demand the punishment of offenders, I do not now enquire; but I assert that this *demand* is not the motive or occasion of human punishment. What would it be to the magistrate that offences went altogether unpunished, if the impunity of the offenders were followed by no danger or prejudice to the commonwealth? The fear lest the escape of the criminal should encourage him, or others by his example, to repeat the same crime, or to commit different crimes, is the sole consideration which authorizes the infliction of punishment by human laws. Now that, whatever it be, which is the cause and end of the punishment, ought undoubtedly to regulate the measure of its severity. But this cause appears to be founded, not in the guilt of the offender, but in the necessity of preventing the repetition of the offence: and from hence results the reason, that crimes are not by any government punished in proportion to their guilt, nor in all cases ought to be so, but in proportion to the difficulty and necessity of preventing them. Thus the stealing of goods privately out of a shop, may not, in its moral quality, be more criminal than the stealing of them out of a house; yet, being equally necessary, and more difficult to be prevented, the law, in certain circumstances, denounces against it a severe punishment. The crime must be

---

*From William Paley, *The Principles of Moral and Political Philosophy* (London, 1785; 7th ed., 1790), Bk. VI, Ch. 9, pp. 268–74, 297–302. Relate to selection 6.

prevented by some means or other; and consequently, whatever means appear necessary to this end, whether they be proportionable to the guilt of the criminal or not, are adopted rightly, because they are adopted upon the principle which alone justifies the infliction of punishment at all. From the same consideration it also follows, that punishment ought not to be employed, much less rendered severe, when the crime can be prevented by any other means. Punishment is an evil to which the magistrate resorts only from its being necessary to the prevention of a greater. This necessity does not exist, when the end may be attained, that is, when the public may be defended from the effects of the crime, by any other expedient. The sanguinary laws which have been made against counterfeiting or diminishing the gold coin of the kingdom might be just, until the method of detecting the fraud by weighing the money, was introduced into general usage. Since that precaution was practised, these laws have slept; and an execution under them at this day would be deemed a measure of unjustifiable severity. The same principle accounts for a circumstance, which has been often censured as an absurdity in the penal laws of this, and of most modern nations, namely, that breaches of trust are either not punished at all, or punished with less rigour than other frauds.—Wherefore is it, some have asked, that a violation of confidence, which increases the guilt, should mitigate the penalty?—This lenity, or rather forbearance of the laws, is founded in the most reasonable distinction. A due circumspection in the choice of the persons whom they trust; caution in limiting the extent of that trust; or the requiring of sufficient security for the faithful discharge of it, will commonly guard men from injuries of this description: and the law will not interpose its sanctions, to protect negligence and credulity, or to supply the place of domestic care and prudence. To be convinced that the law proceeds entirely upon this consideration, we have only to observe, that where the confidence is unavoidable, where no practicable vigilance could watch the offender, as in the case of theft committed by a servant in the shop or dwelling-house of his master, or upon property to which he must necessarily have access, the sentence of the law is not less severe, and its execution commonly more certain and rigorous, than if no trust at all had intervened.

It is in pursuance of the same principle, which pervades indeed the whole system of penal jurisprudence, that the facility with which any species of crimes is perpetrated, has been generally deemed a reason for aggravating the punishment. Thus, sheep-stealing, horse-stealing, the stealing of cloth from tenters or bleaching grounds, by our laws, subject the offenders to sentence of death: not that these crimes are in their nature more heinous than many simple felonies which are punished by imprisonment or transportation, but because the property being more exposed, requires the terror of capital punishment to protect it. This severity would be absurd and unjust, if the guilt of the offender were the immediate cause and measure of the punishment; but is a consistent and regular consequence of the supposition, that the right of punishment results from the necessity of preventing the crime: for if this be the end proposed, the severity of the punishment must be increased in proportion to the expediency and the difficulty of attaining this end; that is, in a proportion compounded of the mischief of the crime, and of the ease with which it is executed. The difficulty of discovery is a circumstance to be included in the same consideration. It constitutes indeed, with respect to the crime, the facility of which we speak. By how much therefore the detection of an offender is more rare and uncertain, by so much the more severe must be the punishment, when he is detected. Thus the writing of incendiary letters, though in itself a pernicious and alarming injury, calls for a more condign and exemplary punishment, by the very obscurity with which the crime is committed.

From the justice of God we are taught to look for a gradation of punishment, exactly proportioned to the guilt of the offender; when therefore, in assigning the degrees of human punishment, we introduce considerations distinct from that guilt, and a proportion so varied by external circumstances, that equal crimes frequently undergo unequal punishments, or the less crime the greater; it is natural to demand the reason why a different measure of punishment should be expected from God, and observed by man; why that rule, which befits the absolute and perfect justice of the Deity, should not be the rule which ought to be pursued and imitated by human laws. The solution of this difficulty must be sought for in those peculiar attributes of the divine nature, which distinguish the dispensations of supreme wisdom from the proceedings of human judicature. A being whose knowledge penetrates every concealment; from the operation of whose will no art or flight can escape; and in whose hands punishment is sure; such a Being may conduct the moral government of his creation, in the best and wisest manner, by pronouncing a law that every crime shall finally receive a punishment proportioned to the guilt which it contains, abstracted from any foreign consideration whatever; and may testify his veracity to the spectators of his judgments, by carrying this law into strict execution. But when the care of the public safety is entrusted to men, whose authority over their fellow creatures is limited by defects of power and knowledge; from whose utmost vigilance and sagacity the greatest offenders often lide hid; whose wisest precautions and speediest pursuit may be eluded by artifice or concealment; a different necessity, a new rule of proceeding, results from the very imperfection of their faculties. In their hands the uncertainty of punishment must be compensated by the severity. The ease with which crimes are committed or concealed, must be counteracted by additional penalties and increased terrors. The very end for which human government is established, requires that its regulations be adapted to the suppression of crimes. This end, whatever it may do in the plans of infinite wisdom, does not, in the designation of temporal penalties, always coincide with the proportionate punishment of guilt. . . .

The *certainty* of punishment is of more consequence than the severity. Criminals do not so much flatter themselves with the lenity of the sentence, as with the hope of escaping. They are not so apt to compare what they gain by the crime with what they may suffer from the punishment, as to encourage themselves with the chance of concealment or flight. For which reason a vigilant magistracy, an accurate police, a proper distribution of force and intelligence, together with due rewards for the discovery and apprehension of malefactors, and an undeviating impartiality in carrying the laws into execution, contribute more to the restraint and suppression of crimes, than any violent exacerbations of punishment. And for the same reason, of all contrivances directed to this end, those perhaps are most effectual which facilitate the conviction of criminals. The offense of counterfeiting the coin could not be checked by all the terrors and the utmost severity of law, whilst the act of coining was necessary to be established by specific proof. The statute which made the possession of the implements of coining capital, that is, which constituted that possession complete evidence of the offender's guilt, was the first thing that gave force and efficacy to the denunciations of law upon this subject. The statute of James the First, relative to the murder of bastard children, which ordains that the concealment of the birth should be deemed incontestable proof of the charge, though a harsh law, was, in like manner with the former, well calculated to put a stop to the crime.

It is upon the principle of this observation, that I apprehend much harm to have been done to the community, by the over-strained scrupulousness, or weak timidity of juries, which demands often such proof of a prisoner's guilt, as the nature and secrecy of his crime scarce possibly admit of; and which holds it the part of a *safe* conscience not to condemn any man, whilst there exists the minutest possibility of his innocence. Any story they may happen to have heard or read, whether real or feigned, in which courts of justice have been misled by presumptions of guilt, is enough, in their minds, to found an acquittal upon, where positive proof is wanting. I do not mean that juries should indulge conjectures, should magnify suspicions into proofs, or even that they should weigh probabilities in *gold scales;* but when the preponderance of evidence is so manifest as to persuade every private understanding of the prisoner's guilt; when it furnishes that degree of credibility, upon which men decide and act in all other doubts, and which experience hath shewn that they may decide and act upon with sufficient safety; to reject such proof, from an insinuation of uncertainty that belongs to all human affairs, and from a general dread lest the charge of innocent blood should lie at their doors, is a conduct which, however natural to a mind studious of its own quiet, is authorized by no considerations of rectitude or utility. It counteracts the care and damps the activity of government: it holds out public encouragement to villainy, by confessing the impossibility of bringing villains to justice; and that species of encouragement which, as hath been just now observed, the minds of such men are most apt to entertain and dwell upon.

There are two popular maxims, which seem to have a considerable influence in producing the injudicious acquittals of which we complain. One is—"That circumstantial evidence falls short of positive proof." This assertion, in the unqualified sense in which it is applied, is not true. A concurrence of well-authenticated circumstances composes a stronger ground of assurance than positive testimony, unconfirmed by circumstances, usually affords. Circumstances cannot lie. The conclusion also which results from them, though deduced by only probable inference, is commonly more to be relied upon than the veracity of an unsupported solitary witness. The danger of being deceived is less, the actual instances of deception are fewer, in the one case than the other. What is called positive proof in criminal matters, as where a man swears to the person of the prisoner, and that he actually saw him commit the crime with which he is charged, may be founded in the mistake or perjury of a single witness. Such mistakes, and such perjuries, are not without many examples. Whereas to impose upon a court of justice a chain of *circumstantial* evidence in support of a fabricated accusation, requires such a number of false witnesses as seldom meet together; an union also of skill and wickedness which is still more rare; and, after all, this species of proof lies much more open to discussion, and is more likely, if false, to be contradicted, or to betray itself by some unforeseen inconsistency, than that direct proof, which being confined within the knowledge of a single person, which appealing to, or standing connected with, no external or collateral circumstances, is incapable, by its very simplicity, of being confronted with opposite probabilities.

The other maxim which deserves a similar examination is this—"That it is better that ten guilty persons escape, than that one innocent man should suffer." If by saying it is *better,* be meant that it is more for the public advantage, the proposition, I think, cannot be maintained. The security of civil life, which is essential to the value and the enjoyment of every blessing it contains, and the interruption of which is followed by universal misery and confusion, is protected chiefly by the dread of punishment. The misfortune of an individual (for such may the sufferings, or even the death of an innocent person be called, when they are occasioned by no evil intention) cannot be placed in competition with this object. I do not contend that the life or safety of the meanest subject ought, in any case, to be knowingly sacrificed: no principle of judicature, no end of punishment can ever require *that.* But when certain rules of adjudication must be pursued, when certain degrees of credibility must be accepted, in order to reach the crimes with which the public are infested; courts of justice should not be deterred from the application of these rules by *every* suspicion of danger, or by the mere possibility of confounding the innocent with the guilty. They ought rather to reflect, that he who falls by a mistaken sentence, may be considered as falling for his country; whilst he suffers under the operation of these rules, by the general effect and tendency of which the welfare of the community is maintained and upheld.

# 47

## Theories of Punitive Justice*
### WESTEL W. WILLOUGHBY
(1867–1945)

Examining the theories which have been brought forward by ethicists in justification of punishment, we find that they may be described as: (1) Retributive, (2) Deterrent, (3) Preventive, and (4) Reformatory, respectively. In determining the value of these theories it will be necessary, as was the case in reference to the theories of justice as applied to the distribution of rewards, to consider them not only from the standpoint of abstract justice, but as to the possibility of realizing them in practice.

*The Retributive Theory.* Beginning with the retributive, or as it may also be called, the vindictive, or expiative, theory, it is to be observed first of all that, in the strict sense of the word, only that pain may be spoken of as punishment which is imposed simply and solely for the sake of the pain to be felt by the one punished. According to the retributive theory, through punishment the offender expiates his offence, suffers retribution for the evil which has been done, and thus is vindicated the principle of justice which has been violated. Thus says Godwin, in his *Political Justice,* "Punishment is generally used to signify the voluntary infliction of evil upon a vicious being, not merely because the public good demands it, but because there is apprehended to be a certain fitness and propriety in the nature of things that render suffering abstractly, from the benefit to result, the suitable concomitant of vice."[1]

Accepting this definition which Godwin gives us as the true meaning

---

*From Westel W. Willoughby, *Social Justice* (New York: Macmillan, 1900), Ch. 10, pp. 322–24, 326–35, 358–61, 378–80. The title of this selection has been supplied by the editor. Compare with selections 9 and 12.

[1] *Op. cit.,* p. 230.

of punishment, it is necessary to hold that, in so far as a penalty is imposed for any other than a vindictive object, as, for example, for the sake of deterrence, prevention, reformation, or social protection, it ceases to be punishment at all. For all of these other objects have a reference to some good that is to be secured in the future; whereas the retributive theory, by its very nature, looks wholly to the past. According to it, pain is inflicted, not in order that some advantage may accrue in the future, but because some wrong has been done in the past.

We have, then, to ascertain the circumstances, if any there be, under which it is ethically allowable for one not only to determine for another the propriety of his acts, but to visit upon such a one punishment in case he commits acts that have been declared *mala prohibita.* *

The idea of retribution or expiation can apply only as between rational beings. It is true that Great Nature (*Natura Naturans*) is often spoken of as inflicting punishment and even as destroying those who violate her laws. But such language cannot be considered strictly correct. Indeed, the very idea of violating a law of nature is an improper one. The so-called laws of nature are but statements of uniformities of experience in the phenomenal world. As such they are not in any true sense commands, and are not possible of violation by men. Certain results, so far as our experience goes, are known to follow from certain causes. That is all. There is no law-giver to be offended. There is not necessarily present any idea of wickedness, nor do the elements of intention and moral responsibility necessarily play a part when, as a consequence of a certain state of facts, certain results, disagreeable or otherwise, are experienced by particular individuals or communities. But in order that the retributive theory may have standing at all, these elements must appear. According to the theory, one is punished because he is supposed to have done a moral wrong, that is, to have committed not simply a formal or legal wrong, but to have sinned in the sight of the power that punishes him. But only that one can be said to have sinned who has freely committed the reprobated act, and who, furthermore, at the time of its commission has been mentally qualified to judge regarding the character of the act committed and, being so qualified, actually intended to commit it.

Having defined now what is meant by punishment in its proper retributive or expiative sense, we come to the vital question whether a true system of ethics requires, or even permits, the existence of a right to inflict pain for this purpose. In short, can there be stated any rational ground for declaring that justice demands, under any conceivable conditions, that

---

*[Acts that are offenses simply in virtue of having been prohibited.]

pain should be inflicted when no possible future good can result? If we answer "No," we of course deny that the idea of punishment, in its proper sense, should play any part whatsoever in our systems of ethics. . . .

That philosopher who, among modern writers, has defended most absolutely the retributive theory of punishment, is Kant. His views upon this point are to be found in his *Rechtslehre*.[2]

"Judicial punishment," says Kant, "can never be administered merely as a means for promoting another good, either with regard to the criminal himself or to civil society, but must in all cases be imposed only because the individual on whom it is inflicted has committed some crime. For one man ought never to be dealt with merely as a means subservient to the purpose of another, nor be mixed up with the subjects of real right. Against such treatment his inborn personality has a right to protect him, even although he may be condemned to lose his civil personality. He must first be found guilty and punishable, before there can be any thought of drawing from his personality any benefit for himself or his fellow-citizens. The penal law is a categorical imperative; and woe to him who creeps through the serpent-windings of utilitarians to discover some advantage that may discharge him from the justice of punishment or even from the due measure of it according to the Pharisaic maxim: 'It is better that one man should die than that the whole people should perish.' For if Justice and Righteousness perish, human life would no longer have any value in the world. What, then, is to be said of such a proposal as to keep a criminal alive who has been condemned to death, on his being given to understand that if he agreed to certain dangerous experiments being performed upon him, he would be allowed to survive—if he come happily through them? It is argued that physicians might thus obtain new information that would be of value to the commonweal. But a court of justice would repudiate with scorn any proposal of this kind if made to it by the medical faculty; for justice would cease to be justice, if it were bartered away for any consideration whatever."[3]

Kant makes this repudiation of the utilitarian element still more emphatic, when he declares: "Even if a civil society resolved to dissolve itself with the consent of all its members,—as might be supposed in the case of a people inhabiting an island resolving to separate and scatter themselves throughout the whole world,—the last murderer living in prison ought to be executed before the resolution was carried out. This ought to be done in order that every one may realize the desert of his deeds, and that blood-guiltiness may not remain upon the people; for otherwise they might

[2] Translated by Hastie under the title *Philosophy of Law.*
[3] *Op. cit.,* p. 195.

all be regarded as participators in the murder as a public violation of Justice."[4]

The vindictive theory is accepted by Kant not only as furnishing the motive for punishment, but as dictating the character of the penalty to be imposed in each case. The doctrine of *lex talionis* is to be applied without reservation. "This right," he says, "is the only principle which in regulating a public court, as distinguished from mere private judgment, can definitely assign both the quality and the quantity of a first penalty. All other standards are wavering and uncertain; and on account of other considerations involved in them, they contain no principle conformable to the sentence of pure and strict justice."[5]

Let us see now what theoretical justification Kant offers for his theory. It is, in short, that the criminal by the deliberate commission of his deed has, in effect, accepted as valid the principle involved in the deed. Therefore, says Kant, if that same principle be applied by society to him, he is in reality but subjected to a rule of conduct which, by his own conduct, he has declared to be a valid one. Thus, in answer to the argument made by Beccaria against the rightfulness of capital punishment, that it cannot be conceived that in the original civil compact the individual could or would have consented thus to dispose of his own life, Kant replies: "No one undergoes punishment because he has willed to be punished, but because he has willed a punishable action; for it is, in fact, no punishment when one experiences what he wills; and it is impossible for any one to will to be punished. To say, 'I will to be punished, if I murder any one,' can mean nothing more than, 'I submit myself along with all the other citizens to the laws': and if there are any criminals among the people, these laws will include criminal laws. The individual who, as a co-legislator, enacts penal law, cannot possibly be the same person who, as a subject, is punished according to the law; for, *quâ* criminal, he cannot possibly be regarded as having a voice in the legislation, the legislator being rationally viewed as just and holy. If any one, then, enact a penal law against himself as a criminal, it must be the pure juridically law-giving reason which subjects him as one capable of crime, and consequently as another person, along with all the others in the civil union, to this penal law. In other words, it is not the people taken distributively, but the tribunal of public justice as distinct from the criminal, that prescribes capital punishment; and it is not to be viewed as if the social compact contained the promise of all the individuals to allow themselves to be punished, thus disposing of themselves and their lives. For if the right to punish must be founded upon a promise

[4] *Idem*, p. 198.
[5] *Op. cit.*, p. 196.

to the wrong-doer, whereby he is to be regarded as being willing to be punished, it ought also to be left to him to find himself deserving of the punishment; and the criminal would thus be his own judge. The chief error of this sophistry consists in regarding the judgment of the criminal himself, necessarily determined by his reason, that he is under obligation to undergo the loss of his life, as a judgment that must be founded on a resolution of his will to take it away himself; and thus the execution of the right in question is represented as united in one and the same person with the adjudication of the right."[6]

What validity is there in this reasoning of Kant? Only this much, we think. It furnishes a satisfactory answer to that school of thinkers who, having not yet thoroughly rid themselves of the social-compact and natural-right theories, declare that all social or political control over the individual, needs, for its justification, the consent of the individual. It is correct to say that in the commission of any given deed, the criminal logically accepts as a valid rule of conduct the principle involved in his act, and therefore that he cannot justly complain if society see fit to subject him to the operation of the same rule that he has already applied in his conduct toward others. But this is all. Kant's reasoning does not have any bearing upon the arguments of those who hold the views which we have accepted in this work. Kant says: "Man ought never to be dealt with merely as a means subservient to the purpose of another. . . . Against such treatment his inborn personality has a right to protect him." This principle is a very true one, and in fact constitutes, as we know, the fundamental fact of social justice, but it does not mean that the infliction of an evil upon a person, in order that some future social good may be achieved, is necessarily a contravention of it.

Kant says that a person should never be treated merely as a means. But a person is treated merely as a means only when his right to be considered as an end is wholly ignored. Now, when it becomes necessary in the interest of society to inflict an evil upon an individual, that individual is *quâ hoc* treated as a means; but he is also treated as an end, if in estimating the social good his individual good is considered, and in the selection of him for punishment the choice has been controlled by empiric facts which make it productive of more good that he, rather than any one or no one else, should be punished. Thus, just as, according to this interpretation of the sanctity of human personality, guiltiness of crime cannot of itself justify the infliction of pain; so, conversely, when the social good demands, innocence from wrong-doing cannot always relieve one from the

[6] *Op. cit.,* pp. 201–202.

duty of subjecting himself to, or release society from the obligation of imposing, an evil which in extreme cases may amount even to death. As Rashdall has well put it: "When a man is punished in the interest of society, he is indeed treated as a means, but his right to be treated as an end is not thereby violated, if his good is treated as of equal importance with the end of other human beings. Social life would not be possible without the constant subordination of the claims of individuals to the like claims of a greater number of individuals; and there may be occasions when in punishing a criminal we have to think more of the good of society generally than of the individual who is punished. . . . The retributive view of punishment, however, justifies the infliction of evil upon a living soul, even though it will do neither him nor any one else any good whatever. If it is to do anybody any good, punishment is not inflicted for the sake of retribution. It is the retributive theory, to my mind, which shows a disrespect for human personality by proposing to sacrifice human life and human well-being to a lifeless fetich styled the Moral Law, which apparently, though unconscious, has a sense of dignity, and demands the immolation of victims to avenge its injured *amour propre.*"[7]

The incorrectness of the retributive theory of punishment becomes manifest when we consider the results to which an attempt to apply it in practice would necessarily lead. In the first place, it would render impossible any penal law whatever, for it would never be possible for courts to gain that knowledge which the theory demands for the just apportioning of penalties. When reduced to their proper meaning, the words retribution, expiation, or vindication, mean the bringing home to the criminal the legitimate consequences of his conduct, that is, legitimate from the ethical standpoint. But this, of course, involves the determination of the degree of his moral responsibility, a task that is an impossibility for any legal tribunal. Conditions of knowledge, of heredity, of training, of opportunities for moral development, of social environment generally, and of motive have to be searched out, which are beyond even the ability of the criminal himself to determine,—far less of others,—before even an approximate estimate can be made of the simplest act. But even could this be done, there would be no possible standard by which to estimate the amount of physical pain to be imposed as a punishment for a given degree of moral guilt. For how measure a moral wrong by a physical suffering? Or, granting what is inconceivable, that such an equivalence could be fixed upon, how would it be possible to inflict upon the culprit just that amount of pain which he might deserve? Individuals differ physically and mentally, and these

[7] *International Journal of Ethics,* January, 1900, article, "The Ethics of Forgiveness."

differences are widened by training and methods of life until it is impossible to determine the degree of discomfort or pain that a given penalty will cause a given individual. The fear of death itself varies widely with different individuals, and the same is true as to the estimation in which all other forms of evil are held. So far, therefore, from there being any certainty that two individuals will be equally punished who are subjected to the same penitential treatment, there is, in fact, almost a certainty that they will not be. . . .

*Utilitarian Theories of Punishment.* To a very considerable extent we have already presented the grounds upon which the other than retributive theories of punishment are based. The retributive theory stands *sui generis* in that it alone looks wholly to the past and rejects as unessential to, if not inconsistent with, itself all utilitarian considerations. In rejecting the retributive theory, therefore, we necessarily accept the utilitarian theory that punishment, to be justly imposed, must have for its aim the realization of some future good. These utilitarian theories differ from each other according to the nature of the good sought. Thus we have: (1) The Deterrent Theory, according to which punishments are inflicted in order that other would-be law-breakers may be dissuaded from crime; (2) The Preventive Theory, the aim of which, as its name implies, is to prevent the repetition of the offence by the surveillance, imprisonment, or execution of the criminal; (3) The Reformatory Theory, the object of which is the moral reformation of the delinquent; and (4) The Educative Theory, of which we have already spoken.

A point to be noticed about these theories is that they are not mutually exclusive. There is no reason why, the utilitarian idea being once accepted, we should not strive to reach in our penitential systems beneficial results in all four of the directions mentioned. It is therefore possible to speak of a given law being founded on one or the other of these ideas only in so far as deterrence, prevention, education, or reformation, as the case may be, is placed in the foreground as the chief end to be realized.

But we may go further than simply to declare that these theories are not mutually exclusive. We may assert that it is rationally impossible to select any one aim and to declare that in any system of penal justice that one should furnish the sole motive for its enactment and enforcement. It may be possible to pass particular laws the aim of which is solely in one or the other of these directions; but to attempt the establishment of an entire criminal code with but a single aim would inevitably lead to absurdities and injustices. If absolute prevention were the sole aim, capital punishment or lifelong imprisonment would be the normal punishment called for; for in no other way could there be furnished a guarantee against a repetition of the offence by the convicted one. If reformation were the sole aim sought, then, not to mention other absurdities, it would be necessary for a court to release from all punishment those hardened and habitual criminals regarding whom experience had demonstrated penal law to be without a reformatory influence. If deterrence were accepted as the absolute canon, we would be obliged to abandon all attempts at reformation, and by the strictness and severity of our punishments give ourselves up to an appeal simply to the fears of mankind. Finally, if the educative theory were to be solely relied upon, we would not be able to modify the character and severity of our punishments so as best to meet threatened invasions of social or political order. This would mean that in times of greatest need the State would find itself powerless. Thus, for example, should a grievous pestilence be threatened, necessity would demand that violations of quarantine and other health ordinances should be prevented at all hazards, and hence that extraordinarily severe penalties should be attached to their violation. Or, again, in a time of great political unrest and disorder, when the very life of the State is threatened, martial law would be demanded. But if we accept any but the deterrent theory as absolutely sufficient in itself, such measures would be unjustifiable.

As we have seen, the retributive theory rests under the embarrassment of predicating as a ground for the right to punish a motive which logically necessitates that the character and degree of the punishments which are inflicted should correspond with the degree of moral guilt of the offenders, whereas the determination of this degree of guilt is inherently beyond the power of any criminal court. From this difficulty the utilitarian theory is free. We have spoken of the ideas of deterrence, reformation, education, and prevention as distinct from one another, and so they are. Yet when viewed in their proper light, they are all but different phases of one supreme idea, the social welfare. The aim of the criminal law, like that of the civil law, and indeed of all laws and principles of conduct, is the general weal. Therefore, in passing upon the propriety of emphasizing in a given piece of legislation any one of these ideas, whether of reformation, education, prevention, or deterrence, it is ever necessary to consider the matter in its social and not in its individual light. There may thus be cases in which, as to the particular criminal or criminals concerned, a remission of punishment would exercise a more beneficial influence than its imposition, but in which social considerations demand a satisfaction of the law's full severity.

The bearing of this upon the question of justly apportioning penalties is that it makes it no longer necessary to attempt the impossible task of making the punishment correspond to the degree of the criminal's guilt, but

leaves it open to the laws and to the courts to arrange their judgments
according to the practical exigencies of each case as determined by the
social need. . . .

. . . However looked at, the strenuous efforts which societies have
made to check crime have at the most done little more than prevent its
increase. This means, then, that little success has been reached either in the
reformatory, educative, or deterrent directions. As a matter of fact, so far as
regards the reformatory idea, there would probably be a consensus of
opinion that, upon the whole, criminal law, as it has actually been administered in the past, has been far more corrupting than elevating to the
individuals punished. And for the future the most sanguine are not inclined
to believe that it will be possible, even with the most approved methods, to
make the reformation obtained more than balance the inevitable corruption that punishment brings by the evil associations it necessitates, and the
blow to pride and self-respect it gives. As for the educative value of
punishment, this is in the highest degree problematical, and many there are
who would reduce its possible influence to a very small maximum. How far
penal laws have been deterrent it is impossible to say; but at the most, as
we have seen, they have been efficient only to the extent of preventing an
increase of crime. As regards, finally, the preventive idea, except where the
punishment of death or imprisonment for life is imposed, little is accomplished.

The one lesson, then, which all these facts teach us is that, for a
solution of the problem of crime, the real effort must be to abolish the
causes of crime, in so far as they are dependent upon conditions within our
control. This means, in truth, entire social regeneration; for wherever there
is injustice, there will be crime. Not all crime, it is true, may be ascribed to
social causes. Some of it is undoubtedly due to the deliberate choice of evil
minds or to the promptings of the passions. But with social justice everywhere realized, with economic and social relations properly regulated, and
with true education, mental and moral, technical and academic, adequately applied, a long step will have been taken towards the solution of
the grave evil we have been discussing. Though possibly exaggerated, there
is yet substantial truth in the declaration of Ferri that "the least measure of
progress with reforms which prevent crime, is a hundred times more useful
and profitable than the publication of an entire penal code."[8]

A deterrent penalty only becomes operative in those cases where it has
failed of effect. A reformatory discipline is only applicable where the
subject of it has already been corrupted. An educative law presupposes an

[8] *Criminal Sociology,* p. 135.

ignorant or biassed mind. In very large measure the necessity for the enforcement of penal laws is a demonstration that proper preventive measures have not been taken. Fundamentally, then, any penal system is unjust in so far as the necessity for it might have been avoided by proper social conduct. Thus, as Green has said, "The justice of the punishment depends on the justice of the general system of rights; not merely on the propriety with reference to social well-being of maintaining this or that particular right which the crime punished violates, but on the question whether the social organism in which a criminal has lived and acted is one that has given him a fair chance of not being a criminal."[9]

[9]*Principles of Political Obligation,* §189.

# 48

## The Institution of Property*

### WILLIAM PALEY
#### (1743–1805)

### Of Property

If you should see a flock of pigeons in a field of corn; and if (instead of each picking where and what it liked, taking just as much as it wanted, and no more) you should see ninety-nine of them gathering all they got, into a heap; reserving nothing for themselves, but the chaff and the refuse; keeping this heap for one, and that the weakest, perhaps worst, pigeon of the flock; sitting round, and looking on, all the winter, whilst this one was devouring, throwing about, and wasting it; and if a pigeon more hardy or hungry than the rest touched a grain of the hoard, all the others instantly flying upon it, and tearing it to pieces; if you should see this, you would see nothing more than what is every day practised and established among men. Among men, you see the ninety-and-nine toiling and scraping together a heap of superfluities for one (and this one too, oftentimes the feeblest and worst of the whole set, a child, a woman, a madman, or a fool); getting nothing for themselves all the while, but a little of the coarsest of the provision, which their own industry produces; looking quietly on, while they see the fruits of all their labour spent or spoiled; and if one of the number take or touch a particle of the hoard, the others joining against him, and hanging him for the theft.

### The Use of the Institution of Property

There must be some very important advantages to account for an institution, which, in the view of it above given, is so paradoxical and unnatural.

*From William Paley, *The Principles of Moral and Political Philosophy* (1785), Bk. III, Pt. I, chs. 1, 2, and 4. The title of this selection has been supplied by the editor. Compare with selections 6 and 46.

The principal of these advantages are the following:

I. It increases the produce of the earth.

The earth, in climates like ours, produces little without cultivation: and none would be found willing to cultivate the ground, if others were to be admitted to an equal share of the produce. The same is true of the care of flocks and herds of tame animals.

Crabs and acorns, red deer, rabbits, game and fish, are all which we should have to subsist upon in this country, if we trusted to the spontaneous productions of the soil; and it fares not much better with other countries. A nation of North-American savages, consisting of two or three hundred, will take up, and be half-starved upon, a tract of land, which in Europe, and with European management, would be sufficient for the maintenance of as many thousands.

In some fertile soils, together with great abundance of fish upon their coasts, and in regions where clothes are unnecessary, a considerable degree of population may subsist without property in land; which is the case in the Islands of Otaheite: but in less favoured situations, as in the country of New Zealand, though this sort of property obtain in a small degree, the inhabitants, for want of a more secure and regular establishment of it, are driven oftentimes by the scarcity of provision to devour one another.

II. It preserves the produce of the earth to maturity.

We may judge what would be the effects of a community of right to the production of the earth, from the trifling specimens which we see of it at present. A cherry-tree in a hedge-row, nuts in a wood, the grass of an unstinted pasture, are seldom of much advantage to anybody, because people do not wait for the proper season of reaping them. Corn, if any were sown, would never ripen; lambs and calves would never grow up to sheep and cows, because the first person that met them would reflect, that he had better take them as they are, than leave them for another.

III. It prevents contests.

War and waste, tumult and confusion, must be unavoidable and eternal, where there is not enough for all, and where there are no rules to adjust the division.

IV. It improves the conveniency of living.

This it does two ways. It enables mankind to divide themselves into distinct professions; which is impossible, unless a man can exchange the productions of his own art for what he wants from others; and exchange implies property. Much of the advantage of civilized over savage life depends upon this. When a man is from necessity his own tailor, tent-maker, carpenter, cook, huntsman, and fisherman, it is not probable that he will be expert at any of his callings. Hence the rude habitations, furniture, clothing, and implements, of savages; and the tedious length of time which all their operations require.

It likewise encourages those arts, by which the accommodations of human life are supplied, by appropriating to the artist the benefit of his discoveries and improvements; without which appropriation, ingenuity will never be exerted with effect.

Upon these several accounts, we may venture, with a few exceptions, to pronounce, that even the poorest and the worst provided, in countries where property and the consequences of property prevail, are in a better situation, with respect to food, raiment, houses, and what are called the necessaries of life, than *any* are in places where most things remain in common.

The balance, therefore, upon the whole, must preponderate in favour of property with a manifest and great excess.

Inequality of property, in the degree in which it exists in most countries of Europe, abstractedly considered, is an evil: but it is an evil which flows from those rules concerning the acquisition and disposal of property, by which men are incited to industry, and by which the object of their industry is rendered secure and valuable. If there be any great inequality unconnected with this origin, it ought to be corrected. . . .

## In What the Right of Property Is Founded

We now speak of Property in Land: and there is a difficulty in explaining the origin of this property, consistently with the law of nature; for the land was once, no doubt, common; and the question is, how any particular part of it could justly be taken out of the common, and so appropriated to the first owner, as to give him a better right to it than others; and, what is more, a right to exclude all others from it.

Moralists have given many different accounts of this matter; which diversity alone, perhaps, is a proof that none of them are satisfactory.

One tells us that mankind, when they suffered a particular person to occupy a piece of ground, by tacit consent relinquished their right to it; and as the piece of ground, they say, belonged to mankind collectively, and mankind thus gave up their right to the first peaceable occupier, it thencefoward became his property, and no one afterwards had a right to molest him in it.

The objection to this account is, that consent can never be presumed from silence, where the person whose consent is required knows nothing about the matter; which must have been the case with all mankind, except the neighbourhood of the place where the appropriation was made. And to suppose that the piece of ground previously belonged to the neighbour-hood, and that they had a just power of conferring a right to it upon whom they pleased is to suppose the question resolved, and a partition of land to have already taken place.

Another says, that each man's limbs and labour are his own exclusively; that, by occupying a piece of ground, a man inseparably mixes his labour with it; by which means the piece of ground becomes thenceforward his own, as you cannot take it from him without depriving him at the same time of something which is indisputably *his.*

This is Mr. Locke's solution; and seems indeed a fair reason, where the value of the labour bears a considerable proportion to the value of the thing; or where the thing derives its chief use and value from the labour. Thus game and fish, though they be common whilst at large in the woods or water, instantly become the property of the person that catches them; because an animal, when caught, is much more valuable than when at liberty; and this increase of value, which is inseparable from, and makes a great part of, the whole value, is strictly the property of the fowler or fisherman, being the produce of his personal labour. For the same reason, wood or iron, manufactured into utensils, becomes the property of the manufacturer; because the value of the workmanship far exceeds that of the materials. And upon a similar principle, a parcel of unappropriated ground, which a man should pare, burn, plough, harrow, and sow, for the production of corn, would justly enough be thereby made his own. But this will hardly hold, in the manner it has been applied, of taking a ceremoni-ous possession of a tract of land, as navigators do of new-discovered islands, by erecting a standard, engraving an inscription, or publishing a procla-mation to the birds and beasts; or of turning your cattle into a piece of ground, setting up a landmark, digging a ditch, or planting a hedge round it. Nor will even the clearing, manuring, and ploughing of a field, give the first occupier a right to it in perpetuity, and after this cultivation and all effects of it are ceased.

Another, and in my opinion a better, account of the first right of ownership, is the following; that, as God has provided these things for the use of all, he has of consequence given each leave to take of them what he wants: by virtue, therefore, of this leave, a man may appropriate what he stands in need of to his own use, without asking, or waiting for, the consent of others; in like manner as, when an entertainment is provided for the freeholders of a county, each freeholder goes, and eats and drinks what he wants or chuses, without having or waiting for the consent of the other guests.

But then this reason justifies property, as far as necessaries alone, or, at the most, as far as a competent provision for our natural exigencies. For, in the entertainment we speak of (allowing the comparison to hold in all points), although every particular freeholder may sit down and eat till he be satisfied, without any other leave than that of the master of the feast, or any other proof of that leave than the general invitation, or the manifest design with which the entertainment is provided; yet, you would hardly permit any one to fill his pockets or his wallet, or to carry away with him a quantity of provision to be hoarded up, or wasted, or given to his dogs, or stewed down into sauces, or converted into articles of superfluous luxury; especially if, by so doing, he pinched the guests at the lower end of the table.

These are the accounts that have been given of the matter by the best writers upon the subject, but, were these accounts perfectly unexceptionable, they would none of them, I fear, avail us in vindicating our present claims of property in land, unless it were more probable than it is, that our estates were actually acquired at first, in some of the ways which these accounts suppose; and that a regular regard had been paid to justice, in every successive transmission of them since; for, if one link in the chain fail, every title posterior to it falls to the ground.

The real foundation of our right is, THE LAW OF THE LAND.

It is the intention of God, that the produce of the earth be applied to the use of Man: this intention cannot be fulfilled without establishing property; it is consistent, therefore, with his will, that property be established. The land cannot be divided into separate property, without leaving it to the law of the country to regulate that division: it is consistent, therefore, with the same will, that the law should regulate the division; and, consequently, "consistent with the will of God," or "right," that I should possess that share which these regulations assign me.

By whatever circuitous train of reasoning you attempt to derive this right, it must terminate at last in the will of God; the straightest, therefore, and shortest way of arriving at this will, is the best.

Hence it appears, that my right to an estate does not at all depend upon the manner or justice of the original acquisition; nor upon the justice of each subsequent change of possession. It is not, for instance, the less, nor ought it to be impeached, because the estate was taken possession of at first by a family of aboriginal Britons, who happened to be stronger than their neighbours; nor because the British possessor was turned out by a Roman, or the Roman by a Saxon invader; nor because it was seized, without colour of right or reason, by a follower of the Norman adventurer; from whom, after many interruptions of fraud and violence, it has at length devolved to me.

Nor does the owner's right depend upon the *expediency* of the law which gives it to him. On one side of a brook, an estate descends to the eldest son; on the other side, to all the children alike. The right of the claimants under both laws of inheritance is equal; though the expediency of such opposite rules must necessarily be different.

The principles we have laid down upon this subject apparently tend to a conclusion of which a bad use is apt to be made. As the right of property depends upon the law of the land, it seems to follow, that a man has a right to keep and take everything which the law will allow him to keep and take; which, in many cases, will authorize the most flagitious chicanery. If a creditor upon a simple contract neglect to demand his debt for six years, the debtor may refuse to pay it: would it be *right* therefore to do so, where he is conscious of the justice of the debt? If a person, who is under twenty-one years of age, contract a bargain (other than for necessaries), he may avoid it by pleading his minority: but would this be a fair plea, where the bargain was originally just?

The distinction to be taken in such cases is this: With the law, we acknowledge, resides the disposal of property: so long, therefore, as we keep within the design and intention of a law, that law will justify us, as well *in foro conscientiæ,* * as *in foro humano,*† whatever be the equity or expediency of the law itself. But when we convert to one purpose, a rule or expression of law, which is intended for another purpose, then we plead, in our justification, not the intention of the law, but the words: that is, we plead a dead letter, which can signify nothing: for words *without* meaning or intention have no force or effect in justice; much less, words taken *contrary* to the meaning and intention of the speaker or writer. To apply this distinction to the examples just now proposed:—in order to protect men against antiquated demands, from which it is not probable they should have preserved the evidence of their discharge, the law prescribes a limited time to certain species of private securities, beyond which it will not enforce them, or lend its assistance to the recovery of the debt. If a man be ignorant or dubious of the justice of the demand made upon him, he may conscientiously plead this limitation: because *he applies the rule of law to the purpose for which it was intended.* But when he refuses to pay a debt, of the reality of which he is conscious, he cannot, as before, plead the intention of the statute, and the supreme authority of law, unless he could show, that the law *intended* to

*[In the forum of conscience.]
†[In the human forum.]

interpose its supreme authority, to acquit men of debts, of the existence and justice of which they were themselves sensible. Again, to preserve youth from the practices and impositions to which their inexperience exposes them, the law compels the payment of no debts incurred within a certain age, nor the performance of any engagements, except for such necessaries as are suited to their condition and fortunes. If a young person, therefore, perceive that he has been practised or imposed upon, he may honestly avail himself of the privilege of his nonage, to defeat the circumvention. But, if he shelter himself under this privilege, to avoid a fair obligation, or an equitable contract, he extends the privilege to a case, in which it is not allowed by intention of law, and in which consequently it does not, in natural justice, exist.

# 49

# Of Property*

## JEREMY BENTHAM
### (1748–1832)

## Of Property

The better to understand the advantages of law, let us endeavour to form a clear idea of *property*. We shall see that there is no such thing as natural property, and that it is entirely the work of law.

Property is nothing but a basis of expectation; the expectation of deriving certain advantages from a thing which we are said to possess, in consequence of the relation in which we stand towards it.

There is no image, no painting, no visible trait, which can express the relation that constitutes property. It is not material, it is metaphysical; it is a mere conception of the mind.

To have a thing in our hands, to keep it, to make it, to sell it, to work it up into something else; to use it—none of these physical circumstances, nor all united, convey the idea of property. A piece of stuff which is actually in the Indies may belong to me, while the dress I wear may not. The aliment which is incorporated into my very body may belong to another, to whom I am bound to account for it.

The idea of property consists in an established expectation; in the persuasion of being able to draw such or such an advantage from the thing possessed, according to the nature of the case. Now this expectation, this persuasion, can only be the work of law. I cannot count upon the enjoyment of that which I regard as mine, except through the promise of the law which guarantees it to me. It is law alone which permits me to forget my

*From Jeremy Bentham, *Principles of the Civil Code,* of the *Theory of Legislation,* chs. 8 and 9 of Pt. I, written approximately 1792; translated from the French of Etienne Dumont (1802) by Robert Hildreth (1864). (Thus this work has never appeared in Bentham's original English.) Compare with selections 9 and 10.

natural weakness. It is only through the protection of law that I am able to inclose a field; and to give myself up to its cultivation with the sure though distant hope of harvest.

But it may be asked, What is it that serves as a basis to law, upon which to begin operation, when it adopts objects which, under the name of property, it promises to protect? Have not men, in the primitive state, a *natural* expectation of enjoying certain things,—an expectation drawn from sources anterior to law?

Yes. There have been from the beginning, and there always will be, circumstances in which a man may secure himself, by his own means, in the enjoyment of certain things. But the catalogue of these cases is very limited. The savage who has killed a deer may hope to keep it for himself, so long as his cave is undiscovered; so long as he watches to defend it, and is stronger than his rivals; but that is all. How miserable and precarious is such a possession! If we suppose the least agreement among savages to respect the acquisitions of each other, we see the introduction of a principle to which no name can be given but that of law. A feeble and momentary expectation may result from time to time from circumstances purely physical; but a strong and permanent expectation can result only from law. That which, in the natural state, was an almost invisible thread, in the social state becomes a cable.

Property and law were born together, and die together. Before laws were made there was no property; take away laws, and property ceases.

As regards property, security consists in receiving no check, no shock, no derangement to the expectation founded on the laws, of enjoying such and such a portion of good. The legislator owes the greatest respect to this expectation which he has himself produced. When he does not contradict it, he does what is essential to the happiness of society; when he disturbs it, he always produces a proportionate sum of evil.

## Answer to an Objection

But perhaps the laws of property are good for those who have property, and oppressive to those who have none. The poor man, perhaps, is more miserable than he would be without laws.

The laws, in creating property, have created riches only in relation to poverty. Poverty is not the work of the laws; it is the primitive condition of the human race. The man who subsists only from day to day is precisely the man of nature—the savage. The poor man, in civilized society, obtains nothing, I admit, except by painful labour; but, in the natural state, can he obtain anything except by the sweat of his brow? Has not the chase its fatigues, fishing its dangers, and war its uncertainties? And if man seems to love this adventurous life; if he has an instinct warm for this kind of perils; if the savage enjoys with delight an idleness so dearly bought;—must we thence conclude that he is happier than our cultivators? No. Their labour is more uniform, but their reward is more sure; the woman's lot is far more agreeable; childhood and old age have more resources; the species multiplies in a proportion a thousand times greater,—and that alone suffices to show on which side is the superiority of happiness. Thus the laws, in creating riches, are the benefactors of those who remain in the poverty of nature. All participate more or less in the pleasures, the advantages, and the resources of civilized society. The industry and the labour of the poor place them among the candidates of fortune. And have they not the pleasures of acquisition? Does not hope mix with their labours? Is the security which the law gives of no importance to them? Those who look down from above upon the inferior ranks see all objects smaller; but towards the base of the pyramid it is the summit which in turn is lost. Comparisons are never dreamed of; the wish of what seems impossible does not torment. So that, in fact, all things considered, the protection of the laws may contribute as much to the happiness of the cottage as to the security of the palace.

It is astonishing that a writer so judicious as Beccaria has interposed, in a work dictated by the soundest philosophy, a doubt subversive of social order. *The right of property,* he says, *is a terrible right, which perhaps is not necessary.* Tyrannical and sanguinary laws have been founded upon that right; it has been frightfully abused; but the right itself presents only ideas of pleasure, abundance, and security. It is that right which has vanquished the natural aversion to labour; which has given to man the empire of the earth; which has brought to an end the migratory life of nations; which has produced the love of country and a regard for posterity. Men universally desire to enjoy speedily—to enjoy without labour. It is that desire which is terrible; since it arms all who have not against all who have. The law which restrains that desire is the noblest triumph of humanity over itself.

## 50

---

# The Right of Property*

## HERBERT SPENCER

(1820–1903)

### I

The moral law, being the law of the social state, is obliged wholly to ignore the ante-social state. Constituting, as the principles of pure morality do, a code of conduct for the perfect man, they cannot be made to adapt themselves to the actions of the uncivilized man, even under the most ingenious hypothetical conditions—cannot be made even to recognise those actions so as to pass any definite sentence upon them. Overlooking this fact, thinkers, in their attempts to prove some of the first theorems of ethics, have commonly fallen into the error of referring back to an imaginary state of savage wildness, instead of referring forward to an ideal civilization, as they should have done; and have, in consequence, entangled themselves in difficulties arising out of the discordance between ethical principles and the assumed premises. To this circumstance is attributable that vagueness by which the arguments used to establish the right of property in a logical manner, are characterized. Whilst possessed of a certain plausibility, they yet cannot be considered conclusive; inasmuch as they suggest questions and objections that admit of no satisfactory answers. Let us take a sample of these arguments, and examine its defects.

"Though the earth and all inferior creatures," says Locke, "be common to all men, yet every man has a property in his own person: this nobody has a right to but himself. The labour of his body, and the work of his hands, we may say are properly his. Whatever then he removes out of the state that nature hath provided and left it in, he hath mixed his labour with, and joined to it something that is his own, and thereby makes it his property. It being by him removed from the common state nature hath

---

*From Herbert Spencer, *Social Statics* (London, 1851), ch. 10, pp. 126–35.

placed it in, it hath by this labour something annexed to it that excludes the common right of other men. For this labour being the unquestionable property of the labourer, no man but he can have a right to what that is once joined to, at least when there is enough and as good left in common for others."

If inclined to cavil, one might in reply to this observe, that as, according to the premises, "the earth and all inferior creatures"—all things, in fact, that the earth produces—are "common to all men," the consent of all men must be obtained before any article can be equitably "removed from the common state nature hath placed it in." It might be argued that the real question is overlooked, when it is said, that, by gathering any natural product, a man "hath mixed his labour with it, and joined to it something that is his own, and thereby made it his property;" for that the point to be debated is, whether he had any right to gather, or mix his labor with that, which, by the hypothesis, previously belonged to mankind at large. The reasoning used in the last chapter to prove that no amount of labour, bestowed by an individual upon a part of the earth's surface, can nullify the title of society to that part, might be similarly employed to show that no one can, by the mere act of appropriating to himself any wild unclaimed animal or fruit, supersede the joint claims of other men to it. It may be quite true that the labour a man expends in catching or gathering, gives him a better right to the thing caught or gathered, than any *one* other man; but the question at issue is, whether by labour so expended, he has made his right to the thing caught or gathered, greater than the pre-existing rights of *all* other men put together. And unless he can prove that he has done this, his title to possession cannot be admitted as a matter of *right,* but can be conceded only on the ground of convenience.

Further difficulties are suggested by the qualification, that the claim to any article of property thus obtained, is valid only "when there is enough and as good left in common for others." A condition like this gives birth to such a host of queries, doubts, and limitations, as practically to neutralize the general proposition entirely. It may be asked, for example—How is it to be known that enough is "left in common for others?" Who can determine whether what remains is "as good" as what is taken? How if the remnant is less accessible? If there is not enough "left in common for others," how must the right of appropriation be exercised? Why, in such case, does the mixing of labour with the acquired object, cease to "exclude the common right of other men?" Supposing *enough* to be attainable, but not all equally *good,* by what rule must each man choose? Out of which inquisition it seems impossible to liberate the alleged right, without such mutilations as to render it, in an ethical point of view, entirely valueless.

Thus, as already hinted, we find, that the circumstances of savage life, render the principles of abstract morality inapplicable; for it is impossible, under ante-social conditions, to determine the rightness or wrongness of certain actions by an exact measurement of the amount of freedom assumed by the parties concerned. We must not expect, therefore, that the right of property can be satisfactorily based upon the premises afforded by such a state of existence.

## II

But, under the system of land tenure pointed out in the last chapter, as the only one that is consistent with the equal claims of all men to the use of the earth, these difficulties disappear; and the right of property obtains a legitimate foundation. We have seen that, without any infraction of the law of equal freedom, an individual may lease from society a given surface of soil, by agreeing to pay in return a stated amount of the produce he obtains from that soil. We found that, in doing this, he does no more than what every other man is equally free with himself to do—that each has the same power with himself to become the tenant—and that the rent he pays accrues alike to all. Having thus hired a tract of land from his fellow-men, for a given period, for understood purposes, and on specified terms—having thus obtained, for a time, the exclusive use of that land by a definite agreement with its owners, it is manifest that an individual may, without any infringement of the rights of others, appropriate to himself that portion of produce which remains after he has paid to mankind the promised rent. He has now, to use Locke's expression, "mixed his labour with" certain products of the earth; and his claim to them is in this case valid, because he obtained the *consent* of society before so expending his labour; and having fulfilled the condition which society imposed in giving that consent—the payment of rent,—society, to fulfil its part of the agreement, must acknowledge his title to that surplus which remains after the rent has been paid. "Provided you deliver to us a stated share of the produce which by cultivation you can obtain from this piece of land, we give you the exclusive use of the remainder of that produce:" these are the words of the contract; and in virtue of this contract, the tenant may equitably claim the supplementary share as his private property: may so claim it without any disobedience to the law of equal freedom; and has therefore a *right* so to claim it.

Any doubt that may be felt as to the fact that this is a logical deduction from our first principle, that every man has freedom to do all that he wills provided he infringes not the equal freedom of any other man, may be readily cleared up by comparing the respective degrees of freedom assumed in such a case by the occupier and the members of society with whom he bargains. As was shown in the preceding chapter, if the public altogether deprive any individual of the use of the earth, they allow him *less* liberty than they themselves claim; and by so breaking the law of equal freedom, commit a wrong. If, conversely, an individual usurps a given portion of the earth, to which, as we have seen, all other men have as good a title as himself, *he* breaks the law by assuming *more* liberty than the rest. But when an individual holds land as a tenant of society, a balance is maintained between these extremes, and the claims of both parties are respected. A price is paid by the one, for a certain privilege granted by the other. By the fact of the agreement being made, it is shown that such price and privilege are considered to be equivalents. The lessor and the lessee have both, within the prescribed limits, done that which they *willed:* the one in letting a certain holding for a specified sum; the other in agreeing to give that sum. And so long as this contract remains intact, the law of equal freedom is duly observed. If, however, any of the prescribed conditions be not fulfilled, the law is necessarily broken, and the parties are involved in one of the predicaments above named. If the tenant refuses to pay the rent, then he tacitly lays claim to the exclusive use and benefit of the land he occupies—practically asserts that he is the sole owner of its produce; and consequently violates the law, by assuming a greater share of freedom than the rest of mankind. If, on the other hand, society take from the tenant that portion of the fruits obtained by the culture of his farm, which remains with him after the payment of rent, they virtually deny him the use of the earth entirely (for by the use of the earth we mean the use of its products), and in so doing, claim for themselves a greater share of liberty than they allow him. Clearly, therefore, this surplus produce equitably remains with the tenant: society *cannot* take it without trespassing upon his freedom; he *can* take it without trespassing on the freedom of society. And as, according to the law, he is free to do all that he wills, provided he infringes not the equal freedom of any other, he is free to take possession of such surplus as his property.

## III

The doctrine that all men have equal rights to the use of the earth, does indeed at first sight, seem to countenance a species of social organization, at variance with that from which the right of property has just been deduced; an organization, namely, in which the public, instead of letting out the land to individual members of their body, shall retain it in their own hands; cultivate it by joint-stock agency; and share the produce: in fact, what is usually termed Socialism or Communism.

Plausible though it may be, such a scheme is not capable of realization in strict conformity with the moral law. Of the two forms under which it may be presented, the one is ethically imperfect; and the other, although correct in theory, is impracticable.

Thus, if an equal portion of the earth's produce is awarded to every man, irrespective of the amount or quality of the labour he has contributed towards the obtainment of that produce, a breach of equity is committed. Our first principle requires, not that all shall have like shares of the things which minister to the gratification of the faculties, but that all shall have like freedom to pursue those things—shall have like scope. It is one thing to give to each an opportunity of acquiring the objects he desires; it is another, and quite a different thing, to give the objects themselves, no matter whether due endeavour has or has not been made to obtain them. The one we have seen to be the primary law of the Divine scheme; the other, by interfering with the ordained connection between desire and gratification, shows its disagreement with that scheme. Nay more, it necessitates an absolute violation of the principle of equal freedom. For when we assert the entire liberty of each, bounded only by the like liberty of all, we assert that each is free to do whatever his desires dictate, within the prescribed limits—that each is free, therefore, to claim for himself all those gratifications, and sources of gratification, attainable by him within those limits—all those gratifications, and sources of gratification which he can procure without trespassing upon the spheres of action of his neighbours. If, therefore, out of many starting with like fields of activity, one obtains, by his greater strength, greater ingenuity, or greater application, more gratifications and sources of gratification than the rest, and does this without in any way trenching upon the equal freedom of the rest, the moral law assigns him an exclusive right to all those extra gratifications and sources of gratification; nor can the rest take them from him without claiming for themselves greater liberty of action than he claims, and thereby violating that law. Whence it follows, that an equal apportionment of the fruits of the earth amongst all, is not consistent with pure justice.

If, on the other hand, each is to have allotted to him a share of produce proportionate to the degree in which he has aided production, the proposal, whilst it is abstractedly just, is no longer practicable. Were all men cultivators of the soil, it would perhaps be possible to form an approximate estimate of their several claims. But to ascertain the respective amounts of help given by different kinds of mental and bodily labourers, towards procuring the general stock of the necessaries of life, is an utter impossibility. We have no means of making such a division save that afforded by the law of supply and demand, and this means, the hypothesis excludes.[1]

## IV

An argument fatal to the communist theory, is suggested by the fact, that a desire for property is one of the elements of our nature. Repeated allusion has been made to the admitted truth, that acquisitiveness is an unreasoning impulse quite distinct from the desires whose gratifications property secures—an impulse that is often obeyed at the expense of those desires. And if a propensity to personal acquisition be really a component of man's constitution, then that cannot be a right form of society which affords it no scope. Socialists do indeed allege that private appropriation is an abuse of this propensity, whose normal function, they say, is to impel us to accumulate for the benefit of the public at large. But in thus attempting to escape from one difficulty, they do but entangle themselves in another. Such an explanation overlooks the fact that the *use* and *abuse* of a faculty (whatever the etymology of the words may imply) differ only in *degree;* whereas their assumption is, that they differ in *kind.* Gluttony is an abuse of the desire for food; timidity, an abuse of the feeling which in moderation produces prudence; servility, an abuse of the sentiment that generates respect; obstinacy, of that from which firmness springs: in all of which cases we find that the legitimate manifestations differ from the illegitimate ones, merely in quantity, and not in quality. So also with the instinct of accumulation. It may be quite true that its dictates have been, and still are, followed to an absurd excess; but it is also true that no change in the state of society will alter its nature and its office. To whatever extent moderated, it must still be a desire for personal acquisition. Whence it follows that a system affording opportunity for its exercise must ever be retained; which means, that the system of private property must be retained; and this presupposes a *right* of private property, for by right we mean that which harmonizes with the human constitution as divinely ordained.

## V

There is, however, a still more awkward dilemma into which M. Proudhon and his party betray themselves. For if, as they assert, "all property is robbery"—if no one can equitably become the exclusive possessor of any article—or as we say, obtain a right to it, then, amongst other consequences, it follows, that a man can have no right to the things he consumes for food. And if these are not his before eating them, how can

[1] These inferences do not at all militate against joint-stock systems of production and living, which are in all probability what Socialism prophesies.

they become his at all? As Locke asks, "when do they begin to be his? when he digests? or when he eats? or when he boils? or when he brings them home?" If no previous acts can make them his property, neither can any process of assimilation do it; not even their absorption into the tissues. Wherefore, pursuing the idea, we arrive at the curious conclusion, that as the whole of his bones, muscles, skin, &c., have been thus built up from nutriment not belonging to him, a man has no property in his own flesh and blood—can have no valid title to himself—has no more claim to his own limbs than he has to the limbs of another—and has as good a right to his neighbour's body as to his own! Did we exist after the same fashion as those compound polyps, in which a number of individuals are based upon a living trunk common to them all, such a theory would be rational enough. But until Communism can be carried to that extent, it will be best to stand by the old doctrine.

## VI

Further argument appears to be unnecessary. We have seen that the right of property is deducible from the law of equal freedom—that it is presupposed by the human constitution—and that its denial involves absurdities.

Were it not that we shall frequently have to refer to the fact hereafter, it would be scarcely needful to show that the taking away another's property is an infringement of the law of equal freedom, and is therefore wrong. If A appropriate to himself something belonging to B, one of two things must take place: either B does the like to A, or he does not. If A has no property, or if his property is inaccessible to B, B has evidently no opportunity of exercising equal freedom with A, by claiming from him something of like value; and A has therefore assumed a greater share of freedom than he allows B, and has broken the law. If again, A's property is open to B, and A permits B to use like freedom with himself by taking an equivalent, there is no violation of the law; and the affair practically becomes one of barter. But such a transaction will never take place save in theory; for A has no motive to appropriate B's property with the intention of letting B take an equivalent: seeing that if he really means to let B have what B thinks an equivalent, he will prefer to make the exchange by consent in the ordinary way. The only case simulating this, is one in which A takes from B a thing that B does not wish to part with; that is, a thing for which A can give B nothing that B thinks an equivalent; and as the amount of gratification which B has in the possession of this thing, is the measure of its value to him, it follows that if A cannot give B a thing which affords B equal gratification, or in other words what he thinks an equivalent, then A has taken from B what affords A satisfaction, but does not return to B what affords B satisfaction; and has therefore broken the law by assuming the greater share of freedom. Wherefore we find it to be a logical deduction from the law of equal freedom, that no man can rightfully take property from another against his will.

# 51

# Property and the Principle of Function*
## R. H. TAWNEY
### (1880–1962)

## I. Property and Creative Work

The application of the principle that society should be organized upon the basis of functions, is not recondite, but simple and direct.† It offers in the first place, a standard for discriminating between those types of private property which are legitimate and those which are not. During the last century and a half, political thought has oscillated between two conceptions of property, both of which, in their different ways, are extravagant. On the one hand, the practical foundation of social organization has been the doctrine that the particular forms of private property which exist at any moment are a thing sacred and inviolable, that anything may properly become the object of property rights, and that, when it does, the title to it is absolute and unconditioned. The modern industrial system took shape in an age when this theory of property was triumphant. The American Constitution and the French Declaration of the Rights of Man both treated property as one of the fundamental rights which Governments exist to protect. The English Revolution of 1688, undogmatic and reticent though it was, had in effect done the same. The great individualists from Locke to Turgot, Adam Smith and Bentham all repeated, in different language, a similar conception. Though what gave the Revolution its diabolical char-

*From *The Acquisitive Society* by R. H. Tawney, copyright, 1920, by Harcourt Brace Jovanovich, Inc., copyright, 1948, by R. H. Tawney. Reprinted by permission of Harcourt Brace Jovanovich, Inc., New York, and G. Bell and Sons, Ltd., London. (Part I is from ch. 5, pp. 52–54, 59–64, 72–83, of the United States edition; Part II is from ch. 11, pp. 222–27, of the British edition.) The title of this selection has been supplied by the editor.

†At the beginning of chapter 2, Tawney says: "A function may be defined as an activity which embodies and expresses the idea of social purpose. The essence of it is that the agent does not perform it merely for personal gain or to gratify himself, but recognizes that he is responsible for its discharge to some higher authority."

acter in the eyes of the English upper classes was its treatment of property, the dogma of the sanctity of private property was maintained as tenaciously by French Jacobins as by English Tories; and the theory that property is an absolute, which is held by many modern Conservatives, is identical, if only they knew it, with that not only of the men of 1789, but of the Convention itself.

On the other hand, the attack has been almost as undiscriminating as the defense. "Private property" has been the central position against which the social movement of the last hundred years has directed its forces. The criticism of it has ranged from an imaginative communism in the most elementary and personal of necessaries, to prosaic and partially realized proposals to transfer certain kinds of property from private to public ownership, or to limit their exploitation by restrictions imposed by the State. But, however varying in emphasis and in method, the general note of what may conveniently be called the Socialist criticism of property is what the word Socialism itself implies. Its essence is the statement that the economic evils of society are primarily due to the unregulated operation, under modern conditions of industrial organization, of the institution of private property.

The divergence of opinion is natural, since in most discussions of property the opposing theorists have usually been discussing different things. Property is the most ambiguous of categories. It covers a multitude of rights which have nothing in common except that they are exercised by persons and enforced by the State. Apart from these formal characteristics, they vary indefinitely in economic character, in social effect, and in moral justification. They may be conditional like the grant of patent rights, or absolute like the ownership of ground rents, terminable like copyright, or permanent like a freehold, as comprehensive as sovereignty or as restricted as an easement, as intimate and personal as the ownership of clothes and books, or as remote and intangible as shares in a gold mine or rubber plantation. It is idle, therefore, to present a case for or against private property without specifying the particular forms of property to which reference is made, and the journalist who says that "private property is the foundation of civilization" agrees with Proudhon, who said it was theft, in this respect at least that, without further definition, the words of both are meaningless. Arguments which support or demolish certain kinds of property may have no application to others; considerations which are conclusive in one stage of economic organization may be almost irrelevant in the next. The course of wisdom is neither to attack private property in general nor to defend it in general; for things are not similar in quality, merely because they are identical in name. It is to discriminate between the various concrete embodiments of what, in itself, is, after all, little more than an abstraction. . . .

William and Robert Cecil were sagacious and responsible men, and their view that the protection of property should be accompanied by the enforcement of obligations upon its owners was shared by most of their contemporaries. The idea that the institution of private property involves the right of the owner to use it, or refrain from using it, in such a way as he may please, and that its principal significance is to supply him with an income, irrespective of any duties which he may discharge, would not have been understood by most public men of that age, and, if understood, would have been repudiated with indignation by the more reputable among them. They found the meaning of property in the public purposes to which it contributed, whether they were the production of food, as among the peasantry, or the management of public affairs, as among the gentry, and hesitated neither to maintain those kinds of property which met these obligations nor to repress those uses of it which appeared likely to conflict with them. Property was to be an aid to creative work, not an alternative to it. The patentee was secured protection for a new invention, in order to secure him the fruits of his own brain, but the monopolist who grew fat on the industry of others was to be put down. The law of the village bound the peasant to use his land, not as he himself might find most profitable, but to grow the corn the village needed. Long after political changes had made direct interference impracticable, even the higher ranks of English land-owners continued to discharge, however capriciously and tyrannically, duties which were vaguely felt to be the contribution which they made to the public service in virtue of their estates. When as in France, the obliga-tions of ownership were repudiated almost as completely as they have been by the owner of to-day, nemesis came in an onslaught upon the position of a *noblesse* which had retained its rights and abdicated its functions. Property reposed, in short, not merely upon convenience, or the appetite for gain, but on a moral principle. It was protected not only for the sake of those who owned, but for the sake of those who worked and of those for whom their work provided. It was protected, because, without security for prop-erty, wealth could not be produced or the business of society carried on.

Whatever the future may contain, the past has shown no more excellent social order than that in which the mass of the people were the masters of the holdings which they plowed and of the tools with which they worked, and could boast, with the English freeholder, that "it is a quietness to a man's mind to live upon his own and to know his heir certain." With this conception of property and its practical expression in social institutions those who urge that society should be organized on the basis of function have no quarrel. It is in agreement with their own doctrine, since it justifies property by reference to the services which it enables its owner to perform. All that they need ask is that it should be carried to its logical conclusion.

For the argument has evidently more than one edge. If it justifies certain types of property, it condemns others; and in the conditions of modern industrial civilization, what it justifies is less than what it condemns. The truth is, indeed, that this theory of property and the institutions in which it is embodied have survived into an age in which the whole structure of society is radically different from that in which it was formulated, and which made it a valid argument, if not for all, at least for the most common and characteristic kinds of property. It is not merely that the ownership of any substantial share in the national wealth is concentrated to-day in the hands of a few hundred thousand families, and that at the end of an age which began with an affirmation of the rights of property, proprietary rights are, in fact, far from being widely distributed. Nor is it merely that what makes property insecure to-day is not the arbitrary taxation of unconstitutional monarchies or the privileges of an idle *noblesse,* but the insatiable expansion and aggregation of property itself, which menaces with absorption all property less than the greatest, the small master, the little shopkeeper, the country bank, and has turned the mass of mankind into a proletariat working under the agents and for the profit of those who own.

The characteristic fact, which differentiates most modern property from that of the pre-industrial age, and which turns against it the very reasoning by which formerly it was supported, is that in modern economic conditions ownership is not active, but passive, that to most of those who own property to-day it is not a means of work but an instrument for the acquisition of gain or the exercise of power, and that there is no guarantee that gain bears any relation to service, or power to responsibility. For property which can be regarded as a condition of the performance of function, like the tools of the craftsman, or the holding of the peasant, or the personal possessions which contribute to a life of health and efficiency, forms an insignificant proportion, as far as its value is concerned, of the property rights existing at present. In modern industrial societies the great mass of property consists, as the annual review of wealth passing at death reveals, neither of personal acquisitions such as household furniture, nor of the owner's stock-in-trade, but of rights of various kinds, such as royalties, ground-rents and, above all, of course shares in industrial undertakings which yield an income irrespective of any personal service rendered by their owners. Ownership and use are normally divorced. The greater part of modern property has been attenuated to a pecuniary lien or bond on the product of industry which carries with it a right to payment, but which is normally valued precisely because it relieves the owner from any obligation to perform a positive or constructive function.

Such property may be called passive property, or property for acquisition, for exploitation, or for power, to distinguish it from the property which is actively used by its owner for the conduct of his profession or the upkeep of his household. To the lawyer the first is, of course, as fully property as the second. It is questionable, however, whether economists shall call it "Property" at all, and not rather, as Mr. Hobson has suggested, "Improperty," since it is not identical with the rights which secure the owner the produce of his toil, but is opposite of them. A classification of proprietary rights based upon this difference would be instructive. If they were arranged according to the closeness with which they approximate to one or other of these two extremes, it would be found that they were spread along a line stretching from property which is obviously the payment for, and condition of, personal services, to property which is merely a right to payment from the services rendered by others, in fact a private tax. The rough order which would emerge, if all details and qualification were omitted, might be something as follows:—

1. Property in payments made for personal services.
2. Property in personal possessions necessary to health and comfort.
3. Property in land and tools used by their owners.
4. Property in copyright and patent rights owned by authors and inventors.
5. Property in pure interest, including much agricultural rent.
6. Property in profits of luck and good fortune: "quasi-rents."
7. Property in monopoly profits.
8. Property in urban ground rents.
9. Property in royalties.

The first four kinds of property obviously accompany, and in some sense condition, the performance of work. The last four obviously do not. Pure interest has some affinities with both. It represents a necessary economic cost, the equivalent of which must be born, whatever the legal arrangements under which property is held, and is thus unlike the property represented by profits (other than the equivalent of salaries and payment for necessary risk), urban ground-rents and royalties. It relieves the recipient from personal services, and thus resembles them.

The crucial question for any society is, under which of each of these two broad groups of categories the greater part (measured in value) of the proprietary rights which it maintains are at any given moment to be found. If they fall in the first group creative work will be encouraged and idleness will be depressed; if they fall in the second, the result will be the reverse. . . .

So the justification of private property traditional in England, which saw in it the security that each man would enjoy the fruits of his own labor, though largely applicable to the age in which it was formulated, has undergone the fate of most political theories. It has been refuted not by the doctrines or rival philosophers, but by the prosaic course of economic development. As far as the mass of mankind are concerned, the need which private property other than personal possessions does still often satisfy, though imperfectly and precariously, is the need for security. To the small investors, who are the majority of property owners, though owning only an insignificant fraction of the property in existence, its meaning is simple. It is not wealth or power, or even leisure from work. It is safety. They work hard. They save a little money for old age, or for sickness, or for their children. They invest it, and the interest stands between them and all that they dread most. Their savings are of convenience to industry, the income from them is convenient to themselves. "Why," they ask, "should we not reap in old age the advantage of energy and thrift in youth?" And this hunger for security is so imperious that those who suffer most from the abuses of property, as well as those who, if they could profit by them, would be least inclined to do so, will tolerate and even defend them, for fear lest the knife which trims dead matter should cut into the quick. They have seen too many men drown to be critical of dry land, though it be an inhospitable rock. They are haunted by the nightmare of the future, and, if a burglar broke it, would welcome a burglar.

This need for security is fundamental, and almost the gravest indictment of our civilization is that the mass of mankind are without it. Property is one way of organizing it. It is quite comprehensible therefore, that the instrument should be confused with the end, and that any proposal to modify it should create dismay. In the past, human beings, roads, bridges and ferries, civil, judicial and clerical offices, and commissions in the army have all been private property. Whenever it was proposed to abolish the rights exercised over them, it was protested that their removal would involve the destruction of an institution in which thrifty men had invested their savings, and on which they depended for protection amid the chances of life and for comfort in old age. In fact, however, property is not the only method of assuring the future, nor, when it is the way selected, is security dependent upon the maintenance of all the rights which are at present normally involved in ownership. In so far as its psychological

404 / R. H. TAWNEY

foundation is the necessity for securing an income which is stable and certain, which is forthcoming when its recipient cannot work, and which can be used to provide for those who cannot provide for themselves, what is really demanded is not the command over the fluctuating proceeds of some particular undertaking, which accompanies the ownership of capital, but the security which is offered by an annuity. Property is the instrument, security is the object, and when some alternative way is forthcoming of providing the latter, it does not appear in practice that any loss of confidence, or freedom or independence is caused by the absence of the former.

Hence not only the manual workers, who since the rise of capitalism, have rarely in England been able to accumulate property sufficient to act as a guarantee of income when their period of active earning is past, but also the middle and professional classes, increasingly seek security to-day, not in investment, but in insurance against sickness and death, in the purchase of annuities, or in what is in effect the same thing, the accumulation of part of their salary towards a pension which is paid when their salary ceases. The professional man may buy shares in the hope of making a profit on the transaction. But when what he desires to buy is security, the form which his investment takes is usually one kind or another of insurance. The teacher, or nurse, or government servant looks forward to a pension. Women, who fifty years ago would have been regarded as dependent almost as completely as if femininity were an incurable disease with which they had been born, and whose fathers, unless rich men, would have been tormented with anxiety for fear lest they should not save sufficient to provide for them, now receive an education, support themselves in professions, and save in the same way. It is still only in comparatively few cases that this type of provision is made; almost all wage-earners outside government employment, and many in it, as well as large numbers of professional men, have nothing to fall back upon in sickness or old age. But that does not alter the fact that, when it is made, it meets the need for security, which, apart, of course, from personal possessions and household furniture, is the principal meaning of property to by far the largest element in the population, and that it meets it more completely and certainly than property itself.

Nor, indeed, even when property is the instrument used to provide for the future, is such provision dependent upon the maintenance in its entirety of the whole body of rights which accompany ownership to-day. Property is not simple but complex. That of a man who has invested his savings as an ordinary shareholder comprises at least three rights, the right to interest, the right to profits, the right to control. In so far as what is desired is the guarantee for the maintenance of a stable income, not the acquisition of additional wealth without labor—in so far as his motive is not gain but security—the need is met by interest on capital. It has no necessary connection either with the right to residuary profits or the right to control the management of the undertaking from which the profits are derived, both of which are vested to-day in the shareholder. If all that were desired were to use property as an instrument for purchasing security, the obvious course—from the point of view of the investor desiring to insure his future the safest course—would be to assimilate his position as far as possible to that of a debenture holder or mortgagee, who obtains the stable income which is his motive for investment, but who neither incurs the risks nor receives the profits of the speculator. To insist that the elaborate apparatus of proprietary rights which distributes dividends of thirty per cent to the shareholders in Coats, and several thousands a year to the owner of mineral royalties and ground-rents, and then allows them to transmit the bulk of gains which they have not earned to descendants who in their turn will thus be relieved from the necessity of earning, must be maintained for the sake of the widow and the orphan, the vast majority of whom have neither and would gladly part with them all for a safe annuity if they had, is, to say the least of it, extravagantly *mal-à-propos.* It is like pitching a man into the water because he expresses a wish for a bath, or presenting a tiger cub to a householder who is plagued with mice, on the ground that tigers and cats both belong to the genus *felis.* The tiger hunts for itself not for its masters, and when game is scarce will hunt them. The classes who own little or no property may reverence it because it is security. But the classes who own much prize it for quite different reasons, and laugh in their sleeve at the innocence which supposes that anything as vulgar as the savings of the *petite bourgeoisie* have, except at elections, any interest for them. They prize it because it is the order which quarters them on the community and which provides for the maintenance of a leisure class at the public expense.

"Possession," said the Egoist, "without obligation to the object possessed, approaches felicity." Functionless property appears natural to those who believe that society should be organized for the acquisition of private wealth, and attacks upon it perverse or malicious, because the question which they ask of any institution is, "What does it yield?" And such property yields much to those who own it. Those, however, who hold that social unity and effective work are possible only if society is organized and wealth distributed on the basis of function, will ask of an institution, not, "What dividends does it pay?" but "What service does it perform?" To them the fact that much property yields income irrespective of any service which is performed or obligation which is recognized by its owners will appear not a quality but a vice. They will see in the social confusion which it produces, payments disproportionate to service here, and payments without any service at all there, and dissatisfaction everywhere, a convincing confirmation of their argument that to build on a foundation of rights and of rights alone is to build on a quicksand.

From the portentous exaggeration into an absolute of what once was, and still might be, a sane and social institution most other social evils follow. Its fruits are the power of those who do not work over those who do, the alternate subservience and rebelliousness of those who work towards those who do not, the starving of science and thought and creative effort for fear that expenditure upon them should impinge on the comfort of the sluggard and the *fainéant,* and the arrangement of society in most of its subsidiary activities to suit the convenience not of those who work usefully but of those who spend gaily, so that the most hideous, desolate and parsimonious places in the country are those in which the greatest wealth is produced, the Clyde valley, or the cotton towns of Lancashire, or the mining villages of Scotland and Wales, and the gayest and most luxurious those in which it is consumed. From the point of view of social health and economic efficiency, society should obtain its material equipment at the cheapest price possible, and after providing for depreciation and expansion should distribute the whole product to its working members and their dependents. What happens at present, however, is that its workers are hired at the cheapest price which the market (as modified by organization) allows, and that the surplus, somewhat diminished by taxation, is distributed to the owners of property. Profits may vary in a given year from a loss to 100 per cent. But wages are fixed at a level which will enable the marginal firm to continue producing one year with another; and the surplus, even when due partly to efficient management, goes neither to managers nor manual workers, but to shareholders. The meaning of the process becomes startlingly apparent when, as in Lancashire to-day, large blocks of capital change hands at a period of abnormal activity. The existing shareholders receive the equivalent of the capitalized expectation of future profits. The workers, as workers, do not participate in the immense increment in value; and when, in the future, they demand an advance in wages, they will be met by the answer that profits, which before the transaction would have been reckoned large, yield shareholders after it only a low rate of interest on their investment.

The truth is that whereas in earlier ages the protection of property was normally the protection of work, the relationship between them has come in the course of the economic development of the last two centuries to be very nearly reversed. The two elements which compose civilization are active effort and passive property, the labor of human things and the tools which human beings use. Of these two elements those who supply the first maintain and improve it, those who own the second normally dictate its character, its development and its administration. Hence, though politically free, the mass of mankind live in effect under rules imposed to protect the interests of the small section among them whose primary concern is ownership. From this subordination of creative activity to passive property, the worker who depends upon his brains, the organizer, inventor, teacher or doctor suffers almost as much embarrassment as the craftsman. The real economic cleavage is not, as is often said, between employers and employed, but between all who do constructive work, from scientist to laborer, on the one hand, and all whose main interest is the preservation of existing proprietary rights upon the other, irrespective of whether they contribute to constructive work or not.

If, therefore, under the modern conditions which have concentrated any substantial share of property in the hands of a small minority of the population, the world is to be governed for the advantages of those who own, it is only incidentally and by accident that the results will be agreeable to those who work. In practice there is a constant collision between them. Turned into another channel, half the wealth distributed in dividends to functionless shareholders, could secure every child a good education up to 18, could re-endow English Universities, and (since more efficient production is important) could equip English industries for more efficient production. Half the ingenuity now applied to the protection of property could have made most industrial diseases as rare as smallpox, and most English cities into places of health and even of beauty. What stands in the way is the doctrine that the rights of property are absolute, irrespective of any social function which its owners may perform. So the laws which are most stringently enforced are still the laws which protect property, though the protection of property is no longer likely to be equivalent to the protection of work, and the interests which govern industry and predominate in public affairs are proprietary interests. A millowner may poison or mangle a generation of operatives; but his brother magistrates will let him off with a caution or a nominal fine to poison and mangle the next. For he is an owner of property. A landowner may draw rents from slums in which young children die at the rate of 200 per 1000; but he will be none the less welcome in polite society. For property has no obligations and therefore can do no wrong. Urban land may be held from the market on the outskirts of cities in which human beings are living three to a room, and rural land may be used for sport when villagers are leaving it to overcrowd them still more. No public authority intervenes, for both are property. To those who believe that institutions which repudiate all moral significance must sooner or later collapse, a society which confuses the protection of property with the preservation of its functionless perversions will appear as precarious as that which has left the memorials of its tasteless frivolity and more tasteless ostentation in the gardens of Versailles.

Do men love peace? They will see the greatest enemy of social unity in rights which involve no obligation to co-operate for the service of society. Do they value equality? Property rights which dispense their owners from the common human necessity of labor make inequality an institution permeating every corner of society, from the distribution of material wealth to the training of intellect itself. Do they desire greater industrial efficiency? There is no more fatal obstacle to efficiency than the revelation that idleness has the same privileges as industry, and that for every additional blow with the pick or hammer an additional profit will be distributed among shareholders who wield neither.

Indeed, functionless property is the greatest enemy of legitimate property itself. It is the parasite which kills the organism that produced it. Bad money drives out good, and, as the history of the last two hundred years shows, when property for acquisition or power and property for service or for use jostle each other freely in the market, without restrictions such as some legal systems have imposed on alienation and inheritance, the latter tends normally to be absorbed by the former, because it has less resisting power. Thus functionless property grows, and as it grows it undermines the creative energy which produced property and which in earlier ages it protected. It cannot unite men, for what unites them is the bond of service to a common purpose, and that bond it repudiates, since its very essence is the maintenance of rights irrespective of service. It cannot create; it can only spend, so that the number of scientists, inventors, artists or men of letters who have sprung in the course of the last century from hereditary riches can be numbered on one hand. It values neither culture nor beauty, but only the power which belongs to wealth and the ostentation which is the symbol of it.

So those who dread these qualities, energy and thought and the creative spirit—and they are many—will not discriminate, as we have tried to discriminate, between different types and kinds of property, in order that they may preserve those which are legitimate and abolish those which are not. They will endeavor to preserve all private property, even in its most degenerate forms. And those who value those things will try to promote them by relieving property of its perversions, and thus enabling it to return to its true nature. They will not desire to establish any visionary communism, for they will realize that the free disposal of a sufficiency of personal possessions is the condition of a healthy and self-respecting life, and will seek to distribute more widely the property rights which make them to-day the privilege of a minority. But they will refuse to submit to the naïve philosophy which would treat all proprietary rights as equal in sanctity merely because they are identical in name. They will distinguish sharply between property which is used by its owner for the conduct of his profession or the upkeep of his household, and property which is merely a claim on wealth produced by another's labor. They will insist that property is moral and healthy only when it is used as a condition not of idleness but of activity, and when it involves the discharge of definite personal obligations. They will endeavor, in short, to base it upon the principle of function.

## II. Porro Unum Necessarium

So the organization of society on the basis of functions, instead of on that of rights, implies three things. It means, first, that proprietary rights shall be maintained when they are accompanied by the performance of service and abolished when they are not. It means, second, that the producers shall stand in a direct relation to the community for whom production is carried on, so that their responsibility to it may be obvious and unmistakable, not lost, as at present, through their immediate subordination to shareholders whose interest is not service but gain. It means, in the third place, that the obligation for the maintenance of the service shall rest upon the professional organizations of those who perform it, and that, subject to the supervision and criticism of the consumer, those organizations shall exercise so much voice in the government of industry as may be needed to secure that the obligation is discharged.

It is obvious, indeed, that no change of system or machinery can avert those causes of social *malaise* which consist in the egotism, greed, or quarrelsomeness of human nature. What it can do is to create an environment in which those are not the qualities which are encouraged. It cannot secure that men live up to their principles. What it can do is to establish their social order upon principles to which, if they please, they can live up and not live down. It cannot control their actions. It can offer them an end on which to fix their minds. And, as their minds are, so in the long run and with exceptions, their practical activity will be.

The first condition of the right organization of industry is, then, the intellectual conversion which, in their distrust of principles, Englishmen are disposed to place last or to omit altogether. It is that emphasis should be transferred from the opportunities which it offers individuals to the social functions which it performs; that they should be clear as to its end and should judge it by reference to that end, not by incidental consequences which are foreign to it, however brilliant or alluring those consequences may be. What gives its meaning to any activity which is not purely automatic is its purpose. It is because the purpose of industry, which is the conquest of nature for the service of man, is neither adequately expressed in its organization nor present to the minds of those engaged in it, because it is not regarded as a function but as an opportunity for personal gain or advancement or display, that the economic life of modern societies is in a perpetual state of morbid irritation. If the conditions which produce that unnatural tension are to be removed, it can only be effected by the growth of a habit of mind which will approach questions of economic organization from the standpoint of the purpose which it exists to serve, and which will apply to it something of the spirit expressed by Bacon when he said that the work of men ought to be carried on "for the glory of God and the relief of men's estate."

Sentimental idealism? But consider the alternative. The alternative is war; and continuous war must, sooner or later, mean something like the destruction of civilization. The havoc which the assertion of the right to unlimited economic expansion has made of the world of States needs no emphasis. Those who have lived from 1914 to 1921 will not ask why mankind has not progressed more swiftly; they will be inclined to wonder that it has progressed at all. For every century or oftener it has torn itself to pieces, usually, since 1648, because it supposed prosperity was to be achieved by the destruction of an economic rival; and, as these words are written, the victors in the war for freedom, in defiance of their engagements and amid general applause from the classes who will suffer most from the heroics of their rulers, are continuing the process of ruining themselves in order to enjoy the satisfaction of more completely ruining the vanquished. The test of the objects of a war is the peace which follows it. Millions of human beings endured for four years the extremes of misery for ends which they believed to be but little tainted with the meaner kinds of self-interest. But the historian of the future will consider, not what they thought, but what their statesmen did. He will read the Treaty of Versailles; and he will be merciful if, in its provisions with regard to coal and shipping and enemy property and colonies and indemnities, he does not find written large the *Macht-Politik* of the Acquisitive Society, the natural, if undesired, consequence of which is war.

There are, however, various degrees both of war and of peace, and it is an illusion to suppose that domestic tranquillity is either the necessary, or the probable, alternative, to military collisions abroad. What is more probable, unless mankind succeeds in basing its social organization upon some moral principles which command general acceptance, is an embittered struggle of classes, interests, and groups. The principle upon which our society professed to be based for nearly a hundred years after 1789—the principle of free competition—has clearly spent its force. In the last few years Great Britain—not to mention America and Germany—has plunged, as far as certain great industries are concerned, into an era of something like monopoly with the same light-hearted recklessness as a century ago it flung itself into an era of individualism. No one who reads the Reports of the Committee on Trusts appointed by the Ministry of Reconstruction and of the Committees set up under the Profiteering Act upon soap, or sewing cotton, or oil, or half-a-dozen other products, can retain the illusion that the consumer is protected by the rivalry of competing producers. The choice before him, to an increasing extent, is not between competition and monopoly, but between a monopoly which is irresponsible and private and a monopoly which is responsible and public. No one who observes how industrial agreements between workers and employers are actually reached can fail to see that they are settled by a trial of strength between two compactly organized armies, who are restrained from collision only by fear of its possible consequences. Fear is a powerful, but a capricious, motive, and it will not always restrain them. When prudence is overborne by rashness, or when the hope of gain outweighs the apprehension of loss, there will be a collision. No man can say where it will end. No man can even say with confidence that it will produce a more tolerable social order. It is idle to urge that any alternative is preferable to government by the greedy materialists who rule mankind at present, for greed and materialism are not the monopoly of a class. If those who have the will to make a better society have not at present the power, it is conceivable that when they have the power, they too, like their predecessors, may not have the will.

So, in the long run, it is the principles which men accept as the basis of their social organization which matter. And the principle which we have tried to put forward is that industry and property and economic activity should be treated as functions, and should be tested, at every point, by their relation to a social purpose. Viewed from that angle, issues which are insoluble when treated on the basis of rights may be found more susceptible of reasonable treatment. For a purpose is, in the first place, a principle of limitation. It determines the end for which, and therefore the limits within which, an activity is to be carried on. It divides what is worth doing from what is not, and settles the scale upon which what is worth doing ought to be done. It is, in the second place, a principle of unity, because it supplies a common end to which efforts can be directed, and submits interests, which would otherwise conflict, to the judgment of an over-ruling object. It is, in the third place, a principle of apportionment or distribution. It assigns to the different parties of groups engaged in a common undertaking the place which they are to occupy in carrying it out. Thus it establishes order, not upon chance or power, but upon a principle, and bases remuneration not upon what men can with good fortune snatch for themselves, nor upon what, if unlucky, they can be induced to accept, but upon what is appropriate to their function, no more and no less, so that those who perform no function receive no payment, and those who contribute to the common end receive honorable payment for honorable service.

# 52

## *What Is Advertising Good For?* \*

### MARTIN MAYER
(1928–    )

Considering the importance of advertising—both as a part of our cultural climate and as a major weapon of competition—the literature on the subject is appallingly feeble. Virtually everything intelligent that has been written about it in the last forty years can be placed on one small shelf—half-a-dozen books, a dozen pamphlets, perhaps twenty speeches.

This failure to treat a serious subject seriously has been, in part, inescapable, because the men who know advertising best are usually ill-equipped to discuss it analytically. Advertising's obvious function is to sell—which means that its ablest practitioners must be people with a highly-developed bump of enthusiasm and a slight depression where the critical instinct ought to be.

But the frivolity of our customary approach to advertising also stems from two American folk myths. Although they contradict each other, most people manage to believe in both:

(1) They are confident that, personally, they are seldom if ever influenced by advertising; and (2) they believe that advertising is immensely powerful in molding the actions of the community.

Neither myth bears much relation to reality, but both survive, feeding on the extreme scarcity of hard facts about the actual effectiveness of advertising in the market place.

It is virtually impossible for a company to find out with any precision how much of a recent sales increase is due to advertising. In fact, it is by no

*From "What Is Advertising Good For?" as it appeared in *Harper's Magazine*, Feb. 1958, pp. 25–31, and subsequently in expanded form in *Madison Avenue, U.S.A.* by Martin Mayer. Copyright © 1958 by Martin Prager Mayer. By permission of Harper & Row, Publishers, Inc., New York, and The Bodley Head Ltd., London.

means easy to determine whether or not a given advertising campaign is creating any sales at all. Too many hands play a part in the selling process. One of the great advertising and sales success stories of 1956, for example, was Procter & Gamble's Gleem toothpaste. Compton Advertising touted it as the substance of choice for those who wished to avoid cavities but could not brush their teeth after every meal. Meanwhile, door-to-door canvassers were on the road, distributing a free tube or a coupon good for a free tube of Gleem to nearly every household in the country. And the Procter & Gamble salesmen, backed by the company's reputation as a very tough outfit, went rolling through the nation's stores with a steamroller of a deal to convince retailers that they should stock and prominently display the new dentifrice.

How much credit for the success of Gleem should go to the advertising? How much more (or less) Gleem would have been sold if the advertising campaign had been different, or if more or less money had been spent on it? How many angels can dance on the head of a pin on which a machinist has engraved the Lord's Prayer?

Another difficulty is that the facts about advertising—even when they can be isolated—will not hold still long enough for the theoretician to catch them. In all the behavioral sciences, a valid insight is good only for the moment of perception, and for an uncertain but probably short time afterwards. And in advertising, where the sands of consumer preference are constantly blown about by the howling winds of competition, it has been extraordinarily hard to find a foundation for a theory which will explain what the industry does and why.

By and large, economists have ducked this problem. Business theorists, who must deal with advertising somehow, have handled the subject by determinedly sweeping it under a wall-to-wall rug which they call "marketing." In recent years, academicians from the fields of sociology, cultural anthropology, social psychology, and even psychoanalysis have descended on advertising with their assorted insights, bodies of theory, and nostrums, and have secured a truly remarkable amount of publicity for their efforts. The disciplines they practice, however, are notoriously unstable, and their work has been aimed almost exclusively at finding something "useful" for the advertiser. With a few exceptions, their contributions toward the *understanding* of advertising have been nonexistent, superficial, or misleading.

## Which Half Is Wasted?

Anyone attempting to grasp what advertising does in our society must account for a large number of balky facts. These are most prominent:

1. *Some advertising is immensely effective in selling a product.*

Though proofs are hard to come by, only a most unreasonable man could deny the success of Leo Burnett's sophisticated touch of a Marlboro man, William Esty's dumb but happy Winston's-taste-good-like-a-cigarette-should, or Ted Bates's smoothly reassuring 20,000 filters in a Viceroy. Generally speaking, there are no important differences among the leading brands of cigarettes except those created by advertising and—although Marlboro's package (the so-called flip-top box) was unquestionably helpful in establishing the brand—no "marketing" elements other than the advertising can seriously claim any major share of the credit for the success of these three filter cigarettes.

2. *Most advertising campaigns are only faintly successful, and many fail utterly.*

The classic statement of the situation goes back to John Wanamaker in the nineteenth century: "I know half the money I spend on advertising is wasted, but I can never find out which half."

Horace Schwerin, who tests television commercials before a theater audience, claims that nearly half of those he screens have no apparent influence on the brand preferences of the people in his theater. Daniel Starch finds that three-quarters of the people who have read a magazine fail to recognize the average advertisement in the issue when it is shown to them in an interview. George Gallup says that as many as one-third of the people who remember many of the details of a television commercial or an advertisement in a magazine have no idea what product (let alone what brand) the sales pitch hoped to sell.

3. *An elaborate and apparently triumphant advertising campaign which sells great quantities of a new product to new customers will not win repeated sales, if the product is in fact perceptibly inferior to its competitors.*

Examples are a soap and a hair dye which sold heavily in their early months and then collapsed, because the first version of each product was defective. The factors which caused failure in both brands have since been corrected, but it is significant that neither has ever been able to regain the public favor it enjoyed shortly after it was launched. Even the most heavily advertised brand cannot hold its market if it is observably inferior to others selling at the same price. On the other hand, however, an advertised brand can command a *higher* price than an identical product sold without advertising.

4. *Most brands of "packaged goods" can attain only a certain maximum share of the market for their sort of product.*

Beyond this saturation level—almost always below 50 per cent of the total market—advertising will not greatly increase sales, however intelligently it is practiced and however much money is spent on it. (Stopping the advertising, however, will produce a loss.) It is axiomatic in the toothpaste business, for example, that a brand with 30 per cent of the market may throw a fresh $10 million into advertising to gain perhaps a 5 per cent increase in sales; while the same $10 million, devoted to advertising a new brand, may give the new brand a 20 per cent share-of-market.

5. *Advertising cannot increase sales for a product if there is an over-all trend against this kind of commodity.* (It may, of course, increase the sales of a *brand* by giving the brand a greater share of a smaller market.)

Brewers spend more than $100 million a year in advertising, but per capita consumption of beer declines every year. Meanwhile, on the rising side of the trend, vintners spend only about $15 million a year and annually increase the per capita consumption of wine. In 1956, the four leading non-filter cigarettes increased their expenditures by at least $3 million—and sold 16.5 billion *fewer* cigarettes.

6. *Given two identical samples, carrying two different brand names and advertised with two different slogans, most consumers will say that one is superior to the other on grounds of taste, aroma, consistency, durability, etc.*

The Philip Morris Company has found that when people puff two cigarettes alternately, they cannot in fact tell the difference between them, and that their preference for one over the other will invariably reflect the influence of advertising. (The practical application of this insight is in the pre-testing of proposed advertisements, which are shown to panels of consumers while they puff.)

Foote, Cone & Belding once tested the strength of a competitor's advertising campaign by packaging two identical batches of an ice-cream mix—labeling one with their client's slogan and the other with the competitor's slogan—and giving away one of each to a large number of housewives. Shortly thereafter, the agency sent an interviewer to ask the women which of the two brands they had preferred. Only one-fifth of them felt there was no difference between the two; all the rest felt a marked preference for one or the other.

## Something Added

Is it possible to put together a self-consistent theory which will explain the facts? If so, we might then begin to understand the role advertising actually plays in our society—and to think about it in real terms, without the usual notion that it is the creature of cherubim or imps.

For the last eighteen months I have been examining facts of this kind at close range, researching and writing a book about this peculiar industry.

I have talked to several hundred advertising men, including most of the acknowledged leaders of the profession. I found them remarkably articulate and thoughtful about the details of their work—about plans and procedures and organizations, and even about the mysteries of creation. But when we discussed the fundamental nature of their profession, their answers were generally fragmentary and disappointing.

Most of them started from the idea that advertising "creates wants." Some said, in John Kennedy's fifty-year-old phrase, that it was "salesmanship in print." Others said that "it moves you closer to the purchase," or it "builds a 'brand image'" which draws you subconsciously toward a product. (There were also a few deplorable cynics who felt that it "doesn't do any damned good at all, but it's a nice living.") Even the most thoughtful of the men I saw were too absorbed in the techniques of advertising, or too concerned about its morality, to look for a more basic rationale for what they were doing.

With some diffidence, I would like to suggest that a valid theory of advertising can be built. Such a theory would be helpful to economists and sociologists. It could be quite useful to mere consumers. And it might work wonders for the morale of the advertising men themselves, who seem to be haunted by recurring doubts about their value to society.

Any realistic approach to such a theory, it seems to me, ought to start with the premise that successful advertising *adds a new value to the product.* Only this hypothesis can account for all of the observed facts. Other theories—especially the argument that advertising "creates wants"—leave some facts unexplained.

Once added value is assumed as the basis, the facts fall into place. Take the case of a soda pill, a placebo, which is advertised as a headache cure. (Carefully advertised, so as not to run afoul of Federal Trade Commission regulations.) The pill may have virtually no medical value; but it will actually cure the headaches of a number of people who take it. The suggestion power of the advertising has created a value for an otherwise worthless product.

Again, a lipstick may be sold at Woolworth's under one name, and in a department store under another, nationally-advertised name. Almost any teen-age girl will prefer the latter, if she can afford to pay the difference. Wearing the Woolworth's brand, she feels her ordinary self; wearing the other, which has been successfully advertised as a magic recipe for glamor, she feels a beauty—and perhaps she is.

For the value of a product to the person who buys it is not limited to the physical use he makes of it. The food faddist who drinks a reconstituted nonfat dry milk solid receives the value of his belief that he is guarding himself against a heart attack. The ambitious young mail boy who twists a lemon peel into his martini feels that he is doing something which is done in the circles to which he aspires—and even if he is sober, the martini tastes the better for it. Whenever a benefit is promised from the use of a product, and the promise is believed, then the use of that product carries with it a value not necessarily inherent in the stuff itself.

Except in extreme cases, such as the placebo pill and the cosmetic, the value added by advertising is small in relation to those values which the product already had. Thus, advertising cannot, as an ordinary matter, sell products which are observably inferior to their competitors. Again, this added value can only rarely be great enough to overcome major trends in product consumption—either in a single area, such as beer, or in the entire community, as in time of economic depression. During a depression, money itself has an added value, and the number on the price tag becomes more important than the values created by advertising. In more prosperous times, however, the extra, intangible values of status or security—made part of a product by advertising—may seem worth whatever extra money they cost. Schweppes tonic sells at a high premium over the price of Canada Dry, largely because of the value added by David Ogilvy's advertising.

One advertising campaign is highly successful because it adds a value which seems important to a large section of the community; another is unsuccessful because the value added is too trivial to interest anybody. Moreover, the *nature* of the value added by the advertising campaign selects the customers who will buy the brand. The Lord Calvert "Man of Distinction" campaign, for example, made that brand of whiskey the favorite of the Negro community.

Since individuals order their lives on different value scales, no brand can hope via advertising to win *all* the customers in a competitive market. This explains the phenomenon of market saturation, which occurs when the great bulk of those who place high importance on the particular values added by this advertising are already purchasing the brand. (This element of individual scales of value also explains the observed fact of limited "brand loyalty.") And the consumer says that he finds differences between identical products which are differently advertised because *the advertising has, in fact, made them different.*

## Is It Real?

In part, the words "added value" are merely another, more accurate and more useful, way of expressing the thought behind the phrase "creating a want." The value of a product to a consumer lies in its fulfillment of a particular desire; increased desire must be reflected across the equation mark by increased value. The old idea of created wants is unrealistic, however, because it assumes an unchanged product. In fact, the application of advertising to a product *must* to some extent change the product. It is remarkable how many people, who readily see that a new package or a new brand name will alter a product, fail to see that advertising inevitably has a very similar effect.

Moreover, the incomplete concept of created wants produces much silliness of argument by advertising's practitioners and its critics. Advertising men, by and large, are hypersensitive and overdefensive about their work, partly because they see it as "the creation of wants." It is possible to rationalize want-creating as a socially admirable activity, but the argument is a tedious one—and subject at several points to a devastating reply which, in Bernard Shaw's phrase, "expresses itself through a symbol formed by applying the thumb to the tip of the nose and throwing the extended fingers into graceful action." Realization within the trade that advertising works on the product, rather than working over the consumer, might make the advertising community less guilt-ridden and contentious. At the same time, a better understanding of what advertising really does might quiet the apparently unceasing attacks on the industry for its alleged fraud, deceit, and "hidden persuasion."

The notion that advertising can somehow "manipulate" people into buying products which they should not buy is both arrogant and naïve. It has been proved false repeatedly by advertising's inability to keep an inferior product afloat, or to sell against primary trends. When an advertising campaign is highly successful, it will almost always be found that the wagon has been hooked onto a strong tendency which existed before the ads were written. It is not a difference in quality or amount of advertising that makes campaigns for filter cigarettes successful, while campaigns for non-filter cigarettes fail; lung cancer is the dominant fact here, though you would not expect to find so obscene an expression in a cigarette ad.

And the consuming public—whatever its failings in the kingdom of abstract ideas—is usually rather shrewd in its evaluations of competing products. The individual consumer appears to make a fool of himself when he says that Brand A "tastes better" than Brand B, though the two are chemically identical. But his difficulty is in expression, not perception. The superior value which he asserts when he says "Brand A tastes better" is not a false or even an artificial value, just because the assertion is false. Though he cannot explain the reasons, the consumer actually does receive greater enjoyment—and thus more value for his money—when he buys Brand A.

Where techniques from the social sciences and the psychological laboratory are used to find advertising ideas (and the success achieved with these techniques has been by no means so great as some propagandists would have you believe), the case is open-and-shut. If a product satisfies a sublimated sexual drive, and advertising can enlarge the consciousness of this satisfaction, then advertising has obviously heightened the value of the product to the consumer. If advertising can convince a consumer that his purchase of a product will promote him to the upper classes (and he cares to be ranked with the upper classes) he will receive an added value that could be described as a thrill. The dry-goods merchant who buys his first Cadillac gets a satisfaction which cannot be measured in terms of the automobile itself. The Cadillac prestige manufactured by advertising man James Adams is as important to him as the Cadillac horsepower manufactured by General Motors.

Many will object that the values created by advertising are "false values." But the truth or falsity of a value enjoyed by a consumer is unimportant in the objective context of getting and spending. Outside standards of judgment cannot measure the *reality* of private gratifications. The history of human vice indicates that values widely regarded as false will always seem real enough to command a price in the market place. So the truth or falsity of the values added by advertising is a question for individual judgment, a matter of opinion, rather than a subject for objective analysis.

## Why Intellectuals Hate It

And, of course, there is only one civilized cultural judgment on advertising: a rousing thumbs-down. The great bulk of advertising is culturally repulsive to anyone with any developed sensitivity. So are most movies and television shows, most popular music and a surprisingly high proportion of published books. When you come right down to it, there is not a hell of a lot to be said for most of what appears in the magazines.

But a sensitive person can easily avoid cheap movies, cheap books, and cheap art, while there is scarcely anyone outside the jails who can avoid contact with advertising. By presenting the intellectual with a more or less accurate image of the popular culture, advertising earns his enmity and calumny. It hits him where it hurts worst: in his politically liberal and socially generous outlook—partly nourished on his avoidance of actual contact with popular taste.

Successful advertising, which must create mass sales, cannot rise too far above or fall too far below the cultural level of the people at whom it aims. Even if an advertising man suspects that he could win results with a more tasteful ad or television program, he is restrained by the fact that he is spending someone else's money. He may risk a new approach in an advertising theme; but he cannot be asked to experiment with cultural standards which may cut him off from his client's market.

Though most advertising must retain the cultural values of its audience, advertising can and does work small changes in public taste. On balance, these changes are probably in the direction of increased sensitivity. Advertising copy and headlines are probably negative forces, helping out with the general debasement of the language. Advertising requires extreme simplification of complicated subjects and the advertising writer must therefore stretch previously precise words to cover large areas. But advertising is a visual as well as a verbal technique. The first purpose of advertising art is to catch the attention of the consumer, in such a way that he is favorably inclined toward the message. Generally speaking, originality in art is more likely to win attention than the same damn thing all over again—so advertising art has kept within reaching distance of advanced design. Through advertising, the public has become familiar with what sensitive people usually regard as "good design"; and familiarity in this area breeds acceptance. In the more general sense, and on its own terms, advertising as a whole seeks to heighten public sensitivity, because a more sensitive perception will be more likely to recognize the values of slight product differences.

The culture must be seen, of course, in a wider focus than mere aesthetics—and in this more general view its horrified critics charge that advertising poisons the wells.

"Advertising has concentrated," writes *Fortune's* Daniel Bell in the *New Leader,* "on arousing the anxieties and manipulating the fears of consumers to coerce them into buying."

Stripped of its emotional language, and rephrased in the terms of an added-value concept, this argument means that advertising creates feelings of insecurity for the purely commercial purpose of increasing the value of a brand. Reduced to cases, the charge is that Listerine and Colgate force people to worry about mouth odors to persuade them to use a product which, it is claimed, eliminates bad breath.

And there is no way around it: the accusation is true. (Though it must be said that advertising has only a relatively minor influence on fundamental attitudes, and cannot create a fear or an anxiety not already present in the consumer—at least in the latent form of an experience not fully considered—before he comes upon the ad.) Advertising undoubtedly does magnify the pains of modern existence so it can sell products which are supposed to soothe them.

Taken by itself, this act seems morally unjustifiable. But the product very often *does* assuage the pains—and it does so, in those areas of health and beauty where the fear appeals are most commonly used, because of the power of suggestion of the advertising itself. The poor old crock who feels tired every afternoon at three, from a complicated set of physical and psychological causes, may be persuaded to believe that what ails him is Tired Blood. So a dose of Geritol, though his condition may be such that it does him no physical good at all, may really cure him of his symptoms. The girl who is ashamed of her pimples may bear them with more grace after she buys a product which is advertised as the greatest pimple destroyer in history—even if it is actually nothing more than second-rate cold cream, aerated (with lanolin added).

Moreover, most of the products advertised as cures for such ills do not work merely psychological wonders; often they actually will produce some of the physical benefits claimed.

In real life, advertising does not plummet untroubled people into a pit of anxiety, for the single, vulgar goal of an advertiser's profit. Advertising probably does increase the number of people who feel some conscious concern about their physical or social failings. But it offers to all people— both those who felt the concern before they saw the advertising and those in whom it is newly aroused—a solution (a guaranteed solution, in the context of the advertising) to their troubles. For a considerable proportion of those who try it, the product actually *is* a solution, and drinking it down frees them of their worries. Measuring the damage done to the national psyche by the additional fears created by advertising, as against the soothing of the national psyche achieved by removing the same fears from a number of people who previously suffered them, is a task for a subtle metaphysician indeed.

## The "Conformists"

Finally, there is the relationship between advertising and what a large number of people call "conformity." This relationship is difficult to discuss, because the alleged "conformity," as a new development in society, probably does not exist outside the imaginations of the people who talk about it. It is true, of course, that a large mass of citizens drawn at random from within a single culture will have more things in common than not. It is also true that modern communications have produced some breaking down of old and perhaps valuable regional distinctions. And it is true that developments in the past thirty years have raised the economic condition of the nation's lowest tenth and lowered that of its highest tenth; raised the educational level of the lowest tenth and lowered that of the highest tenth. So the community appears to be more homogeneous, from a distant look. But the same developments which have created the appearance of homogeneity have also brought about an astonishing increase in the variety of entertainments, of housing and furnishing possibilities, of hobbies, of consumer goods—even of intellectual pursuits, for those so minded.

Actually, "conformity" plagues the impoverished communities, where people work to exhaustion and have neither the leisure nor the income to express their tastes. A prosperous middle-class society may feel, more strongly than a poor community, that it does not like people who rock the boat—but within broad limits its members are free to indulge their individuality as they have never been before.

And advertising's contribution here is, on the whole, to increase diversity. Advertising lives by the product difference, real or asserted—that is, by appealing to different tastes in values. If advertising looks like other advertising (as so much of it does) the fault lies in the limited skill of many practitioners (and in the fact that advertisers, knowing that their competitors are smart, insist on ads quite similar to the competition's). The purpose is not to force anyone to "conform."

What lies behind the cry of "conformity" and the accusation that advertising promotes it is the deep disappointment following upon the arrival of the millennium. We have achieved the nineteenth-century dream: practically everyone has enough to eat and decent clothing; by any standards but our own nearly everyone is well housed; the workday is short and leisure is ample.

But the millennial culture turns out not to be very interesting: the average man remains a mediocre fellow, and pleased with himself, to boot. Which is, certainly, well within his rights. Perhaps advertising *ought* to do something for the culture, but it won't; says it can't; says it shouldn't be asked. In his most defensive moments, the advertising man will hammer on the table and say the majority must be *right* to like garbage because it buys so much garbage. Holding up an inescapable mirror which reflects disappointment, and refusing for reasons of trade to comment on the picture in the mirror, advertising asks to be disliked by that element of the community which aspires to a higher culture. It is.

But dislike of advertising, however strongly felt, is no excuse for silly attacks on it. Like the rest of us, the advertising man does the best he can. He has days when he likes to regard himself as a Machiavellian figure, and for business reasons he has been known to egg on critics who wildly overestimate his power in the community. But he did not create the culture in which, perforce, he has to work; not infrequently, he shares his critics' distaste for the popular, adolescent-oriented aesthetic scene. And he is not the only cobbler who has decided, at least for the time being, to stick to his last.

In our current economy, where personal selling is clearly too expensive a way to move the necessary volume of goods, advertising performs a necessary function—and the more successful it is, the more prosperous everyone will be. Seen objectively, the advertising man's work increases the material comfort and the sum of private gratifications of the nation as a whole. The values which advertising creates may strike a moralist as mangy beasts. But moralists today, like moralists throughout history, must live with the fact that in the dark and democratic world of private gratification all cats are gray.

# 53

## A Deduction of Universities*

## A. PHILLIPS GRIFFITHS
### (1927–    )

## Introduction

I shall try to show what a university essentially is. I shall then discuss how its essential nature is related to those further functions which it sometimes performs, or are thought by some that it should perform: which, not being a part of the essence, may be called accidents.

No philosopher is in a position nowadays to set forth gaily on discussing the essence of something. To many "essentialism," even with regard to institutions, is a methodological Sin against the Holy Ghost. Essentialism— the idea that we must set out to discover the necessary characteristics of things in order to know them—may often be nothing more than the examination of our own definitions. The essences we discover may be merely nominal. Something more than our own classifying activities must be related to the thing if we are to say not merely what it as a matter of fact is, but what it must be. The idea of the end or purpose of a thing may supply this: if we conceive men, trees, the world, as somehow aiming at perfection in their own kind, it becomes possible to speak of their essential nature at least in terms of potentialities. But we do not any longer conceive natural objects in this way, and we do not talk of their essences. Institutions, however, are not natural objects. In their case, essentialism, while still having dangers for the careless, may be unavoidable.

*A. Phillips Griffiths, "A Deduction of Universities," in *Philosophical Analysis and Education,* Reginald Archambault, ed. (New York: The Humanities Press, Inc.; London: Routledge and Kegan Paul, 1965), pp. 187–207.

Even though institutions are not as Mill claimed[1] "at every stage of their existence made what they are by voluntary human agency," they are what they are at any time of their existence because of the quality of the thought of their members. What an institution is, what differentiates it from others, cannot be explicated in terms of empirically observable factors such as physical movements. These may in principle be the same in different institutions; and the differentia can only be the way the members themselves conceive it.[2] If so, for institutions the essence—the idea—is prior to existence: not, of course temporally prior in all or even many cases, but logically prior; in that, unlike stones and the sea, institutions cannot logically be unless they are conceived as such-and-such.

I am not of course suggesting that we can make institutions come and go, appear and disappear, by the magic of thinking; or that we can by thinking make social institutions be whatever we like—even where "we" means not you or me but all of us. For we cannot think whatever we like, and we cannot do whatever we like, and in consequence there are limits on what institutions are possible, and surprises about what institutions become actual. The limits of possibility are set by the (cultural and not merely logical) limits of thought, and by the (physical, cultural, social, economic, etc.) limits of practice. The inner demands of thought may, especially in the face of the pressures of the world, transform the mind that thinks it and revolutionise the institution that embodies it. This is above all true of the institution whose idea is an Ideal which involves values. Where the institution is conceived as aiming at the perfection of some activity, the perfect realisation of which is open, and could not be known until it is long pursued, it may develop according to what seem, in retrospect, inevitable steps, which could never have been predicted from its earlier nature. On the other hand, those institutions whose "end" is limited by articles, such as a project to build a war memorial or to prevent a road running through a park, having clear and definite criteria for deciding when their activities are successful or unsuccessful, complete or incomplete, may be regarded as the product of conscious human will, but incapable of producing the surprises or development that is characteristic of more "open" institutions.

This openness of those institutions whose essence is related to an ideal explains how it is possible both that their nature depends on how men conceive them, and yet at the same time men may argue interminably about what their nature is. What they are arguing about is very often what

---

[1] J. S. Mill, *Representative Government,* Chapter 1.

[2] Consider, for example, what might make a ritual dance an attempt at magic, a form of amusement, or an act of public worship. For further arguments see P. Winch, *The Idea of a Social Science* (London: Routledge and Kegan Paul, 1958).

would count as satisfying the Ideal which constitutes the essence. For this reason the fact that people say the most diverse and even contradictory things about what some institution such as a university is for, does not necessarily mean that they are not all trying to talk about the same thing. And for this reason also, we should not be misled by this bewildering variety of views to think that there is nothing for it but to give up talking about what a university is for and talk only about what it does. What all universities, without exception, do, is warm the air slightly in their immediate vicinities. As soon as we say that it would be idiotic and irrelevant to mention this as an account of what universities do, we are entering on the road to essentialism. We have given up merely observing practices, and are beginning to prescribe them.

What then I propose to do is to present a "deduction" of the idea of a university; attempting to understand the institution in terms of a justifiable Ideal. I shall try to show that there is a region in the firmament of values that must be filled; and that, in general, it is the institution which people tend to call a university that serves to fill it. I shall be saying at once what a university is and what it ought to be. I shall then, in the last section, go on to discuss some of the things which, while remaining itself, a university may or may not also be.

## Essence

What makes an activity valuable considered as an end rather than a mere means?

This question is a vast one. To deal with it in all philosophical rigour, we should first enter into what are called "meta-" questions about the logic, epistemological status, and justification of value judgments. This would take us a long way from the immediate topic and, judging by past efforts, we should probably never get back again. Here, I can make only certain suggestions, based on a consideration of the nature of an activity as such, which I hope will have some plausibility as a general account.

I am speaking of *activities,* and not other states of being or states of mind: of action rather than passion. Many things, such as warmth, pleasure, serenity and excitement, are thought to have value but are not activities at all.

Activities are things people engage in, which they may or may not know how to do. Not all the things people do are activities. If asked "What are your spare time activities?" a man could answer "Oh, breathing, blinking and sneezing," rather than "none," only as a snub or a bad joke.

Nor would we normally speak of "knowing how" to breathe (unless we are talking about operatic singers or swimmers), or how to blink, or how to sneeze; because not being activities these things are not pursued in accordance with rules or standards. We do not do them well or badly, we simply either do or do not do them. If anything is to be an activity it must allow the possibility of effort, for the presence of standards implies the possibility of success or failure, and hence trying. No activity is of much value in itself unless it presents the need for effort to the degree that it is in some way strenuous: standards too easily followed cease to involve conscious attention and become mere habits (e.g. counting, amusing when one first starts on it as a child but a bore after a while). It would be a mistake quite obviously to have a simple linear scale of the value of an activity based only on its degree of difficulty. The more valuable difficulty differs qualitatively rather than quantitatively from the less valuable one. The specific terms of value we use in respect to activities are "absorbing," "interesting," and "fascinating." It would seem that the difficulties an activity presents in order to be satisfying in this sense must be varied, unpredictable in detail, and requiring constant adjustment and the exercise of new modes of action. This must have something to do with the fact that activities are valuable only as modifications of consciousness, and more valuable as these modifications are richer and capable of indefinite development without mere repetition. They are not those that can be done with half a mind, mechanically, or passively. The objects of valuable activities must possess a quality which we might call *reciprocity*. In acting on it, it bounces back again and one may miss it or it may bump one in the nose; or it may return from an unexpected angle which presents itself as a discovery demanding a new response. Bouncing a ball from an uneven wall is more interesting than from an even one. The responses required are more varied and unpredictable, and require more absorption and engagement. Practising boxing with a punchball is more interesting than pummeling a fixed leather bag; boxing with a man, more interesting and difficult still. It is true that if the punchbag is hard and heavy enough it may be even more difficult to hit it than to box with a man; but all this involves is a quantitative increase in one of the many difficulties involved in boxing a man, not the increase in quality of difficulty which arises from the manifold variety of a human opponent's responses. Playing chess against oneself is less satisfactory than playing it with someone else roughly as good; on one's own one gets less or none of the challenging surprises provided by a good player. Activities involving personal relationships, such as fatherhood, possess this quality in the highest degree: every action may elicit a response which requires a new adjustment. An artist in paint or words is, again, frustrated and at the same time satisfied by the response of his material. The permanence and fecundity of the reciprocity of the object of an activity seems to determine much of its value.

Of course the relative difficulty of an activity may present in addition a positive disvalue. It must not be so difficult as to be impossible even to attempt, and it must not be utterly and quickly exhausting. But this does not affect my point; everyone would probably agree that the lazy, the easily tired, the relatively inactive, miss a great deal in life. We pity the weak and the unable, and perhaps try to make up for the poverty of their lives by giving them more from the passive sources of contentment, such as a rubber teat.

Some very important activities derive their value from their effects rather than what they are in themselves. We may continue with them very wisely when they are mechanical, uninteresting, effortless or dull; but unless we are mad this will only be because we are concerned with some further end they happen to serve. Emptying dustbins (trashcans) neatly might, just possibly, be an interesting task at first, but it would make an odd permanent hobby. Nevertheless, the efficient disposal of waste is undoubtedly of the utmost value. But we must not, because impressed by the important by-products of human activity, forget that some human activities have a value of their own. Emptying dustbins will, we hope, one day be done entirely by machines; but not our dancing or our conversation.

Any activity which is pursued as an end in itself is an expression of love. Activities are pursued according to standards, and the objects proper to them are either (as an ideal to be attained) sought or (as in some degree already actual) improved on. For a man to regard something as an end to be sought or cherished or improved rather than harmed, not because of other things but for its own sake, is for him to love it. His activity may be explained by some further end, in which case it is that and not the object of the activity he loves; or he pursues the object because he loves it. Otherwise, his behaviour is unintelligible. To learn to pursue an activity as an end in itself is, then, to learn to love it. I mention this point because the account I have given may seem somewhat soulless. Why should these formal characteristics, so cerebrally detected, have anything to do with what is of value to people? Surely, to be valued, something must be liked or loved as well? My answer to this is "Not *as well;* I am trying to articulate what it *is* to love."

Now the pursuit of learning—the study of physics, history or philosophy—is clearly an activity whose objects possess reciprocity. They provide the kind of interest which is not readily exhaustible, and which provides challenges at every stage which cannot be satisfied except by digging more deeply. Every acquisition of knowledge seems to reveal a host of new and often more subtle and difficult problems. Without care, we get no answers or misleading answers when we put nature to the question, and the next question we ask will be determined by the last one we got. In history, literary criticism, and philosophy, we are engaged in a dialogue with other men, in which we value the unpredictability of their responses and—at least ideally—the unexpected upsetting of our own views. These activities differ, however, from many other valuable ones in one most important respect. Two men who are pursuing them both pursue the same object. Their objects are universal, and at the same time concrete, in that what each man gets is not an instance of, but a relation to, the same thing as his fellow. (All such objects are qualitatively and not numerically identified). The object of the activity of conversation, or fatherhood, is an individual person (conceived under a limiting description) in which every situation is concrete and unique, shared, if at all, by at most a few. The tennis player is faced with an individual opponent, and he faces a series of new situations defined in terms of the numerically distinct participants and hence peculiarly his. They cannot be shared or passed on. Where the object of a non-universal activity—such as a mistress—is passed on, it is pre-empted. But physics, history, or philosophy are not diminished for me if others pursue them. I may be jealous, or, more reasonably, envious, of the better philosophical achievements of others, but I cannot be jealous because there are other philosophers as I might be if my wife had lovers; for I cannot, even mistakenly, conceive philosophy as *mine* in the way that I might— possibly mistakenly—conceive a woman as mine. I cannot speak of my history, my physics, as I can speak of my singing, my son, or my tennis match. As universal and public, physics or history must be pursued under different conditions from those under which non-universal objects are pursued. It is not only that these objects *can* also be pursued by others; they *must* be, if I am to pursue them myself. And I cannot pursue them properly and seriously if I ignore the work of others. They require the check of the opinions of others, and this is possible as well as necessary because they are public and objective in a way that other activities are not. They all involve the pursuit of truth.

The pursuit of learning is, then, an activity having value as an end in itself. But because its objects are distinguished from others by their universality, they can be sought only in a certain kind of environment. It must be one in which there is time to pursue the activity; for the universal objects of the highest excellence are those which demand most systematic attention, and are practically inexhaustible. It must provide the freedom within which the new challenge can survive, in which whether an argument or some fact is considered depends on the standards of the activity rather than any external criterion, such as its social acceptability or its political convenience. It must be an environment in which communication is possible with others who are engaged in the same pursuits.

This environment is one which has been traditionally provided by universities, especially for their senior members. While other societies may have fulfilled this function, such as classical Athens, it was only because they, too, provided the required environment. Leisure in Athens made the pursuit of learning possible; freedom, of the kind idealized by Pericles in his funeral speech, made it live; and the smallness of the community made its sharing easy. The leisure that made learning possible in Athens was, of course, a consequence of the exploitation of others who were not permitted to share in it: the slaves on the land and in the mines, the over-taxed colonies and tributaries, and everyone who was taken advantage of by the commercial superiority of Athens. In this too Athens was similar to the modern university, for there also the pursuit of learning is carried on at the expense of those who have no part in it.

The centre of learning, existing as it must outside Eden, demands a great deal from the community in which it exists. It demands its keep; and (what may be more difficult to give) it demands its indulgence, for it is a place where the most important prejudices, which may be essential for the stability or even the existence of its surrounding community, may have to be questioned, and perhaps destroyed.

As I have described it, there seem to be cogent reasons why anyone who is not a member of a centre of learning should not want it to exist, and no reason why he should. To him, the centre of learning could be justified only in terms of its by-products. Before going on to discuss these, two things need to be said. First, that we, who for our own selfish purposes (or in concern for the selfish purposes of others who love learning) want to defend universities, should be careful, in our zeal for pointing out their useful by-products, that we do not end up forgetting what we were essentially concerned with, rather than the mere by-products. Secondly, we must not too quickly reject the value and importance of selfish activities.

It is only a kind of lunatic puritanism that would condemn all selfish activities. If an activity is supposed to have value only in its contribution to the well-being of others, then value can reside only in effects, only in what is suffered and not in what is done. This is to ignore the value of activities as such altogether. Furthermore, the pursuit of mathematics or history is not *viciously* selfish in the sense that greed is. Pursuing them does not prevent, but rather enhances, their pursuit by another. Except that a mathematician withdraws his hands from the production line, he diminishes no one.

The relevance of the last point might be disputed on the grounds that in practice the pursuit of learning can be the privilege of only a few. It is sometimes said that the pursuit of universal activities as I have described them requires much time and energy; so those who engage in them must be the few who can be spared in the community's productive effort. In any case, only a very few are intellectually capable of the pursuit of universal objects.

Certainly, if history or physics or philosophy are to be advanced, there must be some people who dedicate a considerable part of their lives to them. But once the pursuit of physics or philosophy exists as an institution, others who have much else to do may participate in it. Thus the selfishness of the few is a condition of the satisfaction of the many. That only a few are intellectually capable of the pursuit of universal objects is simply not in accordance with the facts.[3] It will require the presence of those more practised in such pursuits, but it is possible for many to reach a point (as many do who are awarded bachelor's degrees, or attend three-year extra-mural classes) where they produce the guessing, insight and argument that must take place at the growing point of a subject.

## Accidents

There can be no doubt that universities often provide the environment necessary to the pursuit of learning as I have described it. But it is not enough to say this if I am to show that a university must *essentially* be a centre of learning. For universities do other things too. They usually set up to teach; they preserve and even further culture; they help people to acquire useful arts which later enable them to increase productivity, decrease productivity, and perform other desired economic functions; they may be supposed to turn people into better citizens. In addition to these things, which may be and indeed all have been mistaken for the essential function of the university, they do other things too. They are thought by some to be incomparably the best, if the most expensive, marriage bureaux on earth. They are in some places essential to the maintenance of good

---

[3] This will seem to some to be unwarrantable dogmatism. Here I can refer only to the investigations of the Robbins Committee (Committee on Higher Education, *Higher Education* [Report of the Committee under the chairmanship of Lord Robbins, 1961–63; London: H. M. Stationery Office, 1963], esp. Chapter VI), and earlier investigations of the British Association of University Teachers. It is, I fear, true that very many dons in England have bitterly opposed the view that there is a pool of untapped ability, as the ghastly phrase goes. Generally however their remarks seem to have been made on a journalistic, intuitive level. Some now seem to have been convinced by the Robbins Committee report, but find new arguments to oppose the expansion of Universities (one prize example being the claim that while bigger Universities would not necessarily be academically bad, it would diminish the *moral* influence of the writer and other dons over his students. Enough said.).

semi-professional football teams. They are often decorative, places of tourist resort and, as I remarked before, they all warm the air slightly. I shall not think it necessary to concern myself with the second set of university functions. It would clearly be quite idiotic to suggest that they might be considered the essential functions of a university, because it would mean that universities are not at all distinct from correspondence clubs, sporting clubs, national parks or warming pans, respectively. This shows that we do not invent the concept "university" to represent these functions (or we would not have a different concept), we do not conceive the institution in this way. And what it is is how it is conceived. So I need only concern myself with the first set of functions, because some people do conceive universities as essentially distinguished by them. To show that they are wrong, it will be necessary to show that these functions can be conceived as functions of the university only so far as they are dependent on the central function, the pursuit of learning. This however one can only do in so far as one believes they are possible; and as I shall argue, perhaps the last is not.

## (*i*) *Teaching*[4]

Some universities are said to have begun by scholars taking pupils in order to be able to live. Many universities today are full of teachers who are teachers because that is the only way they can get enough money and live in the right surroundings to pursue their subjects. This may be a sufficient explanation of why people who have as a major aim in life the pursuit of universal objects become university teachers (or, perhaps, monks). But it makes the matter look rather too accidental. The activity of teaching is peculiarly compatible with the pursuit of universal objects, in a way that other work, even part-time work, is not. For certain kinds of teaching, at any rate, are nothing but the practice of the activity in public; the pupil and the teacher form the community within which the universal object is publicly possessed. The dialogue between pupil and teacher need not be fundamentally different from that between scholar and scholar. Its avowed end is not the same: it is the initiation of another into a universal activity, not the discovery of truth. But this can be done only by treating the dialogue as if its end were the discovery of truth. The pupil is introduced to the activity by participating in it with someone more advanced who is for the moment more concerned for the state of mind of the individual than the advancement of his subject, but who shows the pupil what a concern for

[4]My argument in this section has been considerably modified in discussion with Professor R. S. Peters.

the advancement of his subject amounts to. It is true that even this is too much to ask of some; there are university dons who hate their pupils for interrupting their real work, until one as advanced and brilliant as himself obtrudes on his attention as would a colleague.

However, to say that teaching is peculiarly compatible with the pursuit of universal objects does not show that it is the pursuit of universal objects which is the essence of the university. It shows merely that university scholars may well teach, not that university teachers must be scholars. But for the latter it is enough to say that for anyone to be introduced to a universal activity, he must be in the presence of someone who practises it, and who does so in a way which shows most manifestly the standards and principles of the activity. There is no way of introducing people to these activities except by helping them to practise them. But no one can simply be *instructed* how to practise them. They possess reciprocity in the highest degree. At every stage they require the stance of doubt: the readiness to meet challenge. Every step must be questioned and one must always be prepared for—indeed look for—refutation. One cannot be prepared for refutation unless one knows what refutation is, and that means knowing what it is to refute. The pupil is from the beginning the critic of his teacher's work, and his aim is to overthrow it if possible (as indeed it must be the scholar's aim, if he is concerned for truth, to see his work overthrown). From the beginning the pupil must take an active part:[5] it is the teacher's cross to bear with initially simple-minded and half-baked objections so that he may eventually be proved wrong with good ones.

So the teacher must be concerned for his pupil as well as for his subject; but if he is teaching history, for example, his concern must be for his pupil as a possible historian rather than as a future wage-earner.[6] What he has to do, whether he himself loves his own subject or pursues it only for

[5] This leads, at least in my own teaching of philosophy, to a pedagogical problem which I have never satisfactorily resolved. To teach students what it is to refute, it is sometimes necessary to give them practice by defending to them a not easily defensible position. A second reason for doing this is that they may be inclined themselves to reject a commonly rejected position—such as psychological hedonism—because it is commonly rejected and not because they have seriously worked through the reasons against it. But taking up the role of devil's advocate sometimes results in the student's doubting the sincerity and seriousness of the teacher. This I think illustrates what I have been saying. There is bound to be a kind of tension resulting from the fact that in teaching one is not primarily seeking truth but must at the same time present to the pupil an example of that search.

[6] This is not a distinction without a difference. Only via such distinctions can one give the concept "love of persons" any content at all. I should argue that there is no such thing as love of a person *as such;* only of a person under a given description. Forms of love of persons are thus discriminated in terms of the description under which their objects are conceived, and the activities which are their expression are consequently very different, as fatherhood differs from friendship, being a good daughter differs from being a good wife, and the love of a wife is different from the love of a Queen (which must lead to difficulties in the life of a Prince Consort).

some further end such as making a living, is to lead the pupil to act as if the pupil loved the subject: for only in this way can he bring the student to see what this love consists in. It is only in this way that the pupil can come to pursue the subject properly, that is, by the standards internal to it, rather than as a mere means which may be restricted to serve an external end. (More about this in section iii). In these circumstances it would be reasonable to expect what does indeed seem to be the case, that the best teachers tend to be those who do love their subjects, for whom their subjects are ends in themselves. Such people will want to be at a centre of learning rather than an institution which does not satisfy this description. They will want people to talk to on their own academic level, the leisure to pursue their subjects, and the freedom to do so not so much as they think fit but as they judge the subject demands. Introducing people to universal objects must be done then at centres of learning, because you must go where the people who can best do it are to be found.

## (*ii*) *Education*

To acquire the practice of a universal activity may not, perhaps, be to become educated. If we regard an educated man as someone who has the knowledge and sophistication which is common to some civilization, his ability to pursue a universal object will not be sufficient for him to be educated. He may be a barbarian in most respects; and this means that every senior member of a university may be a barbarian and still be a satisfactory scholar in his own field. There may be philistine pure mathematicians, philosophers with no aesthetic sense, physicists who never read the newspapers, philologists who spend half their time glued to the telly, and mediaevalists who think science is some kind of hand-soiling tinkering with gadgets. To some extent, this seems to be becoming more generally true, especially of non-scientists: people interested in the arts seem far less able to discuss or understand scientific interests than scientists are able to discuss and understand the arts. At any rate, the common mode of conversation throughout a whole university often seems to tend towards sheer gossip: for personalities seem to be all that each man can talk about other than his own subject.

If this is inevitable, we have a choice: universities either as centres of learning or centres of culture, it would seem. Are universities for turning out educated men of culture, or for turning out people who can do physics or history or philosophy? If the former then they are not essentially centres of learning. If the latter, and the gap is unbridgeable, they will not be centres of culture at all.

But let us now ask, if this is inevitable what, then, would a centre of culture be? It would be a place where people pursue not only physics, but philosophy; not only philosophy, but music; not only music, but engineering (nobody can understand our world and be an all-round cultured man without a knowledge of the nature and problems of engineering); not only engineering, but theology. It is difficult to see why, if they can do all of these things reasonably well, they cannot do one of them well. In which case, the centre of culture is a centre of learning too. But it is also difficult to see why, if they cannot do any one of them well, they should be expected to do all of them reasonably well. If it is inevitable that centres of learning cannot be centres of culture, then it is inevitable that there cannot be centres of culture: it means that our culture is not only fragmented, as C. P. Snow would have it: but that it is necessarily fragmented.

On the other hand, if this is not inevitable, then a centre of learning should provide the environment in which a man can acquire a general culture if he can acquire it at all. For it is there that the growing points of a culture—at least so far as it concerns universal objects—are; and it is there that he will come into contact with those who are most deeply immersed in some aspect of culture. What he may well not do is to meet those who are concerned with the growing points of culture so far as it concerns non-universal objects. He will not meet painters, poets, or international tennis players, and he will not meet many of the best composers. There is no reason why a university should not extend itself to being a patron of the non-universal arts, if it can afford it, as many American universities have done. (Such writers as Frost and Auden, such composers as Schoenberg, who hated teaching harmony, and such footballers as I cannot name, have found niches in American universities from time to time). This should not however be at the expense of its central function as a centre of learning. These other lonelier activities will go on somewhere whether the university environment is provided or not. The university environment, with its air of public criticism, is often inimical to the artist. Artists do not always fit well into institutions, especially ones not primarily dedicated to their purposes. Above all, we do not want to turn poets into literary critics, painters into art historians, or great musical innovators into teachers of elementary harmony: and this not for the sake of universities but for the sake of poetry, literary criticism, painting, art history, and Schoenberg.

### (iii) Useful Arts

In their *Dictionary of Contemporary American Usage* Bergen and Cornelia Evans say of the term "liberal arts": "It means, etymologically, befitting a free man. In practice it means a course of studies comprising the arts, natural sciences, social studies, and the humanities, which is not designed, as are courses in engineering, business administration, forestry, and so on, to have an immediate utility." [7] There may seem to be no obvious connection between the etymology and the present meaning of "liberal arts": can't an engineer, or a dentist, be a free man? But there is this interesting connection. There is a sense in which the pursuit of philosophy or physics or history is the pursuit of a free man whereas business administration or forestry is the pursuit of a slave or at least a servant. It is the sense in which the former pursuits are of value in themselves to those who pursue them,[8] as a pursuit of universal objects; whereas the latter are pursued as a means only, so that people will pursue them only (as slaves) under threat of punishment or (as servants) for the sake of reward. But if this is the reason for the distinction, the examples mentioned are dangerously misleading. The distinction is not really one of different studies. Painting, physics, psychology and Latin may all be pursued "so as to have an immediate utility"; while engineering, business administration, forestry and dental caries may all be studied simply because they are interesting. If, in a university, the study of Latin as a language is robbed of its historical and philological interest because efficient schoolteachers of Latin, who are being processed in the university, have no need of such things, we are treating the students like slaves who have to be equipped with hoes or hammers. If psychology is studied just so far as it might be of use to those who later on will have to advise advertisers about the most efficient methods of deceiving the general public, it has ceased to be the pursuit of a universal object. What makes the distinction is not the field of study but the way it is pursued. It cannot be pursued as a valuable universal object if arbitrary limits are set on what determines the importance and relevance of any question within it; that is, if the standards of relevance become extrinsic to the activity, it loses the fecundity of reciprocity which makes it valuable.

To say that in universities subjects are pursued as ends in themselves is not then to say that they are all useless; it is only to say that their use does not determine the way they are studied. Confusion in this matter may account for the contemptuous attitude displayed by some members of arts faculties to their scientific colleagues; as if the latter were somehow engaged in trade. That their own subjects are largely useless, and many sciences undoubtedly useful, does not necessarily mark any difference in the way in which these subjects may be approached. The same may be said of those

---

[7] B. and C. Evans, *Dictionary of Contemporary American Usage* (New York: Random House, 1957), p. 274.

[8] Ignore the other dimension of meaning of the word "liberal," that a liberal course is a *general course*. I have discussed this issue in the preceding section.

subjects coming under the heading of "technology." Technological problems are objective, public problems, which are related to those trying to solve them in exactly the same way as the problems of physics or literary criticism. That, in solving them, it becomes immediately possible to build a bridge does not mean that, in pursuing them, those who studied them would lose interest if they did not happen to want a bridge. Indeed, far from its being the case that such subjects are not "liberal," their usefulness often depends on their being treated in a disinterested liberal way (as Bell Telephone Laboratories have shown). This is fortunate for universities and for those useless subjects pursued in them; were it not true there would undoubtedly be less of them.

Turning out people with technical abilities is not, then, incompatible with the essential function of a university; but it will become so if this aim is allowed to determine its activities. We may also say that when this aim does become the determinant of its activities, it fails to achieve this aim on the highest level.

## (*iv*) *Preparation for Life*

Education is often held to have as one of its primary aims the training of character; if so we might demand of institutions of higher education that they also have this aim. Not inevitably, however; for we may question, in the first place, whether we should think of universities as being very centrally concerned with *education*, rather than the pursuit and passing on of universal activities; or, in the second place, whether *all* education, at every stage, involves the training of character. But it is a hoary idea that universities should concern themselves with this aim; that they should be turning out good citizens and, indeed, as the highest reaches of the educational system, that they should be turning out the *best* citizens—the aristocrats who will lead.

I shall not concern myself here with the inegalitarian aspects of this view, or with the dangers to the ideals of democracy of leadership cadres. I am writing about universities, not the best way to run society. What I shall ask is whether this aim seems even possible in any institutions which look remotely like universities.

I am not going to argue that leadership, etc., cannot be learnt. But the context in which it is learnt seems as a rule a very different one from an academic institution. In the Army and Police force there are semi-academic institutions such as the Staff Colleges. But no one thinks that it is at such places that the qualities of leadership are developed. The students are those who are already some distance up the ladder of leadership and, being

leaders, are acquiring certain specific information and skills. Trade union-
ists get sent to various educational institutions during their careers, but they
acquire the qualities of a good trade union leader in the work of the union.
Leadership, the ability to handle men and make decisions showing practical judgment, while requiring certain initial qualities of mind and character, seems to be developed by practising *it* and not something else.

On the other hand, graduates do not seem to possess these qualities of
character strikingly more than anyone else. So if we are to regard universities as schools of leadership, we shall have to ask them to do rather different
things from their present practice. It must not be too different or we shall
not call them universities at all. This means that if anyone is going to put
forward the Platonic view that certain studies ultimately produce the
qualities needed in leaders of men, he will be required to make quite
specific suggestions as to which studies, in what way pursued, will have this
effect. Obviously I cannot deal with all such suggestions here. I shall
content myself with the discussion of one such recent suggestion, that made
by Professor Nowell-Smith in his inaugural lecture at the University of
Leicester.[9] It is an interesting one because it involves a very explicit
suggestion that university studies should be limited, in arts faculties, in just
the way that technical subjects may be, by being supposed to have "an
immediate utility": the reverse view to that which takes a pride in the
uselessness of arts subjects. Only here the "immediate utility" is in terms of
desirable effects on the characters and minds of the students, rather than on
their economic value.

What the student should acquire at the university, according to
Nowell-Smith, are the "skills required for living";[10] since university students "are marked out by their talents as leaders and it is they who will
have most to contribute to the solution of our social, moral and political
problems."[11] The academic training should develop not special but general
skills: "creative imagination, practical wisdom, and logical thought."[12]
The view is directly in contradiction to the one I have been putting
forward. These general skills are not simply valuable by-products but
developing them is the essential function of the university. The aim of the
university should explicitly *not* be "to teach literature, history, or philosophy, but those skills that are required for living" to the majority of students.

I think this view is doubly dangerous. In the first place, it may lead us
to neglect those valuable functions which, essential or not, can be per-

[9] *Education in a University* (Leicester University Press, 1958).
[10] *Ibid.*, p. 7.
[11] *Ibid.*
[12] *Ibid.*

formed only by a university. In the second place, and I conclude by arguing this point, the aim is not a possible one. It would be foolhardy to sell universities to the public on such grounds; one fears what might happen when it is seen that the Emperor is nothing but clothes.

Nowell-Smith's suggestion is that the "skills required for living," creative imagination, practical wisdom, and logical power, may be developed by a (partial) study of literature, history and philosophy respectively. If these are skills, they are very odd ones. Notice that most ordinary skills—swimming, tight-rope walking, or carpentry—can be acquired only by practising them; you cannot acquire the skill of swimming without going to the water. But it seems that we can get practical wisdom by studying history and creative imagination by studying literature. Secondly, these skills seem to have no direct manifestation. We can tell that people can swim by seeing them swimming. We cannot tell they have practical wisdom by seeing them do any particular sort of thing. We may be misled on this point because there are sometimes good tests for the possession of qualities of this sort; intelligence tests are an example. But the relation between intelligence tests and intelligence is quite different from the relation between swimming tests and the ability to swim. One could actually learn to swim by doing lots of swimming tests, just as some people learn to play the piano by mastering a series of graded test pieces. One cannot acquire intelligence by doing intelligence tests. This suggests that it is a mistake to regard such qualities of mind as imagination, practical wisdom, and logical power as skills at all, for this will lead us to think they can be acquired in the same way that skills are acquired, and that once acquired they may have one uniform manifestation. In fact such concepts as intelligence or practical wisdom must be "schematised" before they can be applied: that is, given a concrete sense in terms of some particular activity. For different activities performed by the same individual may manifest different degrees of intelligence or imagination. It *may* be true that an intelligent man is more likely to make an intelligent boxer than an unintelligent man; yet an intelligent boxer may be an "unintelligent man." You may be able to tell whether a man is a logical historian by seeing how well he is able to solve logical puzzles; but it is not conceptually impossible to find a brilliantly logical historian who in fact cannot do logical puzzles (for example he may be quite put off by too great a degree of abstraction). We know he is a logical historian because of the *way* he does *history*. Such qualities as logical power or imagination are not skills like the ability to ride a bicycle or blow smoke rings, and they are not manifested as pure intelligence or pure wisdom, as riding a bicycle and blowing smoke rings perfectly manifest the corresponding skills. They are manifested in the *way* some things are done; "imaginative," "wise," "logical" and "intelligent" are adjectives which derive their sense from the adverbial form. Intelligence, imagination and wisdom are the qualities needed to do things intelligently, imaginatively and wisely, and the force of these adverbs will depend on what they qualify (which may be understood by realising that the question "Does an imaginative scientist need more or less imagination than an imaginative poet?" is a nonsensical one). Furthermore, all these qualities are needed to pursue any activity well.

I shall try to illustrate these points by looking at the suggestions Nowell-Smith makes more closely and in greater detail, before drawing my conclusion.

He regards history as involving examples of practical wisdom and as capable of developing it. But the study of history surely already pre-supposes some practical wisdom, and a lot of imagination (sympathetic, if not creative imagination; but I am not too sure of the distinction). It would seem that the study of political institutions is an art: some people have a flair for understanding the nature and processes of such institutions as the Soviet Communist Party, a flair which is essential for any good political analyst. This is also true of understanding the past. If imagination is necessary to the study of history, no less is analytical intelligence. Nowell-Smith says "the historian will be all the better as a historian for some philosophical training." Perhaps. But a historian without considerable logical and analytical intelligence would be no historian worthy of the name. He must be able to detect inconsistencies in his theories, and to characterise the past in meaningful and viable concepts. Probably, he will not consult the philosopher about where he fails: he is more likely to be corrected by other historians, who know better what he is talking about.

The same sort of thing may be said for either literature or philosophy. In literary criticism we do not develop creative imagination, but we surely require that the critic should be imaginative, in that he is able to perceive connections, significances, ambiguities and comparisons of a non-obvious kind in the works he is studying. The connection with practical wisdom is at least as plausible as in the case of history. (It is perhaps more plausible. History might equally be regarded as the record of the manifold follies of men as of their wiser decisions. To distinguish the one from the other means bringing practical wisdom to it, not getting it from it.) In the novel, in drama and in epic and other poetry, there is not only often an abstractable set of situations which are of interest to the moral sense: the moral sense is essential to the appreciation of the work itself, to the significance of its images and its development. Anyone who reads *Lear* without realising its preoccupation with the idea of love and its demands and misuses misses a great part of the value of the work. Equally important to the critic is the capacity for logical thought and careful analysis. As in history, his second order concepts must be consistent, meaningful and viable; but the critic must also bring his logical sense to bear on the work itself. There are arguments in literature, world-views, the posing of problems, even though these are not its primary end; but they are elements of the work, and it is impossible to appreciate or criticise them unless the critic has the necessary analytical equipment.

Again, all these qualities of mind are necessary to the philosopher. The reason why analytical thought is so much more important in philosophy is because it is an absolutely necessary condition of any philosophical view that it should be clear and consistent. It cannot put up with the openness and ambiguities of a literary work—which indeed are a part of the value of literature—and it cannot reflect the empirical modesty of history, which accepts concepts and hypotheses for their working value. So on the critical side in philosophy one can usually make do with analytical expertise. But this merely destructive criticism is not sufficient to a good philosopher. Philosophy never exists in a vacuum; philosophical thought always goes on against a background of other people's philosophical views. Sympathetic historical imagination is necessary to appreciate philosophical work of the past. Furthermore, the power of imagination is necessary to the development of one's own philosophical views: since seeing connections, picking out important and central concepts, and the perspicuous understanding of a language game are not matters of deduction or calculation or mere painstaking analysis.

Imagination, wisdom, and intelligence seem then to be necessary conditions of pursuing any of these three subjects, and, indeed, anything else, well. But it would be a mistake to think that they are *generally* developed by any activity requiring them. In pursuing history or physics, or philosophy, in facing the difficulties of these activities and overcoming them, one becomes better at history, physics or philosophy. Perhaps this means becoming a more intelligent, imaginative, and logical historian or physicist or philosopher. But it certainly does not mean becoming a more intelligent boxer or philologist or soldier, or a more imaginative poet or joke-teller, or a wiser father or trade union leader; or a wiser, more imaginative more logical and intelligent man.

There are human activities which need universities for their pursuit where one may acquire the ability to pursue them, and which require the possession of such qualities of mind as intelligence, imagination and practical wisdom. There is no reason to suppose that the consequence of learning to pursue these activities will be anything other than the ability to pursue them; but being able to pursue them is nevertheless a good thing.

# STATEMENTS ON MORALITY
*Tenth Series*

*71. Justice is the first virtue of social institutions, as truth is of systems of thought. A theory however elegant and economical must be rejected or revised if it is untrue; likewise laws and institutions no matter how efficient and well-arranged must be reformed or abolished if they are unjust. Each person possesses an inviolability founded on justice that even the welfare of society as a whole cannot override. For this reason justice denies that the loss of freedom for some is made right by a greater good shared by others. It does not allow that the sacrifices imposed on a few are outweighed by the larger sum of advantages enjoyed by many. Therefore in a just society the liberties of equal citizenship are taken as settled; the rights secured by justice are not subject to political bargaining or to the calculus of social interests. The only thing that permits us to acquiesce in an erroneous theory is the lack of a better one; analogously, an injustice is tolerable only when it is necessary to avoid an even greater injustice. Being first virtues of human activities, truth and justice are uncompromising.*

John Rawls (1971)

*72. All we need do to secure a just distribution of wealth, is to do that which all theories agree to be the primary function of government—to secure to each the free use of his own powers, limited only by the equal freedom of all others; to secure to each the full enjoyment of his own earnings, limited only by such contributions as he may be fairly called upon to make for purposes of common benefit. When we have done this we shall have done all that we can do to make social institutions conform to the sense of justice and to the natural order.*

Henry George (1883)

*73. In a family based upon mutual respect, tolerance, and understanding affection, the new generation of children—the citizens of tomorrow—stand their best chance of growing up to recognize the fundamental principle of free society—the uniqueness and value and wholeness of each individual human being. . . .*

*. . . The basis of any tolerable society—from the small society of the family up to the great society of the State—depends upon its members learning to love. By that I do not mean sentimentality or possessive emotion. I mean the steady recognition of others' uniqueness and a sustained intention to seek their good.*

Adlai E. Stevenson (1955)

74. *Part of the objective test of a just or good war is the social one that it will bring more good than harm to society as a whole. The test is not in how it affects any one person or group of individuals, or in how they react to the war emotionally, but in its effect upon the welfare of the social whole.*

L. L. Bernard (1944)

75. *All ethics so far evolved rest upon a single premise: that the individual is a member of a community of interdependent parts. His instincts prompt him to compete for his place in the community, but his ethics prompt him also to co-operate (perhaps in order that there may be a place to compete for).*

*The land ethic simply enlarges the boundaries of the community to include soils, waters, plants, and animals, or collectively: the land. . . .*

*In short, a land ethic changes the role of* Homo sapiens *from conqueror of the land-community to plain member and citizen of it. It implies respect for his fellow-members, and also respect for the community as such.*

Aldo Leopold (1948)

76. *The environmental crisis tells us that there is something seriously wrong with the way in which human beings have occupied their habitat, the earth. The fault must lie not with nature, but with man. For no one has argued, to my knowledge, that the recent advent of pollutants on the earth is the result of some natural change independent of man. Indeed, the few remaining areas of the world that are relatively untouched by the powerful hand of man are, to that degree, free of smog, foul water, and deteriorating soil. Environmental deterioration must be due to some fault in the human activities on the earth.*

Barry Commoner (1971)

77. *I think it was a great medieval philosopher who said that all evil comes from enjoying what we ought to use and using what we ought to enjoy. A great many modern philosophers never do anything else. Thus they will sacrifice what they admit to be happiness to what they claim to be progress; though it could have no rational meaning except progress to greater happiness. Or they will subordinate goodness to efficiency; though the very name of good implies an end, and the very name of efficiency implies only a means to an end. Progress and efficiency by their very titles are only tools. Goodness and happiness by their very titles are a fruition; the fruits that are to be produced by the tools.*

*Yet how often the fruits are treated as fancies of sentimentalism and only the tools as facts of sense. It is as if a starving man were to give away the turnip in order to eat the spade; or as if men said that there need not be any fish, so long as there were plenty of fishing rods.*

G. K. Chesterton (1928)

# Bibliography

The Bibliography is arranged under the following headings: Histories; Introductory Works; Fiction; Anthologies; Classics; Theoretical Ethics; Practical Ethics; Values and Ideals; Skepticism and Relativism; Casuistry and Conflict; War and Morality; Institutional Ethics; General.

These categories are not always mutually exclusive. Works that are especially difficult or technical are marked by an asterisk. The symbol "(B)" indicates an especially rich or useful bibliography. Books from which a selection was taken for inclusion in this collection are not relisted here.

## Histories of Ethics and Morals

Bourke, Vernon J. *History of Ethics* (Garden City, N. Y., 1968). (B). Very thorough coverage.

Lecky, W. E. H. *History of European Morals, from Augustus to Charlemagne* (London, 1899). A classic account; the first chapter, "The Natural History of Morals," is an interesting attempt to integrate an account of the development of moral theory with the development of morals.

MacIntyre, Alasdair. *A Short History of Ethics* (New York, 1966).

Mackintosh, James. *Dissertation on the Progress of Ethical Philosophy* (London, 1837). An important and little known work.

Myers, Philip van Ness. *History as Past Ethics: An Introduction to the History of Morals* (Boston, 1913).

Rogers, A. K. *Morals in Review* (New York, 1927). A valuable, readable, and strangely neglected book.

Sidgwick, Henry. *Outlines of the History of Ethics* (London, 1886; 5th ed., 1902). A classic work, still probably the best short history of ethics, and still in print in an edition with an additional chapter by Alban G. Widgery (1931).

## Introductory Surveys and Texts

Brandt, Richard B. *Ethical Theory: The Problems of Normative and Critical Ethics*\*

(Englewood Cliffs, 1959). (B). A text of more than common interest; more difficult than most, therefore not to be read first.

Cabot, Richard C. *The Meaning of Right and Wrong* (New York, 1933).

Drake, Durant. *Problems of Conduct: An Introductory Survey of Ethics* (Boston, 1914; 2nd revised ed., 1935). (B). One of the best of the older texts.

Frankena, William. *Ethics* (Englewood Cliffs, 1963; 2nd ed., 1973). (B). An introductory work by one of the most knowledgeable people in the field.

Garvin, Lucius. *A Modern Introduction to Ethics* (Boston, 1953). (B). Another text of better than average merit; contains a vigorous defense of utilitarianism, good explanation of self-realizationist theories (chs. 12 and 13 *et seq.*).

Hazlitt, Henry. *The Foundations of Morality* (Princeton, 1964). The foundations are egoistic; sprightly reading nonetheless.

Hospers, John. *Human Conduct: An Introduction to the Problems of Ethics* (New York, 1961). (B). A text, of considerable merit, which provides comprehensive coverage of the theories, topics, and problems of ethics, and contains numerous lively examples.

Leys, Wayne A. R. *Ethics for Policy Decisions* (New York, 1952). Emphasis on application of theory to questions of social policy.

Lillie, William. *An Introduction to Ethics* (London, 1948; 3rd ed., 1955). (B). A good beginner's book; see especially ch. 1, "The Nature of Ethics," and ch. 13, "Theory and Practice."

Mabbott, J. D. *An Introduction to Ethics* (London, 1966).

Moore, G. E. *Ethics* (London, 1912). Short, stimulating, influential, clear; not too difficult, not too easy; all in all, a stunning little book.

Taylor, Paul. *Principles of Ethics: An Introduction* (Encino, 1975). (B).

Williams, Bernard. *Morality: An Introduction to Ethics* (New York, 1972).

# Fiction (Novels, Stories, Plays)

These items are rich sources of moral problems and issues; they are also good reading.

Butler, Samuel. *Erewhon* (London, 1872).

Cobb, Humphrey. *Paths of Glory* (New York, 1935).

Coppard, A. E. "The Watercress Girl," in *Fishmonger's Fiddle* (New York, 1925).

Cozzens, James Gould. *The Just and the Unjust* (New York, 1942).

Dostoyevsky, Fyodor. *Crime and Punishment* (1866).

———. *The Brothers Karamazov* (1880).

Fast, Howard. *The Winston Affair* (New York, 1959).

Galsworthy, John. *Justice* (1910).

Goodrich, Marcus. *Delilah* (New York, 1941).

Jackson, Shirley. "The Lottery" (1948), in *The Lottery* (New York, 1949).

Mann, Abby. *Judgment at Nuremberg* (1961).

March, William. *The Bad Seed* (1954).

Maugham, W. Somerset. *The Moon and Sixpence* (New York, 1919).

Rattigan, Terence. *The Winslow Boy* (London, 1946).

Snow, C. P. *The Affair* (New York, 1960).

Steinbeck, John. *The Grapes of Wrath* (New York, 1939). See especially ch. 17.

Tolstoy, Leo. *War and Peace* (1865–69).
———. *Anna Karenina* (1875–76).
Trilling, Lionel. "Of This Time, of That Place," *Partisan Review,* 10 (January–February, 1943), 72–81, 84–105.
Trollope, Anthony. *The Warden* (London, 1855).
Wouk, Herman. *The Caine Mutiny* (Garden City, 1951).

## Anthologies

There are many anthologies and collections in ethics available, and the number steadily increases. Many of them are quite useful, either for collecting in one place a number of valuable selections otherwise not readily available or for some other feature of content or organization. There are, naturally, great differences among them, some containing elaborate editorial and introductory matter, some containing none. Some simply reprint journal articles, uncut and unedited; others reprint from a variety of sources and indulge in internal editing. I list here only some general collections that I regard as most valuable on one count or another. Collections on special topics are listed under other headings.

Abelson, Raziel and Marie-Louise Friquegnon, eds. *Ethics for Modern Life* (New York, 1975). (B). A recent attempt to integrate theory and practice.
Brandt, Richard. ed. *Value and Obligation: Systematic Readings in Ethics* (New York, 1961). (B).
Davis, Philip E., ed. *Introduction to Moral Philosophy* (Columbus, Ohio, 1973). (B).
Frankena, William K. and John T. Granrose, eds. *Introductory Readings in Ethics* (Englewood Cliffs, 1974). (B). A well-edited collection, with informative commentary.
Melden, A. I., ed. *Ethical Theories* (New York, 2nd ed. revised, 1967). Aims at providing "fairly complete selections from the writings of the great moral philosophers of the past"; largely successful.
Pahel, Kenneth and Marvin Schiller, eds. *Readings in Contemporary Ethical Theory\** (Englewood Cliffs, 1970). (B).
Selby-Bigge, L. A., ed. *British Moralists, Being Selections from Writers Principally of the Eighteenth Century.* 2 vols. (Oxford, 1897). (B). A classic collection.
Sellars, Wilfrid and John Hospers, eds. *Readings in Ethical Theory\** (New York, 2nd ed., 1970). (B). A recent though not necessarily improved revision of a fairly standard collection; the material is probably better, the editing is not.
Taylor, Paul W., ed. *Problems of Moral Philosophy* (Belmont, 2nd ed., 1972). A well-edited collection, containing extensive introductory material.
Thomson, Judith and Gerald Dworkin, eds. *Ethics\** (New York, 1968). An outstanding collection of contemporary essays otherwise not easily obtainable.

## Classic Works

Aristotle. *Nicomachean Ethics.*
Butler, Joseph. *Fifteen Sermons Preached at the Rolls Chapel* (also known as *Sermons on*

*Human Nature*) (1726). An excellent discussion is Austin Duncan-Jones, *Butler's Moral Philosophy* (Baltimore, 1952).

————. *Of the Nature of Virtue* (1736).

Hobbes, Thomas. *Leviathan* (1651).

Hume, David. *A Treatise of Human Nature*. Bk. II, *Of the Passions* (1739), and Bk. III, *Of Morals* (1740).

————. *An Enquiry Concerning the Principles of Morals* (1751).

Kant, Immanuel. *Groundwork* [*Foundations, Fundamental Principles*] *of the Metaphysics of Morals* (1785). The best translation is by H. J. Paton, which is contained in his book entitled *The Moral Law* (London, 1948), along with a useful "Analysis of the Argument" and notes to the text. A useful collection of essays on Kant's important work is R. P. Wolff, ed., *Kant: Foundations of the Metaphysics of Morals, with Critical Essays* (Indianapolis, 1969); the translation used is by Lewis White Beck.

Mill, John Stuart. *Utilitarianism* (1861). There is a useful collection of essays on Mill or utilitarianism or both in Samuel Gorovitz, ed., *Mill: Utilitarianism, Text and Critical Essays* (Indianapolis, 1971). (B). An excellent discussion of utilitarianism is Anthony Quinton, *Utilitarian Ethics* (New York, 1973).

Plato. *The Republic.*

Price, Richard. *A Review of the Principal Questions in Morals* (1758).

Sidgwick, Henry. *The Methods of Ethics*\* (1874; 7th ed., 1907). Possibly the best treatise on moral theory that has ever been written; at least it has been so regarded by a number of writers. For commentary, see M. G. Singer, "The Many Methods of Sidgwick's Ethics," *The Monist*, 58 (1974); this whole issue of *The Monist* is devoted to Sidgwick and moral philosophy.

## Theoretical Ethics: Theories and Tests

Broad, C. D. *Five Types of Ethical Theory* (London, 1930). A scintillating discussion of theories of Spinoza, Butler, Hume, Kant, and Sidgwick. Good, lively reading; valuable for its errors as well as its insights.

Dewey, John. *Human Nature and Conduct* (New York, 1922). Dewey's major work in ethics. Should be read along with "The Construction of Good," ch. 10 of *The Quest for Certainty* (New York, 1929) and "Reconstruction in Moral Conceptions," ch. 7 of *Reconstruction in Philosophy* (New York, 1920).

Gert, Bernard. *The Moral Rules* (New York, 1970).

Hare, R. M. *Freedom and Reason*\* (Oxford, 1963). Very widely discussed. Sample: M. G. Singer, "Freedom From Reason," *The Philosophical Review*, 79 (1970), 253–61.

Hobhouse, L. T. *The Rational Good* (London, 1921).

Kaufmann, Walter. *Without Guilt and Justice: From Decidophobia to Autonomy* (New York, 1973). (B). Both silly and provocative, acute and preposterous. Decidedly better than its title, and gets beyond its obvious model, Nietzsche's *Beyond Good and Evil*. "What we need is a new, autonomous morality," we are told portentously (p. vii); and again (p. 119), "We should replace guilt feelings with humbition" ("a fusion of ambition with humility"). So we ought not to feel guilty! This reminds me of a cartoon in which a psychiatrist says to his patient, "All these years of therapy and you still feel guilt? You should be ashamed!" Nonetheless, this is a book to be reckoned with, since it is one of the few books one can find that actually comes out *against justice.*

Lewis, C. I. *The Ground and Nature of the Right* (New York, 1955).

Margenau, Henry. "Ethical Science," *The Scientific Monthly,* 69 (November, 1949), 290–96.

Moore, G. E. *Principia Ethica\** (Cambridge, 1903). Probably the most influential and most intensively discussed ethical work of the century. On matters relevant to the theme of this book, see ch. 5, "Ethics in Relation to Conduct," and ch. 6, "The Ideal."

Murphy, Arthur E. *The Theory of Practical Reason.* Edited by A. I. Melden. (La Salle, 1965).

Prichard, H. A. *Moral Obligation: Essays and Lectures* (Oxford, 1949).

Rawls, John. *A Theory of Justice\** (Cambridge, 1971). An original work of great importance and, unfortunately, immense difficulty; one of the most widely discussed philosophical works of the past fifty years. Some of these discussions are collected in Norman Daniels, ed., *Reading Rawls* (New York, 1975).

Rogers, A. K. *The Theory of Ethics* (New York, 1922).

Ross, W. D. *The Right and the Good* (Oxford, 1930).

Royce, Josiah. *The Philosophy of Loyalty* (New York, 1908).

Sartorius, Rolf E. *Individual Conduct and Social Norms* (Encino, 1975). (B). A defense, very much up to date, of act-utilitarianism.

Sharp, Frank Chapman. *Ethics* (New York, 1928). (B).

Singer, Marcus G. *Generalization in Ethics* (New York, 1961).

Smart, J. J. C. and Bernard Williams. *Utilitarianism, For and Against* (Cambridge, 1973). (B). Contains "An Outline of a System of Utilitarian Ethics" by Smart and "A Critique of Utilitarianism" by Williams. One of the very best discussions to be found.

Stace, W. T. *The Concept of Morals* (New York, 1937). See especially ch. 7, "The General Law of Morals."

Toulmin, Stephen. *An Examination of the Place of Reason in Ethics* (Cambridge, 1950).

## Practical Ethics

Beauchamp, Tom, ed. *Ethics and Public Policy* (Englewood Cliffs, 1975). (B). A useful collection of writings on issues of social policy.

Beck, Robert N. and John B. Orr, eds. *Ethical Choice: A Case Study Approach* (New York, 1970). (B). Not so much a "case study approach" as a collection of interesting essays on questions in practical ethics.

Ellis, Albert. "Sin and Psychotherapy," ch. 7 of *Reason and Emotion in Psychotherapy* (New York, 1962), pp. 132–46.

Girvetz, Harry K., ed. *Contemporary Moral Issues* (Belmont, 2nd ed., 1968). An anthology, interesting though philosophically uneven, that "deals with some of the major moral issues of our time."

Guyon, René. *The Ethics of Sexual Acts,* vol. I of *Studies in Sexual Ethics* (New York, 1934). (Is there such a thing as sexual ethics?)

Heron, Alastair, ed. *Towards a Quaker View of Sex* (London, 1963). Not a collection, but an integrated essay prepared by a group of people; something like a committee report, though it doesn't read like a committee report. One interesting point made in this otherwise revolutionary pamphlet is that "*there must be a morality of some sort to govern sexual relationships.* An experience so profound in its effect upon people and upon the community cannot be left wholly to private judgment. It will never be right for two people to say to each other 'We'll do what we want, and what happens between us is nobody else's business.' However private an act, it is never without its impact on society, and we must never behave as though society—which includes our other friends—did not exist" (p. 40). Is this so?

Hobhouse, L. T. *The Elements of Social Justice* (London, 1922). "The subject of this book is the social application of the ethical principles explained . . . in *The Rational Good*" (*q.v.*)

Knight, Frank H. *The Ethics of Competition* (London, 1935). See especially the first three chapters.

Lecky, W. E. H. *The Map of Life: Conduct and Character* (London, 1899).

Neff, Mary V. *Ethics for Everyday Living* (Chicago, 1958). Very elementary, but pedagogically interesting.

Rachels, James, ed. *Moral Problems* (New York, 2nd ed., 1975). (B). A collection of philosophical essays on "practical moral issues."

Roche, John P. and Milton M. Gordon. "Can Morality be Legislated?" *New York Times Magazine,* May 22, 1955, pp. 10 *et seq.*

Sharp, Frank C. and Philip G. Fox. *Business Ethics* (New York, 1937). (B).

Sidgwick, Henry. *Practical Ethics* (London, 1898).

Stebbing, L. Susan. *Ideals and Illusions* (London, 1941).

Tawney, R. H. *Equality* (London, 1931; 4th ed., 1952).

Wasserstrom, Richard, ed. *Today's Moral Problems* (New York, 1975). (B). Contains selections, "written within the past decade," that "deal with moral issues that have been of special concern to people living in the United States during the past five or ten years."

Wellman, Carl. *Morals and Ethics* (Glenview, 1975). (B). An interesting discussion of a range of practical issues.

Williams, Glanville. *The Sanctity of Life, and the Criminal Law* (London, 1958).

## Values and Ideals

Baier, Kurt. "What is Value? An Analysis of the Concept," in Kurt Baier and Nicholas Rescher, eds. *Values and the Future* (Glencoe, 1969), pp. 33–67.

Dewey, John. *Theory of Valuation* (Chicago, 1939). Especially valuable on the means-end relationship; see chs. 5 and 6.

Hamerton, Philip Gilbert. *Human Intercourse* (Boston, 1885).

Hare, R. M. "Ideals," ch. 8 of *Freedom and Reason* (Oxford, 1963), pp. 137–56.

James, William. "On a Certain Blindness in Human Beings," in *Talks to Teachers on Psychology; and to Students on Some of Life's Ideals* (New York, 1900), pp. 229–64.

Laird, John. *The Idea of Value* (Cambridge, 1929).

Lamont, W. D. *The Value Judgement** (Edinburgh, 1955).

Lindsay, A. D. *The Two Moralities* (London, 1940).

Milo, Ronald, ed. *Egoism and Altruism* (Belmont, Cal., 1973). (B).

Murphy, Arthur E. "Social Science and Social Ideals," Part III, ch. iii of *The Uses of Reason* (New York, 1943), pp. 251–64. On the validity and reality of ideals.

Strawson, P. F. "Social Morality and Individual Ideal," *Philosophy,* 36 (1961), 1–17.

Taylor, Paul W. *Normative Discourse* (Englewood Cliffs, 1961). Characterized by the author as "an essay in general theory of value."
von Wright, George Henrik. *The Varieties of Goodness\** (London, 1963).

## Skepticism and Relativism

Gewirth, Alan. "The 'Is-Ought' Problem Resolved," *Proceedings and Addresses of the American Philosophical Association,* 47 (1974), 34–61.
Ginsberg, Morris. *On the Diversity of Morals* (London, 1956).
Griffiths, A. Phillips. "Justifying Moral Principles," \* *Proceedings of the Aristotelian Society,* 58 (1958), 103–24.
Hudson, W. D., ed. *The Is-Ought Question* (London, 1969). A collection of recent papers on what the editor calls "the central problem in Moral Philosophy." It isn't, but a little hyperbole may be allowed in a collection as stimulating and as well conceived as this one.
Ladd, John, ed. *Ethical Relativism* (Belmont, 1973). (B).
Lundberg, George A. "Can Science Validate Ethics?," *Bulletin of the American Association of University Professors,* 36 (1950), 262–75.
MacBeath, A. *Experiments in Living* (London, 1952).
Melden, A. I. "Reasons for Action and Matters of Fact," *Proceedings and Addresses of the American Philosophical Association,* 35 (1962), 45–60.
Singer, Marcus G. "Moral Skepticism," in Curtis L. Carter, ed. *Skepticism and Moral Principles* (Evanston, 1973), pp. 77–108.
Stevenson, Charles L. *Ethics and Language* (New Haven, 1945). The most thorough and sophisticated presentation of the emotive theory—or *an* emotive theory.
Sumner, William Graham. *Folkways* (Boston, 1906). A bible for relativists.
Urmson, J. O. *The Emotive Theory of Ethics* (London, 1968). A sympathetic and nostalgic eulogy, worth preserving on its own.
Wellman, Carl. *Challenge and Response: Justification in Ethics* (Carbondale, 1971). (B). A perverse, interesting, and provocative book.

## Casuistry and Conflict

Cahn, Edmond. *The Moral Decision* (Bloomington, 1956).
Cox, George Clarke. *The Public Conscience: A Case Book in Ethics* (New York, 1922). Ethics by the case method; an early example.
Davis, Philip E., ed. *Moral Duty and Legal Responsibility: A Philosophical-Legal Casebook* (New York, 1966). A useful compendium.
Fletcher, Joseph. *Situation Ethics* (Philadelphia, 1966). A very bad book, poorly written, weakly argued, astonishingly ignorant, and incredibly inaccurate. Yet it has had enormous appeal. Why? Because it deals with actual perplexities and says something definite about them. Hence valuable.
Fuller, Lon L. "The Case of the Speluncean Explorers," *Harvard Law Review,* 62 (1949), 616–45. Reprinted in *Introduction to Law, Selected Essays from the Harvard Law Review* (Cambridge, Mass., 1968), and definitely worth searching out, since it is one of the most fascinating cases and perplexing conundrums ever devised. (And what would situation ethics say about this case?)

Hartland-Swann, John. "Moral Problems and Problems in Morals," ch. 2 of *An Analysis of Morals* (London, 1960), pp. 18–37.

Kirk, Kenneth E. *Conscience and its Problems: An Introduction to Casuistry* (London, 1927). Not definitive, but probably the most important work on its subject so far.

Levy-Bruhl, Lucien. *Ethics and Moral Science.* Translated by Elizabeth Lee (London, 1905). Hard to find, but worth looking for.

Pollock, Frederick. "The Casuistry of Common Sense," ch. 10 of *Essays in Jurisprudence and Ethics* (London, 1882), pp. 261–86.

## Conflict, War, and Morality

Angell, Norman. *The Great Illusion: A Study of the Relation of Military Power to National Advantage* (New York, 1910; 4th ed., 1913). A classic argument against war, published on the eve of the Great War of 1914–18, an example, presumably, of the power of the pen over the sword.

Clarkson, Jesse D. and Thomas C. Cochran, eds. *War as a Social Institution* (New York, 1941). A useful and unusual collection; see especially the essays by Malinowski (pp. 21–31) and Rosenberg (pp. 189–96).

Kant, Immanuel. *Perpetual Peace* (1795).

Lefever, Ernest. *Ethics and United States Foreign Policy* (New York, 1957). (B).

Merrill, Jean. *The Pushcart War* (New York, 1964). A delightful book. Almost unrivalled as an account of how a war started—was it a war?

Potter, Ralph B. *War and Moral Discourse* (Richmond, 1969). (B).

Royce, Josiah. *War and Insurance* (New York, 1914).

Sidgwick, Henry. "The Morality of Strife," ch. 4 of *Practical Ethics* (London, 1878), pp. 83–112.

Wasserstrom, Richard, ed. *War and Morality* (Belmont, 1970). (B). A slender but useful collection.

Whewell, William. "International Law. Rights and Obligations Between States," vol. II, bk. IV of *The Elements of Morality, Including Polity* (London, 1841; 3rd ed., 1854).

Wright, Quincy. *A Study of War* (Chicago, 1942; 2nd ed., 1965). (B). At 1600 pages, practically an encyclopedia of the subject, and certainly the most comprehensive study extant.

## Institutions and Institutional Ethics

Acton, H. B., ed. *The Philosophy of Punishment: A Collection of Papers* (London, 1969). (B).

Ballard, Lloyd V. *Social Institutions* (New York, 1936). (B).

Bartlet, J. V. and Charles Gore, eds. *Property: Its Duties and Rights* (London, 1914; 2nd ed., 1915). An interesting collection of original essays.

Barzun, Jacques. *The House of Intellect* (New York, 1959).

———. *The American University* (New York, 1968).

Cohen, Morris R. "Property and Sovereignty," in *Law and the Social Order* (New York, 1933), pp. 41–68.

———. "The Dark Side of Religion," in *The Faith of a Liberal* (New York, 1946), pp. 337–61.

Emmett, Dorothy. *Function, Purpose, and Powers* (London, 1958).

———. *Rules, Roles, and Relations* (London, 1966).

Ezorsky, Gertrude, ed. *Philosophical Perspectives on Punishment: Classical and Contemporary Selections* (Albany, 1972). (B).

Hart, H. L. A. *The Concept of Law* (Oxford, 1961).

———. "Prolegomenon to the Principles of Punishment," in *Punishment and Responsibility* (Oxford, 1968), pp. 1–27. A first rate account of the questions that must be considered and disentangled in dealing with the problems of criminal punishment. In the process of disentangling these questions about punishment, draws an intriguing analogy between the institutions of punishment and property.

Haworth, Lawrence. *The Good City* (Bloomington, 1963).

Hertzler, J. O. *Social Institutions* (New York, 1929). (B).

Kent, Edward Allen, ed. *Law and Philosophy: Readings in Legal Philosophy* (New York, 1970). (B).

Liebling, A. J. *The Wayward Pressman* (Garden City, 1945). (B).

———. *The Press* (New York, 2nd ed., 1964). Contains the intriguing remark: "The function of the press in society is to inform, but its role is to make money" (p. 7).

Mecklin, John M. *An Introduction to Social Ethics* (New York, 1920). (B).

Mumford, Lewis. *Technics and Civilization* (New York, 1934). (B). Cultural generalizations galore! And also some profound observations. Check the index for subjects.

Murphy, Arthur E. "The Rewards of Learning," ch. 29 of *Reason and the Common Good* (Englewood Cliffs, 1963), pp. 385–97.

Proudhon, P. J. *What is Property?* Translated by Benj. R. Tucker (Princeton, Mass., 1876). Property is theft, we are told; it is also a lot of other things.

Rescher, Nicholas. "The Ethical Dimension of Scientific Research," in R. G. Colodny, ed., *Beyond the Edge of Certainty* (Englewood Cliffs, 1965), pp. 261–76.

Russell, Bertrand. *Principles of Social Reconstruction* (London, 1916). A valuable and stimulating little book.

Sandage, C. H. and Vernon Fryburger, eds. *The Role of Advertising* (Homewood, Ill., 1960). (B). An excellent collection on advertising as an institution.

Wigmore, John H. and Albert Kocourek, eds. *Rational Basis of Legal Institutions* (New York, 1923). A groundbreaking anthology.

Wolff, R. P., ed. *Political Man and Social Man: Readings in Political Philosophy* (New York, 1966). (B).

# General

There are some useful and even interesting articles scattered through the eight volumes of the monumental *Encyclopedia of Philosophy,* Paul Edwards, editor in chief (New York, 1967). Check the index; and see the entry under "Ethics" in vol. 3. The bibliographies are also useful, though erratic.

For practical ethics, interesting essays often appear quarterly in the journal *Philosophy and Public Affairs* (started 1971), and also in *Ethics* (started 1890 under the title *International Journal of Ethics*). There is a *Seventy-Five Year Index to Ethics,* covering the period October 1890 to July 1965 (Chicago, 1966); unfortunately it lists articles only by author, not by title or subject, but a little browsing will turn up some worthwhile articles. Another periodical of more than ordinary interest is the bimonthly *Hastings Center Report,* for essays and reports on problems of medical ethics.

# Sources and Acknowledgments

Sources and page references (where known) for Statements on Morality are given below. The Editor wishes to thank the publishers and owners of copyright materials for permission to reprint; details are given where required.

## Series I

1. From *Samuel Butler's Notebooks*, ed. by Geoffrey Keynes and Brian Hill (London: Jonathan Cape, 1951), p. 100.
2. Havelock Ellis, *The Dance of Life* (1923), ch. 6.
3. Ernest Hemingway, *Death in the Afternoon* (New York: Charles Scribner's Sons, 1932), p. 4.
4. *Collected Papers of Charles Sanders Peirce*, ed. by Charles Hartshorne and Paul Weiss (Cambridge: Harvard University Press, 1932), vol. I, p. 359.
5. Frank Chapman Sharp and Philip G. Fox, *Business Ethics* (New York: Appleton-Century-Crofts, 1937), p. 3.
6. Samuel Butler, *The Way of All Flesh* (1903), ch. 80.
7. Richard Whately, *Paley's Moral Philosophy* (London, 1859), p. 14.
8. Morris R. Cohen and Ernest Nagel, *An Introduction to Logic and Scientific Method* (New York: Harcourt Brace Jovanovich, 1934), p. 366.
9. A. K. Rogers, *Ethics and Moral Tolerance* (New York: The Macmillan Company, 1934), pp. 2-3.
10. Jean Piaget, *The Moral Judgment of the Child* (London: Routledge & Kegan Paul; New York: The Macmillan Company, 1932), p. 1.

## Series II

11. Henry Sidgwick, *The Methods of Ethics*, 6th ed. (London, 1901), p. 77.
12. John Dewey and James H. Tufts, *Ethics* (New York: Holt, Rinehart and Winston, 1908), p. 212.
13. Arthur E. Murphy, *The Uses of Reason* (New York: The Macmillan Company, 1943), p. 113.
14. Morris R. Cohen, *Studies in Philosophy and Science* (New York: Holt, Rinehart and Winston, 1949), pp. 24-5.
15. R. H. Tawney, *Religion and the Rise of Capitalism* (New York: Harcourt Brace Jovanovich, 1926), pp. 183-4.
16. C. H. Waddington, *The Scientific Attitude* (London: Penguin Books Ltd., 1948), p. 31.
17. From the book *A Guide to Rational Living* by Albert Ellis and Robert A. Harper, p. 103. © 1961 by Institute of Rational Living. Published by Prentice-Hall, Inc., Englewood Cliffs, New Jersey.
18. Ralph Barton Perry, *The Moral Economy* (New York: Charles Scribner's Sons, 1909), p. 2.
19. Richard Whately, *Lessons on Morals* (1855), ch. 8.

## Series III

20. Richard C. Cabot, *The Meaning of Right and Wrong* (New York: The Macmillan Company, 1933), p. 167. By courtesy of Ella Lyman Cabot Trust.
21. Philip Gilbert Hamerton, *The Intellectual Life* (Boston, 1875), p. 120.
22. C. I. Lewis, *The Ground and Nature of the Right* (New York: Columbia University Press, 1955), p. 3.
23. Elizabeth Taylor, *A Wreath of Roses* (London: Peter Davies, 1949), ch. 4.
24. Thomas Nixon Carver, *Essays in Social Justice* (Cambridge: Harvard University Press, 1915), p. 27.
25. Oliver Wendell Holmes, Jr., *Collected Legal Papers* (New York: Harcourt Brace Jovanovich, 1920), p. 304.
26. Albert Schweitzer, *Civilization and Ethics* (London: Adam and Charles Black Ltd., 1923), pp. xvi, 254-5.

## Series IV

27. Niccolò Machiavelli, *The Prince* (1513), ch. 15.
28. Thomas Hobbes, *Leviathan* (1651), ch. 6.
29. Susanna Wesley—source unknown.
30. Morris R. Cohen, *A Preface to Logic* (New York: Holt, Rinehart and Winston, 1944). p. 170.
31. Walter Kerr, *The Decline of Pleasure* (New York: Simon and Schuster), pp. 277-9. Copyright © 1962 by Walter Kerr. Reprinted by permission of Simon and Schuster, Inc.

## Series V

32. John Dewey and James Tufts, *Ethics* (1908), p. 212.
33. William James, *Talks to Teachers on Psychology: and to Students on Some of Life's Ideals* (New York: Holt, Rinehart and Winston, 1900), pp. 265-66.
34. A. Clutton-Brock, *Essays on Life* (London: Methuen & Co. Ltd., 1925), p. 64.
35. W. H. Auden, *The New Yorker,* December 18, 1954, p. 128.
36. Anthony Powell, *A Question of Upbringing* (London: William Heinemann Ltd.; Boston: Little, Brown and Company, 1951), p. 52.
37. From Morris R. Cohen, "Kant's Philosophy of Law," in *The Heritage of Kant,* ed. by George Tapley Whitney and David F. Bowers, p. 298. Copyright 1939 © 1967 by Princeton University Press. Reprinted by permission of Princeton University Press.
38. Thomas Hill Green, *Lectures on the Principles of Political Obligation* (1882) (London: Longmans, Green and Co., 1950), pp. 181-82.
39. *Science,* Editorial, vol. 127 (1958), p. 57.
40. Bertrand Russell, *A History of Western Philosophy* (London: George Allen and Unwin Ltd.; New York: Simon & Schuster Inc., 1945), p. 711. Copyright, 1945, by Bertrand Russell.
41. E. F. Carritt, *The Theory of Morals* (Oxford: The Clarendon Press, 1928), p. 43.
42. Lawrence Sterne, *Tristram Shandy* (1767), ch. 29.
43. David Hume, *An Enquiry Concerning the Principles of Morals* (1751), Sec. IX, Part I.

# Series VI

44. Bertrand Russell, *Human Society in Ethics and Politics* (London: George Allen & Unwin Ltd.; New York: Simon & Schuster, 1954), p. 8. © 1952, 1954, 1955 by Bertrand Russell. Reprinted by permission of Simon and Schuster, Inc.
45. Ralph Waldo Emerson, "The Present State of Ethical Philosophy" (1821), in *Two Unpublished Essays* (Boston: Lamson Wolffe & Co., 1895), p. 58.
46. Thomas Nixon Carver, *Essays in Social Justice* (Cambridge: Harvard University Press, 1915), pp. 18–19.
47. Joseph Butler, *A Dissertation upon the Nature of Virtue* (1736).
48. Brian Medlin, "Ultimate Principles and Ethical Egoism," *Australasian Journal of Philosophy,* vol. 35 (1957), p. 111.
49. From *Psychology and Life,* Fourth Edition by Floyd L. Ruch, p. 464. Copyright 1941 by Scott, Foresman and Company. Reprinted by permission of the publisher.
50. George Santayana, *Winds of Doctrine* (London: J. M. Dent & Sons Ltd.; New York: Charles Scribner's Sons, 1913), p. 151.
51. L. Susan Stebbing, *Ideals and Illusions* (London: Messrs C. A. Watts & Co. Ltd., 1941), ch. 9.

# Series VII

52. From Thomas Carlyle, "Sir Walter Scott" (1838) in Carlyle's *Critical and Miscellaneous Essays* (1869).
53. Jacques Barzun, *God's Country and Mine* (Boston: Little, Brown and Company in association with the Atlantic Monthly Press, 1954), ch. 6.
54. Thomas Szasz, "Moral Conflict and Psychiatry," *The Yale Review* (1960), p. 558.
55. William Whewell, *The Elements of Morality* (London; 1841; 3rd ed., 1854), vol. II, Supplement, ch. 2, sec. 3, p. 305.
56. Anonymous, in *Modern Essays, Reprinted from Leading Essays in "The Times"* (London, 1915), p. 79.
57. E. F. Carritt, *The Theory of Morals* (London: Oxford University Press, 1928), p. 114.
58. Morris Raphael Cohen, *Reason and Law* (Glencoe: The Free Press, 1950), p. 15.

# Series VIII

59. William Edward Hartpole Lecky, *The Map of Life* (London: Longmans, Green, and Co., 1921; 1st ed., 1899), p. 191.
60. Thomas Carlyle, *Chartism* (1839), ch. 5.
61. J. L. and Barbara Hammond, *The Age of the Chartists* (London: Longman Group Ltd., 1930), p. 16.
62. George Santayana, *Reason in Society,* vol. 2 of *The Life of Reason* (New York: Charles Scribner's Sons; London: Constable & Co. Ltd., 1905), pp. 105–106.
63. From *And Even Now* by Max Beerbohm, p. 172. Copyright, 1921 by E. P. Dutton & Co., Inc., and used with their permission.

## Series IX

64. R. H. Tawney, *The Acquisitive Society* (New York: Harcourt Brace Jovanovich, 1920), p. 3.
65. Ralph Barton Perry, *The Moral Economy* (New York: Charles Scribner's Sons, 1909), pp. 147–48.
66. Edward Hallett Carr, *Conditions of Peace* (New York, 1942), pp. 116–117. By permission of Macmillan *London and Basingstoke.*
67. Thomas Hill Green, *Lectures on the Principles of Political Obligation* (1882) (London: Longmans, Green and Co., 1950), p. 190.
68. Henry George, *Social Problems* (New York, 1883), pp. 237, 242.
69. Quintin Hogg, *The Case for Conservatism* (London: Penguin Books Ltd., 1947), p. 97.
70. H. B. Acton, *Kant's Moral Philosophy* (New York: St. Martin's Press, 1970), p. 25.

## Series X

71. John Rawls, *A Theory of Justice* (Cambridge: Harvard University Press, 1971), pp. 3–4.
72. Henry George, *Social Problems* (New York, 1883), p. 120.
73. Adlai E. Stevenson, *What I Think* (New York: Harper & Row, 1955), p. 188.
74. L. L. Bernard, *War and its Causes* (New York: Holt, Rinehart and Winston, 1944), p. 58.
75. From "The Land Ethic" in *A Sand County Almanac with Other Essays on Conservation from Round River* by Aldo Leopold, pp. 239–40. Copyright © 1949, 1953, 1966 by Oxford University Press, Inc. Reprinted by permission.
76. From Barry Commoner, *The Closing Circle,* ch. 8. Copyright © 1971 by Barry Commoner. By permission of Alfred A. Knopf, Inc.
77. G. K. Chesterton, *Generally Speaking* (London: Methuen & Co. Ltd., 1928), pp. 91–2. By permission of Miss D. E. Collins.

# Index of Authors

What follows is an index of the authors who are represented in this collection either by a (regular) selection or by a (shorter) quotation—Statement on Morality. Page numbers of selections are given in boldface; page numbers of statements are in lightface.